FRAMING EUROPE

Princeton Studies in Cultural Sociology

Editors
Paul DiMaggio, Michèle Lamont, Robert J. Wuthnow, Viviana Zelizer

A list of titles in the series appears at the back of the book

FRAMING EUROPE

ATTITUDES TO EUROPEAN INTEGRATION IN
GERMANY, SPAIN, AND THE UNITED KINGDOM

Juan Díez Medrano

PRINCETON UNIVERSITY PRESS   PRINCETON AND OXFORD

Copyright ©2003 by Princeton University Press

Published by Princeton University Press, 41 William Street, Princeton, New Jersey 08540

In the United Kingdom: Princeton University Press, 3 Market Place, Woodstock, Oxfordshire OX20 1SY
All Rights Reserved

British Library Cataloging-in-Publication Data is available

Library of Congress Cataloging-in-Publication Data

Díez Medrano, Juan.
    Framing Europe : attitudes to European integration in Germany, Spain, and the United Kingdom / Juan Díez Medrano.
        p. cm. — (Princeton studies in cultural sociology)
    Includes bibliographical references and index.
    ISBN: 978-0-691-14650-8
        1. European federation—Public opinion—History. 2. Public opinion—Germany—History. 3. Public opinion—Spain—History. 4. Public opinion—Great Britain—History. I. Title. II. Series.

JN15.D54 2004
327'.094–dc21   2003040496

Printed on acid-free paper. ∞

www.pupress.princeton.edu

Printed in the United States of America

1 3 5 7 9 10 8 6 4 2

10 9 8 7 6 5 4 3 2 1

For Pascal

Contents

List of Figures	ix
List of Tables	xi
Acknowledgments	xiii
One Introduction	1
PART I: FRAMES ON EUROPEAN INTEGRATION AND THE EUROPEAN UNION IN THE UNITED KINGDOM, GERMANY, AND SPAIN	19
Two Ways of Seeing European Integration	21
Three Good Reasons for Attitudes toward European Integration	65
Four Journalists and European Integration	106
PART II: NATIONAL CULTURES AND FRAMES ON EUROPEAN INTEGRATION	157
Five Spain: Europe as a Mirror with Two Reflections	159
Six West Germany: Between Self-Doubt and Pragmatism	179
Seven East Germany: A Different Past, a Different Memory	200
Eight The United Kingdom: Reluctant Europeans	214
Nine Frames and Attitudes toward European Integration: A Statistical Validation	236
Ten Conclusions	249

Appendix 1
Selection and Distribution of Respondents, and the
Interviewing Process   263

Appendix 2
Newspaper Selection, Sampling, and Coding Procedures for
Editorials and Opinion Pieces   267

Appendix 3
Frames on European Integration: A Discriminant Analysis,
by City   270

Appendix 4
Sources for Part II: Novels, History Textbooks, and Head of
State Addresses   271

Notes   277

References   299

Index   315

List of Figures

1.1	Trends in net support for membership in the European Union in the largest member states	9
2.1	Group centroids for first and second canonical discriminant functions, based on respondents' frames on European integration and the European Union	57
3.1	Four models of European integration	71
4.1	"Self-Determinists" and "Continentalists" in British history	137
9.1	Average empirical Bayes residuals by country, obtained after estimating hierarchical linear model in table 12	244

List of Tables

1. Net Support for Membership in the European Union in 2000 10
2. Themes Mentioned to Justify Positive or Negative Comments about European Integration or the European Union 27
3. Main Characterizations of Own Country and People 59
4. Main Historical Events Mentioned during Interviews 60
5. Themes Mentioned to Justify Attitudes toward European Integration or Membership in the European Union 68
6. Themes Mentioned to Justify Attitudes by Country and Preferred Model of Integration 102
7. Mean Number of Descriptive or Evaluative Comments in Spanish, British, and German Op-Ed Articles, 1946–97 108
8. Ratios of Negative to Positive Descriptive or Evaluative Comments in Spanish, British, and German Op-Ed Articles, 1946–97 109
9. Percent of Articles and In-depth Interviews with Specific Descriptive or Evaluative Comments 112
10. Positive and Negative Descriptive or Evaluative Comments in Spanish, British, and German Op-Ed Articles, 1946–97 114
11. The Effects of Fearing that the EU Will Harm National Identity and the Degree of Closeness to European Union on Support of Membership in the EU and Preference for an Integrative Model 238
12. The Effects of Economic, Social, and Other Variables on Preference for an Integrative Model 243
13. Distribution of Field Interviews to Ordinary Citizens 264
14. Frames on European Integration: A Discriminant Analysis 270

Acknowledgments

Writing this book has been a remarkable personal and intellectual journey. The project originated in my long-standing interest in and support for European unification. I am less optimistic now than I was ten years ago about the prospects for political unification. Nonetheless, I am happy to have been a witness to the introduction of the euro, just as I was completing the first draft of this book. The best memories I keep from my years of research are what I have learned about the cultures of Germany, Spain, and the United Kingdom and my adventures as I hopped from country to country. I could not have asked for more from my profession. I will always cherish the kindness of all the people I met and interviewed in the six cities in which I conducted my in-depth interviews, and the beauty of some of the literary works I read to prepare part II of the book.

This project would not have been completed without the encouragement, faith in the book's potential, and good advice from several people: Dieter Urban (University of Stuttgart), Mabel Berezin (Cornell University), Michèle Lamont (Princeton University), Ian Malcolm of Princeton University Press, and the anonymous reviewers. I feel very lucky to have interacted with them. At the institutional level, my utmost gratitude goes to the Alexander von Humboldt Stiftung and the University of California, San Diego (UCSD). The former provided me with the funding that made this research possible. I will also never forget its efficiency as an organization and the kindness of its staff. Meanwhile, UCSD allowed me to pursue my research project by granting me generous leaves of absence and through various Academic Senate research grants. I would also like to thank the Deutscher Akademischer Austausch Dienst (DAAD), the Committee for Cultural and Education Cooperation between Spain and the United States, the Center for German and European Studies of the University of California at Berkeley, for complementary financial support granted over the course of this investigation.

Some institutions have provided me with valuable resources and a great intellectual environment, as I collected and analyzed the information for this book. Theoretical and methodological debates among my colleagues at the Department of Sociology of the University of California, San Diego, have been a great stimulus to my work. Other institutions that have significantly facilitated my research are the University of Stuttgart (Germany), the Universidad Pompéu Fabra (Barcelona, Spain), the Centro de Estudios Constitucionales (Madrid, Spain), the

Institut für Publizistik and the Otto-Suhr Institut of the Frei Universität (Berlin, Germany), the Zentrum für Umfrage, Analysen, und Methoden (ZUMA, Mannheim, Germany), the Wissenschaftszentrum Berlin für Sozialforschung (WZB, Berlin, Germany), the Georg-Eckert Institut für Internationale Schulbuchforschung (Braunschweig, Germany), the Berlin Staatsbibliothek (Berlin, Germany), the International University Bremen, and Análisis Sociológicos, Económicos, y Políticos (ASEP, Madrid, Spain).

I have done the bulk of the data collection, coding, and analysis of information myself. Nonetheless, numerous assistants have helped me tremendously by participating in the data collection and coding of this information at different stages of the process: Silvio Waisbord, Natasha Unger, Helena Rigazzi-Hays, Melissa Kenney, Ana Lourdes Suárez, Shannon McMullen, Paloma Díez Hernando, Marga Marí-Klose, Angelica Toscano, Debby Cohen, Caitlin Patler, Kelly Quinley, Mari Choi, Elisa Galán González, and Katharina Welle. I would also like to thank Mauro Porto for valuable bibliographic guidance as I read on the topic of frames.

In the editing phase I have benefited enormously from Jodi Beder's patient editorial comments and suggestions. I am very grateful to her, as I am to the staff at Princeton University Press for their assistance at the production stage of this book.

When a project requires as much ethnographic work and time as this one, it is natural that research and personal life become deeply enmeshed. Although I have had many moments of fun while preparing this book, I have gone through rough times too. The following people have greatly contributed either fun or comfort during those times: José Manuel, Isabel, Magali, Frédéric, Maria Luisa, Paul, Johanna, Ernie, John, Akos, Jesús, Melissa, Carol, Robert, Ruth, Laure, Arachu, Olivier, Enríc, Erika, Alberto, Ana, Javier, Malena, Teresa, Bettina, and Michael. Other people have unknowingly but equally significantly contributed to motivate me during my long periods of solitary work: Georges Delerue, Antoine Duhamel, Boris Vian, Ennio Morricone, Jeff Mills, Jim O'Rourke, Yasuharo Konishi, John Zorn, Ryuichi Sakamoto, Sean O'Hagan, Toru Takemitsu, Pascal Comelade, Bob Dylan, Brian Wilson, and Serge Gainsbourg; their beautiful, cynical, witty, and/or socially engaged creations, as well as those of others in their profession, make life worth living. Finally, I would like above all to thank Beatriz, Marta, and Mari Cruz at ASEP, my parents, my siblings and their families, my parents-in-law, and especially my wife, Berit, for putting up with me, for helping me, and, more generally, for always being there when I needed them.

FRAMING EUROPE

One

Introduction

THE CIRCULATION OF the first euro coins and bills on January 1, 2002, was a milestone in the history of European integration, crowning a sixteen-year period of breathtaking institutional and political transformation. This transformation included the completion of the European single market, the adoption of a Social Charter, and the abolition of passport border controls through the Schengen Treaty. These changes and the way in which they have taken place are unique in the history of Europe, and the resulting polity represents a major challenge to the modern nation-state.

Just as interesting as this transformation is the fact that, except for the single market, the changes have not taken place in all European Union member states; and even then, they often have not occurred simultaneously within the affected states. Over the past sixteen years, the European Union has in fact become a polity with variable geometry. This unexpected shift in the institutional character of the European Union has resulted from political developments in countries that had traditionally shown suspicion toward the European Communities' supranational character.

In this study, we will look at how the attitudes of ordinary citizens and members of the local elites toward European integration are shaped by the histories and cultures of the countries and regions in which they live. In particular, we will listen to their words in interviews, uncovering the different ways in which they conceive of or "frame" European integration. The emergence of these conceptions will then be tracked down historically through analysis of the print media. Finally, they will be matched with the national and regional contexts in which they are rooted, as expressed particularly in high-school history books, in novels, and in public addresses by heads of state. I focus on three of the largest countries of the European Union, significantly distinguished from each other in their histories leading up to the beginning of European integration. By thus using "frame analysis," I hope, one can derive a better understanding of the different meanings European integration has for those in the member states of the European Union.

From European Communities to European Union

The European Union can be broadly conceived as a new form of supranational polity, which combines features of federal states and intergovernmental organizations. Its immediate achievements have included the removal of barriers to trade, the mobility of factors of production and the intensification of cooperation between member states, the implementation of a common currency, and the development of common legislation and standards in many areas.

Throughout the book, I use different names to refer to the European Union. These names correspond to the previous incarnations of what is in fact an evolving set of treaties and institutions. From the signing of the Treaty of Rome (1957) to the Merger Treaty (1965), these treaties and institutions were known as the European Communities. The communities were three: the European Coal and Steel Community (ECSC), created in 1951; the European Atomic Energy Community (Euratom), created in 1957; and the European Economic Community (EEC), created in 1958. The EEC was also known as the Common Market. With the merging of the executive councils of these three communities through the Merger Treaty, the European Communities became the European Community. Finally, the name European Union was coined after the signing of the Treaty of Maastricht (1992), partly to symbolize the broadening of the European integration agenda to two new areas: Foreign Affairs and Security, and Justice and Home Affairs.

The event that triggered the movement toward a European Union with variable geometry was the surprising rejection of the Maastricht Treaty by the Danish population in a referendum held in 1991. More than any other event in the history of the European Communities, the Danish referendum represented the people's triumphant entry onto center stage of the European integration process. Furthermore, it suddenly revealed that international differences in the degree of support for European integration, which had been known about for some time, were not a fluke, and had to be taken seriously. Indeed, the shockwaves of the Danish referendum motivated a referendum in France, decisively shaped the debate on the treaty in the United Kingdom, triggered heated political discussion around newly coined concepts such as "subsidiarity" and "democratic deficit," and eventually led to modifications of the treaty itself. As a result of the debates and political events that surrounded the ratification of the Maastricht Treaty, the United Kingdom only belatedly signed the Social Charter, and opted out of the Schengen Treaty. The United Kingdom, Denmark, and Sweden also opted out of the single currency. The transformation of the European Union into a polity with variable geometry and the significant role that public opinion played in these new developments provided the inspiration for this investigation. More than ever, the main cleavage in the European Union, the one determining the pace and character of European integration, is that between supporters of intergovernmental cooperation and supporters of supranational integration. No progress can be made toward understanding European integration without describing and explaining this stable cleavage.

Studying Attitudes toward European Integration

In the past, political scientists and international relations experts have treated preferences for different models of European integration as given, and the European Union as a case study for the explanation of consensus attainment in processes of interstate cooperation. This approach shows a questionable preference for the goal of developing a general theory of regional integration over that of explaining European unification in its singularity, a phenomenon of major historical significance. In contrast to this tradition, and more attuned to work in the field of comparative politics, this book concentrates on what is arguably the most significant factor in the explanation of the pace and institutional aspects of European integration: the divide between supporters of a supranational and an intergovernmental model of integration. My approach, however, distinguishes itself sharply from current practice in the field of comparative politics in two important ways. First, I focus on the general public rather than on elites. Second, the links I make between the micro-level of individual attitudes and macro-level processes result from a systematic application of analytical tools provided by the sociological literature on frames rather than from mere observation. What emerges is an explanation in which history and culture trump economics and geopolitics as the major forces behind European integration.

Problems in Analyzing International Contrasts in Public Support for European Integration

The study of European integration, explanations of its pace and character, and predictions about what sort of polity will in the end emerge must take into account two major facts: the existence of relatively constant differences in support for supranational arrangements in the countries that form the European Union, and the increasing role of public opinion in determining the course of European integration. In countries like Spain and Germany, for instance, both elite and public support for supranational solutions have been moderately high, whereas in countries like the United Kingdom the opposite has been true.

The divide between pro-integration and Eurosceptic countries contributes significantly to explaining the course of European integration and must be taken into account when making predictions about the future of the European Union. First of all, it explains why, despite general agreement on the need to cooperate in economic and political affairs, European states have taken so long to decide on the specific form—intergovernmental or supranational—of cooperation. Had there been consensus on whether to follow an intergovernmental or supranational path to integration, the European edifice would have been completed some time ago. Second, the divide explains why once the process of European integration began to impinge on core dimensions of sovereignty (e.g., the currency) it became almost impossible to agree on how to cooperate, and a multi-speed or variable-geometry Europe ensued. Finally, if the divide between pro-integration and Eurosceptic countries remains, a European state—encompassing the bulk of the countries of Europe and endowed with most of the trappings of modern states—will not come into being. A "federal" Europe will only be possible if a consensus on the need for supranational solutions develops among the member states of the European Union. To predict whether such a consensus will be reached in the near future, we must focus on the relative stability of levels of support for supranational solutions in the different countries that form the European Union and explain why support has traditionally been higher in some countries and lower in others. This task demands a method, a heuristic that will allow us to shift from people's preferred model of European integration to the micro and macro variables that explain these preferences.

The political science and the international relations literatures do not provide us with the tools needed to address these theoretical and methodological questions. Two reasons account for this inadequacy. First, international relations scholars have often treated country positions on the supranational-intergovernmental divide as given rather than as problematic in explanations of the outcome of cooperation games between European Union states.[1] They have not asked, "Why are some countries more in favor of European integration than others?" or "Why are some countries in favor of or against transfers of sovereignty?" Instead, they have asked, "What structural conditions make cooperation agreements possible when national political elites have different agendas of European integration?" or, more generally, "What structural conditions make cooperation agreements about European integration possible?" Second, scholars who have focused on elite or public opinion attitudes toward different models of European integration use independent variables that do not account for international differences. Thus, while comparative political scientists have been prone to developing long lists of explanatory variables drawn from the observation of correlations between characteristics of the countries

INTRODUCTION 5

that are compared and the dominant attitudes toward European integration in these countries (I will illustrate this problem with respect to the British, German, and Spanish cases), survey researchers have failed to develop adequate statistical models to explain why support for a supranational model of European integration is greater in some countries than in others.[2]

Frames and Support for European Integration

The premise that inspires this book is that a correct understanding of international variation in support for European integration requires taking into account how people conceive of the process and the institutions involved. To determine how people frame European integration in different countries, explain international contrasts in these framing processes, and analyze the role of frames in explaining attitudes toward European integration, I undertook to design and conduct a comparative in-depth study of attitudes toward European integration in Germany, the United Kingdom, and Spain.[3]

The study of conceptualizations of the European Union and European integration connects this book to a multistranded sociological tradition that has emphasized that people's attitudes and behavior toward objects or problems depend on how they conceive of, frame, or represent them.[4] One cannot assume, as does most of the literature, that everybody perceives the European integration process and the European Union in the same way. Some representations of the European Union are shared by everybody, across social and national locations. For instance, most people in the European Union conceive of the European Union as a large market. Other representations are more prevalent in specific social locations. Thus, farmers see the European Union through the lens of the Common Agricultural Policy more than do other social sectors. Still other representations are shared more by people with a particular ideological bent. Some leftist individuals, for instance, conceive of the European Union as yet another plot by monopoly capitalists to better exploit the labor force, whereas more conservative individuals think mainly of the economic advantages of a large single market. Finally, as I show in this book, some representations of the European Union are found more frequently in some countries than in others.

Frames thus vary across sociodemographic, political, and national groups, although they should not be interpreted in essentialist terms, as if a distinct frame corresponds to each group in the population. Frames sometimes distinguish groups from one another; at other times, they are equally prevalent across groups. This applies especially to international differences, the focus of this investigation. Because national states remain a key socialization agency and the bounded space within which individuals spend most of their lives, worldviews and thus framing processes differ across nations. State boundaries are permeable, however, and increasingly so because of globalization in the field of communications. Therefore, as I show in this book, some frames are equally prevalent across national states whereas others are not.[5] It is the frames that distinguish the different countries that interest us most here, however, for they are the ones that contain the clues to the explanation of why support for European integration is stronger in some countries than in others. As I will demonstrate, these distinguishing frames reveal that concern for identity, status, and cultural change rather than for power and plain economic interest is the key to explaining international variation in support for European integration.

Frames mediate the effect of micro and macro sociological factors on people's attitudes toward European integration. As a heuristic device, the focus on frames is useful in a situation like the one researchers confront when studying attitudes toward European integration, in which extant theories have revealed themselves to be insufficient. By examining the frames concerning European integration, we can inductively improve our explanations of people's attitudes and of international variation in these attitudes. More important than this, however, is the information that frames provide about the macro-level forces that shape international contrasts in attitudes toward European integration. This information reflects the fact that the frames' contents draw from the cultures in which they develop.

People approach the topic of European integration equipped with a cultural repertoire that tends to vary along sociodemographic, political, and national lines. This cultural repertoire includes, among other things, knowledge, habitus, stories, memories, and worldviews, upon which people draw more or less consciously when framing objects and problems.[6] Scholars using the concept of culture in the context of discussions about frames have defined it in different ways. Zald defines it as "the shared belief system and understandings, mediated and constituted by symbols and language."[7] Tarrow uses the concept of "ideational materials" to refer to the repertoire of symbols and images in a political culture.[8] In turn, he defines "political culture" as those "points of concern about social and political relations, containing both system-supporting and oppositional elements."[9] In this book, I use the concept of "cultural preoccupation" or, alternatively, Gamson's concept of "cultural theme," to encompass very general beliefs, symbols, and images as well as more concrete topics of discussion in a particular society.[10] Part II of this book systematically examines the main cultural themes in Germany, Spain, and the United Kingdom in the second half of the twentieth century, in order to show how they relate to the frames on European integration that have developed in these countries.

The framing scripts that can be drawn from a culture are almost infinite. But if culture matters in the generation of frames, it is because some cultural fields and features matter more than others. The literature suggests that dominant frames generally draw from the most salient elements in one's national political cultures.[11] Snow and Benford, for instance, refer to the alignment of frames with belief systems and to a frame's narrative fidelity, that is, the extent to which "it rings true with extant beliefs, myths, folktales, and the like," as factors that determine the success of frames used by social movements to mobilize support.[12] Meanwhile, for Gamson, "resonances increase the appeal of a frame by making it appear natural and more familiar."[13] The same explanation for the resonance of frames used by social movements and the media among the population can be applied to the development of frames in general, and frames on European integration are no exception. As I demonstrate in this book, the frames on European integration that distinguish the British, German, and Spanish populations resonate with salient cultural preoccupations in their respective countries.

Beyond demonstrating that salient cultural themes are the main source of inspiration for dominant frames on European integration, this book builds on Gamson's distinction between themes and counterthemes to show that the power of a cultural theme in generating frames depends on the existence of powerful counterthemes. Cultural themes are those that are normative, and cultural counterthemes are those that are oppositional, that is, contrary to normative beliefs.[14] Gamson presupposes, however, that for each theme there is an equally powerful countertheme, which is not always the case. This becomes clear in my examination of West German post–World War II political culture, which shows that three equally salient cultural themes have differed in the extent to which they have succeeded in shaping the frames on European integration that have developed in this part of Germany. I demonstrate that the cultural theme that resonates the most in the population's frames on European integration is one that has generated relatively little controversy over the years, that is, one for which there has not been a salient countertheme in post–World War II political culture.

In sum, frame analysis provides us with a powerful analytical tool to explain attitudes toward European integration. Frames link attitudes toward an object or problem to their structural and cultural causes, and contain encrypted information about these causes. The main goal of this investigation is to decode this information in order to better understand contrasts in support for European integration in Germany, Spain, and the United Kingdom.

A Promising Comparison: The United Kingdom, Germany, and Spain

The scarcity and inadequacy of theories explaining international variation in support for European unification warrants the inductive approach outlined above. In turn, the exploratory nature of the endeavor and the need to systematically collect qualitative information on people's conceptions of European integration and the European Union, as well as on the cultures on which these conceptions rest, makes the comparative approach a suitable compromise between the case study generally favored by historians and the quantitative analysis of survey data for all the European Union's member states. This study focuses on three of the five largest countries and economies in the European Union, as of January, 2003. Large countries not only represent a greater proportion of the European Union's population, but also have more weight in determining the course of European integration. Taken together, the three countries examined in this book represent 48 percent of the population of the European Union and 32 percent of the votes at the European Union's Council of Ministers for decisions adopted by qualified majority.

The focus on large countries is also interesting from a theoretical viewpoint. If one moves from the field of European integration to that of peripheral nationalism, one learns that the effort by culturally distinct regions to loosen or break the ties with the states to which they belong has been greater in more developed than in less developed regions.[15] This is because the leading classes of highly developed regions resent not having political power commensurate with their economic weight and having to subsidize poorer regions. The analogy of the European Union to that of a plurinational state would lead to the prediction that bigger states, especially the oldest ones, are less supportive of European integration than are smaller states, because of the reduction in formal sovereignty that it entails and the net budgetary transfers from rich to poor countries. If one takes the European Union's five largest states, however, it turns out that the "Overdevelopment Thesis" does not hold. With the exception of the United Kingdom, the European Union's biggest states have traditionally been solid supporters of membership in the European Union. If one takes, for instance, the running series of Eurobarometer surveys since 1973 and computes the average net support for membership in the European Union for those years in which the countries were members (percentage who find membership a good thing minus percentage who find membership a bad thing), West Germany ranks ninth out of sixteen (after distinguishing West from East Germany), East Germany ranks eleventh, France ranks eighth, Spain sixth, and Italy third (figure 1.1 shows trends in the six largest countries). The picture is slightly more consistent with

INTRODUCTION

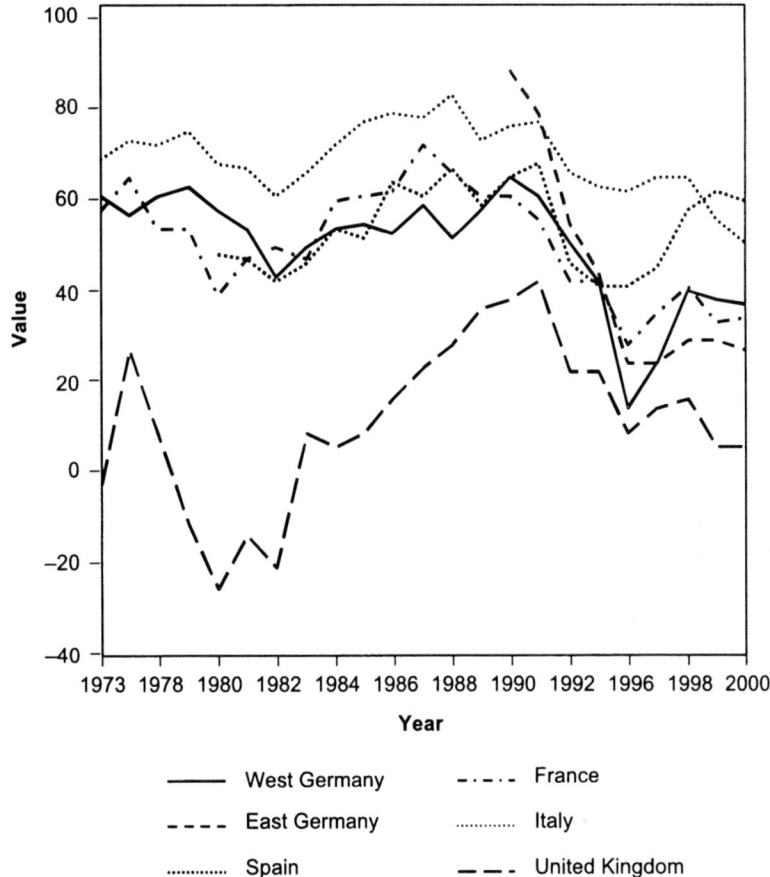

Figure 1.1 Trends in net support for membership in the European Union (percentage who find membership a good thing—percentage who find membership a bad thing; Source: Eurobarometer. 1973–2000) in the largest European Union member states.

Overdevelopment Theory if we just focus on the year 2000 (see table 1). In this year, West Germany ranked ninth, East Germany ranked twelfth, France tenth, Spain fourth, Italy eighth, and the United Kingdom fifteenth. Nonetheless, except for the United Kingdom, levels of support in the five biggest European Union states are still much higher than in some small countries like Austria, Sweden, Denmark, and Finland. In sum, an examination of large European Union states can thus help to clarify why Overdevelopment Theory, which has proven quite valuable for the understanding of peripheral nationalism, does not work so well in an emergent plurinational state structure like the European Union.

TABLE 1
Net Support for Membership in the European Union in 2000 (percentage who view membership as good minus percentage who view membership as bad)

Country	Net Support for Membership in the EU
Luxembourg	75
Ireland	71
Netherlands	64
Spain	58
Portugal	55
Belgium	55
Greece	53
Italy	49
West Germany	36
France	33
Denmark	29
East Germany	26
Finland	17
Austria	14
United Kingdom	5
Sweden	1

Source: Eurobarometer 54.1 (Fall 2000).

A third reason why the three-way comparison between Germany, the United Kingdom, and Spain is useful is that the three countries border with France, both the leading force behind the launching of plans toward European integration and the country that played the most important role in the development of these three countries' national identity.[16] France indeed provided the political and cultural model that influenced the United Kingdom, Germany, and Spain in deciding between a West European and an alternative supranational identity (Imperial or Anglo-Saxon, Central European, or "Hispanic" respectively). Central to this book are then the following questions: How did the three countries solved their identity dilemma? What caused the solution they eventually adopted? What impact had this solution on subsequent levels of support for European integration?

Finally, this three-way comparison allows for controlling for variables that have been used with limited results in previous statistical analyses of survey data, and for variables that have been mentioned in discussions of support for European integration but whose import has not been seriously examined. The level of a country's wealth and the extent to which it depends on trade with the European Union belong to the former category, whereas relative geographic isolation, old statehood, and emotional ties to the populations of former colonies belong to the latter. The contrast between the United Kingdom and Germany—both wealthy countries and with relatively low levels of trade interdependence with the European Union but still showing very different levels of support for European integration—leads to the conclusion that other variables are at play in this category of countries.[17] The contrast between Spain and the United Kingdom—both separated from the center of Europe by geographical obstacles (the Pyrenees and the Channel), very old and plurinational nation-states, and with strong emotional ties to the population of former colonies (Latin America and the Dominions), but at the same time very different in terms of support for European integration—suggests that the effects of geographic obstacles, old statehood, and emotional ties to former colonies are not very strong compared to those of other variables. In this book, I examine to what extent the difference in the British and Spanish levels of economic development explains this contrast, although the comparison between the United Kingdom and Germany already shows that more than rough contrasts in levels of economic development are at stake.

From Statistics to History: Accounts of Support for European Integration in the United Kingdom, Germany, and Spain

Along with quantitative studies, numerous articles and books have been published, written in an essayistic manner and focused on specific countries, which offer interpretations for the levels of support for European integration and for trends in these levels over time. The explanations that have been given for each of the countries can be grouped into several categories. Beginning with Spain, one can distinguish three main hypotheses for the relatively high levels of support. The most frequent argument is that Spaniards have supported membership in the European Union and European integration because they believe that it will contribute to Spain's economic and social modernization.[18] Closely associated with this argument is the hypothesis that Spaniards support European integration because of the significant economic assistance Spain receives from the European Union.[19] Álvarez-Miranda, after carefully comparing political debates in Spain, Greece, and Portugal, concludes that the optimism regarding the effects of membership in the European Union has been stronger in Spain than in the other two countries because Spain was in a better position to compete economically.[20] The second hypothesis one finds in the literature on Spain explains high levels of support for European integration by focusing on the symbolic dimension of membership in the European Union. Authors have emphasized that membership in the European Union is seen as a symbol of acceptance as Europeans and of having become European and democratic.[21] The third frequently mentioned hypothesis is that high support for European integration reflects the Spaniards' expectation that membership in the European Union will reinforce democracy in Spain and prevent the reemergence of nondemocratic authoritarian tendencies.[22] At a deeper level, Álvarez-Miranda has pointed out that in contrast to Greece, where the political elites were divided in their views of Europe and on the issue of membership in the European Union, Spain's consensus about supporting membership in the European Union has been grounded on the lack of conflicting views about the role played by Europe in Spain's recent history.

Similarly, explanations for Germany's relatively high level of support for European integration and membership in the European Union can be grouped into three categories. The most popular type of explanation stresses that the European Union provided a substitute for a conventional national identity and contributed to strengthening the Federal Republic of Germany's state identity after Germany's defeat in World War II.[23] Another argument is that support of membership in the European Union and of European integration resulted from a pragmatic effort to make the FRG acceptable in Europe and facilitate German reunification.[24] Finally, it has been mentioned that German support of membership in the European Union originated in the population's satisfaction with the resulting economic benefits.[25]

There is very extensive literature on the United Kingdom's low levels of support for European integration and membership in the European Union. Furthermore, different scholars often invoke a particular causal factor but then trace it to different historical or structural processes. This makes it difficult to classify arguments. At risk of simplification, however, one can distinguish two sets of causal chains. The first one stresses that the immediate cause of British Euroscepticism is that the British population is afraid of losing its identity.[26] This fear rests on the Britons' lack of identification with Europe and their sense of superiority with respect to other Europeans.[27] This is in turn related to the United Kingdom's long history of strong external ties (Empire, Commonwealth, U.S.-U.K. "special relationship"), further reinforced through collaboration in two world wars.[28] Others trace the British population's fear for their national identity to the United Kingdom's decline after World War II, thus contradicting the former arguments.[29]

The second causal chain used to explain British Euroscepticism begins with the British population's reluctance to lose sovereignty.[30] This reluctance is explained through different factors. For some, victory in World

INTRODUCTION   13

War II spared the United Kingdom from the identity crisis that afflicted most other contenders and that pushed them into European integration.[31] For others, the consequence of victory in World War II was that the United Kingdom emerged with an overblown sense of its world political and economic status and thus adopted political behavior that did not correspond to the country's actual decline.[32] This argument is implicitly disputed by those who contend that the United Kingdom is still in fact a world economic power and that, also because of victory in World War II, it has actually played a stronger role in world politics and thus risks losing more than other countries if it surrenders its sovereignty.[33] Finally, some authors invoke the United Kingdom's long tradition of independence and sovereignty and its history of conflict with France and Germany.[34]

In view of this long list of well-informed explanations, it is not my intention in this book to offer entirely new arguments. What I do hope to accomplish however, is to methodically distinguish between relevant and irrelevant factors in the explanation of ordinary citizens' attitudes toward European integration and membership in the European Union, through the use of the comparative method and the application of frame analysis. The comparative approach allows me to discard hypotheses that look promising only when applied to a single case. For example, it is argued that conflict between the United Kingdom and France is a significant factor underlying British identity and the British rejection of European integration. As I state above, conflict with France has also played a crucial role in the development of Spanish and German identities; but this has not prevented Spain and Germany from being strong advocates of European integration.

This book's analytical and methodological approach also avoids sociopsychological theses that are all but impossible to refute, such as arguments about identity crisis that have been applied to both the United Kingdom and Germany. As a case in point, authors have found ways to explain the United Kingdom's reluctance toward European integration by referring alternatively to the population's sense of superiority and strong identity and to the country's identity crisis resulting from decline. Finally, this book prioritizes factors that explain stable patterns of support for European integration over those that are relevant for only short periods. For instance, Álvarez-Miranda's claim, that the desire to secure Spain's democracy explains the Spanish consensus in support of membership in the European Union, seems untenable in view of the fact that high levels of popular support can be traced back to the early 1960s, when Spain was entirely under Franco's control.[35] A survey conducted by the Instituto de Opinión Pública in 1966, for instance, showed that despite low levels of information (60 percent did not have an opinion), already 33 percent of the respondents were in favor of Spain becoming a member, versus 4 percent who preferred economic autarchy and 3 percent who preferred an economic union with Latin America.

In sum, in contrast to nonrefutable sociopsychological explanations or explanations that apply at most to short periods of time, this book's objective is to let people speak, to determine how strongly rooted their arguments are in discussions of European integration, relate them to broader cultural concerns, and, finally, to provide a plausible interpretation of the interplay between culture, structure, and history in explaining international contrasts. The end product is a parsimonious interpretation of the contrasting levels of support for European integration in the United Kingdom, Germany, and Spain that simultaneously provides clues to understanding variation among European Union member states in general. This interpretation stresses the roles of Empire, World War II, and the Spanish Civil War in shaping the British, German, and Spanish political cultures and, consequently, the way their respective populations have conceived of and positioned themselves with respect to European integration. Culture and history trump economics and geopolitics in the explanation of national contrasts in support for European integration because of their impact on people's degree of identification with Europe and because dominant national self-images and historical interpretations have shaped people's perceptions of the suitability of the European Union as a vehicle for the attainment of individual and national economic, status, and geopolitical goals.

Structure of the Book

This book is structured into two parts. Part I clarifies how ordinary citizens and local elites make up their minds about European integration, analyzes their frames on European integration and the European Union, explores the relationship between these frames and support for particular models of European integration in six different cities of three different countries—the United Kingdom, Germany, and Spain—and examines the stability over time of country-specific frames. This investigation goes well beyond Hewstone's study, the only other comparative research project of this kind, by examining the social representations and attitudes toward European integration and the European Union among ordinary citizens and local elites.[36]

In the first two chapters of part I, I focus on the frames people use when reflecting on European integration and the European Union. In chapter 2, I explore similarities and contrasts between countries, thus testing Lamont and Thévenot's nonessentialist view of national cultural repertoires. Moreover, I examine the different elements that enter justifications for and against European integration and the European Union. The analysis not only supports Lamont and Thévenot's claim, but also reveals the important roles that self-images and collective memory play in such justifications.

Social representations are the most immediate cause of attitudes toward European integration and the European Union. I explore this matter in chapter 3, showing that indeed different social representations are linked to different degrees of support and different desired models of European integration. This discussion offers an opportunity to discuss a classification of models of European integration based on how many competences citizens are willing to transfer to the European Union and how much sovereignty they are willing to surrender. The analysis of the views of German, British, and Spanish respondents suggests that European citizens are not yet ready to fully surrender national sovereignty to the European Union but that they nonetheless favor the transfer of a significant number of competences. It also shows that the fear of a loss of national identity and culture and opposition to a surrender of sovereignty are the most likely explanations for why support for European integration is less widespread in the United Kingdom than in Spain and Germany.

The explanation of the ways people conceive of European integration and the European Union demands an examination of the stability of these social representations over time. Recent images probably reflect the impact of recent causes, whereas long-standing images reflect the impact of past events whose effects are reproduced over time. Interviews do not tell us, however, for how long particular images have been held in the population. The solution I propose is to examine these images through content analysis of the views about European integration that have been transmitted by journalists since the end of World War II. Chapter 4 reveals a close match between the frames used by journalists and those used by ordinary citizens and local elites, as well as constancy in the images people hold of European integration and the European Union. Furthermore, qualitative analysis of the approach to European integration over five decades by the editorialists and commentators of seven major newspapers in three countries provides additional information about the forces that shaped the development of particular frames and attitudes.

In part II of the book, I rely on the concepts of frame alignment and cultural resonance to analyze the cultural and historical factors underlying contrasts in the ways Britons, Germans, and Spaniards frame European integration and the European Union. Chapter 5 is devoted to Spain, chapter 6 to West Germany, chapter 7 to East Germany, and chapter 8 to the United Kingdom. Because of the book's purpose, which is to explain international contrasts, I focus only on the cultural resonance of the country-specific frames described in chapters 2, 3, and 4, that contribute to making Germans and Spaniards more favorable and Britons more opposed to European integration. This section of the book demonstrates that the ways people see European integration are in clear alignment with the broader culture. Chapters 5, 6, 7, and 8 also bear witness to the role of counterthemes in limiting the impact of some cultural themes.

The last chapter of part II of the book, chapter 9, recapitulates the findings of preceding chapters and performs a statistical analysis of survey data from the Eurobarometer Study 51.0 (March–April,1999) to test the roles of frames and broader cultural processes in explaining contrasts in support for European integration. Finally, in chapter 10, I synthesize the main substantive findings of this investigation, and speculate about the future path of European integration.

Sources and Methods

Framing Europe relies on a variety of methods and sources.[37] Chapters 2 and 3 analyze 160 in-depth interviews of ordinary citizens and local elites, which I conducted in a total of six cities in the United Kingdom, Germany, and Spain in 1996 and 1997. To keep the anonymity of the respondents, I will call these cities Weststadt, Oststadt, Quijotón, Catadell, Engleton, and Scotsburg. The cities were selected to represent regions within Germany, Spain, and Great Britain with distinctive national identities, as well as the social and economic structures representative of the regions in which the cities were located (based on distribution by economic sector of the active population, mean income per capita, and unemployment rates). I ended up with a West German and an East German city for Germany (Weststadt and Oststadt), a Castilian and Catalan city for Spain (Quijotón and Catadell), and an English and a Scottish city for Great Britain (Engleton and Scotsburg). Appendix 1 provides a detailed description of the technical procedures I followed to select and interview respondents for the project.

Chapter 4 is based on content analysis of a sample of newspaper editorials and opinion pieces published in British, German, and Spanish quality newspapers between 1946 and 1997, the year I ended my fieldwork. Editorials and opinion articles provide a snapshot of how journalists, members of the educated elites, think at a particular time, and thus facilitate the analysis of change and cross-national comparisons. Moreover, they are short, have a similar format, and are relatively easy to access, which facilitates the systematic analysis of a great number of them. I have examined eight daily or weekly quality newspapers:

The Economist and *The New Statesman* for the United Kingdom,
Die Zeit, the *Frankfurter Allgemeine Zeitung*, and *Neues Deutschland* for Germany, and
El País, ABC, and *Cambio16* for Spain.

Whether these are daily or weekly newspapers should be irrelevant for the purposes of this analysis; it is only important that they differ along ideological and national lines. All the newspapers that I have examined are national newspapers with a very large readership in their respective countries (relative to other newspapers of the same type, daily or weekly). In sum, the editorials and opinion pieces on European integration I have analyzed in quality newspapers are representative enough to allow me to attain the following objectives:

   1. provide an overview of the dominant frames on European integration in British, Spanish, and German quality newspapers and outline the main contrasts in the ways their respective journalists have conceived of European integration,
   2. determine the longevity of the frames that distinguish British, German, and Spanish respondents,
   3. provide a contextualized view of the emergence of these frames, and
   4. describe the main contrasts in the ways more conservative and more progressive British, German, and Spanish quality newspapers have approached European integration in this fifty-year period. In Appendix 2 I provide a detailed description of the techniques I used to select and code editorials and opinion pieces.

To write the second part of this book, I have relied on primary and secondary sources appropriate to the frames' sociopolitical nature. My analysis of primary sources is justified by the comparative focus of this project. Rather than looking for cultural materials that demonstrate the cultural resonance of the frames I analyze, and thus running the risk of overestimating the salience of a cultural theme or countertheme in the different countries, I have systematically examined the same set of primary sources in the three countries. What makes the selection of primary sources problematic is that any single source provides at best a partial view of the countries' national cultures. Finding that a particular frame does not resonate with the cultural themes discussed in a particular source does not necessarily mean that the frame is not culturally relevant: different sources are conducive to the expression of different cultural preoccupations, for they vary in their institutional locations, their functions, their addressees, their styles of presentation, and so on. My choice of sources has been guided by three main criteria:

   1. they should be sources in which one might expect discussion or expression of themes pertaining to the field of political culture;
   2. they should be sources that have been used by scholars for the analysis of national cultures;
   3. they should be easy to compare across national states.

The three types of sources that I analyze are prize-winning novels, secondary school textbooks on contemporary history, and head-of-state

Christmas or New Year's addresses. Although the three sources can be conceived as officially sanctioned cultural products, they are a legitimate entry point to a comparative study of national cultural repertoires to the extent that the themes I examine for each country have been at least as salient among educated and official elites as among the population at large. I follow authors such as Sarah Corse in approaching the national culture through the analysis of canon and prize-winning literature. High-culture literature, says Corse, codifies national elites' visions of their nations and their national experiences, which then in turn helps to determine the content of these nations' identities.[38] She adds that within this high-culture literature, award-winning novels "serve as an on-going validation of nationhood, as markers of a flourishing national culture and identity."[39] In chapters 5 through 8, I also follow Eugen Weber in privileging school textbooks as a source of information about the national culture.[40] History textbooks provide at the very least an indication of the national historical narrative and national self-images that segments of a society's elite would like to instill in the population. Finally, I have chosen to examine head-of-state Christmas or New Year's addresses because they are a yearly power ritual in which the head of state goes over the year's main events and in the process reminds his or her audience of the main markers of the national identity. These addresses offer, among other things, a unique opportunity to examine the collective memory and self-images that state elites, through their highest representative, try to transmit to the population. In Appendix 4 I provide detailed justifications for the selection of novels, history text books, and heads of state addresses, as well as a listing of the selected novels and history textbooks.

The last main source of data I use in this book is the European Commission's Eurobarometer Study 51.0, corresponding to March–April 1999. In chapter 9, I perform statistical analysis with the data contained in this study to examine the validity of some of the arguments developed in the book.

Part I

FRAMES ON EUROPEAN INTEGRATION AND THE EUROPEAN UNION IN THE UNITED KINGDOM, GERMANY, AND SPAIN

Two

Ways of Seeing European Integration

PUBLIC SUPPORT for European political integration is significantly lower in the United Kingdom than in Spain or Germany. Because of this, the British are often portrayed as "deviant," as "spoil-sports" who are unable to adapt to a changing world in which states have become too small. But are they really? Should not we ask instead how it is that the populations of countries like Spain and Germany so easily accept the withering away of the nation-state? It takes a somewhat structuralist-functionalist and ahistorical view of social change to expect that sweeping changes in the economy, such as globalization, will be automatically followed by appropriate political and mental adjustments toward the development of, if not global, at least regional forms of political organization. Rapid and extensive social change inevitably generates resistance. Peasants did not happily turn into industrial workers, local elites did not happily surrender their power to the emergent modern state, the "nationalization of the masses," to borrow a concept from the late George Mosse, did not just happen.[1] The latter, in particular, was a long and often bloody process, in which the state itself was a leading player. To foresee in 1918 that the same century that began with the apogee of nationalism would come to a close under unequivocal signs of an uncoupling of "national" and political identities would have required a good deal of imagination. Therefore, explaining the apparent willingness of some to strengthen European political institutions is as important as explaining others' reluctance to do so.

In this chapter I provide an overview of how ordinary citizens and local elites in Germany, the United Kingdom, and Spain conceive of European integration. I examine the arguments people use when asked to justify their attitudes toward European integration and their country's membership in the European Union (EU), perceptions of the economic effects of membership in the EU for their country, attitudes toward economic and monetary union, and satisfaction or dissatisfaction with the European Union. The answers to these questions and additional commentary provided during the interviews reflect the culturally grounded cognitive frames that bound people's thinking about European integration.

Modes of Argumentation

Thinking about European integration is not people's favorite pastime. They hear about it once in a while in the news, register the information, and then forget.[2] The population has begun to confront the European Union directly, however. Economic and monetary union (EMU) is the most striking example, since it is the first political measure in the process of European integration whose impact will be immediately felt by everybody who resides in the European Union. Apart from this, the European Union makes itself visible in many ways: to farmers, who must adjust what they produce and in what quantities, to meet the requirements of the Common Agricultural Policy (CAP); to fishermen, who can fish only in certain places and certain quantities (in agreement with the Common Fisheries policies); and to producers in general who must confront stepped-up competition from producers in other EU countries or who must meet quality standards decided in Brussels. It also makes itself visible to students, who ponder whether to study in another EU country and apply for an Erasmus Fellowship; to consumers, who weigh the advantages and disadvantages of buying a car in another EU country where taxes are lower, or who now notice a greater range of products in the supermarket; and more generally, to ordinary citizens who travel to other EU countries and rejoice at not having to carry a passport, or who once in a while notice that a road has been built with EU funds. The number of those who at some point or another confront the EU during their daily activities is no longer negligible; but, except for the small few whose livelihood is highly dependent on what the European institutions decide, the majority of the population pays at least as little attention to EU affairs as it pays to TV commercials.

Repetition pays, however, and, as they do with commercials, people have accumulated some knowledge about the EU over the years, enough so as to develop a certain image of the EU: a sketch of what it represents, what it promises, how it works, and what the costs and benefits of membership are. The contours of these images of the EU are thinly penciled, discontinuous, unfinished, full of things that need to be erased or corrected because they do not match the overall design. An hour or two hours of "forced," albeit relaxed, concentration on a topic like European integration hardly suffices for people to assemble all the snippets of reflection stored in lost corners of their minds into a coherent whole—especially if the interviewer refuses to provide any cue as to how to answer questions! The slightly annoying "Why do you think that way?" or "Can you tell me more about that?," patiently and politely repeated by the interviewer after every vague answer to general questions about the EU, does help to stimulate the brain into remembering, even forming arguments. When one puts together all these arguments, sketch over sketch, the contours of individual images of the EU become clearer, and differences and similarities between cities and countries emerge. Respondents may themselves not be totally convinced of the accuracy of these images or of the validity of the attributes they use to praise or criticize the European Union, and they may be incapable of developing their arguments further when prompted by the interviewer. But this is all they have with which to make judgments about European integration; if they think, even vaguely, that the European Union poses a threat to their identity, or that it contributes to better understanding among people from different countries, then that is information that they will use in order to form an opinion about the European Union.[3]

Throughout the interview, respondents had plenty of opportunities to express what they had heard and thought about the European integration process and the European Union, and to justify their answers. The description and comparisons below are based on the respondents' justifications for their answers to four standard questions:

- Are you rather in favor or rather against efforts toward European integration?
- Do you think it is a good thing or a bad thing that (your country) is a member of the European Union?
- Would you say that the economic effects of membership in the European Union have been very beneficial, beneficial, not beneficial, or not at all beneficial?
- In general, would you say that you are satisfied or dissatisfied with the European Union?

Since the interviews were semi-structured, focusing only on those questions asked of everybody provides a safeguard against the possibility that the specific roads taken by the interviews may have prompted different types of comments from the respondents.[4] The quotes that I use to illustrate the major themes covered by these comments are, however, sometimes taken from other sections of the interview.

Participants in this project provided a wide variety of justifications for their answers on issues related to European integration, spanning more than one hundred and thirty favorable arguments and more than one hundred unfavorable ones.[5] In fact, this is only a conservative estimate, since similar answers were coded into broader categories. For instance, respondents who justified their support for European integration by saying "states are too small" or "countries are too small" were coded under the same category.

The broad range of arguments provided by the respondents reflects quite well the different ways in which individuals explain their thoughts and actions to themselves and to others. Some justified their attitudes toward European integration with reference to how they see the world or their country. Answers of the kind "We are all Europeans, therefore we should be united," "It cannot work, because cultures are too different," and "We live in a world where problems have become too big for individual states alone to be able to solve them," fall within this category. The orientation toward European integration or toward a country's membership in the European Union is based on an assessment of how things are. A similar logic underlies answers that originate in the respondents' self-identities, in how they see themselves: "I have always identified with Europe," "I am not concerned with the loss of sovereignty," "I am an optimistic person," "I don't like to be told what to do by another country," or "I don't like the idea of unification." Justifications of this kind often border on circularity, if they are not completely tautologous. When this is the case, they reveal a positive or negative orientation to issues related to European integration that is directly tied to how people feel about the idea of European integration per se rather than to specific aspects directly related to these issues. It is like saying "I am for European unification, because I think European countries should unite," or "I am against membership in the European Union because I don't like my country working together with other countries."

A second category of arguments involved evaluations of what the European Union represents, what it is and does. As mentioned earlier, the European Union can be broadly conceived as a supranational institution whose immediate achievements have been the removal of barriers to trade, the mobility of factors of production and the intensification of cooperation between member states, the implementation of a common currency, and the development of common legislation and standards in many areas. Justification of support for or rejection of European integration or of membership in the European Union that made reference to these achievements falls into this second category, as do arguments used to justify satisfaction or dissatisfaction with the European Union.

A third category of arguments addressed the expected or already perceived effects of European integration or of membership in the European Union. Effects of European integration or membership in the European Union were seen in many areas: the economy, relations between people from different countries, peace, security and defense, a country's prestige or image abroad, social inequalities, national identity, and social modernization. These are the topics to which most of the justifications in this category referred.

By asking respondents to expand on the reasons why they were satisfied or dissatisfied with the European Union, I was able to obtain information on a fourth category of attributes that people connect with the European integration process and with European institutions. Many of the answers referred to the way the European Union functions, to governance issues. This type of argument was also used when people reflected on the positive or negative comments they had heard in connection with the European Unification process or the European Union. Thus, for instance, people criticized the way the CAP works, the huge EU bureaucracy, the fact that there is too much distance between the EU and the citizens, or that most decisions are taken unanimously rather than on a qualified-majority basis. Alternatively, respondents praised the fact that the European Union offers a corrective for bad national government, or the existence of the cohesion and regional development funds.

Finally, respondents praised or criticized, and favored or opposed, European integration or membership in the European Union with reference to where they see the project evolving. Some criticized the slow pace of integration, others criticized the fact that it goes too fast. Some felt uncomfortable about the enlargement to the East, whereas others welcomed it. Some liked the prospect of the EU evolving into something like the United States of Europe, whereas other people abhorred the idea of such a thing ever happening.

Although there is a great deal of diversity in the way people think about European integration, the pages that follow reveal that the respondents' views were predominantly informed by considerations of economic interest, status, and power, in a most Weberian fashion, but also by considerations of good and democratic governance and geopolitical stability. These considerations were in turn guided by past and current individual and collective experience and by expectations about what the future will bring.

The present shapes people's views of European integration through their lived experiences and the information they get from local and national sources. The respondents' comments below show that the European Union is beginning to be experienced in a more direct way than is usually assumed. The national media and, through them, national politicians, intellectuals, interest groups, and the European Union itself, are no longer the only sources of information respondents have about the European Union. Increasingly, people are confronted with the EU's bureaucracy or directly observe its achievements. They also learn about the EU's activities through relatives, friends, or local channels of communication in the communities where they live. The simplistic elite-oriented approach to European unification prevailing in much of the literature has become obsolete.

The past, in the form of collective memory, is also a major factor in the way people conceive of European integration. It conjures up images of better or worse times, to which the present and the future can be compared. The past also makes us conscious of what can happen, and mobilizes us to find strategies to avoid it or bring it back. These strategies are in turn informed by our causal reading of past events. Last but not least, the past reminds us of what we are or once were.

Finally, one's images of European integration and the European Union are informed by what these developments promise for the future. These promises are fundamentally shaped by the messages one gets through the media, but they are also increasingly filtered through one's experiences and interpretations of the effects that European integration has had up to the present. In some cases, these experiences make the promises for the future more credible; on other occasions, they undermine the credibility of such promises.

The Development of a Common View of European Integration

The Benefits of the Common Market

Despite the broad variety of arguments, justifications, and explanations that people offered to clarify their attitudes toward European integration, these tended to converge into a much narrower set of themes (see table 2). On the pro-integration side, the theme that was most frequently mentioned concerns the actual characteristics of and expectations built around the common market. Eighty-one percent of the respondents mentioned the common market and its economic impact as positive aspects of integration. Foremost of all, comments referred to the beneficial effects of the removal of barriers to trade, the formation of a bigger market, and the possibility of working abroad:

> We've got now a huge market on our doorstep, without a lot of the controls and the border controls; that's all been taken down and it allows us to trade in a very big market locally, which must be very cost-effective compared to where we were before. (7, Engleton, Conservative Party representative)[6]

> It is important to be there, so that our products are available, so that our products can go to Europe, so that people can move, easily change address, go and work abroad. (142, Quijotón, 30 or younger, more than High School)

These sorts of comments are based on the assumption that the implementation of the common market will have a direct positive impact on economic well-being and growth. Expected as this finding may be, it is nonetheless remarkable how successful the European Union and its members' governments have been in selling the idea that bigger markets and the resulting greater competition are good for the economy. Early in the

TABLE 2
Themes Mentioned to Justify Positive or Negative Comments about European Integration or the European Union, by City.
(Number of respondents who mention a particular theme)

	Germany		Spain		United Kingdom		
	Weststadt	Oststadt	Quijotón	Catadell	Engleton	Scotsburg	Total
Common Market	23	22	19	20	23	22	129
states too small	12	14	16	14	13	10	79
removal of barriers	13	10	11	8	13	12	67
governance	12	10	9	9	14	16	70
free movement and competion	10	10	1				21
democratic deficit	11	6	4		5	1	27
lessons of World War II	17	2					19
peace	11	9	4	1	9	8	42
understanding	16	5	9	6	11	6	53
modernization	1		8	9	3	3	24
CAP	1	4	15	12	7	8	47
Structural/Regional Funds	1	1	12	10	6	9	39
against isolation		1	7	5	2		15
voice		2	4	8	3	3	20
sovereignty and identity	2	1	2	2	9	9	25
social benefits	1	2	4	4	5	8	24
total respondents	27	29	27	24	27	26	160

century, protectionism was a major source of internal and external political dispute in Europe. Nowadays, however, while the citizenry of the EU may disagree with some of the political aspects of European unification, it is almost unanimous in believing in this basic tenet of economic liberalism.

Not surprisingly, British and German respondents sounded more confident about their chances in the common market than did Spanish respondents. They are, after all, successful export-oriented nations:

> We survive on free trade; we are one of the world's great free trading nations, and Britain exports more per head than the Japanese. You know, we need to have a world where trade, where there are no barriers to trade; otherwise, we'll lose out. So I suspect that I come from that background, that that's my attitude. I want as much free trade as I can possibly get, and the trade across Europe—given that my business is here—a whole market for Europe is important

to me. And the other issue which I think is important is that Britain's businesses largely grew up on tame markets, on the tamed markets of Australia, New Zealand, South Africa, the West Indies, the old colonies; that, you know, we said "Well, you will buy that and the business is good and life is easy." Well, that does not exist anymore, there is no loyalty to UK trade or companies, and so I think that the creation of a single, bigger, home market is ideal.

(8, Engleton, Chamber of Commerce)

We are a country that has produced good products for more than a hundred years. We also think that we have the best vocational training in Europe, and this is the reason why it is advantageous. For us, Germans, it can only be to our advantage. (128, Weststadt, Manual Workers' Chamber)

In Spain, with a tradition of closed markets and trade deficits, the common market was also at the center of people's conception of the European Union, and support for it was very strong. Contrary to British and German respondents, however, Spanish respondents supported the common market with a mixture of hope and fear about its immediate economic effects. Thus, the following comments by a leading representative of the leftist union Comisiones Obreras in Catadell, and of a major farmers' organization in Quijotón:

I believe that it is true that a market of 240 million people offers many more possibilities to everybody than would a much smaller market. Of course, it offers more possibilities but also more challenges, more competition, more problems. (73, Catadell)

I think that it looks very good on paper, in terms of saying "well, we are already all there, there are no borders, all diplomas are recognized," and so on. But what we are seeing is that except in soccer, where Spain has imported all the European players, the truth is that—when we look at other professional areas—the architect who worked abroad before the European Union continues to do so. And here is something that I don't like. If a Spanish doctor or a Spanish engineer has a degree from the Sorbonne or from Germany and has demonstrated his worth, then fine, but for the one who gets his degree from the [University] Complutense, or the [University] Autónoma from Madrid and wants to work in France or Germany, then it is much more difficult. (156, Quijotón)

These last quotes tell us about people's attitudes toward market principles. Popular approval and support of most aspects related to the common market is largely based on belief rather than reasoned judgment. Indeed, when pressed for justifications, few respondents could expand on why a bigger market is better for the economy, why the removal of tariff barriers will stimulate trade, or why the common market must be limited to the European Union rather than be extended to the whole world. They eventually fell back on personal feelings or on what they had read or heard in the media, like the two respondents below:

> In the short term there may be problems, but in the medium and long terms, there will be advantages.
>
> *What sort of advantages?*
>
> A common market, without borders, custom duties, and all these things that still exist.
>
> *Can you explain why this is advantageous?*
>
> I cannot explain it. I've read it in the press that it will be advantageous.
> (128, Weststadt, Manual Workers' Chamber representative)
>
> I think that we will have to wake up to be at their level and that this will have positive economic consequences.
>
> *Where do you get this optimism?*
>
> [Laughter] Well, I guess we have to think positive.
> (81, Catadell, 30 or younger, more than High School)

States Are Too Small

Closely related to the common market theme is the argument that justifies European integration on grounds that states have become too small. About half the respondents in this study mentioned aspects of this argument at some point during the interview. One expression that I often heard during the interviews was the saying "Union is strength" ("Einigkeit macht stark," "La unión hace la fuerza"). People used this expression, apparently convinced of the millenarian authority embodied in traditional sayings. It also served them as a preface to three slightly different points. The first one is that states have become too interdependent and can no longer stand alone. This argument was quite well spelled out by a leading member of the Spanish Socialist Party (PSOE) in Catadell:

> Europe faces the challenge of unity, the challenge of creating a single currency, of belonging to a common market, of having a common foreign and security policy, the challenge of "becoming." We have already overcome the reality of states competing amongst themselves, and we have a universalization of the economy, a worldwide expansion of markets, technological norms that transcend borders. Borders are over and they *must* be over. They don't make sense anymore ... The globalization process has already destroyed the basic elements that sustained states. Nowadays, for instance, a state can no longer maintain the

stability of its currency by itself. In two days the state can be bankrupt because Mr. Soros, or whoever, embarks on a business transaction. Not even Germany can afford to go it alone. (93, Catadell)

To this perception of the globalization of the economy there corresponds a perception of the globalization of problems affecting humanity, which is the second type of argument that respondents used to clarify why states are too small. Thus the comment made by a main representative of the Green Party in Oststadt, for whom,

There are problems in Europe and also in the world that if analyzed pragmatically cannot be financed by the countries individually.

For instance?

The often cited environmental problem, the often cited social domain, social costs from young to old age, which can no longer be solved by the countries alone. (68, Oststadt)

Finally, the respondents' use of the expression "union is strength" corresponded to a widely shared perception that European states can only counter competition from the United States, Japan, and China by forming an economic bloc. The United States, in particular, appeared as both competitor and role model, as in the two following comments:

If we continue to hide in our own countries, none of us will have enough strength to compete in whatever context, whether in defense or in the economic sphere, with the USA, Japan, and China.
(82, Catadell, deputee from Conservative Party)

I would rather have my children grow up in a big nation, a united nation, than a small nation. You know, like the United States. The United Kingdom was great at some time, but you cannot compare it with the United States. And I think that the power of the United States has come from the union.
(52, Scotsburg, 31–50, more than High School)

The Elimination of Borders

Economic arguments played the dominant role in positive images of European unification. The European Union was essentially portrayed as a powerful economic engine, capable of facing up to competition from other world economic blocs in a globalized world. The third positive attribute with significant salience in people's imagined European Union, however, was of a noneconomic nature: the possibility of traveling across Europe without hindrances, such as passports and border controls. This trait was mentioned by almost half the respondents in this study, mostly when asked about what they like in the European Union. One of my English respondents, a married man who works for Royal Mail and who was once stationed in a military base in Germany, illustrated this from personal experience:

> When we lived in Germany, we had to get on a boat to France; you get your passport out, and then you go through France to Belgium; you get your passport out and you go. You could cross from Belgium to Holland without getting your passport out and then, when you got to the German border, passport out again before you can go into Germany. Now you just go, and there isn't any of that. It makes traveling a lot easier. (11, 31–50, less than High School)

The respondents expressed happiness that the borders are gone, at least on paper. Some respondents even reflected on the fact that the removal of borders enhances their sense of belonging to Europe:

> I think that from a psychological viewpoint, one gets a totally different feeling when one travels and there are no borders.
> (112, Weststadt, older than 50, less than High School)

As some respondents indicated, however, the removal of borders would not be a prime reason for them to push for European integration. It simply eliminates a minor nuisance when traveling abroad. Some respondents actually expressed the opposite view, that the removal of border controls poses a threat to the security of Europe's citizens, by facilitating drug trafficking, illegal migration, and other forms of crime. What matters in the context of this chapter, however, is that the removal of border controls is an essential element in people's image of Europe, whether as a source of satisfaction, as is mostly the case, or of dissatisfaction.

Governance

People's positive evaluation of a barrier-free Europe was complemented by a negative evaluation of most aspects related to governance. Almost half the respondents expressed dislike for the administrative side of the European Union. The European Union was portrayed as opaque, distant, inefficient, inadequate to respond to the task of unification, nonaccountable, paralyzed by national egoisms, eroded by corruption, and obsessed with regulating every little aspect of people's lives. When asked to compare the EU bureaucracy with their national bureaucracy along these same parameters, most people remained silent or admitted that indeed their national bureaucracies are not much better. Still, it is an aspect of the European Union with which they were deeply dissatisfied. This general level of dissatisfaction was expressed in slightly different ways in different countries, which one can relate to other national-specific features of images of the European Union. British and German respondents, for instance, especially the former, were more likely to criticize the levels of corruption within the European Union than were Spanish respondents. The following excerpt from an interview with a Conservative leader in Engleton illustrates this and simultaneously shows how national self-perceptions and perceptions of other national groups color people's approach to European integration:

> There is a perception in Britain, whether it's true or not—it's not been helped by certain instances over a number of years—that other countries would sign these documents and on face value agree with them, and then just carry on and totally ignore them. One of the great anomalies! A great example is this European advice on "clean beaches"; they call it "blue flag scale"—you've obviously encountered it. Now, scientifically, if you look at it, geographically, nobody can tell us that a west coast port, in Britain, or west coast holiday resort in Britain can possibly have dirtier beaches than a Mediterranean port, let's say, at the mouth of the Rhône, or any of the other Mediterranean rivers. It does not add up scientifically, yet Britain has less blue flag beaches than any other country in Europe. Now, you have to ask yourself a question. Who does the checking from the European Community? Who does the water testing? Who checks the beaches? Now, I know for a fact that it is a British environmental civil servant. So, I also guess that in Greece there isn't a British environmental agent checking their water, and there is a feeling of—sometimes European politics can be a bit dodgy and you could see handfuls of lira that are being passed at the local, by the local town major to the local water inspector, to make sure that they get a blue flag. Now, that could not possibly happen in Britain.   (12, Engleton)

British respondents also distinguished themselves from German or Spanish respondents in the sensitivity and outrage they expressed toward the European Union's harmonization and standardization tendencies. This outrage, reflected in and exacerbated by the tabloid press in the United Kingdom, reflected the opinion that the European Union should busy itself with more important issues than to determining the shape of cucumbers or how to refer to Brussels sprouts. Underlying this criticism, however, was also the irritation many British respondents felt toward what they perceived to be a breach of the United Kingdom's sovereignty. This is a distinguishing feature of British attitudes that is further examined below. Meanwhile, the following quotes illustrate the respondents' concern about overregulation:

> I work in the bus-building industry and I think that the biggest mistake was when they tried to take the double-deckers off the roads of Britain. These people know absolutely nothing about transport and they try to make that ruling!

They tried to forbid double-deckers?

Yes, they tried to take double-deckers off the roads. I think that over there, on the continent, I think that over there you'll rarely find double-deckers on the roads, very rarely do you find that. In this country, that's the way we do our business. (41, Scotsburg, 31–50, less than High School)

I just remember something now, where they have gone a little bit over the top. In this country, it appears that we are unable to buy milk chocolate as milk chocolate. Now, the EEC has declared that, you know, apparently we don't put enough cocoa in the chocolate and it does not come up to the specified percentage levels that they say makes a chocolate. And that's been known as chocolate in this country; since time immemorial it's always been chocolate. So, that seems a little bit silly. (36, Scotsburg, 31–50, less than High School)

The respondents from Germany, the United Kingdom, and Spain thus seemed to share a basic common sketch of European integration and the European Union. This sketch depicted a Kafkaesque bureaucracy administering a vast market area for goods, labor, and services, in which people move freely and unencumbered by police border controls. In its broadest contours, this image differed very little from city to city and from country to country. Even in Oststadt, which as part of the former GDR only recently joined the EU, common market, globalization, governance, and the removal of border controls were the aspects that people emphasized when justifying their attitudes toward European integration and the European Union.

National Images

The assumption implicit in many comparative quantitative analyses, that the meaning of European integration is the same across countries, would be legitimate if European integration and the European Union were simply understood in the ways I have described thus far. With minor differences, the four themes presented above were very salient in Germany, the United Kingdom, and Spain. However, as I traveled across Europe, reading the newspapers and talking to people, what puzzled me were the national and, occasionally, the regional contrasts. Within each city, the answers in an interview became predictable, after a while, as if scripted by the same author. Not unexpectedly, the themes that came up during interviews reflected what I heard or read in the media quite well. Even those respondents who expressed little or no interest whatsoever in politics, or in the European Union for that matter, were able to repeat published or broadcast comments by politicians, journalists, or representatives of various interest groups. I also noticed that the way people talked about the European Union bore a strong thematic and rhetorical resemblance with other societal preoccupations, even obsessions. As I moved between countries, the themes changed and I needed to readjust my expectations about how respondents would justify their answers to questions on European integration. Each country, and even each city, provided me with a unique opportunity to see European integration and the European Union in a different light, a light quite consistent with the prevailing culture. The description of these contrasts constitutes the object of the rest of the chapter. The question of how they came about is dealt with in coming chapters.

National culture and collective memory are the elements that gave each country's cognitive frame on European integration its distinctive flair. In fact, the examination of these frames helps to assess whether a common national culture and a common collective memory actually exist in a particular country, despite regional differences in identification with the nation. The examination of two cities in each country, representing different subnational identities, responded to the goal of assessing in which ways these different group identities had had an impact on the way people imagined European integration and the European Union. The comparison of cities in Germany, the United Kingdom, and Spain revealed that the subnational cultures affected people's images of European integration only in Germany. The images of European integration and the European Union in the Castilian city of Quijotón and the Catalan city of Catadell were quite similar; the same applies for the difference between the English city of Engleton and the Scottish city of Scotsburg. The East German city of Oststadt and the West German city of Weststadt, however, while similar to each other in ways that differentiated them from the British and Spanish cities, were more different from each other than was either of the other two pairs.

Germany: Labor Competition, Democratic Deficit, and National Socialism

Despite their faith in the common market and its economic advantages, the German population's optimistic approach to European unification was clouded by their anxiety about the effects of differences in wages and general social benefits across the European Union. This anxiety distinguished the German respondents from the Spanish and British respondents, who seldom if ever mentioned this topic. Almost two-fifths of the respondents in Weststadt and slightly more than a third of the respondents in Oststadt mentioned factors related to this inequality in wages and social benefits during the interviews. They typically made this comment when discussing the economic disadvantages of membership in the European Union, but it is also a negative comment that many, especially in Oststadt, claimed to have heard from other people.

Three factors contribute to the explanation of this concern among the German respondents: the high unemployment rates, the completion of the EU's internal market for goods, labor, and capital, and the fact that German wages and social benefits are higher than those in other European Union countries. The last two factors have promoted the relocation of German firms to countries where wages and social benefits are lower and have provided incentives for immigration to Germany from these same countries. Spain and the United Kingdom, where wages and social benefits are set at a much lower level, have no equivalent problems. The inequality in wages and social benefits across the EU is therefore an issue that few Spanish and British respondents mentioned when talking about the European Union. When they did, it was to express their hope that a standardization of social benefits would lead to a higher level than the one prevailing in their own country.

Thus, the problem of unemployment in Germany has become inextricably linked to the problem of wage and social benefits inequality across the European Union. The arguments I heard in the interviews reveal that three possible solutions are currently considered among the population. One solution is to restrict the functioning of the competitive mechanisms of the internal market; respondents suggested that this could be accomplished by immigration quotas, increased taxation of companies that relocate abroad, more stringent controls on labor competition within the national market, or other means. The second proposed solution is the homogenization of labor costs across the EU at a level only slightly below that in Germany. Finally, the third proposed solution is to lower labor costs in Germany. The respondents' comments suggested, however, that only the first two solutions, and especially the first one, are seriously considered at the popular level. Support for the homogenization of labor conditions across the EU is not limited to Germany, however, as I discuss below. Meanwhile, the following two quotes from the representatives of the Manual Workers' Chamber in Weststadt and Oststadt illustrate the dominant views on both the link between unemployment and the European Union and the best way to address the problems that this link creates:

> Faced with renewed competition, the younger generation raises the following question: "what does it mean to become an apprentice or a master craftsman? What do we get out of it? It brings us nothing. We are under heavy financial pressure; we must pay for the exam to become master craftsmen and so on. It costs us a lot of money. And then, after all of this, we experience how craftsmen from other countries come here and start putting things in the market." Eventually, a certain discontent spreads out. We also fear that this training that we have to receive and complete, that this requirement and pressure to complete vocational training, that it will be scrapped. The fact that our labor costs, which

we cannot control, are too high and push prices up plays a decisive role in these developments and prevent us from being competitive. This is the main problem. The quality is there, that can be handled, but we don't prevail because our hourly wage rates are too high, we work too few hours, we have too many opportunities to be sick, or to pretend that we are sick, if I may say so, and all this makes products more expensive, gives a false impression about the real price, the real value of the product....

Is there animosity toward foreign workers?

It has certainly increased over time because of the simple reason that there's high unemployment. The unemployed worker who stands, for instance, in front of a construction site and observes the Polish or English employees who work there—it is natural, it is human—ends up saying: 'Why are you taking my job?' The lords of the construction industry are responsible for this. They are the ones who control the contracts and, instead of signing on local companies, award them to foreign firms. Only later does one realize how many Spanish or English workers have been flown over and work there. This, of course, creates friction and hurts the feelings of some people. (62, Oststadt)

A Portuguese who works here in the construction sector earns more, can actually send more money back home, which leads to a subsequent improvement in the living standards in Portugal, right? On the one hand, I find this a positive thing; on the other hand, it creates serious problems at the moment. We must have competition eventually, but it is currently too difficult and it would create social tensions that would not be altogether good. A large segment of the middle class here in Germany is breaking apart, which has both political and social consequences. Therefore, we need some cushioning; this cannot come so fast. This is the reason why our organization, the craftsmen sector, has demanded a five-year transition period, during which we will still need some protection. During this period we will have to change other things, we will have to bring down our basic costs, social benefits, and additional work-related costs. In fact, I am of two minds: I am for competition, but at the same time this competition must be socially bearable, also to us. This is why what we propose is in fact some form of protectionism. I know it, I am quite conscious about it. I actually consider this a sin but we don't have any other alternative if we want to prevent distress and social problems. That's our predicament.

What sort of problems are you talking about?

Unemployment. You know, I am quite familiar with the history of this century and this is something that we've already gone through, albeit under different circumstances. At any rate, unemployment led to social problems that we must this time prevent at any cost.

Would there be a rise in anti-foreign sentiment?

I don't believe that Germans are naturally predisposed to harbor anti-foreign sentiment. Anti-immigrant feelings could develop, however, if the Germans' situation worsens. Some Germans say, "Why am I worse off? In all probability because there are foreigners among us who live from social benefits financed with our contributions," and so on. I can imagine the development of anti-immigrant feelings from economic factors. The Germans are very spoiled. They have their standards of living and when these go down, they look for culprits; they say things like "we have too many foreigners who live out of our pockets," "it is too costly," and so on, and then we are faced with some kind of reaction. (4, Weststadt)

The quotes above show that many German citizens blame immigrants for the unemployment problem and for threatening both the traditional vocational training system and the system of social benefits. The emphasis on the nexus between labor costs and the German system of vocational training by the Oststadt representative reveals in fact that the understanding of the unemployment debate in Germany must not be framed in simplistic bread-and-butter terms but, rather, in cultural ones. Moreover, the quotes show that many people who analyze the problem dispassionately are giving in to this general sentiment rather than presenting the population with alternative explanations for the unemployment problem that would not undermine the spirit and achievements of European unification. Finally, the references to the German character and to the historical context within which National Socialism came to power in Germany illustrate the role of memory and national self-conceptions in people's reading of the present and their attitudes toward European integration.

Another contrast between German and both British and Spanish respondents concerned the criticism often raised by the former that the European Union suffers from a democratic deficit. Two out of five respondents in Weststadt and one in five respondents in Oststadt raised this criticism, which was often directed at the lack of citizen input in the decisions made by the European Union. The representative of the Green Party in Oststadt best articulated this criticism:

The democratic structures [of the EU] are still insufficiently developed. Too much power is still vested in the Council of Ministers and is executed behind closed doors or at the administrative level; a classic example is the Schengen Treaty that, bypassing national parliaments and the European parliament, was in fact negotiated at the administrative level. Secondly, at this structural level we need more opportunities for majority decision-making, so that one single country can no longer block a decision. Unanimity should be left for very few instances, in which clearly serious national problems or sovereignty are affected.

(58, Oststadt)

In contrast, the democratic deficit criticism was seldom raised in Spain or the United Kingdom. In the United Kingdom, when expressed, it often conveyed a dislike for government from Brussels. When I probed British respondents who criticized the lack of democracy in the European Union and asked them how they would feel if most of the decision-making power was vested in a democratically elected European Parliament, they usually opposed this.

Thus, the results from this study suggest that the democracy criticism of the European Union is more nation-specific than one would think by reading newspapers or internal documents produced by the EU. The origin of this misperception may be that the governance and democracy criticisms are mixed together in the same bag in public discussions. In fact, however, although many people complained about the centralized character of the decision-making process in the EU, about the distance between the EU bureaucracy and the citizen, a much smaller number complained about the lack of democracy. The number of those who did, based on these interviews, was greater in Germany than it was in Spain.

East German and West German respondents shared a very similar cognitive frame on European integration. This is quite remarkable, given that Germany was divided for about four decades and that during this period East Germany's history was practically cut off from the political and socioeconomic developments taking place in Western Europe. In one critical respect, however, their collective representations of European integration differed radically, thus dramatically illustrating the way the shadow of the past extends into the present. This concerns whether or not people mentioned Germany's role in World War II as an explanation for why Germany must contribute to European integration and be a member of the European Union. Seventeen out of 27 respondents in Weststadt offered this as a reason, compared to 2 out of 29 respondents in Oststadt! There were three slightly different versions of this argument. The first version of the argument was that Germany has a moral obligation to cooperate, so as to compensate for Germany's behavior in World War II:

> We have an obligation to work with other countries.
>
> *Why?*
>
> Perhaps because of our past. The world war was lost and it brought a lot of suffering to many countries. I believe that it is the right thing for Germany to engage with other countries and perhaps, once in a while, to make greater financial contributions than do other countries.
> (113, Weststadt, 31–50, more than High School)

This sense of moral obligation often came mixed, as in the following quote, with the view that Germany enjoys better standards of living and more advanced legislation in many areas and is therefore in a position to help other European countries:

> We owe it to other countries to contribute our experience to solving problems in certain areas and to improving the understanding between different peoples. It is not so long ago that Europe was in the midst of war, and I find it a positive thing that such a friendly association develop.
> (132, Weststadt, Young Socialists of the SPD [Social Democratic Party])

The second version of the argument linking Germany's role in World War II to European integration was that Germany should be a member of the European Union to protect itself against its own demons, its tendency to become hegemonic and aggressive whenever it feels strong. This type of comment conveys greater insecurity in the degree to which Germany's political culture has changed since World War II; it represents an internalization of the reservations that other countries have about Germany's intentions and, to some extent, it could be seen as revealing an essentialist and tragic view of the character of the German nation. Often, however, German respondents supported their reservations about their own people by pointing to current anti-foreigner sentiment in Germany. This concern was well articulated by a young university-educated woman in Weststadt, who expressed outrage mixed with anxiety at comments one often hears from young people in Germany:

> *Why are you in favor of Germany's membership in the European Union?*
>
> Because I believe that the Germans will develop the feeling that they are strong as members of a community, and stop thinking that they have to rule over others, as they've always done.
>
> *Do you think that Germany represents a real danger?*
>
> The danger is not political, that is, it does not lie in the political sphere, and in the sense that I would think that someone in the government is planning to conquer the French. But I think that among the population, or in people's thinking, such attitudes are there. For instance, during the weekend, when I was in a bar, I eavesdropped on what a group of young people was saying and I could not believe my ears! I think that it would mean a lot if we could say "we are not German; rather, we are European." That is, we live in Europe and we are also German, Palatines, or part of any other region. I think that if this integration were to take place, that is, in an institutional sense, that this danger would no longer be there.
> (111, Weststadt, 31–50, more than High School)

This sort of comment suggests that the view of membership in the European Union as a safeguard against latent hegemonic and anti-foreigner tendencies must be analyzed in conjunction with people's fear that European integration will lead to higher unemployment because of competition from cheap foreign labor. German respondents conveyed the image of a country that wrestles simultaneously with the burden of World War II and with the problem of consistently high unemployment. They seemed to conceive of the European Union as both a potential problem and a potential solution for Germany's economic troubles: a potential solution if homogenization at a high level of social benefits takes place within the European Union, and a potential problem if this homogenization does not take place, thus triggering anti-foreigner and anti-EU sentiment. Even under this bleaker scenario, however, membership in the EU was seen by some as the best way to keep the ensuing tensions under control.

The third and most frequently heard version of the World War II argument was that Germany should be a member of the European Union to reassure the world about its peaceful intentions; to prove to other countries that Germany does not harbor intentions to channel its economic power into efforts toward political and military hegemony over Europe. Some of my respondents were able to connect this argument to their own lived experience, as did a young philosophy student in Weststadt:

> When one travels to other countries, one notices that there is still a lot of resentment toward Germany. And I think that the more Germany asserts its independence, the greater the problems for Germany, the more critical the view from abroad.
>
> *But, why should Germany worry about how others react?*
>
> Well, there are surely many sides to this problem. I was once in England and was amazed to see that in newspapers, certainly not only in the most critical ones, in magazines, in films, the entertainment industry in general, evil was always represented as associated with Germany. And I think these are signs that there are still bad feelings toward Germany.
>
> (109, Weststadt, 31–50, more than High School)

In another interview in Weststadt, a high school teacher had the following to say:

> When I consider the past, I think it is certainly better to be part of the EU because there are still great misgivings about Germany everywhere.
>
> *Is it really so?*
>
> Oh, certainly! For instance, in Czechoslovakia, where many companies have relocated, they are afraid—it is in the newspapers—they are afraid that the Germans are back! There are misgivings everywhere.

So you think that Germany does not have any other options?

Yes, I mean, it does not depend on us; it depends, rather, on the attitudes of other countries. They should realize that World War II ended fifty years ago and make up their mind about whether we are still the old enemy or partners, and then act accordingly. They should not treat us as one or the other, depending on their mood. Our politicians are partly responsible for this because they are not ready to defend our point of view. I have the feeling that all they do is make financial contributions.

(107, Weststadt, older than 50, more than High School)

These respondents therefore believed that it is time to lay suspicions about Germany to rest. Germany seems in fact to find itself in a catch-22 situation. If it asserts itself in order to defend its national interests, it is accused of going back to the old ways; if it gets too involved in the construction of Europe, then people are suspicious about its intentions. In fact, many British and Spanish respondents, especially the latter, commented on and even complained about the dominant position of Germany together with France in the European Union. Occasionally, I was told that Germany has not really changed, but that what has changed is its methods for achieving hegemony.

The discussion above shows that Germany's role in World War II plays a significant role in the way West Germans think about European unification, but one that is mediated by their perceptions of the current social and political situation in Germany. The finding that this theme played practically no role in the way Oststadt's respondents discussed the European Union is quite puzzling, since studies conducted after reunification do not show substantial differences in the way West and East Germans remember World War II or evaluate Germany's role in it when asked about it.[7] Moreover, East German citizens appear to have internalized in a relatively short space of time the same mental sketch of European integration and the European Union that is found among West German citizens. How does one then explain this obvious discrepancy between the East and West German collective representations of the European Union?

There are three potential explanations: (1) East Germans are so traumatized by the reunification process that all their current thinking revolves around economic issues; (2) World War II has played hardly any role in public discussions of European integration in the period since reunification; or (3) Germany's responsibility in World War II, although remembered and acknowledged, is a much less salient theme in East Germany than it is in West Germany and has not been linked with European integration in public discourse. The validity of the first and second explanations can be seriously questioned empirically. With regard to the first one, it can be noted that 9 out of 29 Oststadt respondents (and 11 out of 27 in Weststadt) justified European integration with the argument that it contributes to peace. If the citizens of Oststadt were so obsessed by the economic disruption brought about by reunification that they could not think but in economic terms, peace would be as absent from their discussions of European integration as the discussion of Germany's responsibility for World War II. As for the role of the media in shaping people's cognitive frames on European integration, it is hard to imagine that public discussions of European integration in East German media would point to the European Union's contribution to peace without simultaneously making reference to World War II. One is then left with the third interpretation for why Germany's role in World War II was not mentioned by Oststadt respondents when justifying Germany's membership in the European Union. The discussion of this interpretation is left for chapters 6 and 7.

A second contrast between respondents in Oststadt and Weststadt in the way they thought about European integration lay in the perceived role of the European Union in improving understanding between people from different cultures. The respondents' comments in this area addressed European unification's expected contribution to cultural exchange, bringing people together, improving trust between countries, and, less often, increasing racial and ethnic tolerance. Whereas 16 out of 27 respondents in Weststadt mentioned this topic, 5 out of 29 did so in Oststadt. This contrast is less striking than is the contrast with respect to Germany's role in World War II. The two types of arguments were often related, however, as in the following words of a young university student in Weststadt who justified Germany's membership in the European Union by saying:

> I am in favor of Germany's membership in the EU out of consideration of the National Socialist past. In general, I am in favor of a multicultural society.
> (110, Weststadt, 31–50, more than High School)

The use of both arguments by respondents means that relations between peoples with different cultures have been made problematic at the level of public discourse and that people are aware of the hegemony of a moral discourse that condemns claims of cultural superiority and political action guided by such claims. When people mentioned Germany's role in World War II as a justification for why Germany should be integrated in the European Union, they revealed two things: first, that Germany's role in World War II and the National Socialist government's racist justification for its territorial ambitions are part of their active memory; second, that they know that the German state's ambitions over Europe in the late 1930s and its ideology of racial supremacy are condemned by today's dominant ideology. When people expressed support for European integration based on the belief that it will contribute to a better understanding between different cultures, to cultural exchange, and to racial and ethnic tolerance, they were implicitly saying more of the same: that they reflect on the relations between cultures and that they are aware of the hegemony of the discourse of cultural equality and tolerance.

The contrast between respondents in Weststadt and Oststadt on these issues reveals a potential difference in the political cultures of East and West Germany that is explored in chapters 6 and 7 below, along with the rest of the themes that distinguish Weststadt from Oststadt and Germany as a whole from the United Kingdom and Spain. At this point, I simply note that the selectivity with which Oststadt's citizens have internalized the different components of the image of European integration that is found among West German respondents is telling about the way cognitive frames develop. It demonstrates that historically grounded cultural processes play a key role in people's selection of the attributes that compose a cognitive frame. Although the media and other agents of political socialization constrain the content of these frames, citizens actively select among their different elements, based on the salience these have for them.

Spain: Modernization, Status, and the Franco Regime

The West German respondents' distinctive thinking about European unification was dominated by the memory of Germany's role in World War II, by concern for relations between cultures, and by the specter of cheap labor competition. In contrast, modernization, status, and opposition to isolationism were the distinctive themes that framed the Spanish respondents' thinking on the topic of European integration. The first theme encompassed statements justifying Spain's membership in the European Union with the belief that membership will contribute to the modernization of the country. The second theme, status, expressed itself in the relatively high frequency with which Spanish respondents stated that membership in the European Union enhances Spain's international prestige. Beyond this, the theme of the nation's status is evident in some of the arguments respondents used when discussing European integration. More often than their British or German counterparts, for instance, Spanish respondents attached extra-economic significance to Europe becoming a strong bloc. Another example is the relatively high frequency, at least in comparison with German respondents, with which they complained about their country not having a strong enough voice in the European Union. The themes of modernization and status are in fact intimately related, for they both reveal a longing to be on a par in terms of wealth and power with the leading European countries, Germany, France, and the United Kingdom. The third theme, the desire to break with Spain's tradition of isolation, relates the attitudes of Spanish respondents to the EU to their memory of the period of Franco's dictatorship and, as I show below, serves as the connecting point for people's preoccupation with modernization and status.

In the aftermath of World War II, Spaniards witnessed how their neighbors to the north developed at a historically rapid pace while Spain remained a traditional rural society. For the few Spaniards who had the opportunity to travel to other European countries in the 1950s, the discovery of the contrast between Spain and its northern neighbors was a traumatic experience. An obsession with becoming like the rest of Europe "to be in Europe," or "to be Europeans," developed then among Spaniards. As I show in chapter 5, this obsession persisted in the 1960s and early 1970s, during the takeoff of Spain's economic development. Over time, Spaniards have come to conceive of membership in the European Union as the road toward modernization, and this was reflected in my interviews in Catadell and Quijotón. Eight out of 27 respondents in Quijotón and 9 out of 24 respondents in Catadell justified membership in the European Union with recourse to this argument. By contrast, few respondents in Germany and the United Kingdom used this type of argument. Some of the comments within this category referred to expectations of greater prosperity and higher standard of living; more general comments referred to the modernization of all aspects of life; finally, respondents expressed the belief that the European Union will be a catalyst for change in the mentality and behavior of the people of Spain. Foremost of all, they said that it would force Spaniards to learn how to compete, as we see in the comments of the president of Quijotón's Chamber of Commerce and a civil servant from Catadell respectively:

> I think that the fact that we were in many ways not so well organized, not so well structured, or, what is worse, that our companies functioned with relatively obsolete systems, has made it necessary for us to be there [in the EU], as a sort of motivating force. I think that we, Greece, Italy, the Mediterranean countries, and Portugal, needed this [to be members of the EU] because, otherwise, it would be very difficult for us, perhaps because of our character, to become up-to-date and thus be able to compete with other countries.   (76, Quijotón)

> One problem in Spain is that changes taking place in Europe have always come late. If we are inside, they will take place at the same time, or at least not so late. Spain needs Europe as an incentive and as an aid to overcome backwardness, to put an end to old-fashioned ideas.   (89, 31–50, more than High School)

Spanish respondents also distinguished themselves from German respondents, although not so much from British respondents, by their higher propensity to mention the Common Agricultural Policy as a source of dissatisfaction, and aid received from the European Union as a source of satisfaction. About half the respondents mentioned the former and 22 out of 53 mentioned the latter. Dissatisfaction with the Common Agricultural Policy was by and large motivated by what for many people is an absurdity, that is, the setting of quotas on certain farm products, such as milk or olive oil, even if farmers get monetary compensation in exchange. Many other respondents echoed the comments by the respondent below:

> Why do we have to buy butter or milk that is brought from elsewhere, when we have such wonderful milk here?! In Cantabria, they have great milk, and when I lived in Galicia, the local milk and the local meat were both very tasty. So why must they bring—and let's not talk about vines! Why on earth do they make us uproot olive and vine trees in order to bring us wine from Nordic countries! How could it be as good as ours?! Impossible. There is a contradiction here in terms of quality. If a country produces with higher quality, one should favor that, or not? (74, Catadell, older than 50, more than High School)

The other side of the coin is that a large number of respondents were quite happy with the Cohesion and Structural Funds that have been flowing to Spain from the European Union. The most visible symbols of this aid, as in the United Kingdom, are the infrastructural projects, such as roads, clearly identifiable because of the large signs that say "Built with European Funds." As in other areas related to the European Union, perceptions of the beneficial impact of financial grants from the European Union were grounded in actual experience or in relatively unmediated observation of what was happening in their communities. Thus the following comment by a respondent:

> In my village, for instance, which is a farming community, some farmers have been able to buy themselves tractors thanks to these grants. I don't know whether it is the right thing or not. The fact of the matter is that we've come together with rich countries. Poor people, despite their good will, cannot afford certain things.
> (150, Quijotón, 31–50, more than High School)

To a large extent the relative salience of the Common Agricultural Policy and the Cohesion and Structural Funds from the European Union in Spain corresponds to the country's socioeconomic characteristics. With agriculture representing a higher percentage of the gross national product than it does in other countries of the European Union and with an income per capita below the average for the EU, Spain's economy is more affected by CAP, and it receives more development funds from Brussels than do Germany and the United Kingdom. On the other hand, one could argue that Spaniards are especially sensitive to economic policy decisions taken by the European Union because they have come to see modernization as inextricably tied to membership in the European Union and to the type of policies the European Union enacts.

The dictatorship of General Franco (1939–75) has the same cultural and political significance for Spaniards that National Socialism (1933–45) has for the Germans, or the Empire and victory in World War II for the British. It was a pivotal historical period whose memory still shapes the Spanish people's image of and aspirations for Spain, as well as their broad political outlook, including the meaning they attach to European integration and the European Union. This role was particularly evident in the high frequency with which Spanish respondents in Catadell and Quijotón justified Spain's membership in the European Union by saying that Spain cannot afford to be isolated. Seven out of 27 respondents in Quijotón and 5 out of 24 respondents in Catadell used this argument. By way of contrast, only one respondent in Germany and two respondents in the United Kingdom mentioned the issue of. Occasionally, German and British respondents said that their country has no alternative but to be part of the European Union; but they did so with no reference to a failed experience of isolation.

The Spanish respondents' desire to avoid isolation was generally framed, as in the example below, with reference to the period of autarchy and isolation of the dictatorship:

> When a country belongs to a community like this one, it is always a good thing; it is much better than to be isolated. With Franco, we went through a long period of isolation and we now see the consequences. We've been forty years behind the rest of the countries.
> (158, Quijotón, 31–50, more than High School)

Sometimes, however, respondents invoked a hundreds-of-years-old tradition of isolation that must be broken:

> *Why are you in favor of Spain's membership in the EU?*
>
> First, for non-economic reasons, almost intuitive or historical reasons, in the sense that Spain has always stayed outside Europe. I think the moment has arrived to finally become a part of Europe, although we are already at a historical stage in which it is not clear what we'll get out of it.
>
> *Since when has Spain been isolated?*
>
> Since always; since the Reformation. We started then and we have not yet come out of it.
>
> *In what sense was Spain isolated?*
>
> In every sense, political, cultural, and economic. From an economic viewpoint, we almost missed industrialization. From the cultural viewpoint, also; everything is related. If you miss industrialization, culture follows, so that you end up even more isolated."
> (141, Quijotón, representative of the union Comisiones Obreras)

The themes of modernization and of breaking with Spain's tradition of isolation are deeply intertwined in the minds of the Spanish people because political and economic isolation during the Franco regime coincided with economic stagnation and backwardness. Even though Spain's economy grew at a very high rate during the 1960s, this economic growth has been explained as resulting from Franco's belated attempts to open up the economy after the failure of the autarchic model of development practiced during the 1940s and the 1950s. Therefore, the enthusiasm with which Spanish respondents embraced the European Union as a vehicle for modernization is partly based on their negative image of autarchy.

The Spanish respondents' rejection of isolation as an option can also be explained with reference to Spain's low international status during the period of the dictatorship. For many Spanish respondents, membership in the European Union symbolized the attainment by Spain of a status comparable to that of other European Union members. This belief is of course consistent with the high frequency with which Spanish respondents indicated that membership in the European Union increases Spain's prestige in the world. The following quote, for instance, reveals the close connection between the concern not to be isolated and the desire to see Spain's prestige increase:

> I think that Spain's prestige increases by being a member of the European Union. More than anything, because of our past trajectory: forty years under Franco, isolation, and all kinds of problems; also, the coup d' etat we had, and so on. I think that becoming a member of the European Union, with countries such as Germany, France, etc., inevitably increases your prestige. It gives you the prestige of being a democratic and stable country.
> (72, Catadell, 30 or younger, more than High School)

The yearning for prestige was also reflected in other themes that emerged during the interviews. For instance, as I noted when discussing the significance of the theme of globalization, it was reflected in the importance that Spaniards attached to being part of a strong bloc such as the European Union. The significance attached to this goes well beyond the economic rationale that inspired British or German respondents. It often reflects the belief, mixed with hope, that being part of a prestigious bloc will necessarily improve Spain's image in the world. At least, as some said, it will offer Spain the opportunity to demonstrate that it has capable leaders able to conduct international affairs. Thus, the pride with which some respondents pointed out how NATO and other international bodies are headed by Spaniards:

> I think that we are now in better shape because of membership. It has contributed to modernizing the state, to modernizing the armed forces, something

that was past due. We have a Spaniard as NATO's Secretary General. That is also a symbol that we've modernized, or that they've modernized us.

(91, Catadell, editor of local newspaper)

The themes of status and modernization intersect in the relatively high frequency with which Spanish respondents note with frustration that Spain's voice is not heard in the European Union. This was particularly true in Catadell, where one out of three respondents referred to this problem. The comments about Spain's lack of voice were sometimes made when evaluating European Union measures that have gone against Spain's perceived interests. In this sense, the comments reflected the high degree of salience that the European Union's expected contribution to the modernization of Spain has in the Spaniards' *collective consciousness*. More often, however, complaints about Spain's lack of voice in the European Union referred to a general feeling among respondents that Spain is being taken advantage of and that its opinions are not taken into account. This, in turn, was frequently interpreted as a sign that Spain is not yet treated as an equal but, rather, as non-European, as "just Arabs":

I think it is a bit of a utopia to think that we are going to be equal to the Europeans. Because they are not going to see us that way, are they? One just has to see, when one goes to France, the kind of treatment one gets from the French people. They look down their noses at us and for them we are just Arabs.

(146, Quijotón, 30 or younger, more than High School)

The European Union has become a mirror for Spain. EU decisions that affect Spain are treated either as major victories or major setbacks, as recognition of Spain's worth or as major affronts. The higher frequency of comments about Spain's lack of voice in Catadell, where support for Catalan nationalism is very strong, than in Quijotón, may also reflect a subtle way of putting down Spain and its leaders. It is an issue that I cannot interpret with the data at hand.

The United Kingdom: Sovereignty, Identity, and the Welfare State

During the public debate on the United Kingdom's participation in the European Monetary Union in the fall of 1997, Labour Party government officials repeatedly stressed that the government's decision to postpone entry was based on economic considerations rather than on principle. They were trying to distance themselves from representatives of the Conservative Party who argued against adopting the euro on grounds of sovereignty. A debate of this kind never took place in Spain or in Germany. Indeed, for all that has been said about the role of the Deutschmark as a symbol of Germany's national identity, the German respondents' opposition to the euro was framed exclusively in economic terms. The character of the public debate on EMU in the United Kingdom finds its correlate at the popular level in the role of sovereignty and national identity in discussions about European integration. The most distinctive aspect of the British respondents' way of thinking about European integration is the significant role played by sovereignty and national identity. Eighteen out of 53 respondents in the United Kingdom mentioned these themes in connection with European integration or membership in the European Union, compared with one or two respondents in each of the German and Spanish cities. The comments were most often made when expressing dissatisfaction with the European Union or in order to oppose economic and monetary union. They covered a broad variety of related issues. In the area of sovereignty, people expressed their opposition to any form of unification, their rejection of supranational forms of government, their desire to protect the country's sovereignty, a dislike of taking orders from Europe, and the feeling that national governments know better or that the country is better left alone. In the area of identity, the comments referred to the fear of losing the nation's identity, culture, or way of life and the desire to protect the nation's identity or culture. A closer look at the respondents' answers shows that they were primarily concerned about the defense of both national identity and culture. The respondents' opposition to the transfer of sovereignty in fact masked the underlying perception that the United Kingdom has little clout in the decision-making process of the European Union and would therefore be in no position to defend its national identity and culture if the European Union increased its supranational character.

Not unexpectedly, respondents had trouble defining what they meant by identity and culture. As one of them put it,

> It's not something that you can easily fit into words; I mean, when it comes down to it, national identity only comes to the fore on important occasions, you know.   (48, Scotsburg, aged 31–50, more than High School)

Upon reflection, however, some respondents came up with lists of things, encompassed by the concepts "outlook" and "way of life," such as the language, the currency, the monarchy, ways of working, and national holidays. Other respondents provided more colorful examples, rooted in everyday life, such as this one provided by the master fencer from Scotsburg quoted above:

> I dislike it [the EU] on the grounds that at times it goes against national identity to a certain degree. You know, "you have to do this, you have to do that." I mean, one of the worst decisions I think they made, as far as this country goes, was that they decided, because of action in the European Court, to get rid of

belting in schools. So, corporal punishment is done away with. And the ramifications of that are obvious. Hardly a week goes past in which you don't see in the television, you know, that they are threatening to close the schools down because the children are unruly.

(48, Scotsburg, 31–50, more than High School)

Comments such as this put the British respondents' previously discussed criticism of governance aspects of the EU in a different light. As shown above, they distinguished themselves from German or Spanish respondents by their critique of overregulation or the European Union's tendency to set common standards for everything. The perceived excess of regulation on the part of the European Union not only seemed ridiculous to the British respondents I interviewed, but it was also sometimes perceived as an infringement of the country's right to self-governance or a threat to the country's identity.

In discussing the topic of identity, British respondents stressed the differences between British culture and the cultures of other European countries. Sometimes, this emphasis on cultural differences led to a Herderian glorification of the advantages of cultural variety, as in this eloquent quote from our master fencer from Scotsburg:

You need your national identity. The human condition is such that variety is what has made us a successful animal. You know, if we were coming from the same culture, the same makeup, then you would grow stale. You would lose the initiative. Because of the culture and the way of life, your mind is made of a specific past. It might be that this culture lends itself toward greater thought in particular cultures, so that in Scotland, in Germany, in France, Spain, Holland, people have a slightly different way of looking at things; faced with the same problem, they come up with different answers, a different thinking process. I think it is very much the case that you want to have as much diversity as you can in order for the race as a whole to grow.

(48, Scotsburg, 31–50, more than High School)

On other occasions, however, comments about the irreconcilable cultural differences between European countries were followed by a nationalist glorification of the British culture. This is, for instance, what a main representative of Engleton's branch of the Conservative Party had to say:

What happens is that the UK system has generally developed over centuries and it is one with which the large majority of the people are very happy; they share a common culture, a common language, a common identity, in the sense that we are all British, there is a tradition of the evolution of the rights of the citizens, the British parliament is the mother of all parliaments; and the way it has evolved is something that is appreciated, that is shared as being very valuable here in the UK; we've had a shared constitutional monarchy for centuries, since the King of England became technically the King of Scotland as well; we've gone through world wars which, particularly the second world war, enabled us to regard ourselves as an island, very much so against the whole world. The fact that we had an Empire and were the strongest country in the world has also strengthened people's perceptions of being a nation, a very independent, very strong nation, which has a lot to offer to the rest of the world. We have, I mean, in many respects many of the older generations in the UK see themselves as having saved Europe from tyranny and disaster as a result of the war. The fact that we struggled in Europe against the Soviet threat, I mean, this is something that I think, I mean, Britain, the fact that it is an island race, an island race, really stands us totally apart, totally apart from the rest of Europe.

(7, Engleton)

As I show later on in a chapter about Spain, the similarity between this discourse and the discourse found in newspaper editorials published during Franco's dictatorship is remarkable. The important point here, however, is that concern for the loss of national identity and culture and the emphasis on the cultural differences between the United Kingdom and other European countries were often expressed alongside comments that reveal fears that the United Kingdom will not have a dominant voice within the EU:

I would not envisage a United States of Europe. I think that with this concept comes the diminution of the national interest, or the danger of that, the potential is there for the more powerful states to dominate. I am quite sure that national interests would find their way into just any debate of any significance, leaving us with a Europe dominated by perhaps a couple of powers, with the smaller areas being less well represented.

(45, Scotsburg, Scottish Nationalist Party City Council member)

Thus, for many respondents the European Union is an extraneous "bureaucracy" that "gives orders" to the United Kingdom, a sort of "dictatorship," instead of an institution in which the United Kingdom is represented and plays a role. In this context, the threat of losing one's national identity and national culture as a result of European integration becomes more real, as indicated by the representative of the Conservative Party in Scotsburg's City Council:

My view is that I wouldn't like to be ruled by bureaucrats in Europe, plain and simple. If we don't have clout in Europe, then the bureaucrats of Europe will rule us.

What is the problem with that?

Well, because we don't like the rules that they produce.

> *But doesn't this sometimes happen in one's own country?*
>
> Well, I suppose so, up to a point. But their way of living, the European outlook is very different to the British way of life. You know, it's an impression; perhaps we have the wrong impression. But we feel that the Europeans are so different to us; perhaps unjustifiably. Speaking passionately, and I really mean passionately: I would rather be the fifty-first state of America than a member of the European Union, but that's me personally. We speak the same language, their way of life is similar to ours, and we can relate to that, you know. I think it is difficult to relate to the Frogs [French] and the Belgians, you know. They are so different. (49, Scotsburg)

The dominant role that the defense of national identity plays in British opposition to Europe's political unification, relative to a principled opposition to a transfer of sovereignty, couldn't be more clearly expressed than in this quote. First, the Conservative Council member opposes European unification on grounds that the United Kingdom will have little clout in the decision-making process. Then, he goes on to stress that the resulting rules would go against British culture and national identity. What is important then is to protect one's identity, even if this means being submerged, probably with even less political clout, as the fifty-first state of the United States! Later chapters provide an interpretation for this choice, based on a comparison with Spain. At this point, it is important to simply retain this link between the British respondents' perceptions of the United Kingdom's power within the European Union, their fear of losing their culture, and their opposition to political unification.

Issues of identity and sovereignty set the British totally apart from the Spaniards and the Germans. On other relevant issues, British respondents distinguished themselves from German respondents, but were close to Spanish respondents. These topics are the Common Agricultural Policy and the Structural Funds from the European Union (mentioned by 15 of the 53 respondents), and the expectation that membership in the European Union will translate into an improvement in social benefits (13 of the 53 respondents).

In the United Kingdom, as in Spain, respondents criticized with passion the Common Agricultural Policy. Beneath this superficial similarity, however, lie significant differences. Spanish respondents were especially outraged by the quota system; in the United Kingdom, I heard this criticism only in connection to fishing. Respondents did not see the rationale behind a system that restricts the British fishing rights at the same time that it fosters competition in British waters from Spanish fishermen:

> They are buying off the ships, buying off the trawlers and everything. The British government has done that. I think it is a disgrace when other trawlers from other countries can come in here and trawl our waters. I think it's a disgrace. How can that lead to unification in Europe!
>
> (32, Scotsburg, editor of local newspaper)

More often, however, criticisms of the Common Agricultural Policy were directed at the surpluses created by the system of guaranteed prices. One of the most indelible memories I have of my stay in Engleton was my visit to the City Hall, a beautiful and very old building, to interview the mayor. As I was leaving, the mayor showed me a room in which a stand had been set up to distribute free packets of surplus frozen meat to retired and needy residents. Scenes like these certainly encourage people in the belief that the Common Agricultural Policy represents a waste:

> The fact is that so much of the world does not have enough food and yet we seem to be stocking up all this food. That's one of the strong things that people still think about Europe, that they can't manage its waste production, and people don't like that. (32, Scotsburg, editor of local newspaper)

Whereas criticisms of the Common Agricultural Policy in Spain and the United Kingdom differed somewhat in terms of content, favorable comments about the Structural Funds received from the European Union and the pressure the EU may create, through the Social Chapter, to raise social standards, were very similar in the two countries. In less prosperous Scotsburg, and to a lesser extent in Engleton, some of the comments expressed the economic and social concerns of a country whose standard of living is lower than Germany's and where the population is quite aware of the differences in the level of social benefits between the United Kingdom and the most socially advanced countries in Europe. A lower standard of living means that the United Kingdom receives Structural Funds from the EU, which are then positively evaluated by respondents in Engleton and Scotsburg. At the same time, lower levels of social benefits mean that for some segments of the population in relatively poor regions, the EU, through the implementation of its Social Chapter, represents the promise of an improvement of living conditions. Many other respondents in Engleton and especially in Scotsburg echoed the following comment by the president of Engleton's Footwear Union:

> I believe that the Social Charter is fair and equitable. If you are working for an employer who is based in Germany, and you're working for an employer in the United Kingdom, why should the Germans have a 48-hour limited week, whereas the English work sixty hours in this country? You know, it's justice really, what's fair and equitable. (24, Engleton)

The Meaning of Silence

In conversations about European integration, German, British, and Spanish respondents distinguished themselves from one another not only by emphasizing certain themes, but also by overlooking others. The omissions tell us as much about the factors shaping people's cognitive frames on the European Union as do the topics that came up in the conversations. German respondents, for instance, hardly ever mentioned issues such as the Common Agricultural Policy, aid received from the Structural Funds, or the feeling that they have little say in the process of integration. This reflects not only the reality of a more developed country within the European Union, less reliant, for instance, on the Structural Funds, but also that of a country that sees itself in a position of leadership. The latter perception was often expressed in the German respondents' belief that without Germany there could be no European Union. The rarity of comments referring to the structural funds in Oststadt was nonetheless surprising, given that East Germany is an important target of these funds. The main explanation for this may be that East Germany relies more on development funds from the German government than on funds from the European Union. In poorer countries, such as the United Kingdom and Spain, the economic significance of EU money is much greater.

Whereas current economic and political factors play a role in explaining why German respondents did not mention certain issues when talking about the EU, historical factors explain why Spanish respondents hardly ever mentioned the contribution of European integration to peace. For British and German respondents it was a major theme, mentioned by 34% of the respondents. For many of them, especially the older ones, the European Union is a guarantee against the outbreak of another war. They did not think that war is likely, but they did not discount the possibility that it could happen, and observed with apprehension the developments in the former Yugoslavia. The following two quotes, one from an editor at Engleton's local newspaper, the other from a representative of Weststadt's Manual Workers' Chamber, illustrate this point:

> Personally, I feel that the closer countries come together, the less likely it is that there will be another war. I think that's very important. I am just old enough to have lived through the aftermath of the Second World War.
>
> *Do you think that at this moment this is a serious concern or something that we should always have in mind?*
>
> I think it is still relevant. We had, for instance, the conflict in Bosnia, not very long ago, which shows how rapidly situations can get out of hand, and could become very dangerous if they were allowed to drag on. And I suppose that if the atmosphere were right, that there's always the possibility that a war could start. I don't think that wars necessarily start for very good and powerful reasons. I think sometimes it is a minor thing that escalates. The more people understand each other, the more contact people have with each other, and the less chance there is of it. (22, Engleton)

I belong to a generation that was ten years old at the end of the war and I obviously remember what happened; therefore, I would like such things never to happen again. We must avoid a balkanization process in the long run.

Was this an important element in the development of your ideas, as you were growing up?

From the start, I was for European unification. I revered Mr. Schuman, who already in the early fifties had met with Adenauer, about which I was enthusiastic. I realized that France and Germany would reach some kind of agreement, which for me was an absolute precondition for peace.

Is the danger of war still a reason?

I think it is a very remote one.   (128, Weststadt)

This sort of comment was nowhere to be found among Spanish respondents, another illustration of how history and its memory influence the way people apprehend the world that surrounds them. Spain has not been involved in any international military confrontation since the war with Morocco in the 1920s; one has to go back to early in the nineteenth century to see Spain involved in a major European war. In fact, in the last two centuries the wars that have really impacted the Spaniards' collective memory, with the exception of the War of Cuba and the Philippines (the Spanish-American War), have been civil wars, whether one thinks of the Carlist Wars in the nineteenth century or the Civil War in the late 1930s. Another historical explanation for the contrast between Spanish respondents and British and German respondents has to do with the timing of entry in the European Community. When Spain applied for membership in the European Community, war in Europe had ceased to be the driving force behind efforts at European integration. Therefore, the finding that Spanish respondents connected European integration to the preservation of peace less often than did German and British respondents is not surprising. It illustrates nicely how a topic becomes irrelevant in people's understanding of European integration both because it lacks cultural and historical significance and because public discussion of European integration fails to stress its significance.

National and City Contrasts: A Statistical Analysis

The examination of the themes that people raised when discussing European integration has permitted us privileged access to the mental sketches that frame their thinking about this topic. These sketches were similar in fundamental ways (e.g., the common market, globalization, governance) but also differed across countries in ways that are no less significant (e.g., the role played by the country in World War II, modernization, identity, sovereignty). Examination of the content of the interviews in Germany, the United Kingdom, and Spain reveals that, except in Germany, where Weststadt and Oststadt differ with respect to how often people connected Germany's role in World War II with European integration, mental sketches of the EU transcended regional boundaries. Respondents from Catadell and Quijotón imagined the European Union in roughly similar ways, and so did respondents from Scotsburg and Engleton. Also, within cities, people thought of the European Union in similar ways, regardless of gender, age, or education. Three exceptions, which become relevant later in the text, are references to (1) Germany's need to reassure other countries, (2) the European Union's expected contributions to Spain's modernization, and (3) the need to break with Spain's isolationist tradition. These three frames were mentioned more often by more educated than by less educated respondents.[8]

One obtains a synthetic view of how well the social representations of European integration discussed above help to differentiate the respondents from the British, Spanish, and German cities through the estimation of a discriminant statistical analysis model. Discriminant analysis predicts group membership (in this case, city membership) based on specific characteristics of the cases that need to be classified (in this case, frames on European integration) and conveys to what extent these characteristics are useful to differentiate members from different groups. It does so through the estimation of a series of canonical discriminant functions. These discriminant functions are linear combinations of the characteristics used in the classification process (in this case, the frames) that maximize the capacity to distinguish between the different groups that one is interested in (see Appendix III). If the information provided helps to distinguish between the different categories, the estimated functions will provide clearly different predicted values for each of the different categories; otherwise, the predicted values will tend to be similar. In this example, two canonical discriminant functions (Eigen values equal to 2.112 and 0.675 respectively) suffice to account for 89% of the variance observed among the respondents in the sample (67% and 22% respectively). Conceptualizations of European integration as a vehicle to reassure other countries about one's country's intentions, as increasing foreign labor competition, as an opportunity to modernize the country and break its isolation, and as a threat to national identity and culture, show the highest correlations with these two discrimination functions. The biggest standardized weight by far for the first function corresponds to the framing of one's country's contribution to European integration as necessary to reassure other countries, whereas the biggest standardized weight in the second function corresponds to people's conceptualization of European integration as a threat to the national identity and culture.[9]

WAYS OF SEEING INTEGRATION 57

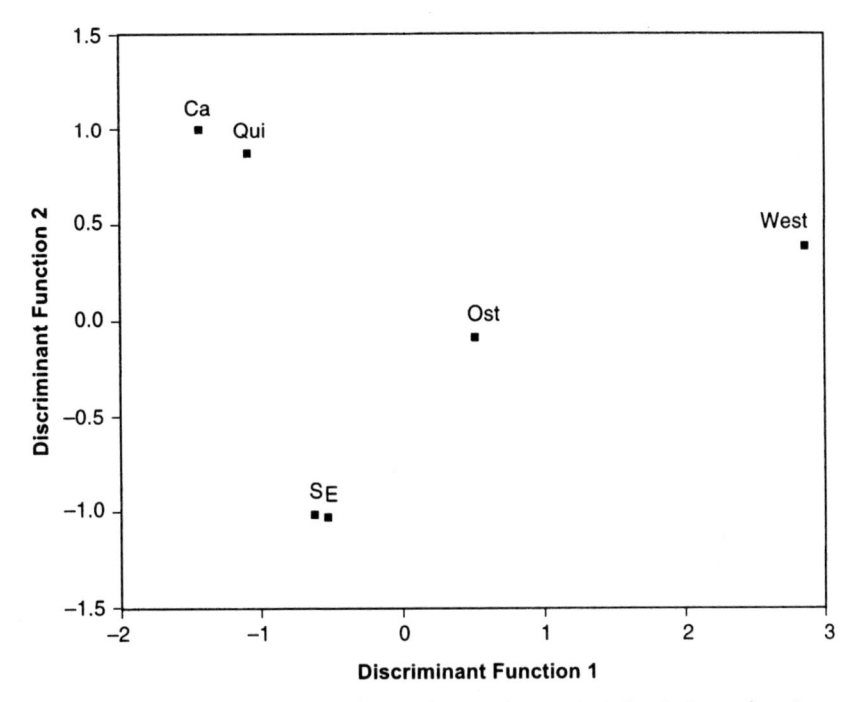

Figure 2.1 Group centroids for first and second canonical discriminant functions, based on respondents' frames on European Integration and the European Union. Qui: Quijotón; Ca: Catadell; S: Scotsburg; E: Engleton; West: Weststadt; Ost: Oststadt.

Figure 2.1 represents these results graphically. Each point represents the centroid, or typical, value, of respondents from the six cities on a two-dimensional space whose axes are the two main canonical discriminant functions. One can perfectly see that the frames on European integration discussed above perfectly distinguish British, German, and Spanish respondents. In fact, the estimated discriminant functions help to correctly predict the country of origin of 89% of the respondents from Weststadt, 83% of the respondents from Oststadt, 85% of the respondents from Quijotón, 79% of the respondents from Catadell, 70% of the respondents from Engleton, and 77% of the respondents from Scotsburg. The graph also confirms that frames on European integration do not distinguish Quijotón from Catadell respondents, or Engleton from Scotsburg respondents, but they do distinguish Weststadt from Oststadt respondents. Therefore, at least with respect to European integration, Catalan and Castillian belong to the same culture, just as English and Scottish respondents do. Meanwhile, the West German and East German respondents appear to come from quite different cultures.

National Self-Perceptions, Collective Memory, and European Integration

The discussion and quotes above reveal the significance of national self-perceptions and collective memory in shaping people's images of the European Union. Thus, respondents often prefaced their comments with expressions such as "we are a country that ...," "we will have to ...," "Great Britain was ...," "The Germans are ...," or they invoked historical events when justifying their comments on European unification or their feelings about their country's membership in the European Union. I have coded these comments in order to detect regularities that may smooth the transition from an intersubjective to an objective and historically grounded explanation of differences in attitudes toward European integration in the United Kingdom, Germany, and Spain. The analysis of these comments will guide us toward a grounded contextualization of these attitudes.

A literal codification of all the comments made by respondents that refer to characteristics of their country or people produces a list of more than three hundred attributes. Many of these comments are quite similar, however, and lend themselves to combination in a smaller number of categories (see table 3). For instance, comments such as "Germany is very wealthy" can be grouped together with other comments such as "the economy of Germany is very strong" or "Germany has a huge economy." This smaller list of categories better allows one to assess the different self-perceptions found in Germany, the United Kingdom, and Spain.

Among German respondents, most of the comments relating to national self-perception were of a positive nature. They saw their country as rich and powerful (13 out of the 56 respondents), as having better legislation and policies than do other countries (7 respondents), and as permeated by a strong work ethic (3). Among Spanish respondents, most of the comments about national self-perception were negative. Spain was seen as a poor and powerless country (12 out of the 51 respondents), a country with bad legislation and policies (3), ruled by incompetent elites (4), and where people tend to lack discipline (3). In the United Kingdom, views were divided. Some respondents viewed the country as rich and powerful (10 out of 27 respondents in Engleton, 4 out of 26 respondents in Scotsburg) and thought that a main feature of its character is fairness (4 out of 53 respondents). Other respondents, however, portrayed the country as being poor and powerless (7 respondents in Engleton), or as a declining power (5 in Engleton). Beyond these positive and negative assessments, respondents tended to portray the British population as anti-European, isolationist or parochial (11 of the 53 respondents), and xenophobic or nationalist (9 in Engleton, 3 in Scotsburg). Sometimes, such comments were meant to be critical, but on other occasions they were simply stated

TABLE 3
Main Characterizations of Own Country and People, by City
(Number of respondents who mention a particular feature)

	Germany		Spain		United Kingdom	
Images of Country and its People	Weststadt (27)	Oststadt (29)	Quijotón (27)	Catadell (24)	Engleton (27)	Scotsburg (26)
rich and powerful	6	7	1		10	4
good laws and policies	3	4				
hard workers	1	2	1			
superiority complex		2			4	1
poor and powerless		1	6	6	7	1
bad laws and policies			2	1	1	
incompetent elites			1	3		
undisciplined			3			
extroverted		1	5			
anti-European		1			2	1
isolationist/parochial			1		5	6
xenophobe/nationalist		1			9	3
declining power					5	2
fair					4	

*Number of respondents for each city.

as fact. These divisions among the British respondents, and the fact that the British made many more comments about their country, their people, and even about other countries than did Spanish or German respondents, convey that there is less agreement about how to characterize the country in the United Kingdom than there is in Spain or Germany. Moreover, the high frequency with which respondents in the United Kingdom critically referred to British nationalism and xenophobia indicates a significant split in the population with regard to national identity, ethnic relations, and attitudes toward the European Union. An issue left unresolved at this point is whether these divisions result from, precede, or are independent of the debate on European integration. This is an issue that I explore later on in the book.

This chapter also shows that respondents often referred, directly or indirectly, to key moments of their history when they pronounced themselves in favor of or against European integration (Table 4). In order to systematically assess the salience of particular historical events in people's

TABLE 4
Main Historical Events Mentioned during Interviews, by City.
(Number of respondents who mention a particular event)

	Germany		Spain		United Kingdom	
Historical Events	Weststadt (27)	Oststadt (29)	Quijotón (27)	Catadell (26)	Engleton (27)	Scotsburg (26)
World War II	14	7	1		12	4
Nazis	6	6				
German reunification	4	13		1	1	2
communism		12				
Franco Period			7	10		
British Empire					10	6
Commonwealth					7	6

discussions of European integration, I coded all historical events mentioned during the interviews. In total, respondents invoked more than fifty different historical events or periods. The distribution of mentioned events shows that West German respondents articulated their reflections around World War II; East German respondents articulated theirs around the reunification process and communism; Spanish respondents articulated theirs around the Franco period; finally, British respondents articulated theirs around the Allied victory in World War II, the Empire, and the Commonwealth.

A careful reading of these results reveals several aspects rarely examined in the humanistic literature on collective memory, which are nonetheless consistent with scientific research on individual memory. For instance, in each and every case, the historical reference points were recent; many respondents have lived through them or are immediate descendants of people who lived through them. They were also dramatic events; they represented a particularly good or bad period or preceded a radical transition to something better or to something worse. The fact that the East Germans' reflections about European integration centered more on the consequences of German reunification and of the Communist period than on World War II seems to indicate that historical memory, albeit multilayered, privileges the most recent dramatic event over preceding ones. Finally, the contrast between Weststadt and Oststadt with respect to how reflection about Germany's role in World War II influences people's discussion of World War II reminds us that the same historical event can be read and remembered very differently, depending on social and political circumstances. It also shows that the lessons people draw from collectively remembered events do not automatically follow from the events themselves. Indeed, the link between Germany's role in World War II and European integration was made by respondents in Weststadt but was not made by respondents in Oststadt. This may mean that public discourse has not emphasized this link, or that in East Germany the memory of World War II is devoid of a critical appraisal of Germany's role in it, or both. This issue is explored in chapters 6 and 7 below.

In conclusion, the images that respondents have of the European Union must be interpreted with reference to the national cultures within which they have developed. The content analysis of the interviews I conducted in Germany, the United Kingdom, and Spain reveals that national self-perceptions and historical memory are the most relevant dimensions of this cultural context. The impression conveyed by my respondents in Weststadt is that they were very proud of Germany's economic and social achievements during the postwar period. In terms of its work ethic, standards of living, and social benefits, they saw Germany as superior to the rest of Europe. Therefore, they said they would like the European Union to be shaped along the German model rather than give up some of its achievements. This attitude becomes especially salient when it comes to facing and addressing current high unemployment levels. One could interpret the current sensitivity to competition from foreign workers and pressure to shape the European Union along the German model as resulting from this combination of pride in past achievements and fear that Germany's economic and social model may in fact be under strain. Respondents tended to blame others rather than to question the German model. On the other hand, West German respondents were well aware that Germany's image abroad is still colored by memories of World War II and the Holocaust; accordingly, they expressed commitment to European unification and a desire to solve Germany's current economic predicament within the framework of the European Union. Hence, the solution that I heard most often was that one should extend Germany's social model to the rest of the countries of the European Union.

The East German respondents I interviewed in Oststadt resembled their West German counterparts only in the degree of confidence they expressed in the superiority of the German model and the German character. Although they considered themselves to be under tremendous economic strain, they attributed this not to failings of the German social and economic model, which they welcomed, but rather to the way reunification was planned and executed. On the national level, they felt abandoned and somewhat betrayed by their Western counterparts, but from a European perspective they saw themselves as part of a prosperous country and, therefore, well above the rest of Europe. Because of unemployment rates that are much higher than they are in West Germany, their reaction when it came to foreign workers was quite similar to that in West Germany: one should prevent foreign workers from coming and, if they do come, one should make sure that they work under the same conditions as the autochthonous population; moreover, one should strive to equalize labor conditions across the European Union. Unlike West Germans in Weststadt, Oststadt respondents rarely justified European unification by referring to the need to reassure other European countries about Germany's intentions or to a sense of obligation based on Germany's actions in World War II. They evaluated European integration in economic terms. This is because their historical memory is dominated by the hardships of the communist period and by the costs of reunification rather than by events such as World War II. Therefore, it is not clear whether, faced with persistently high unemployment levels, East German respondents would express the same degree of commitment to European unification and the European Union as would West German respondents.

The Spanish respondents I interviewed in Quijotón and Catadell approached European unification very differently from the German respondents. Although proud of the recent economic and political modernization of Spain, they expressed the belief that Spain is well behind the rest of Western Europe in social, economic, and cultural aspects. Consequently, and unlike the German respondents, they tended to blame their own country and its people rather than others for such problems as unemployment rates, which are much higher than they are in Germany, East Germany included. In fact, the respondents in Quijotón and Catadell expressed as much awe for the German economic and social model, which they saw embodied in the European Union's institutions, as did the respondents in Oststadt and Weststadt. With memories of the backwardness and ostracism that prevailed during the autarchic phase of the Franco regime still fresh in their minds, the Spanish respondents saw membership in the European Union as the only path toward modernization and international recognition. They complained about specific policies, such as CAP, or protested against attempts to cut the allocation of structural funds to Spain, but they conveyed that they do not entertain other alternatives. European political integration will ensure that Spain belongs to a strong bloc and entails the promise of Structural Funds and an improvement in labor conditions.

Finally, the respondents in Engleton and Scotsburg revealed a major split in British society concerning the United Kingdom's place in the world. Some respondents proudly proclaimed that the United Kingdom is a rich and powerful country with a glorious history. Other respondents had a bleaker view of the United Kingdom. For them, the Empire is a thing of the past, and what remains is a third-rate and not very rich power. When asked about European integration, most respondents, regardless of their national self-perceptions, liked or at least seemed to have come to terms with the United Kingdom's membership in the European Union and with the establishment of a single European market. Their views on further European political integration were not so positive, however. Neither burdened by the past nor concerned about the threat of foreign labor competition as were the German respondents, respondents who believed that the United Kingdom is still a great country tended to be against further European political integration. The rest of the respondents were not enthusiastic, but did not express strong qualms. Interestingly, the "Eurosceptics" did not rely very much on justifications that stress the economic or political advantages for the United Kingdom of a lack of political integration in Europe. Rather, they stressed cultural differences between the United Kingdom and the rest of Europe or expressed outright contempt for other European countries, especially France. Most often, however, as did the majority of the British respondents, they expressed fear of losing their national identity and culture, partly as a result of not having enough clout within the European Union. These are fears that the German respondents did not seem to have. One could interpret this contrast as a sign that national self-doubt is present even among the most assertive British Eurosceptics. To analyze this problem, however, one needs to examine more information, from both the interviews and other sources, which is what I shall do in the chapter on the United Kingdom.

The preceding sections show that the images of the European Union and European integration that people have vary from country to country and, sometimes, as in Germany, from one part of the country to another. These contrasts are interesting per se because they reveal significant aspects of these countries' national cultures and histories as well as the different ways in which the European Union has impacted upon them. They can also begin to explain why the British population harbors more negative attitudes toward European political integration than do the German and Spanish populations. Indeed, the potential loss of identity and sovereignty associated with European unification is part of the cognitive frame of the British respondents but not of the Spanish and German respondents. This potential loss could have been compensated in people's minds by their expectation that integration may lead to improved social rights and benefits. The fact that it hasn't shows either the greater value that British respondents put on sovereignty and identity over improved social rights and benefits, or that they believe that the chances that political integration mean a loss of sovereignty and identity are greater than those of it meaning an improvement in social rights and benefits.

This chapter's discussion of cognitive frames offers cues also as to why Spaniards and Germans are more favorably oriented to political integration than are the British. In Spain, the desire to break the country's isolation and to catch up with other European countries may push up general levels of support for European integration, regardless of the form it takes. This general enthusiasm for European integration does not seem to have been damped by a perception, at least in Catadell, that Spain has little influence over the decision-making process. In Germany, the feeling of responsibility for World War II and the resulting reluctance of Germans to assert themselves as a nation may also push up levels of support for European political integration. This cultural factor could have been more than counterbalanced, however, by the economic expectation that European integration means greater foreign labor competition. The fact that it has not—at least over the long run—may reflect either that this is a recent concern in Germany, triggered by high unemployment, or that, as I have shown, people see opposite solutions to this problem: some react by opposing European integration altogether, and others react by demanding further integration and a homogenization of social rights and benefits across Europe. These issues are further explored in coming chapters. The next chapter, however, analyzes the different European integration projects of the people of the three countries and how they justify them.

Three

Good Reasons for Attitudes toward European Integration

THE EXAMINATION of cognitive frames performed in chapter 2 is indispensable for the explanation of attitudes toward European integration. It is reasonable, for instance, to assume that, other things being equal, evaluations of the European Union will be more positive if it is seen to contribute to peace in Europe than if it is simply seen as a bureaucracy set up to manage the interests of European farmers. The literature on attitudes toward European integration has generally been insensitive, however, to the different ways in which the population conceptualizes European integration and the European Union.

This chapter follows Max Weber and Alfred Schutz by focusing on the "good reasons" people provide to justify their views on European integration.[1] First, it compares the aspects of European integration emphasized by "supporters" and by "nonsupporters" of European integration; then, it describes the various European integration projects that emerged from my in-depth interviews, the arguments with which respondents justified these projects, and the sociocultural characteristics of the different groups of respondents. Finally, it examines the contrasts between the overall views about European unification of respondents who support different European projects.

The Empirical Tradition: Support versus Nonsupport

Underlying the design and analysis of public opinion surveys on European integration has been the dominance until quite recently of theoretical perspectives that granted only a small role to public opinion in the explanation of European integration.[2] Whether we think of theories of regional integration, such as neo-functionalism,[3] or empirically based conceptualizations of popular attitudes toward European integration, such as the "permissive consensus" model,[4] the dominant view in the early '70s, at the time Jacques-René Rabier and Ron Inglehart (two rare dissidents, actually) designed their first Eurobarometer, was that European unification was an elite affair and that public opinion could at most legitimate or, in extreme circumstances, slow down the process. This theoretical climate and the fact that public opinion was indeed much less informed about European integration than it is today, led to the development of survey questions that focused on general support for European unification and evaluation of one's country membership in the European Union.[5] Over the years, researchers have shown a preference for analyzing trends, pooling of cross-national datasets for different time periods, and attaining a low level of nonresponses, over examination of changing conceptualizations of the role of public opinion in the European integration process and developing a more complex measurement of people's attitudes. Because of this data constraint, most empirical research on attitudes toward European integration has focused on the description and explanation of people's answers to the questions on "unification" and "membership" (listed in n. 5).

I begin this chapter with a descriptive analysis of the similarities and differences in the themes mentioned by supporters and nonsupporters of European integration during the in-depth interviews that I conducted in the three countries. The questionnaire for the interviews contained one item of "diffuse" support and another of "specific" support that are roughly similar to the ones included in the Eurobarometer surveys. The first item asked respondents whether they were in favor of or against efforts toward European unification. The second item asked respondents whether they thought that their country's membership in the European Union was a good or a bad thing. Very high percentages among the respondents said that they were in favor of European unification (83% or 133 respondents) and that they found it a good thing that their country is a member of the European Union (89% or 142 respondents). Meanwhile, only 9% (15) of the respondents opposed European unification and 4% (7) thought it a bad thing that their country belongs to the European Union.[6] This imbalance makes a comparison between the arguments used by those who express support for European integration and those who oppose it highly problematic. For this reason, I have computed an index of support that differentiates "supporters" from "nonsupporters" (those who expressed a negative opinion, were undecided, or did not answer) and that combines the answers to the two questions. Respondents who gave positive answers to both questions have been coded in the category "supporters," and the rest have been coded in the category "nonsupporters." This results in a slightly more balanced distribution, with 79% (127) "supporters" and 21% (33) "nonsupporters."

Differences in the comments or arguments used by "supporters" and "nonsupporters" during the interviews help to clarify the extent to which differences in the cognitive frames in the United Kingdom, Spain, and Germany underlie contrasts in levels of support for European integration in these three countries.[7] The images people have of the European unification process may indeed differ from country to country, but not all contrasts polarize public opinion the same way. The total distribution of comments along the categories defined in the previous chapter shows that four main themes distinguish "supporters" of European integration from "nonsupporters" (table 5). "Supporters" emphasize substantially more often than do "nonsupporters" the virtues of the single market and the contributions of European integration to the achievement of peace and a better understanding of people from different cultures. These are, not surprisingly, the goals that were emphasized in the Treaty of Rome. Meanwhile, "nonsupporters" emphasize substantially more often than do "supporters" the threat to sovereignty and national identity represented by European integration. It makes little sense to determine whether these contrasts hold across cities, because of the small number of "nonsupporters" in this sample. One can, however, detect some interesting contrasts by comparing respondents from the three countries. This comparison shows that one additional topic that clearly distinguishes "supporters" from "nonsupporters" in Germany is that the latter often emphasize more the threat of labor competition from other European Union countries. In the United Kingdom, "nonsupporters" emphasize more often than do "supporters" the fact that the United Kingdom's voice is not heard in the European Union. In comparison with German and Spanish respondents, they also mention more frequently the topics of sovereignty and national identity. Finally, in Spain the contrast between "supporters" and "nonsupporters" in the extent to which they mention the benefits of the common market is greater than it is in the United Kingdom and Germany.

Thus, contrasts between "supporters" and "nonsupporters" of European integration correspond to those topics that are most salient in the cognitive frames of all countries taken together and to those that distinguish the cognitive frames of each country. Moreover, the polarizing roles of people's expectations about the contribution of European integration to peace and understanding and about its threat to sovereignty and national identity show that their reflections about the European Union are influenced by what kind of integration project they think it does or should represent. That is, it is doubtful that these topics would discriminate "supporters" from "nonsupporters" if the European Union were simply conceived as a "free trade area." One does not hear much discussion, for instance, about the effects that NAFTA might have on peace and understanding between Mexico, Canada, and the United States, or about its effects on national identity and sovereignty. At least in the United States, the main source of contention has been the effect it might have on jobs, one theme that also distinguishes "supporters" from "nonsupporters" in Germany. The reason why peace, cross-cultural understanding, sovereignty, and national identity polarize public opinion on European integration is that people are more or less aware that what is at stake is whether the European Union will develop

TABLE 5
Themes Mentioned to Justify Attitudes toward European Integration or Membership in the European Union, by Country
(Percentages of "nonsupporters"[NS] and "supporters" [S])

Themes	Germany		Spain		United Kingdom		Total	
	NS %	S %	NS %	S %	NS %	S %	NS %	S %
understanding	15	44	12	33		41	9	39
Common Market	62	86	38	84	67	90	58	87
CAP	31	2	50	53	25	29	33	28
free movement and competition	62	28	12				27	9
democratic deficit		40	12		8	15	6	20
states too small	33	51	38	63	42	44	36	53
governance	33	42	12	40	50	58	33	46
against isolation		2		28	8	2	3	11
voice	8	2	25	23	33	5	21	10
modernization		2	25	35	8	12	9	17
removal of barriers	42	42	25	40	62	41	45	41
social benefits		7		19	8	29	3	18
sovereignty and identity	8	5	25	5	67	24	33	11
Structural/Regional Funds	8	2		51	25	29	12	28
lessons of World War II	25	37					9	13
peace	8	44		12	17	37	9	31
total number of respondents	13	43	8	43	12	41	33	127

Understanding: Contributes to better understanding between peoples and cultures; Common Market: The Common Market is economically beneficial; CAP: The Common Agricultural Policy is a bad policy; Democratic deficit: European institutions suffer from a democratic deficit; States too small: States are too small to face economic or military challenges; Governance: The governance of European institutions is poor, Against isolation: Membership of this country is necessary to break the country's isolation, isolation is disadvantageous for the country; Voice: The country's voice is not taken into account within European institutions; Modernization: The country will modernize as a member of European institutions; Removal of barriers: The removal of barriers to the movement of people is a good thing; Social benefits: The country's social benefits will increase as a result of membership in the European institutions; Sovereignty and Identity: Membership in the European Union has or will have a negative effect on sovereignty and identity; Lessons of World War II: Membership in the Eurpean institutions will reduce misgivings toward the country; Peace: Will contribute to peace; Free movement and competition: Free movement of workers will mean competition from foreign workers; Structural/Regional Funds: The Structural and Regional Funds of the European institutions are a good thing.

into some form of "free trade area," or rather into a state-like political union. Because of this, it becomes relevant to move beyond the analysis of support for European integration broadly conceived to a more thorough discussion of the different projects of European unification that people are considering.

Four Different Projects

While surveys of attitudes toward European integration tend to proceed under the implicit assumption that there is an underlying unidimensional scale of support for European integration and for membership in the European Union, ranging from no support to full support, public discussions frame the political debate on European integration around the issue of how much power should be transferred to the European political institutions. Both of these approaches oversimplify the complexity of attitudes toward European integration and the range of projects of European unification that are possible.

The concentration of survey researchers on the description and explanation of support for European integration has nowadays limited analytical justification, even though their work may illuminate trends and patterns in people's underlying predisposition to support continuing efforts at European cooperation. The focus on survey items that ask respondents to indicate their general degree of support for efforts toward European unification is problematic because there is not such a thing as European unification, no single agreed-upon goal toward which so-called efforts at European unification direct themselves. What, then, is the meaning of asking people about their attitudes toward something that does not exist either in fact or as a project? The focus on survey items that ask respondents to indicate their support for their country's membership in the European Union is also problematic; although answers reflect the European Union's legitimacy, positive answers are often indicative of the simple fact that people do not see alternatives to membership in the European Union.

Meanwhile, the debate on the amount of power that should be transferred to the European Union misrepresents the nature of the problem that European governments and their citizens confront. This approach distinguishes between two different and polar alternatives toward European integration: a "free-trade" and a "federalist" models. The first model refers to the creation of a common market for capital, goods, and services, in which every country retains all or most of its sovereignty, supranational functions are kept to a minimum, and supranational regulation is limited. The second model refers to the creation, on top of the common market, of a series of supranational institutions, vested with sovereignty over a large number of competences, and with a vocation to regulate. This portrayal of the problem of integration is misleading because it confounds transfer of competences, transfer of sovereignty, and regulatory zeal. Conceptually and analytically, these are totally different aspects. I will focus only on the different types of European integration that result if one constrains this discussion to the institutional aspects involving competence distribution and transfer of sovereignty.

Some of the bitterest discussions within the European Union have concerned major institutional change involving the transfer of sovereignty (e.g., economic and monetary union; the power of the European Parliament), rather than the transfer of competences. Public opinion surveys and survey research devote more space, however, to measure people's willingness to transfer specific competences—the "subsidiarity" debate. Thus, they neglect the issue of by whom and how decisions are made in the European Union; that is, the issue of whether decisions are made by majority voting or by unanimity, by the European Parliament or by the Council of Ministers.[8] The omission of voting procedures from public debate is not a trivial and inconsequential omission. First of all, one cannot properly talk about a transfer of sovereignty to the European Union unless decisions are reached through majority voting at the Council of Ministers or by the European Parliament. Second of all, as revealed in the in-depth interviews, people are as concerned about the transfer of sovereignty as about the transfer of competences. Because of the way public debate and survey questions are framed, however, they are not clear at all about what it means to transfer functions to the European Union. Many people who support this transfer turn out to be under the impression that decisions are made unanimously, so that no country can be compelled to abide by European Union legislation against the will of its government. Similarly, many people oppose the transfer of functions to the European Union because they believe that it automatically means that individual countries lose their power to veto the adoption of a decision contrary to their national interests. Therefore, the meaning of survey results concerning support for the transfer of functions to the European Union is highly problematic.

Discussion about the future path of European integration and survey research would be enriched and would better reflect people's concerns if it included discussion of decision-making procedures. This would mean that the discussion about models of European integration would revolve around not two but, rather, four major alternatives, resulting from combining two variables, the extent of transfer of functions and the way supranational decisions are made (see figure 3.1). Thus, one model of integration (Centralized Integration) means that major functions of government are transferred to European institutions and decisions are made through

		Transfer of Competences	
		Low	*High*
Transfer of Sovereignty	*Low*	Decentralized Cooperation (e.g., State system, NAFTA)	Centralized Cooperation (e.g., European Union)
	High	Decentralized Integration (e.g., Germany, U.S.)	Centralized Integration (e.g., France)

Figure 3.1 Four models of European integration.

majority voting procedures. A second model of integration (Centralized Cooperation) means that major functions of government are transferred to European institutions but decisions are mostly made through unanimity voting procedures. This model does not amount to a significant transfer of sovereignty from states to European institutions. Under a third model of integration (Decentralized Integration), most major functions of government are retained by national governments but European decisions are made through majority voting procedures; finally, the fourth model of integration (Decentralized Cooperation) means that most major functions remain at the state level and European decisions are made through unanimity voting procedures. Analytically similar, but not identical, typologies could be developed substituting the predominant type of measures taken by the European Union (e.g., Directives versus Recommendations) or the main locus of decision-making within the European Union (European Parliament versus Council of Ministers) for the predominant voting procedure (Majority decision-making versus Unanimous decision-making). In all three cases, the typology would include the sovereignty dimension, that is, the relative power of supranational institutions agents to regulate state affairs, as well as the competence dimension. As currently framed in public discussions and public opinion surveys, however, the issue of sovereignty has not been properly addressed. People are instead being asked to decide between a decentralized and a centralized type of European administration, and it is left up to them to figure out what this means in terms of the capacity of national governments to stop implementing European Union decisions that they don't like.

The in-depth interviews that I conducted in Germany, the United Kingdom, and Spain revealed that individuals are not sufficiently informed about or interested in European integration to provide a precise and coherent view of how they would like European integration to evolve. The noneconomic themes that differentiate "supporters" of European integration from "nonsupporters," however, as well as general comments made throughout the in-depth interviews, reveal that people are at least as concerned about the power of European Union institutions to determine state policy as they are about the extent to which state functions are transferred to the European Union. I classified respondents along the typology I have described above, based on the answers to my questions and the comments they made throughout the interviews. Among other pieces of information, I relied on the respondents' direct and follow-up answers to a question regarding whether the power of EU institutions to adopt legislative decisions that have to be implemented in all EU members is excessive or insufficient. As part of this general question, I asked respondents about the functions that they thought should be transferred to EU institutions and about how decisions should be made in the European Union. Finally, my classification of respondents along different models of European integration is also based on their answers to a question concerning the aspects of the European Union with which they are satisfied or dissatisfied and on their attitudes toward economic and monetary union (EMU).

In the category Centralized Integration, I have included respondents who are for EMU, who think that the legislative functions of the European Union are insufficient or about right, and who are in favor of the creation of something like the United States of Europe. I also include respondents who do not mind the transfer of sovereignty to the European Union and the adoption of decisions on a majority basis. Finally, I classify in this category respondents who claim to be in favor of the transfer of major state functions, such as defense or the development of a common foreign policy. All respondents in this category meet at least two of these criteria, and more than half of them meet at least three. They are not, however, diehard Euro-centralists: although they support the transfer of sovereignty in significant areas, most of them made it clear that they support the application of the principle of subsidiarity.[9] In all, 29% of my respondents (ordinary citizens and local elites) fall in this category. They tend to be found more in the Spanish cities (24 out of 51 Spanish respondents) and Weststadt (9 out of 27 respondents from Weststadt). They are also more often found among the local elites, tend to be more educated (even after considering ordinary citizens alone), and identify with Europe in addition to their country.

At the other pole of this typology, we have what I call "free-traders," that is, respondents who defend the model of Decentralized Cooperation. One in five respondents belong to this category, which includes individuals who support the existence of a common market and are clearly in favor of their country's membership in the European Union. These respondents think, however, that the legislative functions of the European Union are excessive, oppose EMU (or think it should not take place in the near future), would prefer the maintenance of a European free-trade area to the constitution of a United States of Europe, and reject the idea of the

European Union making decisions on a majority basis. Forty-two percent of those in this category explicitly say that they would prefer the European Union to remain a free trade area, and 59% said that the legislative power of the European Union is excessive. In comparison with those classified in the category Centralized Integration, "free-traders" are more often found in Engleton. Also, they are slightly less educated than "centralized integrationists" and relatively more present among ordinary citizens. In fact, the only city where members of the local elites are classified in this category is Engleton. Finally, 53% of the "free-traders" say that they identify very little or not at all with Europe.

The two intermediate categories in my typology are what I call Decentralized Integration and Centralized Cooperation. Since only two of the people I interviewed fall into the latter category, I focus only on those falling in the former. Respondents in the category Decentralized Integration are respondents who express no objection to some decisions being made through majority-voting procedures or who agree with some transfer of sovereignty, but who otherwise would like to limit this transfer of sovereignty to a minimum. Fourteen percent of the respondents fall into this category, and they are disproportionately drawn from Scotsburg (33% of Scotsburg respondents compared to about 10% of respondents in the other cities). Otherwise, respondents in this category are very similar to those in the category Decentralized Cooperation.

Many respondents (12%) were not informed enough or articulate enough to describe in a coherent way how they see European integration evolving. Almost without exception, those in this group support European integration, and a large majority supports some kind of transfer of sovereignty to the European Union institutions, but it is unclear from their comments or answers how much sovereignty they are willing to give up. Because of this, I have not coded them in any of the four categories. Another group of respondents that are excluded from the categorization includes 21 respondents who were too little informed about European integration and were unable to answer many of the questions on which the categorization is based. Finally, 4 respondents in the sample completely reject European integration.

Therefore, a systematic reading and analysis of the in-depth interviews allows for a classification of two-thirds of the respondents. Twenty-nine percent belongs to the category Centralized Integration, 20% to the category Decentralized Cooperation, and 17% to the category Decentralized Integration. This is not a representative sample, however, and no conclusion can be drawn as to the corresponding distribution of the population of Germany, the United Kingdom, and Spain. As expected, respondents in the United Kingdom fall less frequently in the category Centralized Integration than do respondents from Germany and Spain and more frequently in the categories Decentralized Cooperation and Decentralized Integration. Also, local elites tend to belong more frequently than do ordinary citizens to the category Centralized Integration; the sample is too small, however, to allow disentangling the roles of status, level of education, degree of information, and age, on this association. Finally, respondents in the category Centralized Integration identify with Europe to a greater extent than do respondents in the other two categories. All these results are consistent with what one would expect based on previous research, but need to be confirmed with large representative samples. Meanwhile, the answers to questions and the arguments provided by respondents during the in-depth interviews throw light on the cultural and ideological characteristics of the groups of people who identify with different projects of European integration. Because they represent the two extreme projects of European integration described above, and because they are the most articulate and informed respondents in my sample, I now focus on the respondents whom I have classified in the categories Centralized Integration and Decentralized Cooperation.

"Integrationists"

Twenty-six out of 59 local elite members and 20 out of 101 ordinary citizens belong to the Centralized Integration category. The main distinguishing characteristics of ordinary citizens in this category have already been described. Meanwhile, among the elite members, one finds the majority of the representatives of political parties, unions, and editorial boards of the major local newspapers. Of these groups, only the Conservative Party representatives from Engleton, the representative of the Scottish Nationalist Party in Scotsburg, and the editor of the conservative Quijotón newspaper, support the Decentralized Cooperation European alternative. Since local political party representatives and local newspapers are probably the most influential actors at the municipal level, one can safely say that local elites, especially those of the left, exert a positive influence toward European integration. Only in the United Kingdom is the influence of political organizations, unions, and the press less favorable to the Centralized Integration project. In Engleton, strong opposition by the Conservative Party counteracted the favorable influence of the local newspaper and the coalition formed by the Labour Party and the Liberal Democrats. Meanwhile, the representative of the Footwear Union is ambiguous about the desirability of further political integration. In Scotsburg, neither political party representatives nor the editor of the local newspaper or the representative of the main public workers' union unambiguously favor further political integration. Meanwhile, the representative of the Scottish Nationalist Party expresses views that correspond to what I have called the Decentralized Cooperation project.

Respondents in this category provided a wide variety of arguments to justify their preference for more political integration and a transfer of sovereignty. Four major ones, however, can be outlined: (1) the desire to form a strong economic, political, and cultural bloc, able to compete with the rest of the world, but mostly with the United States; (2) the desire to defend the social market economy, as in Germany, or move further toward it, as in Spain and the United Kingdom; (3) the realization that many environmental and economic problems have become transnational and can no longer be addressed through state policies; (4) the desire to fight nationalist tendencies and create a favorable environment for peace. All respondents present these arguments in multiple combinations, so that one cannot speak of a coalition of various ideological groups, but rather, of a single group, whose members express old and new political themes. What one discovers is a "Rot-Grün" mixture of classic left themes (Social Market economy) and "green" or "postmaterialist" themes (Transnational Problems and Peace). One discovers also an odd shift of the locus of nationalist feelings from the nation-state to the European Union, consistent with the fact that a large majority of these respondents identify quite strongly with Europe. That is, while these respondents proclaim their abhorrence of nation-state nationalisms in order to prevent another European war, they are also expressing a defensive form of European nationalism, aimed at protecting the European social market model against the neoliberal model represented by the United States. The United States is therefore the "other," against which a European identity and a Centralized Integration project are formulated.

To better convey what type of people support the Centralized Integration project and how they justify their views, I now concentrate on six selected interviews conducted in the six cities included in this study. These respondents are (1) a Labor Party member and Head of Engleton's Council, (2) a high school teacher in Weststadt, (3) a prominent member of Oststadt's Green Party, (4) the secretary of the leftist union, Comisiones Obreras (CCOO) of Quijotón, (5) a high school teacher in Scotsburg, and (6) the leader of Catadell's Socialist Party (PSC-PSOE).

STRENGTHENING AND STREAMLINING EUROPE

October 28, 1997

Another gray day in Engleton. The Head of Engleton's Council receives me in his spacious office at City Hall (1, Engleton). My interlocutor is a talkative, energetic, and jovial middle-aged man. Early in the interview, I learn of his experience as a schoolteacher, and as he talks about his students' views and attitudes, he swiftly begins to tell me about the British approach toward European integration and his own reaction to that. Like many pro-integration respondents in the United Kingdom, the head of Engleton's Council, a supporter of the Labour Party, defines himself primarily by opposition to the "Eurosceptics" in his own land. He portrays the British population, including, to his dismay, his students, as dominated by xenophobic attitudes, which are reinforced by the tabloid press:

> I teach in a country school with rural kids, and there is, I think, a general anti-European feeling. I think it is particularly strong among the young, and that's the most depressing; among the young and the old: old people are also terribly anti-European in my experience! Particularly in the ward I represent. It's people like me, in the late middle age or early middle age, or whatever, I think—generally speaking—the people I hang out with in terms of local politics, or in terms of the art world I'm very much involved in, who tend to be very pro-Europe.

What sort of criticism do you hear from people?

> I don't really understand it, but I think the essential criticism is a little xenophobic; I mean, I think there is a racist attitude, hmm, among young people.

About specific countries?

> Oh! I think toward Europe in general; they do not have yet the concept of the scale of Europe. Hmm.... But it's essentially anti-French, there's a lot of sort of pathetic anti-Germanism, anti-German attitudes.... These are people who read *The Sun*; they are genuinely influenced by the mass media. And, you know, it's culturally reinforced by stuff like the Spice Girls; I hate to say it, but they wear the Union Jack and so on. It's quite worrying.

In contrast to these attitudes, the head of Engleton's Council presents himself as someone with a nonessentialist conception of identity, who rejects nationalism, and who does not care about sovereignty. About identity and nationalism, he says the following:

> I change my identity, I think, like every other human being; and if you had been talking to me at a different time in my life ... I began by saying: "You know, I am a Scot." But it's thirty years, forty years since I left Scotland! I'm Scot by birth, that's all; I share some cultural values but I've lived in England most of my life. I don't feel myself particularly English. I don't feel myself particularly Engledite and I've lived here for nearly 25 or 30 years I guess!... You see, hmm, I sometimes would say "I'm European"—more often now actually—when I have to define myself, 'cause I find it very narrow to say "I come from Britain." I find it even narrower to say "I come from England"; I may come from it, but I don't feel of it, in any particular sense.

I've been proud of some of the things our people have done, but equally very depressed. And after eighteen years of a horrible government they kept voting for, I just find it very difficult to understand how people could do that. And so, increasingly—I travel a lot, I enjoy traveling—if I'm in Moscow, I would describe myself as a European, and if I'm in America, or in Canada, increasingly, I feel European....

And about sovereignty:

What the hell is sovereignty! I mean, sovereignty does not mean a damn thing to me, or to most people! Most people expect to have a life, these days, in a reasonably civilized society; they expect a comfortable life, they expect that children will be looked after; they expect that old people will be looked after, they expect quality health care, and they expect a period of working life. And, I don't think that, at the end of the day, they care about who provides it, as long as it is provided....

Like many supporters of the Labour Party in the United Kingdom, my respondent was not always in favor of European integration. He actually voted against entry in the early 1970s because he believed in the Labour Party's portrayal of the European Economic Community as the "European Employers' Federation," that is, an organization solely intent in promoting the interests of multinationals. He characterizes his change of attitudes as a process of growing up, of realizing that, precisely because the world is dominated by multinationals, states have become too small. If what Ford does has global effects, then "perhaps the only way to deal with Ford is to deal with them globally, and to deal within the European Plan." Likewise, people no longer look for work only in their own country. More and more, young workers seek work in other countries, so that national boundaries have lost their meaning. It is this thinking that leads him to defend the implementation of a common currency in Europe. It makes a lot of sense to him, to have a common currency, since many large companies in Europe operate in several countries. In sum, the realization that the world has become too small is the main reason offered by the head of Engleton's Council to explain his change of mind regarding European integration. This by itself, however, does not explain his support for a Centralized Integration model of unification. Underlying this support is his belief that political integration will make Europe more efficient and stronger, and so enable it to counteract the United States' cultural dominance.

In justifying his advocacy of a Centralized Integration model of European unification, my Labour Party supporter speaks both as a citizen and as someone deeply involved in local politics; one might add that he speaks as someone who believes in the now seemingly "old-fashioned" leftist idea of public planning. His vision of Europe is one governed by the principle of subsidiarity, where a significant portion of state power will be transferred to the local level and the rest to European institutions. The resulting administrative and political frame would be one whose scope would ensure both more efficacy in the running of public affairs and a better adaptation to a global economy:

> I can understand the parliamentarian fears that the one level of government that will eventually erode will be the national parliament, and I know what a fearsome battle this will create. But I think it is inevitable, 'cause I think that what one has to see in the context of Europe is planning on a much larger regional basis; it is silly that we are duplicating limited resources throughout Europe; it is absolutely stupid that we have car manufacturing here, here, here, when there are clearly some areas that are better suited. Now, that's not to say that I want to see the UK become the UK Theme Park, but it may be, it may be that that's the best thing the UK could be. But, if that means that the quality of life for most people goes up, if that means that the standard of living throughout Europe, then that's important to all of us. I mean, if people have disposable income in Southern Italy, it might well be that they will eventually want to dispose of their income by touring the Midlands of England. I don't know, but it does seem to me that the best way of using our scarce European resources is to use them on a strategic basis by looking at the whole of Europe and saying what is the best way to plan an economy. And one of the problems of planning a national economy is that, inevitably, some industries are going to be inefficient or uneconomic, or bad, but we keep them going because national pride says, "we must have a mining industry or a shipbuilding industry, or whatever." Why do we need that? If, for instance, shipbuilding could be better down on the Rhine, in Germany, what's to say that we need to keep sustaining the unacceptable simply because "we've always done it that way"? Now, from my point of view, that happening will ensure that the terrible pockets of unemployment and deprivation that occur throughout Europe could be eradicated, because we are using our resources sensibly. It also means quite simply that, in order to administer services—because that's the other side of the coin: first create economic wealth, and the sensible way to do it is by rational planning at a multi, at an international level; but then the question is "How do you deliver the service to all the people?" And the best way of doing that is by local government. So, to me, that seems the two parts of the equation: international cooperation and economic planning at an international level and delivery of services at a very local level.

When I ask him whether this means that he favors something like the United States of Europe, he readily agrees and justifies his answer not only in terms of greater efficiency but, also, in terms of countervailing the United States' current world hegemony:

> I think that having as much legislation as possible, which is common, makes things clearer for people.... I do believe in a Federal United States of Europe,

and I think that will come. I hope it will come in my lifetime, because I think it would be a huge breath of fresh air for the whole world. If we can do that in Europe, then they can do it in other parts of the world. I believe that, in geopolitical terms, in terms of blocs now, it would prevent the view that is still widely held that, you know, there is a cultural domination of America, of American culture. I think that would end. It would be a good thing, also for America. I suspect that one of the things that you've discovered in Europe is tremendous anti-Americanism, have you?

After an hour or so, my interview with the head of Engleton's Council is over. I leave City Hall thinking to myself how odd it is to find such a European-oriented politician leading a town that does not strike me as particularly pro-European. I also reflect on his change of attitude toward Europe over the course of the years. Is he simply repeating party directives and adapting as these change over time? What does this say about the impact of party platforms on people's attitudes toward European integration? Are ordinary citizens as affected as career politicians by changes in a party's political platform? Whatever the answers to these questions may be, he seems genuinely committed to a Centralized Integration model of unification, governed by the principle of subsidiarity. His justifications for this preference, a strong and efficient bloc able to counter the hegemony of the United States, reflect a broad mix of influences: his long membership in the Labour Party, which probably explains his emphasis on planning, his current position as local political leader, with an interest in increasing the power of local government, his living in a country deeply divided along party lines on the issue of European integration, and his life in a world dominated by the United States.

NO MORE WARS IN EUROPE

March 15, 1996

Another gray day. About two miles away from Weststadt's geometrically laid-out and alphabetically arranged city core, I lock my bike on a street lamp. I cross to the other side, making sure not to be run over by one of those inaudible tramways that traverse the city. I enter an old, not particularly pretty, building and climb the stairs to the second floor. A woman about fifty greets me and, following the usual introductions, guides me to the room where we'll conduct the interview. The table sitting in the middle of the room is full with magazines and newspapers, as befits this high school teacher of English, highly interested in public affairs.   (15, Weststadt, older than 50, more than High School)

She tells me about her political sympathies for the Green Party and about her main concern at the moment, unemployment conditions in Germany. I am not surprised, since, almost without exception, this is the main preoccupation of everybody I have interviewed thus far. We then move to discuss European integration. Her definition of the European Union is revealing of her views on this topic: "A necessary institution, to overcome nationalism, create a big market, and, in the future, facilitate the melting together of cultures and the development of a common defense policy."

The development of an institutional environment conducive to peace in Europe dominates her thoughts on the European Union. She was born two years before the end of World War II and she lost not only her father, but also a good part of her family. This experience, she says, and having to confront the memory of Nazism while growing up, have made her very critical of nationalism in general and appreciative of peace-directed efforts:

> I mistrust nationalism; even today, I could well imagine Spaniards or Italians fight each other; or Germans and Englishmen, and the French. Yes, I have a great mistrust of nationalism, and I think that these atavistic attitudes should be channeled.... I believe that individuals need a favorable environment to channel their tendency to be at war with each other. My worldview has been undoubtedly shaped by history, since the history of humanity is a history of wars.

Although her reflection on European integration also includes economic considerations, these are subordinate to her idealistic and peace-oriented identification with the overall project. Thus, when explaining her support for economic and monetary union, she admits having heard and read both positive and negative prognoses, but she eventually chose to believe the former, because they suit better her wish for a united Europe:

> *So you have two types of forecasts, a negative and a positive. Why do you believe the positive ones?*
>
> Why? Because, hmm; if I think that European unification is a positive goal, then I must be willing to do everything to reach this goal. I see the problems, but I hope that in the end it works, so that my wish is fulfilled.

Not only her support for EMU, but also her desire that legislative power be transferred from the Commission to the European Parliament and her preference for majority over unanimous decision-making procedures, justifies classifying her in the Centralized Integration category. She is cautious, however, about the pace of European integration, and although she supports progress toward the constitution of a United States of Europe, she does not think that it is for tomorrow. Before that happens, she says, legislative power must be transferred to the European Parliament, and mechanisms must be developed to increase the accountability of European Union officials. Other reasons she gives for her cautious approach are her fear that someone like Berlusconi or Le Pen could rise to power in a united Europe or that German legislation will become watered down. In the end, I develop the feeling that my respondent is torn between her deeply engrained desire for peace and her status as a secure, middle-class citizen in democratic and socially advanced Germany. Whereas the former explain her idealistic and uncompromising support for European integration, the latter could explain her gradualism.

A STRONG AND PEACEFUL EUROPE

November 10, 1997

Another gray and, alas, rainy day. After locking my—now wet—bike to a fence in the faculty's parking lot, I enter the redbrick building that functions as one of Scotsburg's biggest high schools. I identify myself at the reception desk and I am brought to a small, book- and paper-filled office, and am told to make myself comfortable and wait for my respondent. I set up my recording equipment and review my interview schedule. Ten minutes later, she comes into the office, preceded by a huge stack of student essays. My respondent, in her mid-thirties, strongly bound to Scotland and, like most Scotsburg residents, supporter of the Labour Party, is one of the high school's history teachers. We have barely one hour and fifteen minutes before her next class, so we proceed right away with the interview.   (47, Scotsburg, 31–50, more than High School)

It does not take much effort to figure out her attitudes toward European integration:

Would you say that you are in favor of or against efforts toward European unification?

Very much for; particularly, for political unification.

She is actually for a creation of a federation of states, something like the United States of America. This means that many policy domains should be transferred to the institutions of the European Union: defense, environment, health, economics, and employment. Economic and monetary union should also take place, and the United Kingdom should be there from the start. Otherwise, "if we postpone it for too long, it will bring all the negative consequences that we've had since 1947 for not being part of Europe." She also thinks that legislative power should be transferred from the Council of Ministers to the European Parliament.

In justifying this project of European integration, my respondent combines the arguments of Engleton's head of the Council and the high school teacher from Weststadt:

First and foremost, to maintain peace in Europe. Second, to be a third force economically, a proper third force economically, against Japan and America; to safeguard the jobs of the Europeans against the Pacific Rim; and to bring greater prosperity.

Although competing economically against Asia is for her an important consideration, the economic and political assertion of Europe and, within it, of the United Kingdom, vis-à-vis the United States of America plays a more important role:

I don't want Britain to be hanging on the coattails of America.

Consistent with this position, later on in the interview she justifies European unification by saying that the United Kingdom cannot really defend its international interests as long as Europe lacks a common defense policy and continues to depend on NATO.

In Scotsburg, however, as well as in the other cities in my study, "integrationists" do not advocate a full transfer of sovereignty to the European Union. Whereas Engleton's head of the Council justified the subsidiarity principle on efficacy grounds, and Weststadt's teacher justified it appealing to the notion of accountability, Scotsburg's history teacher invokes cultural reasons. Because of cultural differences across Europe, the United States of Europe should not be identical to the United States of America:

It is very difficult when you have ancient states like, for example, Denmark, France, England, that are so different culturally; and I don't think that you could impose on that a common language. I think you have to allow for cultural variation; even in the United Kingdom, our tradition in Scotland is very different from England. We have great differences in religion, in education, and in law. I think that these traditions should not be allowed to die. They must allow the individual areas to develop in their own way, I think.

In practical terms, what this means for her is that areas such as education should remain the prerogative of states and, within them, of regions. The role of one's biography and professional experience in giving meaning to such an abstract notion as European integration manifests itself, as it did in the preceding two interviews, when my respondent opposes the idea of a common history curriculum across the European Union. History teachers should be allowed total freedom to teach what they want and to adapt the content of their courses to the historical peculiarities of the place or region where they are teaching:

"In European history there's a lot in common, but there's also a lot which is peculiar to each area."

The maintenance of peace and Europe's economic assertion with respect to the rest of the world, especially the United States, are among the most frequent arguments that "integrationists" use to support political unification in Europe. The three interviews above illustrate this, while at the same time showing that personal biography and national peculiarities color the way respondents present their case and set limits on the amount and pace of integration. The next interview introduces two new arguments for integration: the defense of Europe's social market mechanisms and the existence of transnational problems that only supranational institutions can address.

A SOCIALLY AND ENVIRONMENTALLY CONSCIOUS EUROPE

May 20, 1996

Sunny day in Oststadt! After a three-mile walk on the main artery that stems from the train station and crosscuts the entire town, I turn left to a quiet street with single-family homes on both sides. My immediate impression of being somewhere in the Midwest of the United States is enhanced upon entering my guest's house. Sparsely, comfortably, and tastefully furnished, I am reminded of some of my colleagues' homes back there. Perhaps it is no accident. My respondent is an academically involved chemist and active member of the local Green Party. (4, Oststadt)

I begin the interview, as I always do, asking him about the local community's views on European integration. He tells me that people are generally happy to be part of the European Union, although the initial enthusiasm, on the eve of German reunification, has certainly faded. People especially value the enhanced freedom to travel to other countries brought by reunification and by membership in the European Union. It is a source of satisfaction that he shares. He tells me of having traveled to Western Europe only once between 1960 and the fall of the Berlin wall, to attend an international conference on the Chernobyl accident in 1986. For political reasons, crossing the Iron Curtain was heavily restricted, but even within Eastern Europe, people confronted numerous travel obstacles, because of limitations on how much currency they were allowed to exchange.

People in Oststadt are much less enthusiastic today about membership in the European Union, for the same reasons that they are less satisfied about Germany's reunification. The impact of competition with the West has been of such magnitude, in terms of economic restructuring and rising unemployment, that many wonder whether reunification was worthwhile after all. My respondent's European project is heavily influenced by this experience. Turning upside-down the neoliberal pro-integration argument, he envisages the European Union primarily as an instrument to restrain and steer competition, rather than as an institutional framework to strengthen the single market:

> The issue is not whether one wants or does not want European unification; it is, rather, whether one wants to steer the process or leave it in other people's hands. We have had similar experiences during what is known as, in rather euphemistic terms, the reunification of Germany. It was then the case that economic and monetary union took place before political measures were

adopted to steer the process. This delay is responsible for much of the destruction and unemployment since then. Because of this experience, I think that East Germans are very sensitized to the need of political steering mechanisms, so that European unification is not directed by people who pursue their own interests rather than the European interest.... We cannot leave European unification only in the hands of the economic sector. We cannot leave it in the hands of the Mafia; or in those of the multinationals—whose boundaries with the former are actually often difficult to discern.

Three main arguments, in order of importance, underlie my respondent's support for political unification: (1) avoid social dumping, (2) address transnational problems, and (3) secure peace in the face of growing conflict over the distribution of wealth.

The defense of Germany's Social Market economy is by far his main concern. Under this umbrella he includes labor rights and benefits, consumer rights, and regional balance. Political integration is necessary to protect this system against the threats of cheap foreign labor, cheap foreign products of lesser quality than local ones, and big multinationals, respectively. His views on the effects of the single market on East Germany's economy, as he himself acknowledges, are theoretically informed by Marx's overproduction thesis—that is, the idea that we are about to reach a point in which production exceeds the capacity of the market to absorb it; therefore, we need to develop mechanisms that are better suited to administer and distribute current wealth than to increase production. To this Marxist foundation, he adds reflections about the ecological limits to growth, developed by the environmentalist movement.

During the interview my respondent lays out various measures that the European Union could pass to protect the German Social Market economy model. The European Union could, for instance, specify that contract bids (e.g., in the construction sector) be open to foreign firms only for large projects. Also, one could tax the transport of goods in direct proportion to the traveled distance, so as to protect local producers. Furthermore, one could promote the standardization of labor rights and benefits and the quality standards of products. Finally, one could support regional economies by introducing local currencies side by side with the euro. Wages and salaries would be paid in a set mix of European and local currency (e.g., 70% and 30%), so that the local currency could be used for exchanges involving regional products and services only. On the issue of economic and monetary union, he expresses support, but thinks that it should not be implemented until the political steering mechanisms are in place. He justifies this again with reference to East Germany's experience during reunification:

> That is, I am afraid that the single currency leads toward a situation in which economic policy would be determined by multinational corporations.... We

need steering mechanisms; otherwise, the same thing will happen as during the process of German reunification. That is, that the strong ones, the strong firms, the strong regions, benefit at the cost of the rest of the population.

As a person highly involved in evaluating the environmental impact of the Chernobyl accident, my respondent is quite sensitive to the existence of transnational problems that are not easily addressed through state measures:

> Police, environmental policy, the fight against internationally organized crime, are problems that single states can no longer manage, because the wind—this is not such a big country like the United States of America— blows beyond East Germany, much farther, and rivers flow across different countries. Europe needs to be united, or at least a certain degree of unification.

He therefore believes that greater police cooperation is needed, as well as common environmental standards. Furthermore, he thinks that the war in ex-Yugoslavia and Germany's experience of receiving a large number of refugees call for a common foreign policy. Although it may still be too early for a common defense policy, the European Union should invest in creating effective institutional mechanisms for conflict prevention and resolution. He stresses that the danger of not controlling crime, of not preventing conflicts such as the one in ex-Yugoslavia, and of not sharing equitably the burden of accepting refugees, could be growing antiforeigner sentiment. Again, these reflections are very much influenced by my respondent's concern over current political tensions in East Germany: in particular, increasing xenophobia among the East German population, fueled by a belief that foreigners are responsible for rising unemployment and crime rates.

Finally, my respondent thinks that European political integration is needed to prevent growing social conflicts over the distribution of wealth from degenerating into nationalism and then war in Europe:

> The economic situation will not improve very much. Ideal would be to be able to maintain current standards of living, but this will not be possible everywhere. Therefore, there is the danger that everybody will look out for their own national interest, which will create tensions. There will always be national interests, but we must try to find ways to pursue them by working together.

When asked about the institutional changes that he thinks are necessary to achieve the objective outlined above, my host replies that, as part of the effort toward political integration, the European Parliament should be empowered, and majority decision-making should be extended to a larger number of areas. He also supports transferring sovereignty to the European Union, which he sees as consistent with Germany's federal tradition. He does not think, however, that the time is yet ripe for the creation of the United States of Europe, partly because of cultural differences. Furthermore, he believes that political integration should go hand in hand with a strict application of the principle of subsidiarity.

I have a bitter taste when I leave my respondent's house. Yes, he is an articulate supporter for European integration; but all I remember from the conversation are justifications and proposals solely moved by local—should I say egoistic—interests. Where's the European ideal? Or should I hope for Mandeville's principle to apply to European unification as well as to the economy, so that people's egoistic pursuit of political integration in the end produces an institutional model that benefits the largest number?

DEFENDING EUROPE'S SOCIAL MODEL

November 10, 1996

Freezing in Quijotón. Going up the stairs is a challenge when your right ankle is puffed up like a balloon. The old Communist union's headquarters remind me of a public administration building: a maze of corridors, people who run from office to office, the rhythmic noise of photocopy machines. But also, not quite like it: political posters calling for mobilization, announcements of upcoming assemblies or demonstrations, information on learning opportunities for workers.... The secretary of Comisiones Obreras (CCOO) in Quijotón greets me in her large office. She is businesslike but eager to talk about something that will distract her from her daily routine. (141, Quijotón)

The leadership of the coalition led by the reformed Communist Party, Izquierda Unida, has been critical at times of the way European integration is proceeding. It is also critical of the draconian budget measures that the Conservative Party of President Aznar has taken to ensure that Spain meets the convergence criteria of the economic and monetary union.[10] But the local representative of Izquierda Unida in Quijotón does not share this criticism. The same can be said about the secretary of Comisiones Obreras. This 45-year-old ex–high school teacher has been resolutely favorable to European integration since her first travel abroad as a teenager. Like many other members of her generation, she immediately sensed that Spain's hope for modernization was inextricably tied to breaking its traditional isolation and becoming a member of the European Economic Community (EEC). She is convinced that, as a member of the European Union, Spain will be motivated to assimilate positive values of other countries, such as the discipline and organizational capacity of the Germans, and to improve its educational and competitive standards. Her only current sources of anxiety are high unemployment levels and the danger that Spain may eventually turn into a tourist resort, where everyone is a waiter.

She is totally committed to political integration because she cannot accept a European Union solely conceived as an economically driven project:

> Without political union, it is as if we were there solely to see who grabs more of the collective wealth. Money is essential, the economy is essential, but there are other things in life. Man needs more than bread and butter to live. The mere satisfaction of material needs is unsatisfying.

More specifically, she wants political union because it will contribute to the improvement of Spain's labor legislation and worker benefits:

> I am convinced about that, even though the Welfare State is currently under attack. We will still benefit, even if the Right continues to govern here and in countries like Germany. We are still a long way before the end of the Welfare State and there's therefore room for our level of workers' rights and benefits to improve.

She also favors political integration as the only option that Europe has to defend its culture and values against the United States of America:

> Europe would then be a world power. It would be a counterweight to the USA. The USA has economic development but no human face. I deeply dislike that. Europe, on the other hand, has yet to lose its values.

For all these reasons, and although her project lacks in concretion, my respondent favors the strengthening of the European Union's common institutions, the development of a common European foreign policy, and the formation of a European government. Also, and against the opinion of many union militants, who complain about the sacrifices convergence policies have demanded from them, she is strongly in favor of a rapid adoption of the common European currency. Asked whether she minds losing sovereignty, she has this to say:

> It does not bother me at all. Why should it, when all the multinationals are already here?

A STRONG AND SOCIALLY CONSCIOUS EUROPE

March 22, 1997

Mediterranean sun. "I hope he is there this time," I tell myself as I climb the stairs to the second floor of this small building, not far away from Catadell's train station and outside the town's medieval quarters. Heavy sigh of relief, as the receptionist takes me to the office of the Socialist Party's representative in Catadell. Local affairs occupy only a small portion of the time of this career politician. Fate has chosen that I interview someone who has experienced European integration from positions of responsibility in European institutions and who therefore spends a great deal of his time abroad.   (93, Catadell)

People who are in the habit of reflecting about the obscure topics that interest the researcher often volunteer their own sociological explanations of their attitudes, before we have a chance to ask:

> The fact is that, because of my background, I am very open, not only to universalism, but also to the idea of Europe. I got my doctorate at the Sorbonne, I have studied abroad, and, therefore, feel very emotionally tied to Europe. And for me, let's put it this way, there is not such a thing as the European barrier. There isn't because I don't face linguistic limitations; at least, I have enough grip on foreign languages that I can travel across Europe at ease, without feeling that I am a foreigner.

My host is therefore very committed to the construction of Europe and to Spain's membership in the European Union, which he sees as a *sine qua non* for the country's modernization. Unless it unites, he says, Europe cannot survive in an age of globalization that has eroded the states' capacity to influence the course of the economy and their capacity to compete against giants such as the United States. Integration is also necessary to steer competition within Europe instead of allowing it to degenerate into a wild struggle, a zero-sum game where the gains of one country are the losses of another:

> Globalization has rendered obsolete all the control mechanisms that were available to the state in the past. Nowadays, for instance, states can no longer ensure the stability of their currencies. Any big speculator can decide to play at buying or selling Hong Kong's currency and, two days later, this state has gone bankrupt; and this happens, simply because Mr. Soros, or whoever, has decided to make a big profit. That is something that no state can endure by itself. We also have the problem of the hi-tech industries, the world of space exploration and of space technology, the satellites; no state can, by itself, put the necessary resources together. The only exception to this is, of course, the United States of America. Not even Germany can afford doing this alone anymore. Then, there are the economic advantages of unity: it is obvious that a bigger market, one with 380 or 400 million consumers, offers more opportunities for economic dynamism and wealth creation than do small or middle-sized entities of about 40 million consumers. Last but not least, to forego the creation of large organizations such as the European Union would result in an exacerbation of competition between European states up to Smithian levels, in which the only way people become rich is by fucking up [*sic*] their neighbors; this would mean a total waste of energy and also, that what you would win on one side, you would lose on the other. I think one must tend toward large regional blocs. Otherwise, they eat you, they eat you!

The respondent's last comment, on the need to form a European bloc in order to restrain competition within Europe, reflects a political ideology that questions the primacy of market principles in social organization. Considerations of social justice and solidarity must, according to him, balance market mechanisms in the allocation of wealth. This justification, undoubtedly shaped by Spain's heavy dependence on structural funds from the European Union and its relatively lower levels of labor rights and benefits, is the main justification my respondent offers to strongly advocate European political integration.

> I am interested in the European project only if the citizens of Europe, the citizens of my country, the citizens of Catadell, can expect better standards of living, more social justice, and more equality. Otherwise, I am not interested.

He thus criticizes the European Union for having approved a Social Charter that, in his view, is too vague and not as ambitious as a related Council of Europe proposal that he helped to draft. Furthermore, he makes the British conservative government, opposed to political integration and to extending common rights and benefits to the workers of the European Union, the target of his most vitriolic criticism:

> First, they must learn once and for all that in order to create a real single market, a single currency, and a single economic system, one needs to develop political and juridical mechanisms. Everything is interrelated. For instance, if you want to liberalize financial markets, you have to agree on common legislation as to what constitutes an illegal financial practice. Second, they must confront the fact that they are in a situation of total decline—never in my whole life have I seen so many rats as in London's subway; it is time that they figure out how to get rid of them. They are going backwards. For twenty years they have been deluded into thinking that they were Rudyard Kipling's Empire; well, it turns out that they lost their Empire more than sixty years ago. Then, they have this thing with their "American friend" and this strange attitude toward "the Continent." It's been a catastrophe. And one just needs to have a look at Great Britain: one of the greatest countries in the world finds itself in a situation of total decay; one just needs to visit London to see it.

When outlining the actual contours of his European project, the representative of Catadell's Socialist Party is rather cautious and pragmatic. He is certainly in favor of transferring more competences to the European Union and of giving more power to the European Commission and the European Parliament. He is aware, however, that states will not give up sovereignty easily, especially on matters of defense, and that national identities are deeply ingrained among the population. Therefore, he advocates application of the principle of subsidiarity at the municipal, regional, state, and European administrative levels.

"Free-Marketeers"

I have classified nineteen ordinary respondents and thirteen local elite members in the Decentralized Cooperation category. Aside from this group's socio-demographic characteristics, which I have outlined above, two features about the local elites can be highlighted. First of all, all but four are British respondents; second of all, speakers for women's, houseworker, and agrarian organizations are disproportionately represented in this category. Other local elite members represented here are the two local conservative leaders I interviewed in Engleton, a Scottish Nationalist Party's council member in Scotsburg, the Student Union's representative in Engleton's main college, a Young Labor member in Engleton, the president of Scotsburg's Chamber of Commerce, and the editor of Quijotón's conservative newspaper. In all, and with few exceptions (e.g., Young Labor, Student Union, and Chamber of Commerce), the organizations represented in this category could be described as conservative. They are certainly conservative when compared with the organizations to which the local elite members in the Centralized Integration category belong.

Respondents in this category are quite overtly opposed to European political integration. Although they applaud the European single market, and in some cases go as far as supporting the creation of the single currency, they oppose majority decision-making procedures in the European Union and want to restrict as much as possible the transfer of competences. Furthermore, in contrast to respondents in the Centralized Integration category, free-marketeers hardly identify at all as Europeans.

Culture and sovereignty are the two main themes that respondents in this category use to oppose political integration. The culture argument takes two forms: some oppose political integration because it would erode national identity; others claim that cultural differences would make it too difficult to reach consensual decisions and implement these decisions. The sovereignty argument rests on a principled opposition to any transfer of sovereignty. Finally, between those invoking culture and sovereignty as reasons to oppose political integration are respondents who do not think that a supranational organization would be efficient; also, respondents who think that it will damage British interests.

As in the previous section, I have selected several respondents to exemplify the different themes outlined above. These respondents are the Scottish Nationalist Party's representative at Scotsburg's City Council, a university student from Quijotón, the president of Weststadt's Housewives Association, a high school teacher from Weststadt, and one leading member of Engleton's branch of the Conservative Party.

PROTECTING NATIONAL IDENTITY

November 6, 1997

> Westward from Edinburgh, eastward from Glasgow: Scotsburg. Five minutes away from the local library, my temporary headquarters, lies the town's City

Council, a modern, nondescript building. I have never met a Scottish nationalist leader. What does the Scottish Nationalist Party's Council member think of Scotland's current autonomy? I must remind myself that my research topic is no longer Basque and Catalan nationalism, but rather, European integration. But aren't the two topics related? Didn't I undertake this project to better understand collective identities?

In contrast to some of the people that I have already interviewed, for whom Scotland is now independent, my respondent is aware that the degree of autonomy granted to Scotland pales in comparison with that granted to Catalonia and the Basque country. He is optimistic, however, and thinks that the new Scottish parliament will transform this limited autonomy into something worthwhile. (45, Scotsburg)

Something that autonomy will not change for the time being is Scotland's dependence on the British government when it comes to relations with the European Union. This is a source of concern for my respondent. It prevents Scotland from defending its own interests and thus makes it more vulnerable to a loss of identity. Identity is the theme that dominates the SNP councilman's reflections on European integration. He is extremely supportive of European cooperation and of the creation of a European single market. The economic opportunity represented by this big market alone justifies membership in the European Union and a severing of ties with traditional partners, such as the Commonwealth countries. Moreover, one cannot ignore the European Union's contribution to peace. When it comes to political integration, however, my host is resolutely opposed. The dominance of some states within the European Union would mean that the national interests of small countries are overlooked, and this would result in those countries' loss of identity.

Several times during the interview, I ask my respondent what he means by "identity." Like many other people, he has trouble finding a definition. Sometimes, he describes identity as self-determination, as the ability for a country to decide on its own affairs. On other occasions, he defines it in terms of a sense of belonging to a particular country, with particular values, a particular history, and a particular culture. He thinks, for instance, that identity so understood would be diluted if Scotland were part of a politically integrated European Union. My host's most elaborate definition of national identity, however, rests on the notion of a people's self-confidence, a conception that one also finds in Saint-Exupéry, Mounier, and the 1960s writings of Catalonia's nationalist leader, Jordi Pujol. Scotsburg's SNP councilman puts it this way:

> There is a question of national confidence that comes with the question of identity. I think it has been eroded in Scotland. One of the reasons why we are only now embarking on this modest form of parliament is that people very often hold the attitude: "We, yes, we want to retain our Scottish history, our Scottish culture, but we really couldn't manage without England, we

could not survive in the real world, in the economic world; in the world of international affairs we require England." That's something that has gradually diminished over the last, I would say, thirty, forty, years. There is a greater sense of confidence now; I think that comes from political action. I think it's primarily caused by the SNP, which has been, not the only, but the primary vehicle of the Scottish independence movement....

... There's nothing worse than uniformity, a uniformity of ideas, a uniformity of approach, a uniformity towards considering yourself to be of slightly lesser importance in the scheme of things than others; I think it leads to a poorer quality of life. People don't demand, people do not strive, people do not tend to achieve the same level as others. I think that this is a damaging feature. Let's take the United States, for example. The Negroes have made fewer strides forward in that they really see themselves as being an inferior group within the society; they expect to be inferior, and a great many of them, probably with abilities, don't strive to make the most out of those abilities. And I think that this must have applied to other ethnic groups, because the ruling group, if you want, the dominant group tended to say: "No, you are not one of us, therefore you must be inferior." And it did not take people long enough to start seriously to believe it.

Because of this concern for Scotland's identity, Scotsburg's SNP councilman opposes political integration, including the single currency, whether or not Scotland is directly represented in the European Union's institutions. Instead, he proposes "an association of independent states, working together toward the economic benefit of the whole, the political benefit, the social benefit of the whole." Such conception of the European Union does not preclude altogether the development of common policies or common legislation. For instance, he is not against the adoption of the Social Charter. What it means is that no country should be forced to adopt legislation or policies that its representative government opposes. It also means that most of the European Union's power should be vested in the Council of Ministers and that the legislative and policy-making capacity of the European Union should be kept to a minimum.

ANGLOS VERSUS LATINS

November 6, 1996

Northeast from Madrid, on the road to Barcelona: Quijotón. Five- or six-story building; redbrick. Date: probably 1960s. I am in a residential neighborhood, one of many built during the years of Spain's economic development: identical houses; great business for speculators.

It may well be that the young generations are more favorable to European integration. I have yet to find, however, an idealistically oriented and well-informed young respondent. Many of my twenty-something respondents are like the history major I'm interviewing now. Nice, polite, and uninterested in current affairs. (146, Quijotón, 30 or younger, more than High School)

How often do you read the newspaper?

Almost everyday.

What paper or papers do you read?

The sports newspapers.

Despite this lack of interest, however, my respondent provides me at least with a perspective on European integration that I am not used to hearing in Spain. Like most Spaniards, he agrees with Spain's membership in the European Union. He is particularly satisfied with the possibilities of traveling abroad without a pass and of working in other countries. Also, like many other Spaniards, he is not overly optimistic about the economic benefits of membership: the European Union's agricultural policy and the budgetary and other policy measures taken to be part of economic and monetary union have been particularly onerous for the middle classes. Despite these problems, Spain has no alternative. Rich countries will benefit more than poorer countries like Spain; staying out, however, would make things worse, since markets and the possibility of getting funds from the European Union would be lost. The same logic applies to EMU, although he is not particularly happy about it and would rather follow the British approach.

Where my respondent really differs from the standard discourse on European integration I hear in Spain is in his attitudes toward political integration. Totally against it, he justifies this opposition on the basis of cultural differences:

I believe that the European Union's power to legislate is excessive. I don't buy this idea that Europeans approve laws that we have to respect in Spain. The standpoint of an English person cannot be similar to that of a Spaniard. His needs, his way of looking at things are not comparable. For instance, I have heard this story about bullfighting: that Europe is against it. Perhaps this is not very important but, my God, if they prohibit bullfighting! It is something that hurts the national feelings. If Europeans prohibit bullfighting ...! Ultimate decision-making power should remain at the state level. The Latin way of thinking has nothing to do with the Anglo-Saxon. Because of this difference, it quite problematic to think of a common decision-making frame.... A political union is a serious matter; it is not a mere economic union. A committee made up of foreigners that tells you what to do ... I don't know.

The interview does not last much longer. After this burst of eloquence, my host sinks into short, dispassionate answers to my questions.

How strongly do you identify with Europe . . . ?

Not at all.

EFFICIENCY AGAINST INTEGRATION

February 27, 1996

> An hour away from Frankfurt; an hour away from Mainz: Weststadt. I enter the headquarters of Weststadt's Housewives Association (Hausfrauenverband) just as a large number of women are leaving the premises, after listening to one of the weekly talks organized by the association. At the back of the auditorium is a table full of documents about the association and the state of the economy, as well as leaflets with consumer advice. The president of the association, 48, upper-middle-class, voter for the CDU, invites me to go to her office to conduct the interview. (130, Weststadt)

My respondent, whose career background is banking, tells me that she is quite familiar with the implications of European integration. Her husband works for a firm that has subsidiaries in many countries, so that she gets to travel often with him and thus learns about the pros and cons of the single market. One of the topics that worries her the most is the difference in labor costs across Europe. She is very critical of the unions for driving those costs so high in Germany, which makes firms less competitive in European markets. Therefore, she sees it as a good thing that European firms, employing cheaper foreign labor, get contracts in Germany, thus putting pressure on the unions to accept cuts in labor benefits.

Her views on the single market are extremely positive. From an economic perspective, German producers benefit from the bigger market and the possibility of moving abroad to countries where labor costs are lower. The single market is also a source of advantages for consumers, because it broadens the range of products they can buy. She tells me, however, that her association always recommends that its members give priority to local products, to boost the local economy. The president of Weststadt's Housewives Association is also very satisfied with the cultural advantages of European integration. The greater freedom of movement it entails facilitates contacts between people from different cultural backgrounds. Thus, she tells me about a Franco-German exchange program in which her children are involved and how programs like this contribute to overcoming the historical mistrust between the two countries.

When it comes to political integration, my respondent's views are much less favorable. She would certainly welcome standardization in some areas, like labor benefits and criminal law. She justifies the need for the latter, for instance, by saying that the removal of border controls within the European Union has made it easier for criminals to move across countries. Police cooperation and a homogenization of criminal law would help to fight crime more effectively. In general, however, my respondent perceives the legislative competences of the European Union as excessive and believes that the ultimate power to decide whether a European decision is implemented in one's territory ought to reside in the national parliaments. Rather than invoking cultural reasons, like the previous two respondents, she justifies her views with reference to administrative efficiency. First of all, previous experience shows that when a country opposes a directive from the European Union, it does very little to enforce it:

> People do not comply with decisions in which they have not participated. We see this in the case of Yugoslavia. Decisions made by external organizations are not obeyed by those who do not agree with them. One must bring interested parties into the decision-making process and rely on persuasion before making a decision. Only then is it possible to implement measures and monitor compliance.

Second of all, national administrations know the country and how best to address its problems better than do European institutions:

> National parliaments know the structures of the country better, they know regional problems better, and they should have influence in the decision-making progress. This does not mean that they should adopt measures alone but rather, that they should play a determinant role in the decision-making process.

My interview ends with a discussion about economic and monetary union. She thinks it is a good idea because it would make exchanges easier and contribute to the development of a "we" feeling in Europe. Like many German respondents, however, she would rather postpone it because she is afraid that the euro will be a weaker currency than the Deutschmark.

PROTECTING NATIONAL INTEREST

March 26, 1996

Still in Weststadt. I get out of the tramway in one of the suburbs that surround the city; a typical middle-class neighborhood, formed by forty- to fifty-year-old individual family homes. Five minutes later, I am sitting in my host's living room, coffee and *Kuchen* included. She is a teacher in a modern secondary school (Realschule), one of the three main types of high school in Germany, less vocational than the Hauptschule and less academically oriented than the Gymnasium. She declares herself conservative and a supporter of the CDU. Very concerned about the erosion of values in our society, she complains about how this is reflected in rising crime rates. She herself has recently been the victim of street theft by, she adds, a foreigner. She is also concerned about high unemployment rates, for which she blames Germans, who have been too complacent and allowed social benefits to skyrocket. (107, Weststadt, older than 50, more than High School)

Politicians have assumed that Germany will always be able to increase production levels and export its goods, although we all know that these have become too expensive, that wages are too high, that social benefits are too high, that people go on vacation too often in comparison with America or Japan. Politicians and businesspeople are responsible for that, for not having put the brakes on in time, and now they try to rescue what remains to be rescued, especially their own heads.

Early on, she sets the tone for the interview by saying that the idea of European political integration is a joke and by complaining about the way Germany is treated by its partners in the European Union. There is nothing wrong with the European single market, she says. A bigger market is to Germany's advantage, and she likes the idea that there is free movement of labor across the European Union. Furthermore, she welcomes the fact that European cooperation has contributed to smoothing out relations between Germany and its former enemies in World War II, the United Kingdom and France. Finally, she likes the European Union's efforts to reduce economic inequalities between its members, although she questions the honesty of national officials responsible for spending the EU's Structural Funds.

What angers my respondent the most is the feeling that Germany is being taken advantage of—mainly the fact that it pays far too much in comparison with what it receives. She finds it outrageous, for instance, that Germany contributes so much to the development of poorer countries in the EU and then is left alone to deal with the costs of German reunification. Europeans and Germans, especially German politicians, are equally responsible for this state of things. Europeans blackmail Germany through constant reminders of its role in World War II, whereas Germans themselves do not seem to have digested this history and are so naïve as to believe in the European ideal, when everybody else is just looking out for their own national interests:

> Germany should make it clear that the war ended fifty years ago and Europeans should decide whether we are the old enemy or their partners. One should not take one stance or the other depending on the circumstances....
>
> ... Here in the West there are people who are very pro-European, for whom the word Germany sounds foreign; they don't want anything to do with Germany, they want to be European. They are young people, especially, who have been tricked or who are still digesting the history of Germany. These are those who identify with Europe. But Germany is still there! One wonders for how long, but it is still there! I am loyal to my Homeland. That does not mean that I approve of everything that is being done, but I am German in the first place and only then European.

My respondent does not consider herself a nationalist, but thinks that Germany should look out for its self-interest, and in this sense she thinks that Germany has more to lose than to win from European political unification. In a situation in which Germany is not treated as an equal, it is not likely to succeed in having its national interest prevail. This means that EU legislation in areas like environment or food quality standards will probably be less advanced than legislation in Germany.

This skepticism toward European political integration is compounded by a deep mistrust of EU bureaucrats and by a belief that the economic and cultural differences between the different EU states are so dramatic that solutions satisfying all of them would be impossible to find. This logic leads her, of course, to oppose EMU.

> There is France, there is Germany, there is Italy, and they are very different, from a historical perspective, from the perspective of their mentality, from the perspective of their economic development, and why should someone in Brussels or Strasbourg say how they should live, what currency they should use, what measurement system they should use?

She then illustrates what would happen if the European Union followed the path of political integration with the example of the United States, a country that, in her opinion, is about to explode because of its extreme cultural diversity.

> A united Europe, a European state à la USA, is sheer foolishness. The European states are too different: culturally, from the standpoint of language, economically. The USA itself is about to collapse because of too many Latinos and Hispanics. And then there are the blacks. I am sure that it will split into three parts.

Therefore, she advocates De Gaulle's concept of a Europe of the Fatherlands, a loose organization in which countries cooperate with each other whenever they have common interests:

> So that all states look after their own interest, while trying at the same time to get along with each other, cultivating good relationships, helping those who need help, economically if necessary.

I must confess that I do not agree at all with what she says. It even scares me at times. But I enjoy the discussion for the passion, sincerity, and level of articulateness with which my respondent defends her viewpoint. If only all respondents were like this one!

IN THE NAME OF SOVEREIGNTY

October 15, 1997

An hour north of London, between Oxford and Cambridge: Engleton. It's pitch dark and pouring when I finally find the home of the Conservative Party official I am interviewing today. Fortunately, he does not mind that I am somewhat late. (7 Engleton)

My respondent, mid-thirties, highly educated, son of Polish immigrants, combines his activity as a politician with work in corporate finance. Partly because of his significant business dealings with Eastern Europe, the process of European integration is central to his preoccupations. He therefore articulates his ideas forcefully and with clarity. For him, what matters is the creation of as large a market as possible, one that will include the former communist bloc. Political integration, on the other hand, is out of the question; nobody should be telling the United Kingdom what to do. As an example of the European Union's unacceptable intromission in the United Kingdom's affairs, he cites the function of the European Court of Justice as a Court of Appeals above the House of Lords itself.

Despite his objections to the European Union's interference with British affairs, my host thinks that the United Kingdom should remain a member. As a member of the European Union, not only does the United Kingdom benefit—if only slightly given its high contributions to the EU budget—by the bigger market, but it also has the opportunity to shape the process:

> It's more effective being inside the tent pissing out than outside the tent pissing in.

Throughout the interview, I try to determine why he opposes political integration. His readiness to debate ideas affords me the opportunity to better understand the hidden meanings behind people's standard justifications for disapproving of European political integration. At several points during the interview he, like other respondents, refers to the unaccountability and unelected character of those who make the decisions at the European Union. I ask him then whether he would be happier if legislative power in the European Union was transferred to the European Parliament, an elected and, in principle, accountable institution. He then replies that the European Parliament is too far from the citizen and that districts in a European election are too big to really ensure representation:

> If you are now suggesting that we should have a European wide body, where you have a half a million people electing one representative, or no matter how you have the electoral system, so that this person would have lawmaking powers, that is something that goes against the grain of the UK, the UK's political system. I mean, it is far better to devolve down decision-making than devolve it all the way up.

I then offer the example of the United States as a model of organization that might solve these problems. His reaction is that the United States' model is inapplicable in Europe because "of sheer diversity, cultures, history, politics, economies, everything." I counter that Scotland, Wales, Northern Ireland, and England are also quite different and yet I doubt he would question the viability of the British model. Now somewhat impatient, my respondent finally begins to recite the longevity and superiority of the British system of government (the British Parliament as the "mother of all parliaments"), and proclaims the uniqueness of the United Kingdom as "an island race, an island nation," which sets it apart from the rest of Europe, as sufficient reason to oppose European unification.

The parallels between this discussion with this Engleton Conservative Party representative and another one I had in Scotsburg, with an equally eloquent and extremely engaging Young Labour representative, are remarkable. Although the latter was much more favorable to political integration than the former, the following exchange ensued when I asked the Young Labour representative about his willingness to transfer some taxation power to the European Union.   (42, Scotsburg)

> But if you give up your fiscal policy…what are you controlling? What's the point of voting? At the moment in Britain you can vote for higher taxes, for higher spending, you can vote for lots of things if you want to. You give up your fiscal policy, forget it, what's the point of voting? If that happens, it could really lead to trouble. Because that's not a democracy!
>
> *But there could be a European democracy, like the one in the U.S.*
>
> (Great laughing).
>
> *Regardless of the problems, it's still a democracy.*
>
> Yes, yes, and what was the turnout for the Presidential election? Twenty-five percent? No, I would not be for that.
>
> *Why?*
>
> Because Britain is not, say, like a state in the United States.
>
> *Why?*
>
> Basically, because Britain has been an independent country for a thousand years.
>
> *But at some point the German principalities were also independent, and yet they came together to form Germany, and the same happened in Italy. The U.S. ex-colonies were independent and then they formed the United States.*
>
> Sure, but I think that in a democracy, decisions are taken at the closest level possible, you know. A common policy for Europe, I don't like the idea.
>
> *But in the U.S., for instance, there are federal structures and states have a great deal of autonomy. Wouldn't you agree with something like that?*
>
> Not at the moment. I don't like the sound of that, it doesn't sound right.

What is the main reason? Imagine a United States of Europe organized democratically, with power vested in the European Parliament, and a federal structure.

I see what you are saying but the point is, Britain is not like a state in the United States of America, it's not Florida! Britain is a country, you know, we are an independent nation and that is a step too far. I would not be for that.

Because you want to preserve Britain's independence?

Yes.

What do you think is the value of that?

What is the value of what?!

I simply say that because I have heard from people in Germany and Spain that they don't care about losing their sovereignty.

(Silence) You've got to remember that Britain is different. Ok, it sounds a little bit Eurosceptic, but Britain is different to [*sic*] continental Europe; we are different, you know, I don't know what it is but...

How can you define this?

I don't know what it is. It really sounds like an old person's view actually, it really does (great laughter).

The fact that a pro-integration and a free-trader respondent from the same country end up using such similar arguments testifies to the power of culturally grounded cognitive frameworks in constraining people's responses to European integration. I will further characterize and trace the origins and strength of this cognitive framework in the United Kingdom in a later chapter. At this point, the previous interview above illustrates the fact that respondents often oppose European political integration because they simply do not want to give up sovereignty.

My interview with this Conservative Party representative ends amicably. We've both had a great time arguing, and it matters little whether we end up agreeing or not.

Cognitive Frames and European Political Integration

Chapter 2 has shown that people's images of the European Union vary from country to country and, sometimes, as in Germany, from one part of the country to another. These contrasts are interesting because they reveal significant aspects of national cultures and histories as well as the different ways in which the European Union has impacted upon them. The current chapter has also shown that "supporters" and "nonsupporters" of European integration tend to emphasize different themes. "Supporters" emphasize the contribution of European unification to peace and understanding and the benefits of the common market. "Nonsupporters" emphasize the loss of sovereignty and national identity entailed by European integration. In previous pages, I have moved beyond this distinction between "supporters" and "nonsupporters" to a more complex differentiation between supporters of a Centralized Integration and a Decentralized Cooperation form of European integration. Those who support a Centralized Integration model, more progressive and overrepresented in the local elites, argue for political integration by invoking transnational problems, the need to defend the social market economy, the creation of a strong bloc that competes against the United States and, to a lesser extent, Japan, and the maintenance of peace in Europe. Those who support a Decentralized Cooperation model, latter, more conservative, more concentrated in the United Kingdom, would be happiest if the European Union were a free-trade area in which states cooperate with each other without giving up sovereignty. They defend their viewpoint by stressing five major factors: the defense of the states' national identity, differences between the EU members, administrative efficacy, national interest, and the intrinsic value of sovereignty.

I now go back to the respondents' cognitive frames and analyze the contrasts between "integrationists" and "free-traders." This analysis provides clues as to the underlying explanation of differences in support for European political integration in the United Kingdom, Germany, and Spain. The tabulation of these differences (table 6) shows that "integrationists" (those who prefer the Centralized Integration model) were more prone than were "free-traders" (those who prefer the Decentralized Cooperation model) to say that states have become too small, and to associate the European Union with a rise in social benefits and with an improvement in understanding between people from different cultures. On the other hand, "free-traders" mentioned more often than did "integrationists" the themes of sovereignty and national identity.

Because of the small size of the sample, it is not worth trying to determine to what extent these contrasts between "free-traders" and "integrationists" correspond to actual differences in the way the two groups saw the European integration process, or to differences in other variables, such as the level of information the respondents have.[11] Actually, even if it were possible to control for differences in levels of information, the interpretation of the results would be obscured by the fact that the causal direction of the relationship between levels of information and support for different forms of European integration would not be easy to determine.

TABLE 6
Themes Mentioned to Justify Attitudes toward European Integration or the European Union, by Country and Preferred Model of Integration (Percentages in the Decentralized Cooperation [DC] and Centralized Integration [CI] categories)

Themes	Germany DC %	Germany CI %	Spain DC %	Spain CI %	United Kingdom DC %	United Kingdom CI %	Total DC %	Total CI %
understanding	33	50		42	18	50	18	46
Common Market	78	79	83	96	76	88	78	89
CAP	22	7	50	50	35	38	34	35
free movement and competition	33	36					9	13
democratic deficit	33	50		12	12	25	16	26
states too small	33	64	50	71	41	88	41	72
governance	22	50	33	54	65	88	47	59
against isolation			17	30		12	3	17
voice		7	17	25	24		16	15
modernization			17	46	12	12	9	26
removal of barriers	44	64	50	29	59	62	53	46
social benefits		21		29	12	38	6	28
sovereignty and identity	11		17	4	41	12	28	4
Structural/ Regional Funds		7	33	50	41	25	31	33
lessons of World War II	33	50					9	15
peace	11	57		8	24	62	18	35
Total number of Respondents	9	14	6	24	17	8	32	46

It is perfectly conceivable, for instance, that "integrationists" have more interest in European integration and therefore gather more information about it.

The data limitation represents no obstacle, however, to the use of the different pictures of European integration held by "free-traders" and "integrationists" to better understand why the British population supports political integration less than do the Spanish and German populations. Most of the contrasts between "free-traders" and "integrationists" are irrelevant in this respect, because they refer to themes for which no difference was found between British, German, and Spanish respondents. For instance, although "integrationists" were more prone to say that states have become too small than were "free-traders," British respondents mentioned this theme almost as frequently as did Spanish or German respondents. In other instances, the contrasts between "integrationists" and "free-traders" are irrelevant because they refer to topics in which differences between British, Spanish, and German respondents ran counter to what one would have expected in explaining why the British are less favorable to European political integration than are the Spaniards or the Germans. The theme of governance is a case in point. "Integrationists" criticized the governance aspects of the European Union slightly more often than did "free-traders." Since we know that British respondents mentioned this topic slightly more often than did Spanish or German respondents, this contrast would lead to the expectation that the British are more favorable to European political integration than are the Germans or the Spaniards. This is clearly not the case.

The only contrast between "integrationists" and "free-traders" that can be used to explain differences in support of political integration between the British and the Spaniards and the Germans is the one concerning national identity and sovereignty (which encompasses, among others, the different classes of arguments developed during the typification of "free-traders" above). In all three countries taken together, 28% of the "free-traders" mentioned this topic, as opposed to 4% of the "integrationists." It is reasonable then to infer that, since British respondents were more likely to mention the topics of national identity and sovereignty than were the Spanish and German respondents, a concern for national identity and sovereignty underlies the relatively low level of support for European political integration found in the United Kingdom compared to Spain or Germany. This point would sound like a circular argument if concern for sovereignty predominated over concern for national identity among British respondents. As the discussion in chapter 2 and the comparison between "supporters" and "nonsupporters" make clear, however, fear of the loss of national identity and insecurity about the clout that the United Kingdom has or may have within the European Union are the two concerns that dominated the British respondents' references to issues of national identity and sovereignty. There is no circularity here. Instead, the puzzle that needs to be solved is why concern for national identity and power within the European Union is greater in the United Kingdom than in Spain or Germany. This issue is addressed in the chapters on Spain, the United Kingdom, and Germany below.

In sum, the content analysis of in-depth interviews in the last two chapters throws light on the cognitive frames on European integration within which British, Germans, and Spaniards have developed their views on European integration. The benefits of the common market, the removal of internal border controls, the realization that states have become too small, are social representations of the European Union shared by respondents in the three countries. The same can be said of negative aspects associated with poor governance within the European Union institutions. This chapter has also illuminated the issues that polarize public opinion in these countries into "supporters" and "nonsupporters" and into "integrationists" and "free-traders." The contribution of European unification to peace and cross-cultural understanding and the fear of loss of sovereignty and national identity are themes that differentiate people across the two dimensions. Meanwhile, the emphasis on the advantages of the common market differentiates "supporters" from "nonsupporters" but, as one might expect, does not differentiate "integrationists" from "free-traders." Also, the perception that states have become too small and the expectation that European integration will bring about a rise and equalization of social benefits across the European Union differentiate "integrationists" from "free-traders," but do not differentiate "supporters" from "nonsupporters." This preliminary finding that characterizes "integrationists" as relatively progressive in comparison with "free-traders" is quite significant because the literature has generally depicted supporters of European integration as more conservative than its opponents.[12] This image, which contrasts with all that I heard in my in-depth interviews, may be due to the focus of previous research on the factors that explain broad support for European integration and to the fact that this research has not paid much attention to the factors that have historically moved some leftist groups to a rejection of European institutions. Much of this rejection was based not so much on a desire to defend the nation-state against supranationalism but, rather, on a critique of a model of integration that was excessively focused on the creation of a common market and was solely guided by economic considerations. In this sense, the rejection of Inglehart's hypothesis of a positive relationship between postmaterialism and support for European integration may have been premature.[13] Postmaterialists may be critical of the way European integration is proceeding, but they may still be better predisposed toward a supranational form of integration, as long as it is political and addresses their major concerns.

The analysis presented in the previous two chapters also points out significant contrasts in the cognitive frames of the British, Spanish, and German populations when they think about European unification. Some of these national-specific contrasts happen to play a fundamental role in differentiating "supporters" from "nonsupporters" of European integration and "integrationists" from "free-traders." National identity and sovereignty, for instance, are central and distinctive elements in British social representations of European integration, which clearly differentiate "supporters" from "nonsupporters" and "integrationists" from "free traders." In turn, the fear of foreign labor competition helps polarize Germans into "supporters" and "nonsupporters" of European integration, but does not differentiate "integrationists" from "free-traders." I have shown, however, that "integrationists" in general expect the European Union to move in the direction of higher and homogeneous social benefits. In the German case, this means that public anxiety about the consequences of increased competition in the labor market—in part caused by rising unemployment—takes two radically different forms: a rejection of European integration or a push for more political integration. Finally, the results for Spain presented in tables 5 and 6 show that "supporters" and "integrationists" differentiate themselves from "nonsupporters" and "free-traders" by their emphasis on the role that the European Union may play in the modernization of the country and in breaking its traditional isolation. These two highly related topics are central in the Spaniards' cognitive frame, and differentiate Spain from Germany and the United Kingdom.

Sovereignty and identity, voice, the welfare state, and modernization are thus topics that play a major role in distinguishing the cognitive frames on European integration in the United Kingdom, Germany, and Spain and in polarizing their respective populations with respect to this process of state transformation. The next chapter explores the long time span over which these themes have distinguished the debate about European integration in the three countries.

Four

Journalists and European Integration

THE VIEWS of European integration articulated by ordinary citizens and local elites, fragmented and ill-expressed as they are, differ from country to country because they reflect preoccupations that are rooted in the countries' histories and cultures. These conclusions from chapters 2 and 3 are strengthened and clarified upon examination of the reflections of journalists on the construction of Europe over the past fifty years. They are strengthened because journalists in many ways repeat what we already know from in-depth interviews with ordinary citizens and local elites. They are clarified because the journalists' numerous written reflections on European integration give us better interpretive access to the contexts, both cognitive and historical, within which these interviews were produced.

The examination of the British, Spanish, and German intelligentsia's printed legacy, in the form of editorial and opinion pieces in the quality press, reveals substantial constancy over time. British journalists have consistently advocated a decentralized cooperation model of integration, whereas Spanish and German journalists have defended a more centralizing and integrating model. The fact that European integration has been flexible enough to accommodate different projects of integration is part of the explanation for this stability. The other reason why the projects of European integration defended by journalists in Germany, the United Kingdom, and Spain have remained largely unchanged is the persistence of the broader questions that generated those projects in the first place. These questions are the British "heroic" attempt to preserve the United Kingdom's role as an independent world power between the United States and the Soviet Union, the Spaniards' "desperate" effort to regain some role in the international arena after centuries of decline, and the Germans' "pragmatic" attempt to effectively defend their economic and political interests without raising world condemnation.

Toward a Genealogy of Frames

This chapter analyzes these questions through an examination of arguments made by elite journalists in favor of or against European integration and through a detailed account of how and in what contexts these arguments developed. The logic underlying this approach to a genealogy of frames on European integration and the European Union is that the frames that most distinguish the British, German, and Spanish populations do not refer to direct, observable consequences of European integration and the European Union for people's lives. Rather, they represent long-term expectations of the impact of European integration on the national collectivity, the type of abstract frames that more often than not originate in the reflections of the most educated groups in society, even though they eventually become part of the national cultural repertoire through tortuous diffusion processes.[1] Because of these features, a useful strategy to trace the origin of these frames is to examine how journalists and public commentators, members of the educated classes, have reflected about European integration since the late 1940s in the quality press.

I have focused on the quality press rather than the popular media because it is indeed unlikely that the topics that distinguish the British, German, and Spanish social representations of European integration have been addressed, not to mention discussed in articulate form, in tabloid newspapers or on TV.[2] The reader should therefore be clear about the strategy followed here: my goal is to trace the genesis of the frames that distinguish British, German, and Spanish populations, as revealed by in-depth interviews conducted with representative samples of these populations, through use of a valid and reliable indicator. Based on the nature of these distinguishing frames, I have selected a source of information most likely to contain discussions of those frames, so as to get the most accurate picture possible of when they were formulated initially and in what historical and political contexts.

The analysis below reveals that concerns about sovereignty, about modernity and breaking with the country's traditional isolation, and about the country's image abroad were formulated as journalists confronted national dilemmas: the United Kingdom's ties to the Commonwealth and the United States, the British Labour Party's desire to defend its vision of socialism, the struggle between democratic and antidemocratic forces in Spain, and the problematic relations between the Federal German Republic and its neighbors. By analyzing how these national dilemmas were debated in connection with decisions about European integration, how arguments changed under changing circumstances, the introspective explanations that journalists used to interpret their own views or changes in these views, and the contradictions embedded in those reflections, one begins to uncover the hidden preoccupations with power and status behind the different projects of European integration.

General Patterns of Support for European Integration

Editorials and opinion pieces in the three countries differ in the extent to which they include descriptive comments about the process of European integration and the European institutions. Spanish articles, in particular, contain much less descriptive information than do German and British articles. This is the conclusion one reaches after examination of how often the articles refer to the topics or attributes mentioned by the participants in the in-depth interviews: on average, 0.7 per article in the Spanish newspapers, 1.6 in British newspapers, and 1.3 in German newspapers (see table 7). Moreover, 57% of Spanish articles, as opposed to 30% and 37% of the British and German articles, respectively, do not contain a single descriptive statement. Comparatively speaking, Spanish articles tend more to report what has happened or express positive and negative evaluations of what has happened than to make descriptive or programmatic statements about the process of European integration and its different institutions.[3] This singularity of Spain in comparison with Germany and the United Kingdom is not coincidental, and I discuss it below. It reflects the fact that, in general, Spanish elite journalists have been more concerned about Spain being a member of the European Union than about the characteristics and direction of this supranational institution.

The degree of support for European integration, membership in European institutions, and a transfer of sovereignty to European institutions varies across countries and across newspapers. Although overt opposition has been uncommon (I exclude the former-GDR newspaper *Neues Deutschland* from this and the next section's analyses because European integration was not an issue in the GDR for most of the period considered here), there are significant contrasts in the extent to which the articles contain explicit calls for transfers of sovereignty. Whereas 31% of the articles from Germany (excluding *Neues Deutschland*) support transfers of sovereignty, only 16% and 15% of the articles from Spain and the United

TABLE 7
Mean Number of Descriptive or Evaluative Comments about European Integration in Op-Ed Articles, 1946–97

	Spain	*United Kingdom*	*Germany*
pre-1973	1.136 (44)	1.436 (101)	1.272 (92)
1973–1997*	0.633 (150)	1.845 (110)	1.282 (110)
Total*	0.747 (194)	1.649 (211)	1.277 (202)

( ) Number of cases.
*Country differences significant at .05 level, two-tailed.

TABLE 8
Ratios of Negative to Positive (N/P) Descriptive or Evaluative Comments about European Integration in Op-Ed Articles, 1946–97

	Spain	United Kingdom	Germany
1946–1958	0.2 (13)	0.5 (31)	0.1 (39)
1959–1972	0.1 (31)	1.4 (70)	0.6 (53)
1973–1985	0.7 (77)	1.8 (51)	1.1 (49)
1986–1997	1.1 (73)	1.1 (59)	0.4 (61)
Total	0.5 (194)	1.3 (211)	0.8 (202)

( ) Number of cases.

Kingdom, respectively, do so. The similarity between Spain and the United Kingdom is in fact only superficial, since there is much more consensus among British than among Spanish newspapers. Together with *Die Zeit* (39%), *Cambio16* and *El País* are the newspapers where op-ed articles make the most frequent calls for transfers of sovereignty (38% and 27% respectively), whereas *Abc* is the newspaper where one finds the lowest percentage of such calls (8%).[4] Table 8 provides another indication of the British newspapers' relatively negative attitude toward the European integration process: the ratio of negative to positive descriptive and evaluative comments contained in the articles. Whereas the ratio is 1.3 in the United Kingdom, it is only 0.5 and 0.8 in Spain and Germany respectively.

These results already tell us a story about the attitudes toward European integration and the European institutions of center-right and center-left elite journalists in Germany, the United Kingdom, and Spain. In Germany, lead and op-ed articles tend to present positive images of the European integration process and the European institutions. Furthermore, they do not question the unification process or membership in the European Union. Last but not least, they are the most consistently pro-federalist in the set, especially when they come from *Die Zeit*. In the United Kingdom, op-ed articles portray European integration and the European Union in negative terms and occasionally denounce or oppose membership in the European institutions. They also contain fewer expressions of support for transfers of sovereignty than do German articles. In Spain, op-ed articles differ from the German and British ones in that they contain many fewer descriptive statements of European integration and European institutions. More often than in the other two countries, they simply state what happens or praise or criticize particular countries or individuals. Beyond this, the Spanish articles tend to have a positive bent and hardly ever criticize European integration or its institutions. On average they also express federalist views less often than do German articles. In contrast with the similarity in the models of integration defended by center-right and center-left newspapers in Germany and the United Kingdom, however, these federalist views are found much more often in the center-left than in the center-right Spanish newspapers.

Images of European Integration

The existence of a permanent dialogue between journalists and the rest of the population with respect to European integration is reflected in the strong similarity between their images of European integration and European institutions, as well as in the meaning they both attach to the membership of their respective countries in the European Union. Indeed, the correlation between the percentages of newspaper articles and the percentages of respondents that mentioned each of various themes displayed in table 9 is equal to 0.75.[5] As one would predict, because of the similarity in social position of elite journalists and the population's most informed and educated segments, there is also a greater correlation between the thematic content of newspaper articles and the thematic content of the in-depth interviews with local elites, than between the thematic content of such articles and that of the in-depth interviews with ordinary citizens (0.77 and 0.69 respectively).[6] Dominant themes of op-ed articles (as of interviews) are the economic advantages of creating and being part of a single market (18%), the realization that European states are too small to compete economically and militarily against the United States, the Soviet Union (Russia), and Japan (19%), and criticism of the functioning of European institutions (15%) and the Common Agricultural Policy (CAP) (12%) (see table 9).[7] One of the greatest contrasts between the themes emphasized in the op-ed articles and those emphasized by participants in the in-depth interviews concerns the frequency with which they referred to the removal of border controls. Whereas it was the fourth most mentioned topic in the interviews, it was only the thirteenth most mentioned topic in the op-ed articles. The population is clearly not exclusively dependent on understandings of the European integration process provided by elites, even though the latter may contribute to focus discussions, directly or indirectly, by emphasizing certain topics.

The analysis of frames on European integration also reveals that the topics that dominate the content of op-ed articles have done so for a very long time. This is certainly the case for comments about the economic consequences of the common market and the belief that states have become too small. Meanwhile, criticisms of governance and CAP became dominant themes in the period between 1973 and 1985. In sum, we are in the presence of a fairly stable image of European integration and European institutions: the European Union as an economic and political necessity, but needing reform of farming policy and style of government.

The images of European integration and European institutions presented in op-ed articles in each country separately also mirror those provided by respondents in their respective countries. In Germany, for instance, the topics of peace and consideration for other countries' misgivings about Germany play a significant role in the articles included in this sample (14% and 7% of the newspaper articles respectively), compared to the much smaller role of the topic of peace in the United Kingdom and Spain and the absence of discussion of Germany's past. (see table 10).[8] In the past, German elite journalists have been particularly sensitive to the implications of an East-West confrontation, and today, following the breakup of the Soviet Union, they are concerned with the potential for political instability in Eastern Europe. Both before and after the breakup, despite some debate, the conclusion at which they have arrived is that European institutions offer the best safeguard against these potential threats. Similarly, German op-ed articles have continually stressed how important it is for Germany's image abroad, to be an active partner in the building of Europe. In fact, the data reported in table 10 drastically underrepresent the degree to which German elite journalists have been concerned about other countries' misgivings toward Germany. If instead of counting direct references to the role that German commitment to European unification has on other countries' fears of Germany, one counts all references to other countries' misgivings toward Germany, the overall percentage for the entire period jumps from 7.4% to 11.4%.

A comparison between the views on European integration of German elite journalists and those of ordinary citizens reveals overall similarities but also one significant contrast, which concerns the absence of comments in the German sample of op-ed articles referring to a fear of competition by lower-paid foreign workers. As I showed in the previous two chapters, this was a very salient theme among German respondents, which distinguishes them from British and Spanish respondents. The contrast between German journalists and respondents may not be a coincidental one. In fact, it could well reveal the care German elites take to present a good image of their country, one that is consistent with their desire to reassure Germany's neighbors. The rest of the citizens, on the other hand, may have been influenced by news that links unemployment in Germany to the greater mobility of firms and labor throughout Europe. In 1995–96, when I conducted my interviews, there were a good number of informative pieces in the media concerning conflict in the construction sector caused by the presence of large numbers of workers from other countries of the European Union who were working for lower wages.

TABLE 9
Percentage of Articles and In-depth Interviews with Specific Descriptive or Evaluative Comments about European Integration (Absolute values and standardized scores)

	News	Interviews	Ordinary Interviews	Local Elites Interviews	News Z-score	Interviews Z-score	Ordinary I Z-score	Local Elites I Z-score
understanding (P)	1.3	33.0	34.7	30.5	−0.85	0.30	0.46	0.04
Common Market (P)	17.6	82.0	80.2	81.4	1.82	2.82	2.86	2.48
CAP (N)	12.2	29.0	33.7	22.0	0.94	0.09	0.40	−0.37
democratic deficit (N)	6.1	17.0	12.9	25.4	−0.06	−0.55	−0.69	−0.21
states too small (P)	18.9	49.0	47.5	52.5	2.04	1.14	1.13	1.09
governance (N)	14.7	44.0	31.7	64.4	1.35	0.88	0.30	1.66
against isolation (P)	5.4	9.0	9.9	8.5	−0.18	−0.97	−0.85	−1.02
voice (N)	2.8	13.0	12.9	11.9	−0.60	−0.76	−0.69	−0.86
modernization (P)	2.5	15.0	11.9	20.3	−0.65	−0.65	−0.75	−0.45

	607	160	101	59	607	160	101	59
removal of barriers (P)	2.3	42.0	44.6	37.3	−0.69	0.77	0.98	0.36
social benefits (P)	1.3	15.0	9.9	23.7	−0.85	−0.65	−0.85	−0.29
sovereignty and identity (N)	4.0	16.0	17.8	11.9	−0.41	−0.60	−0.44	−0.86
lessons of World War II (P)	2.5	12.0	12.9	10.2	−0.65	−0.81	−0.69	−0.94
peace (P)	8.6	26.0	21.8	33.9	0.35	−0.72	−0.23	0.20
free movement and competition (N)	0.0	13.0	14.9	10.2	−1.06	−0.76	−0.59	−0.94
Structural Regional Funds (P)	1.3	15.0	9.9	23.7	−0.85	−0.65	−0.85	−0.29
N =	607	160	101	59	607	160	101	59

Note: Differences in magnitude between the percentages obtained in the in-depth interviews and those obtained after coding the op-ed articles are partly due to the different ways in which the information was obtained. Respondents were always asked a specific set of questions about European integration, whereas one does not have any control over the content of the newspaper articles. To facilitate rank comparisons, I also report standardized scores for each of the variables: (P) = positive mention; (N) = negative mention.

TABLE 10
Positive and Negative Descriptive or Evaluative Comments about European Integration in Op-Ed Articles, 1946–97
Percentage and (number of cases)

	Spain	United Kingdom	Germany	Total
understanding (P)	1.0 (2)	—	3.0 (6)	1.3 (8)
Common Market (P)	14.9 (29)	19.0 (40)	18.8 (38)	17.6 (107)
CAP (N)*	4.6 (9)	19.4 (41)	11.9 (24)	12.2 (74)
democratic deficit (N)*	1.5 (3)	10.0 (21)	6.4 (13)	6.1 (37)
states too small (P)*	21.1 (41)	9.5 (20)	26.7 (54)	18.9 115)
governance (N)	12.9 (25)	18.5 (39)	12.4 (25)	14.7 (89)
against isolation (P)*	8.8 (17)	7.1 (15)	0.5 (1)	5.4 (33)
voice (N)	1.0 (2)	3.8 (8)	3.5 (7)	2.8 (17)
modernization* (P)	5.2 (10)	2.4 (5)	—	2.5 (15)
remove barriers (P)	1.0 (2)	2.4 (5)	3.5 (7)	2.3 (14)
social benefits (P)	0.5 (1)	2.4 (5)	1.0 (2)	1.3 (8)
sovereign/identity*(N)	1.5 (3)	8.5 (18)	1.5 (3)	4.0 (24)
lessons of WWII (P)*	—	—	7.4 (15)	2.5 (15)
peace (P)*	5.2 (10)	6.2 (13)	14.4 (29)	8.6 (52)
free movement and competition (N)	—	—	—	—
Structural/Regional Funds (P)*	5.7 (11)	3.8 (8)	1.0 (2)	3.5 (21)
N =	194	211	202	607

*Chi-square, significant at .05 level, 2-tailed.
(P) = positive mention; (N) = negative mention.

What we have in this case is an illustration of the different factors that contribute to the development of popular frames on European integration. Elite journalists may play a role, even if indirect, but so do actual experience and observation, regular news about the European Union, and other news that, because of its high degree of salience, the population relates to the consequences of European integration and the European Union.

The comparison of journalistic and popular views on European integration in West Germany thus shows that there is a shared perception that Germany must contribute to efforts toward European unification in order to reassure other West European countries. The salience of this topic if anything increased in the post-German reunification period, especially in *Die Zeit*. How is it, then, that East German respondents hardly ever mentioned the need to reassure other countries about Germany's ambitions when discussing European integration? One possible answer is that, as one would expect, the press of the German Democratic Republic, especially the newspaper *Neues Deutschland*, lost legitimation and readership upon reunification.[9] Therefore, had post-reunification East German elite journalists framed European integration as journalists did in West Germany, they would have found it difficult to reach their potential public. It is telling, nonetheless, that in seventeen op-ed articles published by *Neues Deutschland* between 1990 and 1991 (the end period of my sample for this newspaper), none of them mentioned the need for Germany to reassert its commitment to European integration or advocated further European integration to reassure other countries about a too strong Germany. Another potential explanation is that the West German press, including the quality press, has encountered difficulties in setting foot in East Germany.[10] These difficulties, which already reveal a certain mismatch between the political preoccupations and worldviews of West Germans and East Germans, should have made it difficult for West German ideas about European integration to reach the broader East German public. Finally, it is possible that negative depictions of European unification by East German journalists in the pre-reunification period have had lasting effects on the East German population because of having lost all legitimacy but not having yet been fully replaced by positive ones in the East German press.

In sum, it is quite likely that the images of European unification currently held by the East German population have been mostly shaped by factual news information about the day-to-day functioning of the European Union, rather than by the concerns of West or East German journalists and other elites. This context and the radically different set of cultural values in which the East German population was brought up would probably explain why the Oststadt respondents hardly ever expressed concern about other countries' misgivings toward a strong Germany in their discussions of European integration. More than any other contrast discussed in this and previous chapters, the contrast between Weststädter and Oststädter reflects the role of the broader culture in shaping public discussions about European integration and the way they influence the population's views of European integration.

In Spain, the desire to break the country's traditional isolation by becoming a member of the European Union and the expectation that membership in the European Union will contribute to the modernization of the country are mentioned with greater frequency than other topics (9% and 5% respectively). The frequency with which these themes recur in Spanish op-ed articles is somewhat higher than it is in the United Kingdom, even more so if one adjusts for the difference in the number of topics mentioned in Spanish and British newspaper articles (10% and 6% of all mentions touch on the topics of isolation and modernization in Spain, compared to 6% and 2% respectively in the United Kingdom). Needless to say, these topics are all but absent in discussions of European integration in German op-ed articles.

Upon comparing the content of Spanish op-ed articles with that of the in-depth interviews conducted in Quijotón and Catadell, one finds that the CAP and the Structural and regional funds are much less salient topics in the former than in the latter. As noted for the topic of foreign worker competition in Germany, this is an illustration of the plurality of sources of information that shape people's frames on European integration. Journalistic and other elite views are just one source of information. Factual news and direct observation and experience also play a role. The Structural Funds and the Common Agricultural Policy are examples of EU policies that have been observed and experienced directly by the population, especially in the last ten years. They are also policies about which there has been abundant factual coverage in the press. The contrast between the low level of debate about the CAP among elite journalists and the high salience of this topic among the general population reveals different sensitivities as to what is important about the European Union. The fact that the CAP is less mentioned in the Spanish op-ed articles than in the British and the German is also interesting, but can be easily explained by the fact that Spain was not yet a member of the EEC in the late 1970s, when most disputes concerning the reform of the Common Agricultural Policy took place.

Several features distinguish British op-eds from those published in German and Spanish newspapers. First of all, they place less emphasis on the need for European institutions to make European states more competitive and secure, both economically and militarily. Only 10% of the articles mention this topic, compared to 21% and 27% in Spain and Germany respectively. In fact, trends over time show that this has always been so, which contrasts with the large number of British respondents who mentioned this theme during the in-depth interviews. These findings ought to be examined jointly with the tendency of British op-ed articles to attribute negative economic effects to the United Kingdom's membership in the European institutions. Overall, elite journalists and public commentators in Britain do not appear to have been persuaded as much as those in Spain and Germany of the economic and political advantages of a supranational organization like the European Union.

A related feature that distinguishes British from German and Spanish articles is the relatively high frequency with which they refer to the negative consequences that European integration and membership in the European institutions has for national sovereignty and national identity.[11] German op-ed articles also frequently discuss the topic of sovereignty and identity, but only to point out that a transfer of sovereignty is a good thing. Indeed, a remarkable 22% of German articles mention the transfer of sovereignty as a good thing (compared to 12% in the United Kingdom and 4% in Spain), whereas only 2% mention it as a bad thing (compared to about 9% in the United Kingdom and 0% in Spain).[12]

Sovereignty is thus a highly debated topic among British and German elite journalists writing about European integration, and an irrelevant issue in Spain. But whereas the transfer of sovereignty has been highly contested in the United Kingdom, it is overwhelmingly supported in Germany. The examination of temporal trends shows that the period of greatest opposition to a transfer of sovereignty in the United Kingdom was the period between the creation of the EEC and EURATOM (1957) and the United Kingdom's accession (1973). Between the British accession and the signing of the Single European Act (SEA) (1986), the debate continued, but comments favorable to a transfer of sovereignty became more numerous than those against it. Finally, in the last decade, the intensity of the debate has declined considerably, and comments in favor of specific transfers of sovereignty have more than tripled over those against these transfers.[13] This is yet another instance where popular attitudes toward European integration do not exactly correspond to what is said by elite journalists at that particular moment: while British respondents often argued against European integration by criticizing the erosion of sovereignty and, more significantly, of their identity, op-ed articles in the center-right and center-left quality press had basically abandoned this type of discourse. The debate on economic and monetary union is a case in point. Writers for both *The Economist* and *The New Statesman* have expressed lukewarm support for the single currency, but criticism of the process of monetary unification has not been made on grounds that it violates British sovereignty. Rather, such criticism has been directed at the convergence criteria and the lack of popular legitimacy. When British respondents criticized EMU, however, they mostly referred to issues of sovereignty and identity.

In sum, op-ed articles about European integration in Germany, the United Kingdom, and Spain commend its economic and politico-military aspects and criticize its governance aspects and CAP. The ultimate goal of this examination of European integration among elite journalists is to determine the longevity of the frames on European integration that differentiate British, German, and Spanish respondents. The conclusion that one draws from the examination of elite journalist frames since the 1940s is that these singularizing frames have been salient all along. To better unveil the context within which they were activated and thus advance in our understanding of the causes of contrasts in support of European integration between the United Kingdom, Germany, and Spain, we need a more qualitative analysis of the op-ed articles in this sample, one that makes full use of the richness and complexity of information that they contain. My goal is to sketch a history of how the quality press, through its op-ed articles, has dealt with European integration for fifty years. This qualitative examination of the information reveals the underlying and broader political, economic, and cultural preoccupations that have shaped public discourse on European unification in Germany, the United Kingdom, and Spain.

Germany: The Quest for Sovereignty

The position of the *Frankfurter Allegemeine Zeitung* (*FAZ*) and *Die Zeit* toward European integration has been almost unequivocally favorable for the past fifty years. This unwavering pro-integration attitude, however, is less the product of idealistic Europeanism than of a pragmatic quest for sovereignty. It also encompasses two slightly different European projects, the more intergovernmental one advocated by the *FAZ* and the more integrationist one advocated by *Die Zeit*. Based on the articles' content, one can divide the analysis of discussions about European integration into four periods: before the Treaty of Rome (1946–57), before the United Kingdom's accession to the EEC (1957–72), before the Single European Act (SEA) and admission of Spain and Portugal as members of the European Community (1973–85), and the post-SEA period (1986–97).

Between 1946 and 1957, most of the discussion about European integration evolved around the main dilemmas faced by the Federal Republic of Germany (FRG) after World War II: how to regain sovereignty, how to rebuild the economy, how to best protect the FRG against the Soviet Union, and how to keep the door open for German reunification.[14] The immediate context within which these dilemmas were played out in the articles' discussions of European integration was debate about the fate of the coal-producing Saar region and about the FRG's remilitarization in the face of the Cold War. The two discussions were in fact related because of the significant role that the Saar, like the Ruhr, had played in Germany's prewar military buildup. Confronted with two equally dreadful potential scenarios, a Soviet or a new German aggression, the Allies were divided about how to deal with the FRG. The French mistrusted Germany and thus resisted the return of the Saar to Germany and German remilitarization. The Americans and the British, on the contrary, more worried about the Soviet threat, had a greater interest in Germany's economic recovery and remilitarization as the best strategies to prevent the FRG from falling prey to communism. Within this context, everybody welcomed the Schuman Plan for the constitution of the European Coal and Steel Community (ECSC). It allowed for a rational use of natural resources that would accelerate Europe's economic recovery and unlock the process of German remilitarization by putting the ECSC founding members' coal and iron resources, including the Saar's, under the control of the High Authority of the ECSC. The *FAZ* and *Die*

Zeit supported the idea, despite initial reluctance to do so out of concern that it would be economically disadvantageous for the FRG.[15] Later on, satisfied with the ECSC experience, the *FAZ* and *Die Zeit* also welcomed the creation of the European Economic Community (EEC) and EURATOM by the treaty of Rome (1957).

The creation of the ECSC did not allay French misgivings about the constitution of an independent German army, even if integrated in the incipient Brussels Treaty (1948) and Atlantic Alliance (1949). This is why, in 1952, the French prime minister Pléven proposed the creation of a European Defense Community (EDC), molded on the ECSC. According to Pléven's plan, the FRG would have militarized under a joint European military command. Needless to say, the Soviet Union reacted immediately to the prospect of the EDC. Banking on German postwar antimilitarism and the strong popular support for German reunification, it made a counterproposal that read like "German neutrality in exchange for German reunification." Like most European leftist parties, the German SPD initially wavered and leaned toward the Soviet proposal. The *FAZ* and *Die Zeit*, however, put little trust in the Soviet Union's plan. They thus supported Pléven's plan and criticized the neutrality initially expressed by German Social Democrats.[16] This support of the EDC was in vain, as is well known. In 1954 the French Assembly, dominated by socialist, communist, and Gaullist deputies, all opposed to giving up sovereignty on defense matters, sacrificed Pléven's plan, and thus compromised the entire European integration project.

In sum, from the very first moment, the *FAZ* and *Die Zeit* welcomed proposals toward European unification. They did so, however, out of necessity. A recovery of the Saar, remilitarization, the withdrawal of Allied troops from West Germany, and German reunification, were the main goals orienting Adenauer's West German foreign policy, largely adhered to by the *FAZ* and *Die Zeit*.[17] In the end, German reunification was provisionally given up in exchange for the security that the Atlantic umbrella offered against the Soviet threat, while the remaining goals were achieved at the cost of giving up some formal sovereignty to the newly created European Communities. The fear of the Soviet Union that both the *FAZ* and *Die Zeit* expressed in articles about European unification during this period cannot be overstated. Notwithstanding the primarily pragmatic reasons for supporting European integration, the *FAZ* and *Die Zeit* made virtue out of necessity and discussed the different aspects of integration as well as ways of improving the functioning of the new institutions. The project they defended was both economic and political. Specifically, their op-ed articles stressed the obsolete character of old European states when justifying transfers of sovereignty, and praised the European Communities' contributions to peace and economic development.[18]

Between 1957 and 1973, the *FAZ*'s and *Die Zeit*'s articles on European integration were dominated by the debate over the United Kingdom's admission to the European Communities. De Gaulle's strong personality and nationalist convictions, displayed in his vetoes against the United Kingdom's entry (1963 and 1967), forced Germany to confront and test the limits of its recently recovered sovereignty and of the European arrangements. De Gaulle's opposition to the enlargement of the European Communities, his intergovernmental European project, and his anti-American rhetoric, backed by his decision to develop an independent nuclear deterrent and to withdraw from NATO, stood in total contradiction to the principles upon which the FRG had been founded.[19] Germany was put in the delicate position of siding with or against De Gaulle. The first option threatened to compromise its ties to the United States, its security, and its power to pursue its economic and political interests without scaring neighbors. The second option compromised its ties to France and could thus reawaken the specters of the two world wars.

The *FAZ*'s and *Die Zeit*'s op-ed articles of this period deal with these issues and reflect contrasting reactions. Contributors to these newspapers condemned De Gaulle's decision with respect to the United Kingdom and continued to express commitment to a political Europe. The *FAZ* presented European integration as the best defense against the Soviet Union and the most promising strategy toward German reunification and an autonomous Germany that would not raise suspicions in other countries. *Die Zeit* emphasized the need to create a strong Europe that would stand between the United States and the Soviet Union. The *FAZ* and *Die Zeit* differed in the strength of their opposition to De Gaulle and in the model of European integration they advocated. The *FAZ* expressed greater understanding for De Gaulle's concept of a Europe of the Fatherlands. Thus, its editorials and opinion pieces called for a decision-making philosophy based on the search for consensus, and subtly criticized the Federalophilia of large segments of German society. In an article published in 1962, Jürgen Tern said:

> The key to the difference of opinion [between France and Germany] concerns what the nation means or should not mean in Europe and for European unification. Some believe that the nation-state has irreversibly lost economic viability and whatever remains of it after the political catastrophes must be done away with. Others view this as a malicious distortion of the situation, which, were it to lead to a new form of politics, would mean a fatal impoverishment of Europe.
>
> Many Germans who have had very bad experiences with their nation-state and who have suffered because of the heavy blow to the material and moral substance of the nation, tend to share the former opinion, and have become, with their characteristic zeal and perfectionism, resolute supporters of integration. For the French, it is another matter. They have been able to protect the nation,

with all that this represents for the state, their cultural life, and their self-understanding; they still see themselves as the classic European nation that sets the standards for the rich Western civilization. Their nation-state remains more intact than a cursory glance at its surface would suggest. And they do not see any reason or gain in sacrificing its continued existence and its wealth to a process of integration simply based on functional interconnections.

("Das Europa De Gaulles,'" *FAZ*, February 10, 1962)[20]

Die Zeit's attitude toward De Gaulle was much more critical than the *FAZ*'s. Rather than go along with the concept of "L'Europe des Patries," the contributors to this weekly newspaper intensified the federalist character of their European project, calling for a common defense, extensive majority voting, and common social policies.[21] Federalism and the inclusion of the United Kingdom in the European project were presented as the key to Germany's political autonomy in the face of France's hegemony within the European Community and international mistrust. *Die Zeit*'s view was that a strong federal Europe would be less dependent on the United States for its defense. Furthermore, its journalists argued that as part of a strong Europe, Germany would raise less suspicion from its neighbors when making overtures to Eastern Europe as part of efforts to reunify Germany. Finally, op-ed articles in *Die Zeit* reflected the view that entry of the United Kingdom into the European Community would give Germany more political leverage in the event that Communists were elected to office in France and Italy, a not too remote possibility at the time. Thus, on March 17, 1967, Marion Grafin Dönhoff criticized the government for not pushing hard enough for the United Kingdom's membership in the European Community:

> And how will the Bonn government feel the day it finds itself—with the Communists to the East, across the Elbe River—sitting at the EEC with a French Popular Front without De Gaulle, and with Italy, where, like in France, support for the Communists is at 25%? At that time, England, if kept outside the gates of Europe, will probably have already strengthened its ties to America and built the pillars of a bridge going from Washington to Moscow. The bulk of the political and economic activity would then bypass a now small continental Europe. Is that what we want? ("Entrée für England," *Die Zeit*)

In fact, *Die Zeit*'s underlying objective, a national foreign policy less conditioned by conflict between the superpowers, was not all that different from De Gaulle's. The difference between France and Germany lay in the fact that France enjoyed the freedom to go it alone, whereas Germany needed the European umbrella. Therefore, whereas the *FAZ* was closer in practice to De Gaulle's European project, *Die Zeit* was closer to its spirit.

Between 1971 and 1973, the articles in *Die Zeit* toned down their hopes and demands for a more federal Europe, in keeping with the then prevailing pessimistic mood about European integration and in order to sweeten the pill for the United Kingdom, as it prepared itself to become a member of the European Community. Ralph Dahrendorf, in particular (under the alias "Wieland Europa"), published a piece calling for a radical reconceptualization of the European integration process. The core of his proposal was to increase the intergovernmental character of unification, in order to move beyond economic integration into political integration:

> The Germans have always passionately engaged in a theological debate about supranationality and the surrender of sovereignty. In this respect, it was the readiness to give up sovereignty that almost characterized the traditional, indeed the official, German position. In order to compensate for the highly improbable reunification of the country, out of embarrassment for a nonexistent foreign policy—whatever the reasons—the Federal Republic of Germany has systematically weakened itself and Europe through supranational illusions. There are probably still many Germans who think that the Luxembourg Compromise, the following, with few exceptions, of the rule of unanimous decision-making, has decisively weakened Europe. But this applies only to a Europe of the visionary and the academics.
> (Wieland Europa [Ralph Dahrendorf], "Ein neues Ziel für Europa,"
> *Die Zeit*, July 16, 1971)

Based on other pro-integration articles published in *Die Zeit* around that time, one cannot say that Dahrendorf represented the weekly's view; his article illustrated, however, a toning-down of the federalist aspirations traditionally espoused in this publication, or, at least, less confidence in the achievement of the federalist goals. In the early 1970s, the views expressed in the *FAZ* and *Die Zeit* had thus become quite similar and less idealist under the impact of De Gaulle's European policies.

The period 1973–85 was marked by the effects of the oil price crisis and by the institutional crisis of the European Community. The oil crisis and subsequent monetary instability revealed the lack of solidarity between the Community's members and the absence of mechanisms for policy coordination. Meanwhile, the policy of subsidized farm prices in the Community came to absorb most of the budget, which compromised the development of other integrative policies, and even the enlargement of the Community to include southern Europe. Under these conditions, the mood in Europe was somber. Any optimism created by the prospect of the first direct election to the European Parliament was soon dissipated by the low turnout. The articles in the *FAZ* and *Die Zeit* reflected this pessimistic mood.

The *FAZ* warned against the negative consequences that the crisis of the Community could have for the security of Europe, for the chances of German reunification, and for the prosperity of Europe. One reads repeatedly in this newspaper that the security of Europe would be compromised if the economic crisis brought the Communists to power in some of the European Community's countries, or if Europe were unable to negotiate as one with the United States and present an image of unity in East-West relations. Also, op-ed articles stressed that a divided Europe would jeopardize German reunification by forcing Germany into an individual foreign policy toward the East that would inevitably create unrest among Western allies. Finally, the *FAZ* editorialists claimed that a real European single market would not be achieved unless followed by political union in areas such as monetary policy. To avert all these problems, the *FAZ* contributors called for Germany to take the lead toward more policy coordination and institutional reform. Among other recommendations, they proposed putting an end to the Luxembourg Compromise and called for the creation of an economically and politically strong Europe that would work in partnership with the United States. By the early 1980s, however, the *FAZ* had lost hope. Frustrated because of the slow pace of institutional reform and completion of the single market, which was proving costly to Germany, its contributors grew increasingly skeptical about the grandiose projects for political unification that were periodically made. This skepsis led them to talk about a multiple-speed Europe and about concentrating on deepening relations with France.

The content of op-ed articles published in *Die Zeit* during this period was very similar to that in the *FAZ*: frustration with national egoisms and with the slow progress in solving institutional problems. The only relevant contrast between the two newspapers concerned foreign policy views on East-West relations. For the *FAZ* contributors, a strong Europe was primarily necessary to protect Europe from Soviet aggression.[22] For *Die Zeit*'s contributors, Europe needed to be strong in order to pursue a policy toward the GDR and Eastern Europe that would be independent of U.S. policy (even though the partnership with the United States through NATO was never questioned).[23] The bitter conflict between Christian Democrats and Social Democrats with respect to the latter's *Ostpolitik* loomed in the background. Both the *FAZ* and *Die Zeit* had their sights on an eventual German reunification, but whereas the *FAZ* bet on a policy of strength, *Die Zeit* bet on the strengthening of relations between East and West.

Between 1986 and 1997 the mood in the *FAZ* and *Die Zeit* became much more positive because of the implementation of institutional reforms in the European Community and enlargement to southern Europe. The two newspapers welcomed the creation of the single market and the Treaty of Maastricht. Moreover, they agreed on the idea that a unified Europe would reassure other countries about Germany's intentions and facilitate the resolution of conflicts. Finally, after the initial Danish "No" vote on the Maastricht Treaty, they both concluded that the future European Union would have to emphasize the subsidiarity principle. The divisive issues in this period were the economic and monetary union (EMU) and, to a lesser extent, the role of the European Parliament. The *FAZ* contributions to the EMU debate were quite ambivalent up to 1997. Although the articles were in favor of the single currency, they constantly stressed that EMU should not take place at the cost of monetary stability. This was the message sent by Gerard Braumberger in an article published early in 1992:

> Many members of the central council of the Bundesbank share the misgivings (both rational and emotional) of the "man in the street." Moreover, one wonders in Frankfurt whether the abolition of the tried and tested D-Mark, because of the priority given to political considerations, is really as necessary as claimed by the German government. Do the statutes of a future European central bank, acceptable from a German standpoint, provide a real guarantee toward a stability-oriented policy? One also wonders in the Bundesbank whether this readiness to relinquish sovereignty rights soon after the achievement of national unity is a politically reasonable idea.
> ("Die Bundesbank und Maastricht," *FAZ*, February 10, 1992)

The *FAZ*'s articles depicted a bleak scenario that suggested that EMU would not take place, or would do so only after a very long period of convergence. They also criticized countries for trying to meet the EMU criteria on time at the cost of economic stability.[24] Finally, they often floated the idea that EMU should not take place without a previous political union, or advocated a multiple-speed Europe in which Germany and a few other countries would go ahead with monetary union until other countries met the required economic criteria. At some point, they even suggested that it would never take place because enlargement to Eastern Europe would make it impossible. In general, the *FAZ*'s approach consisted not so much in opposing EMU outright but, rather, in stressing the problems associated with it.

Die Zeit's approach was quite different. It was spearheaded by former chancellor Helmut Schmidt, who passionately advocated a prompt and one-speed EMU for political reasons, even if this required a flexible, "political" interpretation of the EMU criteria. For Schmidt, EMU was primarily necessary in order to calm other countries' fears about a united and much stronger Germany.[25] He also pointed out the need to strengthen Europe so as to counterbalance potential political instability in Eastern Europe, and to harness the spread of nationalism both in the European Union and Eastern Europe. Finally, he argued that EMU was necessary to strengthen Europe vis-à-vis the United States and Japan. As in the *FAZ*, some articles in *Die Zeit* discussed the possibility of a multiple-speed Europe or a Europe of variable geometry, but only to prevent countries like the United Kingdom from blocking progress toward integration. Consistent with this view of Europe, contributors to *Die Zeit* during this period advocated a strengthened European Parliament, whereas the *FAZ* op-ed articles called for a limitation of its powers.

In sum, the main underlying goals orienting debates about European integration from the end of World War II to the late 1980s remained largely the same: German reunification, security concerns about the Soviet Union, and the desire to create a common market. The deep mistrust the Allies had toward Germany in the postwar era meant that the FRG's elites, both political and cultural, hardly saw any other option but to pursue their interests within the framework of the European institutions. Because of this, the European project sponsored in the FRG was by necessity not only economic but also political. Until the fall of communism, contributors to the *FAZ* and *Die Zeit* continually stressed the need to build a strong and stable political Europe to resist pressure from the Soviet Union and communism in general. Over the years, however, the foreign policy priorities and the conceptions of a unified Europe expressed in the op-ed articles of the *FAZ* and *Die Zeit* came to diverge significantly. The SPD's *Ostpolitik* was the first major issue that divided them. Whereas the *FAZ* articles insisted on putting pressure on the Soviet bloc and criticized Europe's assertion of autonomy vis-à-vis the United States, *Die Zeit*'s articles advocated a more intense dialogue between Europe and the Soviet bloc and emphasized the singularity of Europe's interests with respect to those of the United States. Two contrasting views about the FRG's foreign policy therefore translated into two contrasting views about Europe's foreign policy.

With the fall of communism, many foreign commentators and politicians feared that a reunited Germany would loosen its commitment to a united Europe. It is too early to say whether they were right or wrong, but analysis of op-ed articles from the *FAZ* and *Die Zeit* suggest that the post-1989 transformations led to quite different views about the future of European integration among German elite journalists. The *FAZ*'s op-ed line up to 1997 seemed to corroborate the aforementioned concerns. To be sure, the *FAZ*'s articles did not question the achievements of the European Union. But their reservations about the euro in the period considered here, their stress on subsidiarity, and their calls for a limited transfer of powers to the European Parliament, all spelled out a view of a united Europe that was close to the decentralized cooperation model that I sketch in chapter 3. They also signified a more assertive view of Germany, with less concern about what other countries might think about Germany's home and foreign policies. Some of this spirit was already captured in an article published in May 1984. The article decried the fact that because of the coincidence between the celebration of the day of the popular uprising in the GDR of June 1953, known as the Day of German Unity (Tag der Deutschen Einheit), and the European election, some commemorative events in the Bundestag had been postponed. The author of this piece saw this as an indication that, contrary to what the Germans had been made to believe, European integration would make it more difficult to attain German reunification:

> The sudden postponement of the Day of German Unity with the improvised argument that it unfortunately coincides with the European election is not only a "technical" issue. It is an eye opener. It solves the old question about whether Europeanist sanctity—real, invented, or perhaps even dishonest—in the end will lead to developments that completely collide with the efforts to achieve German unity. In recent years there have always been isolated, usually timid, but gradually louder voices that consider this to be a possibility. They have asked with increasing urgency whether a European policy that aims toward the United States of Europe and a German policy, like the one prescribed by the Basic Law, are perhaps incompatible.... The coalition parties must prove that their European policy does not run against a properly understood German policy, precisely on the day of the European election. If they don't demonstrate this symbolically, the number of those who believe that the roads to Europe and to a united—or at least a not so divided—Germany seem to point in different directions may grow.
> (Ernst-Otto Maetzke, "Für Europa preisgegeben," *FAZ*, May 23, 1984)

In retrospect, one may conclude that for the *FAZ*, European integration was almost exclusively instrumental toward German reunification. Once this goal was achieved, the range of options open to German foreign policy was broader and the *FAZ* contributors seem to have chosen the European cooperation road. The opposite can be said about *Die Zeit*. Although primarily concerned with the same goals as the *FAZ*, *Die Zeit* increasingly deviated from the uncompromising approach toward Eastern Europe advocated by the United States, the CDU, and contributors to the *FAZ*. The change in orientation expressed in the *Ostpolitik* was only the starting point for a growing consciousness of distinctively German and European foreign policy interests that diverged from those of the United States. Helmut Schmidt was a main proponent of the *Ostpolitik* as leader of the SPD, and he has continued to spearhead the movement toward a more integrated Europe through contributions to *Die Zeit* and other newspapers. The same can be said about Theo Sommer and the late Marion Gräfin Dönhoff, editors of *Die Zeit*. How close their views are to that of a decentralized but integrated Europe is difficult to tell, but their support for the single currency and the arguments they advanced to support it in the early 1990s are consistent with their persistent appeals for an assertive and autonomous Europe that dates back to at least the late 1960s. Furthermore, their rethinking of the role of Europe in the aftermath of the transformations in Eastern Europe, pointing out the dangers of renewed nationalism both in Western and Eastern Europe, reveals the educational aspect of the experience of the *Ostpolitik*. It taught the editors of *Die Zeit* to see the specificity of German and European interests and thus allowed them to set new goals for the European Union in the post-communist, post-German reunification era.

The previous pages have focused on the Federal Republic of Germany because in the pre-reunification years only the FRG was affected by and participated in efforts toward European unification. But to better understand how German citizens, East and West, think about European integration and the European Union, we must pay attention to how these were portrayed in the GDR media in the pre-reunification years.

The image of European integration and of the European Communities sketched in articles published between 1949 and 1991 was simple and persistent, the same official story being constantly hammered on the readers of *Neues Deutschland*. The process of European integration, both economic and military, was portrayed as a plot concocted by capitalist monopolies, predominantly American and German, to dominate Western Europe and its colonies and prepare a military aggression against the Eastern bloc. Initially, the United States was given the primary role in this alliance, but over time West Germany appeared as the prime mover, a country ruled by old Nazis intent on accomplishing what they could not accomplish in two world wars. This version of the story emerged time and again, whether during discussion of the Paris and Rome Treaties or during the negotiations for the United Kingdom's accession.

Needless to say, *Neues Deutschland* predicted that the European Communities were bound to fail, because of competition between the different countries. The articles during the period emphasized four negative consequences of European integration: transfer of sovereignty to European institutions, rising prices, declining social standards and worsening conditions for the workers, and the impossibility of achieving German reunification. A frequent variation of this last theme consisted in the prediction that the Federal Republic would take over the German Democratic Republic. Moreover, *Neues Deutschland* did not miss a single occasion to point out the imperfections of the EEC, be they national disputes over the CAP or over the budget, the monetary crises of the 1970s, the expected decline in the living standards of workers, or the resistance of the working classes in the United Kingdom and Scandinavian countries to membership in the EEC.

Only in the late 1980s did the paper warm up to the EEC, as the prospect of commercial treaties between the EEC and the GDR arose.

However, in the years immediately following German reunification and before the Maastricht Treaty, *Neues Deutschland* remained ambiguous about European unification. While supporting the Maastricht Treaty and even the EMU and the strengthening of the European Parliament, it stressed the need for subsidiarity, and constantly decried the threats to Germany's social standards, the economic costs the European Union meant for Germany, and the Schengen Treaty. It also criticized the European Union's militarism and, more specifically, German militarism, as in Yugoslavia, and its lack of consideration for other European Union members (e.g., the unilateral German recognition of Croatia and Slovenia). Finally, it floated alternative projects to the European Union, such as a proposal for a Central European Union centered in Austria or the reliance on the Conference for Security and Disarmament in Europe as the springboard toward a demilitarized model of European unification that would have a strong social dimension.

This summary of the content of editorial and opinion pieces published in *Neues Deutschland* between 1949 and 1991 shows that European integration was portrayed in very negative terms for the entire period. The fact that Oststadt respondents presented an image of European integration that was much closer to that expressed by Weststadt respondents and in the West German press demonstrates the delegitimation of the Communist regime and the rapidity with which cognitive frames are transmitted. Oststadt respondents did not, however, internalize a theme that was present in a very large number of Weststadt interviews and in the *FAZ* and *Die Zeit*: the role that German commitment to European integration plays in reducing other countries' misgivings toward Germany. Why did this issue stick in the West Germans' consciousness but not in the East Germans'? I have already pointed out some potential explanations early in the chapter: the lack of penetration of the West German elite press in East Germany, the ambiguous support of European integration in the delegitimated East German elite press, and the long-lasting effects of portrayals of the European integration process in the pre-reunification period. I pursue this issue in chapters 6 and 7. But now I will examine how British elite journalists writing op-ed articles for the United Kingdom's quality newspapers have addressed European integration and British membership in the European institutions.

The United Kingdom: Reckoning with Decline

In the second half of the century, contributors to two major British weeklies, *The Economist* and *The New Statesman*, debated European integration as the United Kingdom declined from world hegemon to middle-sized power. A systematic and sequential reading of op-ed articles in the two weeklies reveals an unchanging preference for cooperative rather than integrative arrangements in Europe. Because of the United Kingdom's decline, however, the two weeklies came to accept the United Kingdom's membership in the European institutions and, once this was accomplished, strove for a decentralized cooperation model of European integration with democratic accountability.

The United Kingdom confronted serious dilemmas in deciding to become a member of the European Communities. The maintenance of commercial, political, and emotional ties to the Commonwealth and the Labour Party's goal of implementing socialist policies were perceived as incompatible with the European framework. Therefore, seeing no major reason to surrender sovereignty to a supranational institution, contributors to *The Economist* and *The New Statesman*, like the Conservative and Labour parties, resisted as long as they could before giving up and accepting membership. Underlying this struggle against a surrender of sovereignty was in fact a struggle to preserve the United Kingdom's self-image as a world power. This explains the pathos that entry negotiations with the EEC involved. During the intense debates that preceded the conclusion of these negotiations, a particular language to conceive and discuss European integration took shape, centered on sovereignty and idealized British history and institutions. For purposes of comparison, the discussion that follows uses the same chronology employed to examine the German newspapers, even though some major turning points in discussions about European integration in *The Economist* and *The New Statesman* do not coincide with this chronology.

The United Kingdom emerged victorious from World War II, having served as the leading geographic, political, and military base for the Allied war effort in Europe. With an empire largely intact, the Commonwealth at its core, the United Kingdom aspired to play a major role in shaping the postwar world order, together with the United States and the Soviet Union. The country's economy was in shambles, however, and the empire's foundations shaky. In the following twenty years, this empire would unravel, exposing the rusty mechanisms of an economically dynamic, socially advanced, but inflation-prone and conflict-ridden kingdom.

Between 1946 and 1957, contributors to *The Economist* and *The New Statesman* reflected the unfolding drama in their discussions about European integration. Confronted with proposals for the creation of the ECSC, the EDC, the EEC, and EURATOM, they dismissed them, trumped them with alternative plans, and eventually rejected them altogether. Contributors to *The Economist*, like those to *The New Statesman*, recognized three main problems: the rebuilding of the British and European economies, the defense against the Soviet Union, and the need to prevent another German aggression. During these years, the editorials in *The Economist* delineated the contours of an Atlantic Community with military and economic dimensions. This Atlantic Community, encompassing the United States, the United Kingdom and its old Dominions, and the western half of continental Europe, was meant to have an intergovernmental character. *The Economist* hoped, in fact, to use the Commonwealth as its model. The economic philosophy of the project was free trade and its military components, the Brussels Treaty and the North Atlantic Treaty Organization. *The Economist* was cognizant that the Soviet threat and the German question posed special problems. Furthermore, it was well aware that the United States would not provide economic and military aid to Europe unless Europe demonstrated a firm commitment toward economic and political unification. *The Economist* therefore supported the creation of special supervisory organizations to manage the continental coal and iron resources, and welcomed the proposal for a European Defense Community, as long as it was closely linked to NATO.

The Economist observed the ECSC and EDC developments as an interested outsider and with skeptical eyes, blind to the idea that the United Kingdom would at some point take part in a supranational project, which at any rate it considered to be an unpopular and poor solution to the problems faced by Europe. Its worldview was one in which the United Kingdom was a world actor at the same level as the United States and the Soviet Union, and separate from Europe:

> Where the British interest in these matters lies is surely clear. It is to co-operate most fully where progress is easiest and the need most urgent. Britain's position compels it to seek not new responsibilities but new strength; it is, therefore, strongly attracted by the United States and by the links already existing between the Americans and three members of the Commonwealth, Canada, Australia, and New Zealand. It follows that the British, wherever the debate on western unity is engaged, insist on the possibilities of partnership in NATO rather than on integration with Europe.
>
> ("Prescriptions for Unity," *The Economist*, September 10, 1949)

In 1952, for instance, under U.S. pressure to step up efforts to strengthen Europe's defense because of the Korean War, *The Economist* proposed that the Americans and the British be part of the councils of the EDC, and that the British assign their troops in the Continent to the European army. This is as far as *The Economist* would go: to have the United Kingdom play the role of advisor (together with the United States), to have it commit some troops, but not to recommend its becoming a member of the EDC. From its perspective, the United Kingdom lay as far outside Europe as did the United States.

From early on, contributors to *The Economist* were well aware that the Western Europeans did not share the United Kingdom's and *The Economist*'s image of the country and that, in fact, they saw it as natural that the United Kingdom would participate in the development of the incipient European institutions. But what really forced *The Economist* to treat European developments seriously were the success of the ECSC and plans for EURATOM and the EEC. Here were two projects that threatened not only the United Kingdom's military standing but, most importantly, its economic interests. The EEC, because of its common external tariff, was indeed bound to impinge on the United Kingdom, whether the UK joined or remained outside. Staying out would threaten the access of British products to the expanding European market, whereas joining would mean subjecting farm products from the Commonwealth to the external tariff. This would in turn deteriorate relations between the United Kingdom and its old Dominions and potentially make food prices higher in the United Kingdom. Confronted with the uncertainties involved in both solutions, *The Economist* tried to square the circle by making alternative proposals. Most of these proposals were variations on the same theme: how to prevent Commonwealth farm products from being penalized by an eventual entry of the United Kingdom in the EEC. In the end, *The Economist* settled for the Conservative government's decision to stay out and its proposal of a Free Trade Area between the EEC and the United Kingdom:

> The Government can hardly commit itself today to a full customs union with wide delegation of powers to federal institutions; for one thing, such a union would cover only one eighth of British trade, at the expense of the Commonwealth trade that accounts for one half. But a free trade zone, in which Britain would gradually abolish trade restrictions with Europe but retain independent tariffs for the rest of the world, is another matter. It would associate her with the common market while preserving the great majority of imperial preferences. ("Free Trade with Europe," *The Economist*, September 22, 1956)

Under the Conservative Party's plan, the United Kingdom's trade with the EEC would have not been affected and would not have been subject to the common external tariff. It is thus understandable that when the plan was rejected by the EEC, *The Economist* reacted angrily both against the EEC and, most significantly, against the British government, for not having taken the Schuman Plans more seriously:

> Czechs, Swedes, Spaniards, and Englishmen, resentful of being left high and dry without a continent to belong to, may feel that it would have been more tactful to leave some title in abeyance for a possible "big" Europe of the future.

... [T]he British government made a mistake in fixing, or appearing to fix, its sights exclusively on the tariffs and the quotas, vital though these matters are in any practical consideration; irritating as it may be, the planners and dreamers of the Six do see their union as much more than a commercial arrangement.
("Europe—Big or Little," *The Economist*, October 18, 1958)

Contributors to *The New Statesman* saw European institutional developments from a different perspective. In line with the Labour Party, *The New Statesman* was no enthusiast of the Atlantic Alliance or of militarism in general, and did not share *The Economist*'s pro-American affinities. In fact, it supported a peace treaty with the Soviet Union and an unblocking of trade relations with the East. More than *The Economist*'s, *The New Statesman*'s worldview was centered in the United Kingdom-Commonwealth binomium and rested on the twin principles of socialism at home and free trade with the Commonwealth. While it opposed NATO and the EDC because they contradicted *The New Statesman*'s antimilitaristic ideology, it opposed the Schuman Plans for the ECSC and EEC because of their capitalist character. Like *Neues Deutschland* in the GDR and the radical wings of Western European leftist parties in general, *The New Statesman*'s articles portrayed the ECSC and the EEC in ominous terms, as a capitalist plot led by Americans and German Nazis:

> There is much of the weary atmosphere of 1926 about all this, though the Schuman-Adenauer Plan for the "union" of heavy industry is, after all, a slender imitation of Locarno.
> (Basil Davidson, "Europe Inc.," *The New Statesman*, June 3, 1950)

From the perspective of the British left, the risks involved in the United Kingdom's involvement in the EEC were indeed too big. At the time, the United Kingdom had a large nationalized sector and an advanced welfare state. Fear that these achievements by the Labour Party might be compromised by membership in the EEC underlay *The New Statesman*'s opposition to the United Kingdom's membership. Instead, the leftist weekly proposed intergovernmental approaches that would involve the different social partners in plans for the use of productive resources in Europe. These proposals were, however, halfhearted and not very detailed, for, in fact, *The New Statesman* did not seriously consider the prospect of the United Kingdom participating in the construction of Europeanwide institutions. It did not see any need for giving up sovereignty rights and did not feel that the United Kingdom had run out of options.

Between 1957 and the early 1980s, op-ed articles in *The Economist* and *The New Statesman* came to accept the United Kingdom's membership in the European Communities. It was a gradual process, with three distinct phases that one could label as reflecting "Denial," "Grudging Acceptance," and "Embrace." *The Economist* completed all the phases before the United Kingdom's entry in the European Communities; *The New Statesman* completed only the first two, and always a few years later than *The Economist*. The context for these developments were the economic success of the EEC, the first steps by French president De Gaulle to develop an independent nuclear deterrent, the orderly British withdrawal from its former imperial possessions (punctuated by the traumatic Suez fiasco of 1956), and the failure of British governments to break with the pattern of growth–trade deficit–inflation–recession–social conflict. The structural crisis of the British economy rapidly condemned the United Kingdom's alternative to the EEC, the European Free Trade Area (EFTA), to failure, which forced the Conservative cabinet led by Macmillan to apply for membership in the European Communities.

During the first entry negotiations, *The Economist*, while supportive of the United Kingdom's membership in the European Communities, did not hide its dislike of the institutions, and predicted quite optimistically that the United Kingdom would manage to minimize the negative effects of membership. Its writers took it for granted that they would be able to reverse the European Communities' drift away from the United States and attain lower tariffs at the World Trade Negotiations:

> Doubtless some people in Paris, and some elsewhere on the Continent, at present see Britain as an American Trojan horse. In a sense it is, and quite rightly....
> ("Europe or Atlantis?," *The Economist*, July 14, 1962)

In view of this confidence, De Gaulle's first veto came as a shock, met with undisguised anger in some of *The Economist*'s subsequent editorials. *The Economist* then predicted an unraveling of the European Communities and warned about the dangerous vulnerability of Europe to Soviet aggression. It also saw an opportunity to again recommend its concept of an Atlantic Community, both at the economic and military levels. Overall, the tone of *The Economist*'s articles up to and immediately after De Gaulle's 1963 veto was still one of confidence in the United Kingdom's power and leadership. Soon after, however, *The Economist* somberly reassessed the United Kingdom's role in the world, conceding that it was no longer a dominant player. Thus, a milestone lead article entitled "Breaking out from the Past" (May 18, 1963) began as follows:

> The six and a half years of the attempt to come to terms with the European common market, since the free trade area was proposed in 1956, are the Great Divide of modern British history. For the time being, the attempt has failed; and British opinion is still far from wholly won over to the idea that the European communities qualify as a "good thing." But the effort alone has dealt a mortal blow to the Festival of Britain spirit, the happy pursuit of parochial self-

esteem that still dulled the country's awareness of facts in the nineteen-fifties. In the great debate on the common market, the British have seen through some of their own shibboleths; this is something.

The grandest victim of the common market's cold douche has been the illusion that Britain was still a world power, an illusion fostered by a heroic war record and by a touching faith in the welfare state—so half-hearted, so incomplete—as a model for others to emulate, much as British parliamentary institutions were taken as models in the nineteenth century.

The Economist's leaders began to convey that membership was not only necessary to maintain the political and military cohesion of the Atlantic Alliance but also the only economic option for the United Kingdom. The change of attitude in *The Economist*'s articles of this period was conveyed by the weekly's reevaluation of the costs of entry for the United Kingdom and of the European institutions themselves. During the 1963–67 period, *The Economist* stressed that the incompatibility between membership in the European Community and relations with the rest of the Commonwealth was not all that great after all. Also, rather than express the intention of transforming the Community from inside, it called for accepting it as it was.[26] It even discussed the advantages of membership with regard to cooperation in the fields of industry and technology.

When De Gaulle again vetoed the United Kingdom's entry in the European Community in 1967, *The Economist*'s reaction was no longer one of defiance but rather of resignation and resolution to persevere with entry negotiations. Introspection about the changed world status of the United Kingdom continued during this period. *The Economist* presented the United Kingdom as too small to stand alone:

> The British have farther to go, less on specific issues of policy than in attitudes. For most of this century it has been natural for Englishmen to think of themselves as part of the English-speaking world, of which the United States has become the visible leader. Only now are they beginning in any number to think of themselves as Europeans as well.
>
> ("And Now," *The Economist*, October 14, 1967)

To buttress its call for entry in the European Communities, the editorials in *The Economist* trivialized the Commonwealth and food editorials by challenging other groups' interpretation of statistical data and pointing out that statistical interpretations are quite often guided by emotional predispositions:

> Why is this sort of clamor set up whenever any new hope of entering the EEC dawns? The truth is that there are some people in Britain who are bitterly opposed to union with Europe on emotional grounds, or on the grounds of what they call the "bureaucratic monster" at Brussels and in that it interferes with

Britons' independence to run their own affairs. Such people are to be found in the economics profession, politics and the civil service; and this quite clearly does affect their sense of statistical balance.

("Oh Moo," *The Economist*, July 12, 1969)

Also, *The Economist* countered opponents of a transfer of sovereignty by arguing that parliamentary sovereignty had, at any rate, been eaten away by the British Home civil service and by NATO. Finally, it asserted that the United Kingdom, as a large country, would have clout in the decision-making process. This was an important point to make at a moment when the United Kingdom's self-image as a world power was contradicted by its decision to enter institutions that its governments and publications such as *The Economist* had formerly dismissed.

The content of editorials published by *The Economist* at the time immediately before and after entry in the European Community amounted to what one could call a religious conversion. Moving beyond justifications for membership, and against a background of public skepticism, *The Economist* justified European integration by referring to the growing internationalization of capitalism and the need for larger markets; also, by stressing the political need to hold Germany in check, at a time of growing concern in the West about its Social Democratic government's *Ostpolitik*. Furthermore, *The Economist* made idealistic federalist proclamations and called for the extension of common European policies and for a democratically elected European Parliament vested with real power. Finally, its editorials capitalized on British antipathy toward the French, by contrasting the federal approach it now defended with France's intergovernmental approach. In sum, gradually awakened to the lack of options for the United Kingdom, *The Economist* moved in a little more than a decade from a disdainful attitude toward the European Community to embracing them as the best of all worlds.

The New Statesman did not go as far as *The Economist* in reassessing the merits of membership in the European Communities. Before 1967, its op-ed articles insisted on the arguments already put forward in the previous period. In particular, they reiterated that the achievements of the British Labour movement in previous decades would be compromised through membership in the European institutions. Moreover, they raised the specter of rising unemployment caused by an influx of immigrants from poorer countries to the United Kingdom. Far from conceding that Britain's economy could not survive outside the European Communities, *The New Statesman* expressed unremitting faith in the promise of socialist planning and restrictive consumption policies, and in the advantages of a strengthening of ties with the Commonwealth:

> Without publicly-directed planning, it is impossible to reconcile economic growth and social justice. Yet such planning, even on the modest scale which

Labour set out in Signposts for the Sixties, will be gravely hindered—if not excluded—once Britain signs the Treaty of Rome.... Outside the Market, it would be equally necessary to restrain consumption in the cause of high investment and capital export. But, with public planning and progressive social policies designed to enlist the cooperation of the trade unions, effort could at least be concentrated in the decisive sectors of the economy and the social burden spread fairly. It would, moreover, be possible to create closer links with Europe on the basis of mutual interest and, thanks to the most-favoured nation clause, on the same terms as the United States.

("Labour's Alternative to Europe," *The New Statesman*, May 4, 1962)

The tone of the op-ed articles of this period was unmistakably nationalist, expressed not only in content but also in form, based as it was on an epic language that drew heavily on the imagery of World War II. Thus *The New Statesman* constantly referred to its opposition to a "surrender" of sovereignty, used terms such as "*diktat*" when discussing decisions by the European Communities and "*Zollverein*" to describe the EEC, and portrayed the EEC as controlled by recycled Nazis.[27] Complementing this rhetoric was the effort by some contributors to *The New Statesman* to reconstruct British history as a history of struggles between "Self-Determinists" and "Continentalists" (see figure 4.1). A prime example of this is Paul Johnson's piece "The Lessons of History":[28]

The existence of the Channel has always given the inhabitants of the British Isles a degree of choice in their reception of Continental ideas and institutions, though it was some time before they formed societies cohesive enough to exercise it....
The problem which faced Britain's rulers was a perennial one (it has faced all pre-colonial peoples): to what extent could they take advantage of proximity with a dynamic commercial, social and military system without risking absorption in it?
... Yet a grouping on the lines of the EEC was originally a German concept, and remained Germany's principal war aim in both world conflicts.... It was the Kaiser who seized on the phrase "the United States of Europe" as something to flourish in the face of rising American and Russian power....
... Britain is turning to the EEC, as she turned to imperialism in the 1880s, to escape from the economic difficulties, which have changed remarkably little in the past century....
... A significant aspect of the present debate over Britain's relationship with Europe is that, despite the fact that the Continentalists control virtually all the press and all radio and television channels, the self-determinists still constitute the overwhelming majority of the nation.... [The] arrogant confidence [of the Continentalists] in the superiority of their own judgement over that of the great mass of their fellow-countrymen should be sobered by the thought that, in the past, overweening Continentalists have usually been punished by exile or worse ...
... If Britain goes it alone once more, the last quarter of this century will see

Self-Determinists	Continentalists
Caractacus	Gildas
Pelagius	St. Wilfred
Arthur	Edward Confessor
William I	St. Anselm
Henry II	Thomas Beckett
Wyclif	Stephen Langton
Henry V	Richard II
Thomas Cromwell	Thomas More
Elizabeth I	Queen Mary
Oliver Cromwell	Charles I
Milton	James II
Walpole	Bolinbroke
Burke	Castlereagh
Canning	Wellington
Gladstone	Disraeli
Baldwin	Edward VII
Eden	MacMillan

Source: Paul Johnson, "The Lessons of History," *The New Statesman*, May 21, 1971, p. 69.

Figure 4.1 "Self-Determinists" and "Continentalists" in British History.

profound changes in British habits and institutions, many of which will be painful. But Britain has always, in the past, chosen the adventure of sovereignty in preference to the presumed security of a Continental system. And history shows that, in the end she has always chosen rightly.

(*The New Statesman*, May 21, 1971)

In contrast with today's perception of anti-EU rhetoric in the United Kingdom as originating in the British far right, and as being transmitted through the Murdoch-controlled tabloid press, the examination of *The New Statesman* editorials reminds us that this rhetoric owes much of its content to the British left and was sketched long before Murdoch's newspaper revolution.

The New Statesman's attitudes toward the European Community began to change after De Gaulle's second veto. While restating that membership in the European Communities would probably result in rising inequalities and a loss of sovereignty, it noted that the European Community had become more intergovernmental and that the Labour Party would at any rate be able to change it from within, by forging alliances with workers' parties in other countries. In a remarkable turnaround, it also began to criticize the isolationism and chauvinism of some of the Labour Party's militants and political representatives.[29]

During the 1975 Referendum campaign, *The New Statesman* went further and adopted the practice of presenting "pro" and "con" views, while announcing the editors' pro-membership attitude. Those "against" portrayed the EEC in extremely negative terms, emphasizing bad policies—social, regional, environmental—and lack of unity on foreign policy issues. They also repeated the line that socialism could only be achieved outside the European Community. Those "for," on the other hand, stressed the idea that the United Kingdom did not have any other option, and expressed confidence in the potential for coalitions between leftist parties in Europe that would change the spirit of the European Community. Furthermore, like *The Economist*, they distinguished between formal sovereignty and actual sovereignty in order to assert that the latter would increase with membership.

As fate would have it (with help from De Gaulle and Pompidou), the United Kingdom became a member of the European Community just as the oil crisis and the breakdown of the Breton-Woods monetary system were exerting a heavy impact on the European economies. Thus, rather than improve, the British economy continued to suffer from the same problems that afflicted it before the United Kingdom became a member of the European Community. Under these conditions, the fact that most of the EEC's small budget was devoted to subsidizing farmers through the Common Agricultural Policy, from which the British population hardly benefited, provided ammunition to those who for years had opposed the United Kingdom's membership. Between 1973 and 1985, especially after the 1975 Referendum, *The Economist* and *The New Statesman* regularly used their editorial and opinion pages to decry both CAP and the national contributions to the European Community, and to call for reform.

For *The Economist* the period 1973–85 was one of disillusionment and retreat from previous pro-federalist enthusiasm. While loyal to membership in the European Community and supportive of common policies in selected areas, the pursuit of the single market, enlargement to Southern Europe, the existence of a European Parliament, the Regional Fund, and plans for economic and monetary union, *The Economist* stressed the cooperative approach over the integrationist (federalist) approach, especially on defense issues. *The Economist*'s European vision was no longer an all-encompassing Atlantic Community but, rather, a two-legged construction, made up of the Atlantic Alliance for foreign policy and defense and the European Community for economic issues.[30]

For *The New Statesman*, the period between 1973 and 1985 was also one of disillusionment, augmented by the perception that EEC legislation set limits on the types of policies that the Labour Party could aspire to implement at home. Contributors to *The New Statesman* mentioned areas such as subsidies, capital flow controls, trade policy, and welfare benefits, where the Labour Party's autonomy was seriously curtailed. The

Conservative Party's 1979 election victory, however, and Margaret Thatcher's subsequent dismantlement of the British welfare state, privatization measures, and limitation of workers' rights, put an end to the Labour Party's and *The New Statesman*'s dream of a socialist United Kingdom and forced them to take a new look at the European Community. Op-ed articles published in *The New Statesman* began to express a more positive and constructive approach to the European Community. Some articles included the familiar argument that in a global world states have become too small and formal sovereignty has lost meaning. Others stated that supranational organizations offer the only way of preserving actual sovereignty. *The New Statesman* advocated a more political European project than did *The Economist*. As in Germany, European political integration began to emerge as the project of the left, a left that would not countenance that Europe remain a quasi-dependency of the United States, and that advocated a self-assured Europe standing tall between the United States and the Soviet bloc. This project was not necessarily federal, but it encompassed a strong European Parliament, a single currency, a social and regional dimension, and a European defense.

Between 1985 and 1997, discussions of institutional reform took precedence over discussions about policies, as the European Community underwent three major institutional reforms: the Single European Act (SEA), the Maastricht Treaty, and the amendments to the Maastricht Treaty by Amsterdam's Intergovernmental Conference. For most of this period, the contrasts between *The Economist* and *The New Statesman* outlined above persisted. In the mid-1990s, however, under the impact of the Blairite revolution within the Labour Party, the views of *The Economist* and *The New Statesman* converged into a decentralized cooperation model of European integration.

Before Maastricht, *The Economist* further refined its two-legged project consisting of an economically integrated Europe and a Western alliance responsible for political and defense matters. It did not oppose further foreign and defense cooperation between the members of the European Community but expressed dislike of a political Europe that would distance itself from NATO. Consequently, *The Economist* stressed the need for the European Community to concentrate on the completion of the single market, on CAP and budgetary reform, on enlargement of the EC toward Southern Europe, and on drafting plans for a future economic and monetary union. Moreover, *The Economist*'s European vision was non-federal. To justify its non-federal approach, *The Economist* pointed out irreconcilable cultural differences between the European countries, differences that would become greater as enlargement to Central and Eastern Europe took place.

> Peering ahead, it is now easy to imagine a Community with two dozen members and would-be members. That is the prospect that should determine the shape of

something as grand as political union. This union is less likely than ever to be a single superstate, and more likely to be a confederation of sovereign countries. Added diversity will create a still stronger argument for keeping as much law making as possible at the national level. The central rules that are needed—and mutual economic openness demands a surprising number of them—will go on being made by votes between many member governments rather than in one European Parliament. The reason is that the more disparate the EC's membership, the less will its voters think of themselves as Europeans first, and only second as Poles, or Spaniards, or Latvians, or French. (November 2, 1991)

The Economist also stressed that the United Kingdom had broader interests when compared with other countries, because of its ties to the Commonwealth and its international financial role:

Some of the difficulties Britain has with the Community's evolution are genuine, some imagined, some self-inflicted. The genuine ones stem from the fact that Britain has a wider set of distinctive interests than most EC members do. It has its own nuclear weapons. It is home to one of the three big financial centers of what is the most global of industries. Because the sun never sets on the British Empire, it still does not set on a swathe of countries with which Britain retains ties of blood, commerce, language and cricket. Most of the other EC countries are happy to embrace "Europeanism," however woolly the notion; it is all they have. It defines what they were, are, will ever be. Only France has a history, and a sense of independence, as particular as Britain's. Perhaps the real oddity is not that Britain finds it hard to fit itself into a solely European framework, but that France has so far found this easy.
("The Road to Maastricht," *The Economist*, November 23, 1991)

There was therefore no point in pushing for institutional reforms that would make the European Community more federal. On the contrary, what was needed, according to *The Economist*, was an institutional reform that would accentuate the European Community's cooperative, intergovernmental aspects. In particular, *The Economist* proposed to transfer the power to initiate legislation from the European Commission to the European Council of Heads of State. In the absence of this reform, *The Economist* expressed reluctance toward increasing the number of decisions made through majority-voting procedures.

Another element of *The Economist*'s European project was its democratic character. In the past, *The Economist* had made much of the undemocratic nature of the European Communities and had even supported the democratic election of a European Parliament. In the context of debates about institutional reform, however, *The Economist* reconceptualized what it meant by democracy. It did not mean more power to the European Parliament but, rather, more power to control the work of the

Council of Ministers, through greater transparency of Council deliberations and decisions. This approach was consistent with *The Economist*'s assumption that cultural differences in Europe prevented further steps toward a more federal Europe.

The Economist's discussions of institutional reform in the post-Maastricht period centered fundamentally on subsidiarity and EMU. The initial Danish "No" vote to Maastricht, the bare "Yes" in France, and Major's trouble getting the Maastricht Treaty approved by the British Parliament were interpreted by *The Economist* as support for its Decentralized Cooperation model of integration. In this period, *The Economist*'s leaders stressed the lack of popular support for further political integration and called for strict application of the subsidiarity principle. Otherwise, *The Economist*'s main proposals of the pre-Maastricht period remained unchanged.

Discussions of EMU in *The Economist* mirrored those in the *FAZ* in Germany, as described earlier. *The Economist* had traditionally expressed support for EMU. It was seen as fitting the logic of the creation of a single European market. As a timetable was set for EMU, however, *The Economist*'s support became more ambiguous. While periodically stressing that it found EMU desirable, *The Economist*'s editorial pieces continually stressed the lack of popular support for EMU and the unlikelihood of it ever happening because of poor economic performance and lack of discipline among the countries. It eventually advocated a multiple-speed process that would allow those countries that wanted to go ahead to do so, thus clearly indicating that the United Kingdom was not ready to participate in it.

In the second half of the 1980s *The New Statesman* went through a Euro-enthusiastic phase reminiscent of the one experienced by *The Economist* in the early 1970s. In one of the most Euro-enthusiastic editorials ever published in *The New Statesman*, "Now is the Hour," the author says the following of Delors's project:

> He has realised, as world-weary British commentators have not, that the most promising antidote to xenophobic and destructive nationalism is supranationalism; that the best way to prevent frontier quarrels is to make frontiers irrelevant; that the twin imperatives of national identity and transnational interdependence can most easily be reconciled in a community based on the principle of union in diversity.... He has also realized two other things—both of them even less palatable on this side of the Channel. The first is that the attractions of supranationalism depend on its being genuinely supranational.... The second thing Delors has realised is that the single most explosive element in the witches' cauldron of the past was the German Question. A Europe of nation-states is bound to be dominated by Germany.... In a federal Europe, on the other hand, no nation-state would predominate, because there would be no nation-states.
>
> (January 26, 1990)

This embrace of the European Community, like *The Economist*'s a few years earlier, was prefaced by a sobering reassessment of the United Kingdom's identity. This reassessment questioned the validity of myths that *The New Statesman* itself had contributed to creating in the 1960s.

> The dominant idea of Britishness has rested on a series of associations: between a physical space, a political tradition, a particular state form, a claim about cultural unity and continuity, and an arrogant assertion about being the original home of democracy. None of these associations is true, even if you're only looking at the very short historical timescale of 300 years or so.
> ("Home and Away," *The New Statesman*, March 24, 1989)

The New Statesman's new pro-European discourse contained a critique of the provincialism of the elites and of their ability to share power. It concluded that Britain would gain from integration, both in terms of democracy and accountability.

For some years *The New Statesman* remained true to its reassessment of British identity. It thus advocated a federal Europe, both political and economic. Its project included almost everything that has ever been proposed for the European Union: a stronger European Parliament, common Regional, Social, and Development Aid policies, economic and monetary union, a Social and an Environmental Charter, and enlargement to Central and Eastern Europe. The main justifications for the political aspects of integration were, as in *Die Zeit*, the need to contain the spread of nationalism and to control a much stronger Germany. Instead of viewing cultural differences as a reason to slow down political integration, *The New Statesman* argued that only a political and decentralized European Union could protect national identities in a globalized world. EMU, on the other hand, was advocated on economic grounds, as a means to avoid inflation, to reduce transaction costs, and to prevent currency speculation. Regional, Social, and Structural funds were advocated to facilitate convergence between the countries and thus make EMU possible.

In the second half of the 1990s, the programmatic and leadership changes in the Labour Party had a profound effect on the content of op-ed articles published by *The New Statesman*. The federal tone of previous years, for instance, became more subdued, as some contributors expressed reservations about strengthening the role of the European Parliament, and, like *The Economist*, called instead for stronger control mechanisms over the Commission and more transparency in the work of the Council of Ministers. Also, when discussing EMU, *The New Statesman*'s contributions reflected the indecision and divisions within the Labour Party on this issue. Some op-eds, for instance, questioned the economic advantages of the single currency and its effects on social benefits. Other articles represented the views of the government by saying that the United Kingdom should only join EMU when economic conditions were right. Finally, when discussing common policies, *The New Statesman*'s articles began to echo the New Labour's market-oriented approach; thus, they expressed less enthusiasm for an ambitious Social Charter or for large Structural Funds.

In sum, it took about thirty years before both the Conservative and the Labour parties in the United Kingdom accepted membership in the European Communities. This means that for more than half of the postwar period, the British population, unlike that of other European countries, has been exposed to negative characterizations of and nationalist discourse against the European Community, as illustrated here with respect to two major quality newspapers in the United Kingdom. The discussion has shown that resistance to membership was mostly driven by the perception that the United Kingdom could do well economically on its own; also, that the United Kingdom did not face the constraints on its ability to rebuild its economy and its military that Germany faced at the end of World War II. Europe was after all not born out of idealism, but out of the combined effects of fear of Germany and of the Soviet Union. The United Kingdom, a world power at the end of World War II, did not face German constraints or French fears. Therefore, it did not perceive the need to participate as a member in the creation of European institutions with a supranational component. Had the United Kingdom remained a world power, the issue of membership would not have been raised. It did not, however, and the divisions in the United Kingdom concerning membership in the European Community reflected the confusion resulting from having to process the dramatic changes that took place in the country during the 1950s and 1960s. When the United Kingdom finally became a member, it did so out of necessity and after a protracted negotiation process with France that made membership look more like a capitulation than a freely taken initiative. Moreover, the population of the United Kingdom carried into the European Community negative images of these institutions developed during years of internal political debate and difficult entry negotiations. These negative preconceptions would be the screen through which information about European integration would be filtered in coming years. Furthermore, they could be periodically mobilized and reproduced whenever the Conservative and Labour parties debated the European Communities or whenever there was conflict between the British government and the European Community.

Although the United Kingdom eventually became a member of the European Community, nothing compelled the British elites to adopt an integrationist program. The dramatic conditions that created the impetus toward European supranationalism at the end of World War II were no longer there, and other members of the European Community were not strongly pushing for it, at least until the mid-1980s. Consequently, except for short periods of Euro-enthusiasm that coincided with their switch from opposition to resolute acceptance of the United Kingdom's membership in the European Community, *The Economist* and *The New Statesman* tended to propose a decentralized cooperation project of European integration. This is more clearly the case in *The Economist* than in *The New Statesman*, which between 1985 and 1995 defended a decentralized integration project similar to that of *Die Zeit* in Germany. Thus, while *The Economist*'s articles, like the *FAZ*'s, expressed reluctance to accept EMU and political union, *The New Statesman*'s were more resolute about EMU and stressed the need to strengthen Europe with respect to the United States and the Soviet Union by building up its political and military dimensions.

With the accession of New Labour to power in the United Kingdom, however, *The New Statesman*'s enthusiasm toward EMU and political union lost much of its impetus, so that the positions of *The Economist* and *The New Statesman* were quite comparable by the end of 1997. One can only speculate about the reasons why New Labour began to waver on EMU as soon as it was elected. The press focused on the official explanation, which was that the economic cycles of the United Kingdom and the rest of the European Union were not in sync and that much needed to be done at the institutional level to prepare the country for membership; and on speculation that Labour did not want to risk alienating a large segment of the British population and thus jeopardize a future reelection. Both explanations are plausible, but our examination of *The Economist*'s and *The New Statesman*'s discussions about membership in the European Communities reveals that, all too often, problems of economic incompatibility between the United Kingdom and the European Community (e.g., Commonwealth, socialism) that were presented as insurmountable, seemingly lost all their significance as soon as *The Economist* or *The New Statesman* decided it was time to commit the United Kingdom to the European Community. The same applies to justifications for not pushing ahead with further European integration on the basis of lack of popular support. *The Economist* repeatedly used this argument during the 1946–97 period; yet when it finally supported membership in the European Community, it did try move public opinion to this view. At this point, however, it is of little importance whether *The Economist*'s and *The New Statesman*'s explanations for postponing the introduction of the euro are sufficient or not, or to perfectly understand the motivations underlying these explanations; what matters is that the political and media elites' lack of commitment to EMU directly and indirectly reinforced popular resistance toward European integration during the last period analyzed here: directly, because of the influence that elites exert on people's views; indirectly, because this lack of commitment to EMU opened the door to the re-expression in the United Kingdom of anti-European and nationalist themes that were developed by publications such as *The Economist* and *The New Statesman* during the membership debates of the 1960s and 1970s.

Spain: The Struggle to Count in the World Scene

After a cruel civil war (1936–39) and five years of dictatorship under General Franco, Spain emerged from World War II economically and demographically exhausted, and internationally ostracized. Against all odds, however, the dictatorial regime survived for three more decades, and at the time of Franco's death (1975) Spain was already a member of major international organizations (e.g., UN, OECD) and had joined the club of highly developed industrial nations. An explanation for this apparent miracle lies beyond the scope of this book, although factors such as the Cold War, American aid, economic liberalization measures in the late 1950s, remittances from emigrants to the rest of Europe, tourism, and foreign investment have often been highlighted.

One goal that Franco failed to achieve was Spain's admission as a member of the European Community. His patient pursuit of this goal, however, and the public debate and expectations that ensued, lie at the root of the mythifying of Europe in the Spanish collective consciousness and of the meaning that European integration acquired for the Spanish population. Editorial and opinion pieces in *Abc* (1946–97), *Cambio16* (1971–75), and *El País* (1976–97) reveal that in the Spanish public sphere European integration has mostly been understood in terms of Spain's membership in the European Community, and of ensuring that Spain be among the countries leading the process of integration. Underlying this understanding of European integration has been the desire to break with Spain's international isolation and irrelevance. One good example of this attitude was the announcement by a leading member of the Spanish Conservative Party, upon winning the 2000 general election, that the driving motivation behind the new government's foreign policy would be to reinforce Spain's international presence. He did not specify, however, what tangible benefits were expected from this greater international presence. The finding that op-ed articles in the newspapers examined in this chapter included a smaller number of descriptive statements about European integration and the European institutions than did the British and German is thus not surprising. Public debate about Spanish foreign policy with respect to Europe has been driven more by the desire to "be there" than by a systematic discussion of the merits and drawbacks of different integration projects. Despite this lack of definition, by 1997 one could detect two projects of European integration in the Spanish press that mirrored, in an exaggerated way, the contrasts already examined between the *FAZ* and *Die*

Zeit in Germany: the decentralized cooperation project of *Abc*, and the decentralized integration project of *El País*.

Whereas practical issues guided the German and British press's orientation toward European unification, more ideological and philosophical concerns guided op-ed articles published immediately after World War II in the newspaper *Abc*.[31] Consistent with one of the main tenets of Franco's ideology, the main justification for European integration offered in *Abc* was the fight against communism, a fight that was conceived as much in ideological as in military terms. From early on, however, *Abc*'s op-ed articles also contained some anti-American rhetoric and called for a strong Europe vis-à-vis both the United States and the Soviet Union. According to these articles, only by becoming stronger could Europe aspire to defend the essential and unifying element of its culture, Christian values, from the onslaught of both socialism and capitalist materialism, whose influence had been eroding Europe's spiritual foundation since the French Revolution:

> Europe's mission consists of two successive tasks, although not necessarily immediate. The first is the creation of universally valuable works and the discovery of all the valuable aspects of human creation, including those from outside Europe.... The second and final task of Europe's mission is that of offering to God, lucidly and intentionally, the truth and value of all human creations.
> (Pedro Laín Entralgo, "Misión de Europa," *Abc*, June 12, 1947)

> Nobody is unaware that the great enemy of a united and free Europe is found in the Kremlin. But one must not forget that Communism usually sneaks into Power by taking advantage of the freedom of the press, universal suffrage, and the principles of the inorganic [*sic*] democracy. There lies the great weakness of Europe. One does not want evil, but loves and cares for the things that produce it. The exemplar character of our war of Liberation is that one fought against Communism with military means and against the Republic, revolutionary democracy, suffrage, and the parties, and all the things that drove us toward Communism, with a quill. The unity of Europe will never be forged on the principles of the French Revolution, but rather, on those of Christianity.
> (L. M. Ansón, "El Porvenir de Europa," *Abc*, July 15, 1960)

The defense of Christian values was the dominant but not the only justification provided in *Abc* for supporting European integration. Other articles reflected on Europe's economic and military prostration and explained it with respect to the obsolescence of the sovereignty principle. Finally, some articles, published as early as the mid-1950s and representing liberal views, advocated European unification and Spain's participation in these efforts on economic grounds, pointing out the small size of European national states.[32] Finally, *Abc*'s op-ed articles recounted Spain's past contributions to European civilization, and conveyed the expectation that

Spain would contribute significantly toward the goal of European unification:

> We, as Spaniards, are unpleasantly surprised and annoyed upon noticing that our collaboration in this task [European unification] is not invited; they do not even ask us to express our opinion. There is passion there, but also blindness. Spain, western nation, the fourth in Europe from a demographic viewpoint and in terms of its potential, and the oldest constituted nation within western civilization, to which it adhered twenty centuries ago, is fully entitled to be taken into account.... Any attempt to unify Europe in which Spain is not present will lack viability: it will be condemned to failure.
> (Alfredo Kindelán, "Sin España no habrá una Europa eficaz," *Abc*, October 19, 1956)[33]

This expectation, which betrayed a broader aspiration to see Spain play a leading role in the international community, rested on an understanding of European unification as a "moral crusade" against communism. Rather than focus on the cultural similarities between European nations, this interpretation emphasized a shared unity of purpose as the main justification for efforts toward European unification. The philosophical and speculative tone, and the content of early *Abc* op-ed articles, reflected Spain's international isolation in the immediate post–World War II years and the Franco regime's desire to break this isolation. It also followed in a tradition dating back to the nineteenth-century debates between those favorable to linking Spain with the dominant European political and intellectual currents and those favorable to maintaining Spain's idiosyncrasy. These debates regained new intensity in the twentieth century, with the opposition between "Casticistas" and Europeanists, the former more focused on discovering and developing Spain's essence (e.g., the later-period Unamuno) and the latter more interested in strengthening the ties with Europe (e.g., Ortega y Gasset). The interesting turn in *Abc*'s invocation of the concept of "unity of purpose" is that it blended a Europeanist aspiration, participating in a common project with other European countries, with a "Casticista" emphasis on the singularity of the different European nations.[34]

Despite the peculiarity of the pro-European message, the important fact was that public opinion was already told at this early stage that Spain was European and that the government intended to participate in unification efforts in Europe. Moreover, to justify this aspiration and enhance the value of Spain's decision, Europe's image was embellished and mythified. For instance, it was often portrayed as the cradle of rationality, liberty, and creativity:

> Here are in condensed form the three flagships of Europe, which summarize its outstanding qualities: an orderly and tolerant way of living, within the limits of reason; a will to preserve the arts, that is, the noblest spiritual traditions; and, fi-

nally, the breeding of inventions, a faculty for which it still retains the lead, even though these inventions are often put to the service of geographical regions with neither sense for living together nor will to tradition.

(J. M. de Cossío, "Fe en Europa," *Abc*, January 16, 1951)[35]

Once European unification became a reality, however, contributors to *Abc*'s op-ed pages had to confront the fact that Spain was not a democracy and was thus not allowed to become a member of the nascent European organizations. Franco himself tried to distract the population from focusing on the European Communities, by pointing out in an interview that strengthening ties with Europe did not necessarily mean becoming a member of the European Communities; he commented on the fact that being a member of the Organization for Economic Cooperation and Development (OECD) was actually more important for Spain:

> Modern life no longer allows for nations to remain isolated. They need to trade abroad and exchange their products.... Our main market is the European one, and therefore every development in this area affects us directly.... The OECD, which includes the main European nations, and the Common Market, which only concerns six among them, are two different things. The case for the OECD is clear, and we advance in this direction. As for the Common Market, it is still too soon to make any pronouncement. At any rate, there is a trend and an evolution among the peoples of Europe in which we must participate, keeping an eye on our interests, about which there is total unanimity.
>
> (*Abc*, interview published on April 30, 1959)

Franco's apparent coolness about the subject of membership in the Common Market was soon contradicted by his actions, when on February 9, 1962 his Foreign Affairs Minister, Castiella, submitted a letter to the European Communities with a proposal to begin entry negotiations.[36] The letter, of course, was not answered, thus placing Spain in the position of a suitor who has been rejected by the object of his affection.

If the goal was to break the country's isolation and not be left behind, Spain had even fewer options than did the United Kingdom, which had already applied for membership. Its sentimental ties with Latin America were at least as strong as, if not stronger than, those of the United Kingdom with the Commonwealth, but not so much its economic and institutional ties. Although occasional articles discussed the possibility that Spain concentrate on Latin America and the Arab world, this alternative was never followed seriously. Another contrast between Spain and the United Kingdom was that the democracy prerequisite was not negotiable. The Treaty of Rome was quite clear about allowing only democratic countries to be admitted to the European Communities. The consequence of this obstacle to Spanish membership and of the lack of realistic alternatives was that the problem of Spain's admission to the European Communities inevitably triggered a public debate, cautious but nonetheless open, about the costs of authoritarian rule. Although the dominant reaction in *Abc* was to attack De Gaulle and to stress the commonalities between the Spanish and the British situations, some authors began to call for political reforms or to subtly comment on the singularity of Spain's political arrangements compared to those of other European countries:

> In all the countries that belong to the Common Market or EFTA—with one single exception—there are political parties, open parliament, freedom of expression, a non-confessional state, and free trade unions. That is, a system that rests on an individualist—not means-based, not family-based—form of democracy ... today's Europe rests on free newspapers, free weeklies, uncensored books, on a radio and a TV that—while state-owned—maintain a balance between the different political tendencies.... [F]rom the Pyrenees to Finland, fourteen countries live in and are governed by roughly comparable political regimes. (J. M. de Areilza, "La primera década," *Abc*, July 13, 1967)

Spain's relationship with the European Community monopolized *Abc*'s discussions about European integration in the period between 1967 and 1975, the year of Franco's death. The conservative newspaper's op-ed articles stressed how crucial it was for Spain's survival to secure at least a trade association with the European Community. In fact, the government quite skillfully sold to the Spanish population the signing of a Preferential Trade Agreement with the EEC in 1970, which it presented as a victory and a first step toward membership. *Abc*'s op-ed articles during this period reflected a broad range of reactions to the European Community's resolute refusal to consider Spain's application for membership. Some articles expressed nationalist outrage against the European Community's stance and argued that membership was actually not needed, since the Preferential Treaty was actually quite beneficial to Spain. Other voices represented in the newspaper called for minor political reforms, with the expectation that they would be sufficient to secure membership. Finally, some contributors called for a true reform of political institutions, to transform Spain into a democracy.

In the context of a lack of alternatives to membership, the transformation of the negotiations with the European Community into a debate about democracy had the unintended consequence of raising the salience and value of membership. On the one hand, the Franco regime persisted in its attempts to negotiate membership in order to silence those who claimed that democratic institutions were a precondition for entry; on the other hand, the pro-democracy movement of opposition to Franco stressed the contrast between a democratic Europe and a nondemocratic Spain. In fact, even if some of the opposition's members were more interested in instrumentalizing the entry negotiations toward their democratic goals than they were in membership, the end result of this instrumentalization was to further idealize the European Community.

Another effect of the debate over democracy that also contributed to mythifying Europe was that it precipitated a further debate about what it means to be European. It goes without saying that the Europeanists had long before won their secular debate against the "Españolistas" or "Casticistas"; they had done so from the moment that Franco began his attempts to establish diplomatic and economic relations with the rest of Europe. The debate that raged in the late 1960s and early 1970s was instead a debate about the definition and appropriation of the concept of "Europeanness." There were, on the one hand, those who claimed that to be European meant to adhere to democratic values, and, on the other hand, those who insisted that to be European had nothing to do with one's political values, or with a country's political system.[37]

These two debates were also central to discussions about European integration in the center-left weekly *Cambio16* in the period 1972–75. Moreover, the examination of its editorials reveals the efforts by members of Spain's opposition to Franco to stereotype the political right and left as representing isolationism and openness respectively; also, to portray Spanish history since King Phillip II as dominated by an isolationist and traditionalist mentality that the modern Spanish democratic left was now set to subvert. In sum, the messages transmitted by the democratic opposition were that to be leftist meant to be European and to be European meant to be open to foreign influence, to be modern, and to be democratic. At the same time, Spain's membership in the European Community came to symbolize breaking with the nondemocratic, traditionalist, and isolationist past; it meant to become modern, open, and democratic, regardless of its immediate economic impact.

Because of the intensity of the debate described above, op-ed articles in *Abc* and *Cambio16* devoted little space to discussing where the European Community was going, why it was needed, and how it functioned. The few comments that were made portrayed Europe as an emergent powerful bloc between the United States and the USSR. This image of Europe of course added further urgency to the removal of political obstacles to Spain's membership. Therefore, when Franco died in 1975, and Spain became a democracy, many thought that entry into the European Community was imminent. They were soon disappointed, however, when they learned that the political obstacles were only the tip of the iceberg, and that economic factors were likely to complicate the entry negotiations. Spanish agriculture was the main stumbling block, because of its competitiveness in European markets, its large role in the Spanish economy, and the disputes about CAP and budget reform that were paralyzing the functioning of the European Community. The resolution of these problems dragged on for ten years and was the focus of most newspaper discussions about the European Community. During this period, membership in the European Community acquired a new symbolic role, that of sanctioning Spain's democratic credentials and its status as a modern, economically advanced society. In *Abc*, the reaction to the long duration of the negotiations was one of pessimism. European institutions and the unification projects were discussed in generally critical terms, and Europeans were portrayed as holding age-old animosities toward Spain:

> The Europe of the Communities, the one that recently undertook the unifying task, by building on efforts to overcome a deep crisis through the pooling and balancing of resources and economic, technical, demographic, ideological, and defensive means, carried within it, hidden in its well armored frame, a disdainful sentiment toward everything Spanish.
> (J. M. Alfaro, "Los desdenes de Europa," *Abc*, March 9, 1978)

Proudly, however, contributors to *Abc* vowed not to give up the negotiations or turn their backs on Europe. Spain, they said, has a right to be part of Europe, because it is European and because of its immense contributions to European civilization. Moreover, they stressed how important membership in the European Community was for Spain's modernization and, after the attempted coup of 1981, for the consolidation of democracy. In this context, *Abc*'s op-ed articles hardly discussed European unification per se. At most, they indicated support for the integration efforts, which they presented as a way to strengthen Europe, or supported reforms adopted by the European Community, such as the extension of majority voting in the decision-making process.

Instead of debating the contours of European unification, *Abc*'s op-ed articles continued to dramatize the struggle between left and right about what it means to be European. The newspaper defended the view that Spain had always been European and opposed this view to that of the left, which equated being European with identification with the values of progressive European forces and with membership in the European Communities. This criticism of the Spanish left was extended to what contributors to *Abc* presented as the ruling Socialist Party's careless efforts to rush Spain into the EEC. In their view, a poorly negotiated Accession Treaty would be worse than the extension of the 1970 Preferential Trade Agreement.

The content of discussions about European integration in the newly founded (1976) newspaper *El País* was not very different from that in *Abc*'s. Like *Abc*, *El País* decried the duration of the negotiations and France's delaying tactics; also, it emphasized how important it was for Spain's modernization and democratic stability to become a member of the European Community. Spain's modernization and democratic stability arguments in fact weighed more in the decision to support membership than did economic ones, for time and again op-ed articles stressed that in the short term Spain would find it hard to compete in a borderless market. Finally, like *Abc*, *El País* spent little space discussing the direction of European integration. Its editorials conveyed support for a federal Europe, including a strengthened European Parliament, but few additional details were offered. The few contrasts between *Abc* and *El País* were more a matter of style than content. For instance, *El País*'s reaction to the long duration of the negotiations was also one of impatience and defiance, but the tone tended to be less nationalistic.[38] Also, *El País* contributed to the construction of pro-European attitudes as a project of the left, which it contrasted to the isolationist and anti-European project of the right:

> In Spain, Europeanist feeling has generally been part of an endless and continuous civil war, cold or hot, latent or overt. One part of the population has always understood that in Europe, taken as a whole, ideas had been developed and proposals for societal transformation had been made that were beneficial to the entire population, and that through these ideas—about culture, education, equality of rights—one entered a stage of wealth distribution, of accumulation of technical, scientific, and economic benefits, in which one needed to participate. Meanwhile, another part of the population took Spain for a private estate that was defended, behind barbed wire and rifles, through traditional ideologies, hierarchical social structures, and truths that did not need to be proven.
> ("Europa en Madrid," *El País*, June 21, 1981)

Abc's and *El País*'s discussions about European integration became more focused on the project itself, and their overall approach began to differ, during the period of institutional reform of the EC that began upon Spain's and Portugal's accession in 1986. Between 1986 and 1997, *Abc*'s op-ed articles tended to be critical of the European Community and its successor, the European Union (e.g., for its handling of the Bosnian crisis and EMU), and approached European integration exclusively from the perspective of Spain's national interests. The main principles of this approach were to resist integration when it damaged Spain's short-term national interests and not to let Spain lag behind if other countries moved ahead with further integration plans. Thus, *Abc* stressed the need to maintain Spain's voting power in the EU in the face of enlargement, pushed for a delay of or a giving up of EMU, resisted the idea of a two-speed Europe in which Spain would be pushed into the back seat, opposed encroachment of the European Parliament on Spain's sovereignty, and was in favor of cooperation on foreign policy and defense matters. *Abc* also presented the European Union as an arena where Spain could prove its worth. Thus, when Spain came to preside over the Council of Ministers, an editorial emphasized that this was an opportunity for Spain to demonstrate its management skills and its ability to complete the agenda that lay before the Council; nothing was said about the content of this agenda or about Spain shaping that agenda. The same concern about Spain's status was apparent in the newspaper's criticism of Spain's dependence on Structural Funds from the European Union, which, in its view, transmitted the image of a country that is always begging.

In contrast with *Abc*, *El País*'s op-ed articles during this period paid much more attention to the institutional aspects of European integration. The project outlined and advocated in these articles was in fact similar to *Die Zeit*'s and *The New Statesman*'s (before New Labour). The contributors to *El País* thus called for a political and cohesive Europe, for EMU, and for a strengthening of the power of the European Parliament. Its ultimate goal was the creation of a Social Europe.[39]

Like *Abc*'s, however, *El País*'s approach to European integration was also guided by a desire to defend Spain's national interests. Contributors to *El País* made it clear that part of the attraction of membership in the European Union was that it would ensure a stronger voice for Spain in international affairs and that it would be a good source of economic assistance. The newspaper's ambivalence toward enlargement to Central and Eastern Europe, which would diminish Spain's role in the decision-making process and probably mean a reduction in the cohesion funds it receives from the European Union, is a case in point. Yet, *El País*'s support for further European integration went beyond the simple defense of national interests found in *Abc*. This is illustrated by the contrast in the two newspapers' views on EMU. While contributors to *Abc* repeatedly asked for a postponement and even shelving of EMU, *El País* insisted on accelerating the process and on including the largest number of countries possible. Its position, like *Die Zeit*'s, was that the expected contributions of European unification to peace and to addressing the problems of globalization justified allowing political considerations to take precedence over economic ones.

In his speech to the Library of Congress of February 24, 2000, King Juan Carlos I of Spain made the following remark:

> In this new international context, Spain looks with special interest towards Europe and the Atlantic. After years of absence, Spain is once more actively involved in the political life of Europe. Accession to the European Union constituted a watershed in the recent history of my country. Within a short time, Spaniards made an exceptional effort to adapt their entire economic, industrial, and even social structures to the regulations of the new environment where we have chosen to live. We can say, and I as a Spaniard am proud to do so, that this effort has been rewarded by considerable success. Spain today is an open and modern country, with a plural, highly motivated and thriving society, which faces the future with optimism and aims to play a leading role in the community of developed nations.[40]

This excerpt from King Juan Carlos's speech perfectly captures the meaning of European integration and the European Union as transmitted by op-ed articles published in *Abc*, *Cambio16*, and *El País* since the late 1940s. Consistent with the views of Spanish political elites during this period, contributors to these newspapers have never doubted that Spain's economic survival required becoming a member of the post–World War II European institutions. Consequently, Spaniards were from very early on exposed to positive images of European integration. Moreover, these positive images were reinforced by the 1960s political debates between advocates and opponents of Franco's dictatorship about the need to democratize Spain and the meaning of being European. These debates added new meaning to membership in the European Community: it came to represent not only an economic necessity, but also the means to break with Spain's secular isolation and to modernize the country. Finally, as centrist and socialist democratic governments negotiated entry in the European Community, membership came to acquire yet another meaning, which was that of sanctioning the political and economic transformations that Spain had experienced since the death of Franco.

The centrality that the goal of membership has occupied in public discussions of European integration in Spain has detracted from the formulation and debate of a clear unification project. The message conveyed in *Abc*'s and *El País*'s op-ed articles is that Spain should always keep up with those countries setting the pace, regardless of the direction. Only in recent years have *Abc* and *El País* begun to develop clearly distinct approaches to integration. While *Abc*'s approach has prioritized national interests and the protection of the country's sovereignty, *El País* has expressed more favorable views toward a decentralized integration project.

Summary

For more than fifty years, elite journalists in Germany, the United Kingdom, and Spain have reflected on European integration, thus providing the population with understandings about what it means, how European institutions work, and where Europe is headed. This chapter has revealed that the frames that differentiate British, German, and Spanish representations of European integration and the European Union have existed since the discussion began. Also, it has also shown that despite the existence of a strong similarity between the themes invoked by elite journalists and those present in the rest of the population, there are significant contrasts that demonstrate that ordinary citizens are not just passive recipients of messages publicized by these elite journalists. Part of the similarity between the images of European integration transmitted by elite journalists and those observed among the general population may simply reflect that all are exposed to the same type of information. In fact, many respondents probably get only indirect access or no access at all to the elite journalists' discourse on European integration.

When discussing contrasts in the way German, British, and Spanish respondents portray European integration and their country's membership in the European Union, I have shown that Germans distinguish themselves by their greater emphasis on foreign labor competition and a concern about other countries' misgivings toward Germany; also, that the Spaniards distinguish themselves by their focus on the roles that membership in the European Union plays for Spain's modernization and toward breaking with Spain's traditional isolation; and that Britons distinguish themselves by their refusal to surrender sovereignty and fears that the United Kingdom's identity would be eroded as part of the European Union. In chapter 3, I also showed that a concern about identity is what best differentiates those who favor a decentralized cooperation model of integration from those who lean toward a centralized integration model of integration. Finally, in this chapter I have argued that contrasts between German, British, and Spanish frames on European integration have a long history.

This chapter has discussed the historical and political context within which these frames developed and the dilemmas faced by elite journalists when confronting European integration and the issue of membership in the European Union. What it does not tell us is why some ways of conceptualizing the European integration process became more prevalent than others, or why basic political decisions such as becoming a member of the European Union became a dilemma and a source of deep introspection, as in the British case. The story is still incomplete because it neglects the roles that these countries' political cultures have played in creating the differences in attitudes. Also, it does not completely explain why certain issues became so central in the elite journalists' approach toward European integration: in the United Kingdom, sovereignty; in Spain, isolation and modernization; and in Germany, reassuring Europe about Germany's intentions. Undoubtedly, West German elite journalists emphasized other countries' concerns regarding Germany's intentions with good political reasons. Conservative British elite journalists, however, could have exclusively stressed economic problems related to the Commonwealth, and leftist British elite journalists could have exclusively stressed the incompatibility between a socialist United Kingdom and a more conservative EEC. Also, the Spanish elite journalists could have exclusively stressed the role that membership in the European Communities would play in Spain's economic development and in anchoring Spain to a community of democratic countries.

The need to move beyond these frames on European integration into a discussion of political culture is best illustrated by the contrast between West Germany and East Germany. As I have discussed, one of the most puzzling findings in this investigation is the fact that the respondents in Oststadt hardly referred to other countries' concerns about Germany when discussing European integration, even though this was a widely discussed theme in West Germany in general and in West Germany's quality press in particular during the post-reunification years. In this chapter, I have concluded that the most promising explanation for this anomaly is that in the immediate years after reunification, in the context of a delegitimized East German public sphere and a somewhat alien West German public sphere, East Germans forged their views of European unification by relying on factual information reported in the print media and on TV, and on a way of seeing largely formed under socialism. This view excluded, as I show in chapter 7, a sense of guilt vis-à-vis other European countries or a sense of pressure to act in a way that would not raise suspicions or fears. The next chapters explore some of the broader cultural preoccupations within which national discourses about European integration were developed in the United Kingdom, Germany, and Spain.

Part II

NATIONAL CULTURES AND FRAMES ON EUROPEAN INTEGRATION

Five

Spain: Europe as a Mirror with Two Reflections

> One of Spain's problems is that changes that take place in Europe have always arrived late. If we are inside [the European Union] changes will take place at the same speed, or at least will not arrive so late.
>
> The outcome of the nurturing of isolation and the subpyrenaic singularizing fact has been a discrepancy between the history of Spain and that of many European countries. The failure to catch the train of industrialization, the bloodshed of our civil wars, and the lack of tolerance expressed in the Celti-berian excesses were the tangible fruit of the isolationist phenomenon.
>
> It has been my goal to develop more extensively the idea that ... Spain's mental misery originates in the isolation in which a whole way of doing things, guided by inquisitorial protectionism, puts us, one that strangled at birth the internal ["Castiza"] Reformation and blocked entry to the European one ... ; that only by opening our windows to European winds, imbibing the continental environment, trusting that we will not lose our personality by doing this, Europeanizing ourselves in order to make Spain, and immerging in people, will we regenerate this moral desert.

THREE DIFFERENT people, three different social actors, three different periods, but yet the same message: Spain needs to break a long period of isolation in order to join and catch up with Europe. The first quote comes from one of my respondents, a mid-level civil servant working for the police department in the Catalan city of Catadell. A middle-aged high-school graduate and regular newspaper reader, he was very informed about the European Union but expressed little interest in it and in politics in general. The second quote comes from an op-ed piece published in 1972 in the newspaper *Abc* by Federico Silva, a respected moderate liberal who was talked about as potential prime minister during the early months of the democratic transition but then faded from the political scene.[1] In this piece, Silva called for cosmetic changes to the Francoist constitution that would give Spain a more democratic profile and thus enable it to become a member of the EEC just as the United Kingdom was about to do. The third quote comes from Miguel de Unamuno, a leading member of the literary and intellectual movement known as the "Generación del 98" that contributed greatly to shaping the cultural and political landscape of twentieth-century Spain. The words come at the end of a long essay entitled "En torno al casticismo," published in 1895, in which Unamuno decried Spain's long decline, diagnosed its causes, and proposed the Europeanization of Spain as a remedy.[2] Later in his life, Unamuno would with the same self-assuredness reverse his views about the need to Europeanize Spain and proclaim, "let them invent!" ("them" meaning "the rest of Europe"), but that is another story. What matters here is that the idea of "rejoining" Europe, both in a cultural and political sense, has been a recurrent and influential theme in Spain during the twentieth century. When ordinary citizens or elite journalists justify their support for Spain's membership in the European Union with the argument that Spain needs to end its isolation with respect to Europe in order to modernize, they are expressing a general preoccupation with Spain's isolation and modernization among the leading segments of Spanish society in the second half of the century that predates the European Union itself.

The respondents from Quijotón and Catadell who mentioned the topics of isolation and modernization were better informed than were the rest of the respondents: whereas 70% of those who did not mention these topics (23) were quite or very informed, 89% of those who did (28) were. The latter conceived modernization and the end of isolation from various angles, which can be traced to two different discursive and historical origins. The great majority of them understood modernization narrowly, as economic modernization and as catching up economically with leading European countries. Some in this group saw membership in the European Union as an incentive to rationalize organizational and production practices following the European model:

> Let's take the meat industry. One used to kill the pig, chop it, and ship it automatically from Catadell to the Barcelona or whichever market. Now, they've had to invest large sums in freezing facilities. They must kill the pig, place it in these facilities, leave it there—I believe six or seven hours at a specific temperature—and then chop it, and all this because of European Union norms. If they want to stay in business, they have to do it. And they do it quite happily!
> (84 Catadell, representative of party Convergencia I Unió)

> I'd like to be part of a better planned, more rationalized environment. In this sense, Germany can teach us a lot in terms of discipline, to the benefit of the Spanish economy.
> (73 Catadell, representative of the Union Comisiones Obreras)

Other respondents in this group, however, expected modernization to affect not only the economy but also all sectors of society and culture. A leading representative of Catadell's Chamber of Commerce referred, for instance, to the prospects of an overall change in mind-frame or, as he put it, the "Europeanization" of Spain. Another respondent, member of the editorial board of Catadell's local newspaper, expressed satisfaction at the fact that membership in the European Union had helped to modernize the state and Spain's armed forces. Yet another respondent, a representative of the party Izquierda Unida's Quijotón branch, was confident that membership in the European Union was necessary in order to "promote the modernization of the country," to insert Spain in a "democratic dynamic with no return," and "to end the narrow-mindedness prevailing in the country until recently, and still visible in many small localities."

References to isolation equally reflected two distinct understandings. Some respondents, a minority, invoked their own experiences and welcomed the fact that membership means no longer to feel, be treated, or be seen as different from other Europeans as was the case during Franco. For instance, because of membership in the European Union, said one respondent, Spaniards were no longer treated with suspicion and disrespect when trying to cross the border to France. Also, as another respondent said, membership has helped Spaniards to overcome the inferiority complex that they felt toward European tourists who benefited from favorable exchange rates when traveling to Spain, regardless of their social background. For these and other respondents, not being isolated meant achieving equal status with other Europeans. The majority of those who mentioned the topic of isolation, however, simply thought that isolation had had catastrophic consequences for Spain. These respondents traced Spain's isolation from Europe variously to the Franco regime, the nineteenth century, or even the Counter-Reformation.

The analysis of arguments in newspaper op-ed articles also reveals differences in the way modernization and isolation have been conceived. Modernization has been understood either in narrow terms as economic modernization, or in broader terms as including both political and cultural modernization. Meanwhile, arguments referring to isolation have sometimes invoked narrow economic reasons but more often expressed a general rejection of what was portrayed as a long tradition of political and cultural isolation from Europe with disastrous consequences for Spain.

In general terms, one can therefore distinguish between respondents and elite journalists who use the modernization and isolation arguments in an instrumental-economic fashion and those who use them in order to position themselves ideologically. For the former, membership in the European Union is necessary to solve particular economic or practical problems that Spain would not be able to solve if it stayed outside the European Union. For the latter, membership in the European Union means embracing a series of ideas attributed to Europe—thus referred to as "European"—and positively evaluated as "modern," and rejecting another set of ideas, negatively evaluated as "traditional" and perceived as having characterized Spain over the past few centuries.

As I show in the rest of this section, justification of Spain's membership in the European Union in terms of the virtues of breaking with isolation and the European Union's expected contribution to Spain's modernization is generally rooted in a desire to narrow the economic gap between Spain and the wealthiest European countries, a desire intensified by memories of the miserable conditions of the post–Civil War period and by the rapid economic growth of the 1960s. At the same time, the conceptualization of this project by many respondents and elite journalists as an "Europeanization" project, as a progressive break with a traditional and autarkic Spain, best exemplified by the Franco regime, reflects the gradual ascendancy of a liberal narrative of Spain's history that has been told and retold throughout the twentieth century.

Franco's Authoritarian Modernization Project

The quests for prestige, modernization, and isolation have certainly been major facts of Spain's contemporary history. The channeling of these aspirations through participation in the process of European unification required, foremost of all, discarding alternative routes and their associated supranational identity projects that had been debated in the first third of the twentieth century. These alternative routes reflected a general phenomenon throughout Europe: the continental European states' attempt to compete both economically and politically with the British Empire, through maintaining or developing their own overseas empires or, at least, privileged economic spaces bound together by an imagined commonality of culture. Spain, almost irrelevant to begin with, was out of the race before it could pick up steam, as it lost its last overseas colonies in Cuba and the Philippines in 1898 and proved incapable of getting a foothold in Africa in the following years. Repeated failures did not prevent Spanish intellectuals and politicians from dreaming up a geographical space dominated by Spain, if not politically or economically, at least culturally. This space was supposed to encompass all the Spanish-speaking world, and the values that were to preside over it were Christian values, of which Spain was seen as the most ardent historical representative. It was known as the Hispanidad, formally celebrated every October 12 as the Día de la Raza, and its most passionate exposition was Ramiro de Maeztu's *En Defensa de la Hispanidad*.[3] At the end of World War II, however, the Hispanidad as cultural surrogate of a long-lost empire and the even less ambitious non-European project of an inward-looking and autarkic Spain lay moribund. In this context, the route through Europe toward modernization was gradually perceived as the only alternative.

In 1945 the country was bankrupt and internationally isolated. The catastrophic economic, demographic, and cultural consequences of the 1936–39 civil war, the period of repression that immediately followed Franco's victory, and the ill-fated policy of supporting the Axis forces under the guise of neutrality had turned Spain into a wasteland. Furthermore, the Allies initially bet on an economic and political blockade of Spain as a means to force Franco out of power. Franco's suicidal autarkic economic policy, dating back to 1939[4] and intensified because of the blockade, simply made things worse for the Spanish economy.

By the late 1940s, however, the Allies' gave up their inefficient and halfhearted blockade, since they realized that it was not working to oust Franco from power and instead was hurting the Spanish population. Furthermore, the beginnings of the Cold War made the United States uneasy about the revolutionary potential of the Spanish situation at the same time that the geopolitical value of Spain for Western defense increased. Thus, the new decade witnessed a series of diplomatic steps aimed at facilitating Spain's insertion in the international scene,[5] just as Franco gradually sacrificed his autarkic economic policy, made governmental changes in a more liberal direction, and exploited his achievements in the international arena for domestic purposes.

As the European Steel and Coal Community (ECSC) got under way in 1951, Spain was thus beginning to break free from the externally and self-imposed economic and diplomatic isolation of the 1940s. But the diplomatic and economic challenges ahead were daunting. In the diplomatic sphere, Spain had missed out on some milestones of the reconstruction of Europe: the creation of the Council of Europe and the signing of the Atlantic Treaty in 1948, the Marshall Plan, the Organization for European Economic Cooperation (OEEC) created to administer the Marshall Plan funds, and the creation of the ECSC. Furthermore, although the West was ready to tolerate Franco, it refused to treat Spain as an equal for as long as it would remain a dictatorship. Therefore, the door to both NATO and the European Communities stayed shut until the end of Franco's regime. On the economic front, despite the resumption and gradual acceleration of growth as the decade advanced, Spain remained in a state of ruin, with the national income below prewar levels until about 1957. In fact, the economic and cultural gap with the rest of Western Europe continued to increase during this decade.

Whereas the 1950s represented a partial end to Spain's international isolation and the gradual abandonment of economic autarky, the 1960s witnessed an extremely rapid economic, social, and cultural transformation.[6] Two key policy developments in this period were the "Plan de Estabilización" (Stabilization Plan) and the "Planes de Desarrollo" (Development Plans). The former, aimed at reining in inflation and implementing reforms recommended by the IMF and the OEEC, created an appropriate institutional context for economic development. The latter, designed and implemented by the "Tecnócratas," a very influential and highly competent political clique tied to the Opus Dei Catholic religious organization, were the instrument that the government used to stir this economic development. The 1960s were characterized by the transition from an agrarian to an industry- and service-based economy, the development of a broad middle class, the depopulation of the countryside, the emigration of millions of workers to other countries of Western Europe, the arrival of millions of tourists, secularization, and the erosion of traditional values regarding sex and the family. These transformations were followed by growing labor and university unrest, which was met with a combination of repression and some political reform toward more freedom of expression and the democratic representation of workers' and students' interests.

In the half-decade preceding the end of the dictatorship, these transformations continued, at the same time that Franco, physically and intellectually incapacitated, revealed himself unable to steer a coherent political course, alternating stepped-up repression with timid proposals for the legalization of political associations. These years signaled the entry of the Basque separatist organization ETA onto the political scene, heralded by their assassination of Franco's most trusted advisor and likely successor, Vice President Carrero Blanco, in December 1973. Franco reacted to challenges to the dictatorial regime by ETA and other military organizations with predictable violence, which culminated in the executions of September 1975, two months before his death.

It is impossible in only a few pages to thoroughly examine Spanish political culture in the post–World War II period.[7] One can, however, outline some of its elements in order to understand the rhetorical use of arguments about prestige, isolation, and modernization in today's discourse about European integration. The fact that Spain was a dictatorship for most of this period recommends a distinction between official culture and oppositional culture. The official and oppositional political cultures of this period of Spanish history used the Civil War and the Franco regime as their main referents. The official version was freely expressed during the entire period, whereas the opposition led a clandestine existence until the mid-to-late-1950s and began to seriously challenge official culture only in the late 1960s, coinciding with the relaxation of the dictatorial regime's repression mechanisms.

The topics of prestige, economic modernization, and isolation that, as shown in previous chapters, distinguish Spanish from German and British popular and public discourse on European integration, played a salient role in the Francoist official narrative. The three topics were in fact strongly interrelated: Spain's integration in the international market was presented as necessary to attain economic modernization; Spain's integration in the international political arena and economic modernization were presented as contributing to Spain's prestige; and Spain's prestige, "earned by its unwavering anti-communist stance," played a role in its access to international markets and international organizations. One gets a glimpse of the salient role of these three themes through examination of Franco's speeches, secondary school history textbooks, and winners of the National Literature Prize during the dictatorship.

One very important feature of Francoist official discourse was its mistrust of foreign countries and its rejection of what were referred to as "foreign ideas"—"foreign" because they went against the hegemonic ideology and were viewed as inappropriate or dangerous for Spain. When history textbooks of this period discussed the political conflict between liberals and defenders of the Old Regime in the nineteenth century, they portrayed it as one between "followers of the principles of the French Revolution" set on "forcing these principles upon Spain," and "Traditional, Catholic, and Monarchic Spain" (notice the use of the impersonal form here) respectively;[8] when the Second Republic was criticized, it was described as "anti-Spanish";[9] and when Franco justified his system of government, he reminded Spaniards about the "sad and disastrous consequences that the reliance on foreign doctrines in order to solve problems has had for Spain,"[10] referring to both liberal and communist ideas.

Of all the destructive foreign ideas that, according to Francoist discourse, threatened to slowly erode Spain's spiritual foundations, liberalism and communism received privileged attention.[11] Against political liberalism, Franco proposed an organic form of democracy, which he presented as "more modern" and "adaptable," that enshrined the principles of hierarchy, order, and discipline,[12] against the dehumanizing effects of economic liberalism and the leveling effects of communism, Franco proposed a capitalist system with strong state intervention to attain both economic and social goals.[13] Emphasis on the pitfalls of liberalism peaked in the 1940s and was still significant in the 1950s; in this decade, however, the communist threat became the main target of Franco's invectives; later on, direct disquisitions on communism would slowly give way to general references to "the enemies of Spain" and "foreign influences" as responsible for internal and external mobilization against the dictatorship.

Francoist mistrust and dislike of anything defined as "foreign" combined with an obsession with the deeply engrained hostility toward Spain attributed to foreigners and foreign countries. Thus, official discourse saw anti-Spanish plots in every revolutionary episode before the Civil War, in demonstrations of opposition to Franco, and in foreign condemnations of the Franco regime. One year before his death, as the movement of opposition to the dictatorship both inside and outside of Spain rekindled its efforts, Franco was still convinced that it was nothing but a "foreign" conspiracy:

> I know that we still suffer, even as our Truth and our Reasons ["Razones"] gain acceptance, from the effects of a secular foreign hostility, fed by those who systematically refuse to acknowledge what they see and those who do not pardon us for our progress and our peace.[14]

This "secular" hostility was often presented as a continuation of the "Black Legend" about Spain.[15] In *El otro árbol de Guernica* by Luis de Castresana, winner of the 1967 National Literature Prize, this theme played a central role. The book tells the story of a group of Basque children, from Republican families, who are sent to Belgium during the Spanish Civil War and return at war's end. In a fairly sentimental and patriotic tone, it describes the homesickness experienced by the children and their efforts to assimilate to a foreign culture while retaining their Spanish identity. The message of the story is that children are better able to see the deep unity of the Spaniards, which adults have forgotten. The children are portrayed as representing the only hope that Spain might live again in peace. More significantly, however, the book emphasizes the bad image that Spain had abroad—poor, uncivilized, populated by dirty, dishonest, and cruel people, and not having contributed anything to Europe's history: in sum, the themes generally attributed to the "Black Legend." At one point in the narrative, for instance, the book's main character, Santi Celaya, is outraged when he attends a lecture in school and hears what the teacher says about Spain:

> The assistant portrayed Phillip II and the Duke of Alba in a merciless way, while Santi listened attentively and respectfully, thinking that it was perfectly all right for Belgians to observe history through Belgian eyes and not through Spanish eyes. But then, the assistant somehow began to ramble and to talk about the discovery of America and about the Civil War, and to say that Spain was a country full of beasts that had never contributed anything to the world. Judging from what the assistant said, in Madrid and Barcelona, in Seville and Bilbao, and all around Spain, one dressed pretty much in loin cloths and there were neither tramways nor anything; only matadors and flamenco dancers. One got the impression that there were neither workers, nor school teachers, doctors, good and cultivated people concerned with progress, liberty, and justice, or any Spaniard, from the North or the South, from here or there, from this side or the other side, whom one could trust. He also suggested that the Spanish women were all slave-like, slovenly, or something worse.[16]

Given the opposition of Francoist official culture to foreign ideas and its deep-seated conviction that there was a foreign conspiracy against Spain, one strategy for the Franco regime could have been to simply ignore the rest of the world. Instead, Franco sought to increase his legitimacy at home by breaking Spain's diplomatic and economic international isolation, by stressing the privileged relations between Spain and Latin America[17] and the Arab world, and, more significant in the present context, by making foreign recognition the primary benchmark of his performance. Spain's increasing prestige abroad was emphasized at every opportunity, and this is reflected not only in Franco's speeches but also in secondary school history textbooks. In the 1950s, the world was depicted as admiring Spain for having been the first to recognize the threat of communism and for having defeated it; with a certain condescension toward other countries, Franco stressed in his speeches that the world had initially misjudged and unjustly treated Spain, until it was forced to confront reality and to concede Franco's prescience by readmitting Spain into the international community.[18] A 1957 secondary school history textbook, after listing three recent major breakthroughs of Franco's diplomacy—the treaty with the United States, the Concordat with the Vatican, and membership in the UN—ended with the following sentence: "And it is only right to note that Spain's international prestige has a name: Franco."[19] Later, in the 1960s, official discourse shifted emphasis to stress the world's admiration of Spain's political stability and pace of economic development.[20]

Paradoxically, then, the same foreigners whom Franco mistrusted and who allegedly hated and misunderstood Spain were also the ones called on to judge the achievements of the dictatorship. This paradox is resolved if one realizes that the emphasis on the Black Legend and the emphasis on the world's admiration of Spain were two sides of the same concern about what the world thought of Spain. This concern could be interpreted as manifesting either insecurity about the legitimacy and achievements of the dictatorship and the status of Spain in the world, or implicit recognition of the illegitimate character of the dictatorial regime and of the validity of some of the images other countries held of Spain. Regardless of the motivation, the fact remains that by turning the developed world into the judge of Spain's achievements, the Franco regime was contributing to increasing the value of that developed world in Spanish eyes. For all their talk of the danger of foreign ideas and the Black Legend, the Franco regime was turning the world—the world that counted, which was the West and, within the West, Europe—into Spain's referent, into Spain's "obscure object of desire."

Official Spain not only contradicted itself by seeking legitimation in what the world said or thought about Spain, it also did so by trying to assert Spain's presence in the world through membership in every international forum. The dictatorship was always isolationist with respect to politics and culture, and until the mid-1950s, isolationist in terms of economic policy; but it was never isolationist in the diplomatic sphere. Before the end of World War II, the regime's intellectual elites were even willing to support a united Europe built around Germany, in which Spain would pursue the re-creation of Christian unity.[21] Although some intellectuals were concerned with the racist elements of Germany's unifying philosophy, they were even more concerned with the spread of Anglo-Saxon materialism and communism.[22]

After the defeat of the Axis forces, Franco adapted his foreign policy to the new geopolitical environment and invested a great deal of effort in making Spain visible internationally. Thus, from the 1950s, the concept of "isolation", frequently used in official discourse, was generally associated, not with diplomatic isolation but, rather, with something Spain did not want and had to move away from. The experience of Spain's isolation during the 1940s was in fact portrayed as traumatic, as in Franco's 1950 New Year's address. Upon discussing Spain's gradual integration in the international arena, Franco said: "While the pain experienced may be erased from the Spaniards' consciousness, in the book of history the condemnation of this forced isolation and of the lack of assistance in this period of general need will remain forever." Castro's 1965 secondary school history textbook reiterated this same idea, and with a mix of sarcasm and pride, commented that after years of unjustly and mistakenly ostracizing Spain, the international community now begged for Spain's cooperation in international conferences and organizations.[23] In fact, the idea conveyed in official discourse was that Spain's presence in international organizations was something the world needed and demanded.[24]

The dictatorship's efforts to insert Spain in the international community were part of a politics of prestige for internal consumption, but also the result of the regime's need to secure material support for rebuilding the Spanish economy and catching up with Europe. Franco's uprising was not moved by the desire to modernize Spain economically. His priorities were instead to restore law and order and reestablish Spain's prestige. Nevertheless, after victory in the Civil War and ten years of miserable economic conditions in Spain, he had to confront the fact that meeting these objectives and surviving in power in the long run would be greatly facilitated by Spain's economic recovery and development. Franco's discourse in the 1950s and 1960s presented Spain's economic modernization as a challenge, "not a whim but, rather, a necessity."[25] The regime's preoccupation with economic modernization and the use of all available technical expertise was conceived and justified as compatible with a lack of political and cultural modernization. This policy is what ideologues of the regime close to the Opus Dei referred to as "Españolización en los fines y europeización en los medios" ("Spanish-ization" of the goals and Europeanization of the means).[26]

The General certainly did not create the preoccupation with economic development, nor was Francoist discourse necessary to instill in the population the belief that the desired economic transformations were taking place: economic performance is something that the citizens see and feel. Nonetheless, official discourse gave public expression to this preoccupation among the population, shaped popular perceptions of what was happening, increased the centrality of economic and social change in Spanish life, and turned this topic into a familiar one that could be used later on to justify Spain's membership in the European Communities. Furthermore, the policies that followed from this official discourse on modernization made economic development possible, triggered a migration wave from rural to urban areas and to other Western European countries, and opened the door to a massive influx of European tourists. Thus, Franco's modernization discourse and the changes experienced by the population combined to turn the topic of modernization into the major theme of Spain's political culture in the 1960s and early 1970s.

In 1950, the focus on economic modernization was already a significant element in Franco's New Year's address. In it he referred to Spain's growing vitality, despite the high degree of isolation that Spain had suffered in previous years. In 1955, he began to instrumentalize for legitimization purposes the alleged success of his government's economic policies: "We restored our economy and transformed our nation at a pace and to a degree never achieved before."[27] In 1957, in a speech given in Asturias, he made it clear that the age of autarky was over and that Spaniards had to "go out and fight in the Common Market."[28] In 1958, he began to refer to what would become the centerpiece of the regime's economic modernization efforts and achievements during the 1960s, the Development Plans. In his 1963 New Year's address, Franco labeled the Development Plans "the great achievement of our time" and invited "all Spaniards to this great task that will bring so many benefits to our Homeland." There would be three such plans (1964–67; 1968–71; 1972–75[29]), promoted by the technocratic team around López Rodó, minister of the Franco government since the 1957 government reshuffle. For the formulation of these plans, the government enlisted the collaboration of experts from all fields in the social sciences, with hardly any attention to political affiliation. Because of the central role that these plans played in Franco's policy during the 1960s, the expressions "Planes de desarrollo" (Development Plans) and "Polos de desarrollo" (Poles of Development) became familiar catchwords during the 1960s, as did the expression "La década del desarrollo" (the decade of development).

The development of Spain became the dictatorship's war cry of the 1960s, as anticommunism had been in the 1950s. The "mission" for which Franco wanted to mobilize the country, however, was not only to develop the country, but also to catch up with the most advanced economies: "We must and can aspire to attain the living standards of the most advanced peoples," he said in his 1958 New Year's address. The attainment of this objective required that Spaniards learn to compete in international markets and that the agrarian and industrial structures be transformed. It also required, however, that workers sacrifice short-term gains (e.g., salary increases above the rate of inflation) for long-term objectives.[30] In the opening address of the 9th legislative period of the Spanish Cortes on November 17, 1967, Franco was already confident enough to proclaim victory in the regime's battle to close the gap with the advanced European economies. He pointed out that whereas the time lag with respect to European industrialized countries (France, Italy, Germany, and the United Kingdom) had been of fifteen to twenty years early in the decade, it had now decreased to four or five years. This comparison with the big countries in the Common Market thus became a permanent fixture of official discourse during the late 1960s, helping to establish the rest of Western Europe as the main cultural, economic, and social referent for the Spanish population.

A telling piece of evidence of the role that economic modernization played in official discourse during the 1960s and of the salience of Spain's modernization in Spanish culture during this period is the 1971 winner of the National Literature Prize. Angel Palomino's highly successful novel *Torremolinos Gran Hotel* is a satirical description of life in a hotel in the booming tourist resort of Torremolinos, at the end of the 1960s.[31] The literary value of the novel is not particularly high, but the story it tells stands as a monument to the official version of Spain's economic and social transformations of the 1960s. The life and characters of this hotel can be taken as a representation of the economic, social, and cultural transformations of Spain during the 1960s, from a rural country to an industrial nation whose economy was centered on tourism. The main characters are the staff of the hotel and its guests. The guests, represented in stereotypical ways, are predominantly American and English, although references to Swedish women, as erotic objects and representations of liberated European morals, also figure prominently in the novel. The main national characters are a middle-aged, wealthy businessman and his wife. The businessman is portrayed as a sex-obsessed person, constantly trying to cheat on his wife. He is made to represent Spain's nouveau riche, the guy who has made a fortune through devious means (speculation with real estate; capital evasion to Switzerland). Other characters that loom large in the story are members of a decadent and extravagant aristocracy, similar to the characters in later films by director Luis García Berlanga (e.g., *Patrimonio Nacional*). Completing the tableau of the new Spanish power elite, the author inserts bureaucrats and high government officials in the novel. Working for, observing, and often enduring this new power elite are representatives of a new middle class, such as the hotel director, and of the working classes, who try to adapt to the surrealistic life of tourist resorts. The hotel director in particular is portrayed as an educated, honest, professional, and hardworking man, whose relationship with his wife, in contrast to marital relationships among the power elite, is one of mutual understanding and love. At the story's end, the "gangsters" lose some money but are spared jail. The honest hotel director, who rebels against them, loses his job at the Torremolinos Hotel; nevertheless, his talent is recognized and he is hired as director of a hotel in Barcelona, which, because of its image as historic center of Spanish capitalism, is meant to represent a more fitting place than Torremolinos for a representative of Spain's emerging bourgeoisie.

Torremolinos Gran Hotel is thus a literary symbol of the centrality of economic and social modernization in official and popular culture during the 1960s. Official discourse and policies signaled the Franco regime's determination to modernize the country economically and helped to enshrine the rest of Western Europe as the standard of economic development to which Spain should and could aspire. Meanwhile, actual economic development, for all its unevenness, started to teach some sectors of Spanish society how to compete in international markets, and instilled in Spaniards the consumerist mentality that characterized other European societies. The conditions were thus established for economic modernization to work as an argument for membership in the European Communities. The majority of the comments that my Spanish respondents made with respect to the effects of membership in the European Union on Spain's modernization largely reflect this official discourse developed during the 1960s. Another type of comment made by other respondents and by elite journalists during the 1970s belongs, however, to a different tradition, a liberal tradition dating to the early part of the twentieth century that coexisted on a second plane with the dominant culture during the dictatorship.

"Spain as Problem": The Liberal Europeanizing Project

For most of Franco's dictatorship, the majority of the Spanish population was solely exposed to the official discourse examined above. This state of things began to change in the mid-1950s with early manifestations of political unrest at the university (1956 student demonstrations) and the workplace, with mass worker migration to the rest of Europe, and with the first waves of European tourists visiting Spain. In the 1960s, student and working-class unrest met with timid reforms allowing a small amount of representation of these groups' interests. Also, a loosening of the grip on the free expression of ideas, exemplified by the 1966 Press Law, allowed access to a fairly broad range of perspectives on politics, culture, and society, to those looking for them.

Broadly speaking, oppositional culture contained three main elements: (1) a critique of the regime's reading of Spanish history, (2) a critique of Spain's political and social foundations, and (3) a critique of Spain's cultural foundations. The critique of the dictatorship's reading of Spanish history resulted from the joint influence of foreign historians and a new generation of Spanish historians.[32] The latter distinguished themselves from previous generations of Spanish historians because of their systematic empirical approach, their focus on social and economic history, and their liberal political attitudes. The most significant results of their efforts were a critical reappraisal of the period of the Spanish Conquest and Spanish Empire (seen as containing the seeds of the crisis of the seventeenth century), a more positive evaluation of the eighteenth century and its enlightened reformers, and a new interpretation of the crises and conflicts of the nineteenth century. They blamed the failure of liberal reform rather than the pernicious role of liberalism and the ineptitude of politicians, as did Francoist historiography. The influence of these authors at the popular rather than the elite level was felt especially after Franco's death, as I show below.

The critique of the political and social foundations of the Francoist regime was the dominant theme in this oppositional culture, and its intensification paralleled the intensification of political mobilization against the dictatorship. Before the 1960s, literature was arguably the main vehicle of this critique. "Tremendista" novels of the 1940s, such as Camilo José Cela's *La familia de Pascual Duarte* (1942), some realist novels of the 1950s, such as Ana María Matute's *Los hijos muertos* (1958 National Literature Prize), and some theater pieces such as *Historia de una escalera* (1949, Lope de Vega Prize), by Antonio Buero Vallejo, depicted what some sectors of Spanish society viewed as the darkest side, the traumatized character, and the immobility of Franco's Spain. *Los hijos muertos*, for instance, depicts the emptiness that the Civil War left in many families because of the death of thousands of members of the younger generation, victims of miscarriages, stillbirth, murder, or bombs. There are no good or bad sides in this story: the different characters are depicted as belonging to one side or the other, but there is no discussion of the virtues of either. Still, the majority are Republicans, and it is their suffering that is predominantly reflected (in contrast to two previously cited National Literature Prize recipients, *Los cipreses creen en Dios* and *Los muertos no se cuentan*, that emphasize the suffering of those siding with Franco's army).

In the 1960s and early 1970s, political mobilization was increasingly the main and most effective vehicle of the democratic and peripheral-nationalist opposition to Franco. At the university, children of the progressive bourgeoisie predominantly led this movement, whereas at the workplace, underground communist organizations and progressive segments of the clergy predominantly led it. Meanwhile, groups of bourgeois origin, inspired by social-Catholic and Christian-democratic convictions in Catalonia and socialist and revolutionary groups of lower-middle-class origins in the Basque country, mobilized behind peripheral nationalist organizations.[33]

More relevant for the purposes of this chapter was the questioning of the cultural foundations of the Franco Regime. This questioning began from very early on, as in the mid- to late 1940s progressive members of the Falange and of the Catholic factions of the regime appropriated and promoted Spain's Europeanizing tradition. To understand what this meant, however, we need to trace the history of the Europeanizing tradition. This history may be said to begin with the penetration in Spain of Enlightenment ideas in the eighteenth century, but it is only with the "Crisis of 1898" that this tradition established itself, coinciding with the legitimacy crisis of the ideology of traditionalism and the coming of age of a brilliant generation of Spanish intellectuals and reformers known as the "Generación del 98."[34] The members of the Generación del 98 borrowed some of their ideas and their self-description as "Europeanizers" from reform proposals aimed at catching up with Europe made some years earlier by leaders of what was known as the Regeneracionista movement. To the Regeneracionistas' reform-minded attitude, the members of the Generación del 98 added a reflection about the causes of Spain's decline and the ways to overcome it. They developed a very harsh critique of Spain's historical evolution that they traced to Spain's betrayal of its essential nature. They thus invested much of their energy in the tasks of rewriting Spanish history, rediscovering the essential nature of Spain, locating the moment when it deviated from its true nature, and finding the spiritual and intellectual remedies for its problems.[35] In their early proposals they coincided with the Regeneracionistas: their goal was the Europeanization of Spain. Ganivet, for instance, argued that one should not fear the penetration into Spain of imported ideas because the rapid flow of ideas facilitated by modern means of communication guaranteed that no imported idea would ever be strong enough to become threatening. Furthermore, he thought that Spain was in such a critical state that, regrettable as that might be, the adoption of foreign ideas could only be beneficial.[36] Unamuno, on his part, criticized Spain's isolationism and argued that Spain would be able to rediscover its essential nature only through a thorough process of Europeanization, a thorough assimilation of the principles of modernity.[37] In later years, Ramiro de Maeztu, also member of the '98 Generation, and Unamuno himself, abjured Europe: whereas the former redirected his energies to formulating a supranational identity project around the idea of Hispanidad, the latter proposed a regeneration of Spain solely based on its own character and values. The initial concerns and proposals of the *Generación del 98* were taken up by the "Generación del 14," whose main representative was the philosopher and essayist José Ortega y Gasset.

Ortega, firmly anchored in a liberal and lay tradition, maintained—and regretted—in newspaper articles and in his books *Meditaciones del Quijote* (1914) and *España Invertebrada* (1922) that Spain's culture lacked clarity of thought and intellectual rigor. He traced this to a corrupted and insufficient form of Germanization of Spanish culture.[38] To counter this deficit, Ortega proposed a thorough reform of Spain's educational system toward facilitating the spread of the main tenets and habits of modernity.[39] Only then would a healthy symbiosis of the clarity of seeing, which he ascribed to Mediterranean peoples, and the clarity of thinking, which he ascribed to Germanic peoples, ensue, leading Spanish culture toward the intellectual heights reached by Cervantes.

The Europeanization project advocated from the Regeneracionistas onwards amounted to Spain's assimilation to the modern spirit. Admittedly, it advocated only a partial assimilation, for it emphasized freedom of thinking and reason, but was often critical of or ambiguous toward economic and technical progress and parliamentary democracy. It is precisely this version of modernity, however, that was embraced during the 1940s by intellectuals like Laín Entralgo and Ridruejo, leading supporters of Falange who had gradually veered toward a liberal form of Catholicism. Laín's highly influential book, *España como problema* (1948), perfectly synthesized the main contributions to the debate about Spain since the last third of the nineteenth century, and proposed a third way between the isolationist traditionalist and the Europeanizing progressive views.[40] This third way, which according to the author represented the views of his generation, the "Grandchildren of '98" (Los nietos del 98), contained a very strong Catholic component and also echoed ideas formulated earlier by the founding leader of Falange, José Antonio Primo de Rivera. Nevertheless, Laín made a conscious effort to connect with Ortega's ideas, and argued that one could be Catholic and simultaneously cultivate and value scientific and intellectual contributions, whatever their national or political origin. Contrary to the progressive tradition, he opposed the rejection of everything achieved in Spain in the past centuries and the blind imitation of every European import, for he believed that, whether one liked it or not, Spanish culture would always be a national translation of European influences. He then applied the same argument against traditionalists and recommended against opposing foreign influences; instead, he advocated taking these foreign ideas as a source of inspiration and then transforming them so as to adapt them to the Spanish cultural tradition.

Laín's call for Spain to remain part of the main European public debates of its time, despite Franco's cultural isolationism, represented an early and significant strategy of opposition to the dictatorship. It was echoed by numerous intellectuals of his and younger generations in the 1950s and 1960s, heirs of Costa, Unamuno, and Ortega (e.g., Joaquín Ruiz Giménez, Julián Marías, José Luis Aranguren). The extent of their influence was such that in 1970, five years before the end of the dictatorship, Aranguren considered Ortega's liberal tradition hegemonic in Spanish culture.[41] One may certainly argue that there is some degree of exaggeration in this statement, since Franco's official discourse remained strong in schools and in the state-controlled media. If anything, it applied to the educated segments of Spanish society, and even they were starting to listen to a younger leftist generation, the May '68 generation, quite critical of the tradition that preceded them.[42] Still, this leftist generation did not modify the equation between Europeanization and modernity that had been established since Costa; it simply emphasized aspects of modernity, such as democracy, that had played a minor role in past discussions of the *Problem with Spain*, and introduced new ones, such as a Marxist critique of capitalist development.

Since democracy was restored in Spain after Franco's death, the hegemony of the liberal tradition has been well established. The standard-bearer of this tradition has been the leading Spanish newspaper *El País*, founded in 1976.[43] *El País* skillfully absorbed and gave voice to the two main unofficial intellectual currents of late Francoism: the Orteguian liberal establishment and the moderate left.[44] Consistent with this intellectual heritage, its founding charter and subsequent op-ed pieces published over the years proclaimed the newspaper's commitment to the political, economic, and cultural modernization of Spain, which it equated with its assimilation of European values and norms of behavior.[45]

El País was not the only vehicle transmitting the messages that modernity was equivalent to Europeanization and vice versa. Secondary school history textbooks of the democratic period emphasized this link, by insisting on the development gap between Spain and the rest of Western Europe, by portraying progressive forces in twentieth-century Spain as pro-European and in a more favorable light than the conservative forces, and by opposing a modern and open Europe to a backward and autarkic Francoist Spain.

During the Franco regime, secondary school history textbooks consisted mostly of a monotonous recounting of facts, told in rigorous chronological order and referring mostly to the political-institutional sphere. Furthermore, very little space was devoted to twentieth-century history. In the mid-1970s this approach to secondary school history changed radically because of the delayed implementation of reform legislation approved in 1970, the democratic transition, and the influence of works by foreign, economic, and social historians mentioned above in the discussion of the 1950s and 1960s oppositional culture.[46] The content of post-Franco history textbooks was heavily influenced by the work of economic and social historians. They stressed Spain's slow and uneven industrialization in the nineteenth century, which they explained as resulting from insufficient political modernization and conservative politics, and traced back to this failure most of the social and political ills of the twentieth century, including the Spanish Civil War. Europe was presented as the yardstick for Spain's economic achievements and the model to imitate. Thus, for instance, when Edelvives's 1977 history textbook discussed the bourgeoisie's efforts to enact desirable political, economic, and social reforms in the context of the 1868–74 revolutionary years, it referred to these as attempts to enact "European-style" reforms.[47] When Edelvives's 1977 and 1998 and Anaya's 1986 history textbooks discussed economic change in the nineteenth and early twentieth centuries, they always stressed that it was slow when compared to Europe's.[48]

Written from a democratic, center-left perspective that showed greater sympathy for the progressive than for the conservative phases of nineteenth and twentieth-century Spanish history, post-Franco secondary school history textbooks differentiated clearly between progressive Europeanizers (e.g., the Regeneracionistas, the young members of the Generación del 98, Ortega) and conservative isolationists (e.g. Menéndez Pelayo, Cánovas).[49] What is more significant, they constructed the Francoist regime as isolationist and antimodern. When discussing the Franco regime's vision of history, for instance, Anaya's 1986 history textbook used the dictatorship's own anachronistic language to describe its negative attitudes toward foreign ideas. Read in the 1980s, this rhetorical device made the regime sound ridiculous and conveyed the opposite message, that is, that there was nothing dangerous in foreign ideas:

> Eyes were turned toward the *"glorious Imperial period,"* to the time of the Catholic Monarchs and the Habsburgs. Meanwhile, the history of the 17th century was seen as a regrettable mistake, for the arrival of *foreign* ideas (the masonry and liberalism, then Marxism) had almost *asphyxiated the genuine Hispanic essential nature*, now rescued by way of the *saving Crusade*.[50]

Another example comes from Edelvives's 1977 history textbook. Within a broader narrative that condemned fascism in its different manifestations, the textbook portrayed Europe and Franco as opposites, the former representing good and openness and thus deserving prosperity, the latter representing evil and isolationism, and thus deserving economic backwardness:

> It would take Europe many years to view our country with sympathy, simply because Francoist Spain had developed in the camp opposed to the Allies (although it did not participate in the war on Germany's side except for sending a division made up of volunteers to fight against Russia).
> ... The consequences of this were felt very soon. The famous "Marshall Plan" of American aid for winners and losers did not affect Spain, which was left excluded from it. Europe succeeded in its recovery effort, first because of the above-mentioned aid (20,000 Million dollars between 1945–1948) and then because of the creation of a European Economic Community (Treaty of Rome, of 1957). Meanwhile, Spain maintained its arrogant isolationist, autarkic, position, which resulted in a considerable lag with respect to the world economy.[51]

Paragraphs such as these strongly and unambiguously conveyed that European (and American) approval of Spain was a prize to be won through redemption of past sins (e.g., through becoming a democracy and abandoning isolationist policies), and that the direct consequence of winning this prize would be economic prosperity through membership in the European Economic Community. Thus almost at the end of this 1984 history textbook published by Anaya, one reads that "the recovery of democracy has also meant for Spain its full integration in Europe."[52]

The previous pages demonstrate that the expectation that the European Union would contribute to Spain's modernization and international prestige and the desire to put an end to Spain's isolation were conceived and became effective arguments for Spain's membership in the European Union because they were salient topics in Spanish culture for more than a century. A liberal intellectual tradition dating back to the last third of the nineteenth century conceptually equated modernization and Europeanization and, after a period of abeyance during the early years of Franco's dictatorial regime, gradually rose from obscurity in the 1950s and 1960s and finally became hegemonic under the leadership of the newspaper *El País* after democracy was restored in the late 1970s. This Europeanizing project initially faced the opposition of alternative identity projects, some of them isolationist and autarkic, others organized around Christian universalism and the community of Spanish-speaking people (Hispanidad). These alternative supranational identity projects were abandoned in the aftermath of the Spanish Civil War and effective defeat in World War II, however, because of the desolate economic situation in which Spain found itself and the greater opportunities for recovery offered by Europe. Autarky was given up early in the 1950s and the Hispanidad, apart from occasional references to it in articles published early in the late 1940s,[53] became an anachronism, invoked only rhetorically by Franco on special occasions in order to strengthen relationships with Latin America.[54] Therefore, the Generalísimo himself strongly pushed for Spain's presence in the European diplomatic arena, placed Spain's economic modernization at the center of his policies, and established Europe as the mirror for Spain's economic development. The Francoist and the progressive Europeanizing projects inspired two different modes of argumentation about European integration that are now reflected in justifications for Spain's membership in the European Union and for pursuing the goal of European unification. One of these modes of argumentation, echoing Francoist discourse on European integration and certainly compatible with the liberal tradition, emphasizes an instrumental-utilitarian view of modernization and rejects isolation in simple terms as something bad for the country. The other mode of argumentation, rooted in the liberal tradition, conceives of Spain's membership in the European Union as contributing to the country's cultural, political, social, and, indeed, economic modernization, and as breaking with a long isolationist tradition that is made responsible for Spain's relative gap with respect to the most advanced countries in Europe.

Six

West Germany: Between Self-Doubt and Pragmatism

> The twelve years of Nazi dictatorship in Germany and Europe overshadow centuries of German history; Nazi rule is still the dominant paradigm for research and analysis of contemporary Germany.... Different from Japan, [West] Germany is still evaluated against the wartime background of the twelve years of Nazi fascism.[1]

IN THE spirit of this quote, taken from a study of the way West Germany and its population have dealt with the Nazi past, one could argue that the 1933–45 period was, for most of the second half of the twentieth century, the main anchoring point of West German collective memory and identity. Moreover, the characteristics and behavior of the Nazi regime were a major conditioning factor of West German national and foreign policies, and of foreign attitudes and behavior toward Germany, during this same period. It is thus not surprising to see Nazi Germany referred to so often both in interviews about European integration with ordinary citizens and local elites and in newspaper editorials and opinion pieces about the same topic. The Nazi past provided arguments for European integration and facilitated the spread of these arguments to broader groups in the population.

These arguments for European integration were readily accepted partly because the political consequences of World War II—defeat, economic destruction, occupation, partition—had turned Western Europe into the only plausible supranational identity for the population of the Federal Republic of Germany. Alternative supranational identities, such as *Mitteleuropa*, that had competed with a Western European identity in the interwar period were thus buried after Germany's defeat in World War II. The idea of *Mitteleuropa* had been popularized by the liberal intellectual Friedrich Naumann in 1915,[2] and was linked with other former liberal political and economic proposals developed by diplomats like Metternich and economists like List for the creation of a political federation or a customs union involving primarily Germany and Austria, but also neighboring countries in Central and Eastern Europe.[3] These proposals, including the attempt to develop a German empire overseas, had been circulating since the 1814

Congress of Viena and, like the idea of Hispanidad in Spain, reflected the German elites' attempts to find a strategy to compete with the British empire.[4] The Continental blockade during World War I frustrated Germany's attempts to build an empire overseas and made the idea of a Central European space even more attractive for people like Naumann.

Like the idea of Hispanidad, the Central European project was prone to distortion and instrumentalization by antidemocratic nationalist groups, for whom Western Europe embodied the dreaded ideals of the French Revolution. This was especially so in the aftermath of World War I and the signature of the Treaty of Versailles. For instance, in his 1931 book *Paneuropa oder Mitteleuropa?*, the German nationalist Hans Krebs, German deputy in Prague's Parliament, compared the concept of Mitteleuropa, which he favored, to the concept of Paneuropa, forerunner of European integration, which had been proposed by the Count Coudenhove-Kalergi. Krebs, like many German nationalists outraged by the Versailles settlement, not only rejected the idea of European integration, which for him did not correspond to any racial, economic, or political reality, but saw power-hungry France, freemasonry, and Roman Catholic Church circles, behind it.[5] Rather than a Central European federation formed by equals, as conceived by Naumann and others, German nationalist groups, influenced by the idea of *Lebensraum* (space necessary for life) and juristically backed by Carl Schmitt's adaptation of the Monroe doctrine,[6] came to envisage a large political entity dominated by Germany. This political entity was supposed to have a Central European core but was not necessarily limited to Central Europe, as World War II was to show. Under the Nazis, the idea of Mitteleuropa was thus gradually subsumed into a Pan-Germanist project.

The end of World War II put an end to the Mitteleuropa and related projects, heirs to the idea of the "great spaces" that had been so influential since the nineteenth century. The concept of Mitteleuropa reemerged occasionally in the FRG during the 1980s and then after German reunification.[7] There were even occasional references to it in *Neues Deutschland*, the newspaper of the former German Democratic Republic, as an alternative to the European Union in the early 1990s. In general, however, the only viable supranational identity for West Germans in the post–World War II period was the Western European identity, an identity that the FRG's political establishment was quick to adopt as its own, both in pronouncements and actions. This embrace of a Western European identity by the FRG's political elites and the absence of alternative supranational identity projects facilitated the development of positive attitudes toward European integration in the FRG. The justifications that people developed for their attitudes toward European integration were shaped, however, by the dominant political culture themes and counterthemes in post–World War II West Germany.

As noted in chapter 2, 17 out of 27 West German respondents mentioned Germany's role in World War II when discussing European integration. The strong salience of the Nazi period in conversations about European integration distinguishes German from Spanish and British conceptions of European integration and membership in the European Union. Analysis of the quality press (chapter 4) further reinforces these conclusions; frequent references to the Nazi period and Germany's role in World War II also distinguish German op-ed articles on European integration from those published in the United Kingdom and Spain.

Respondents who mentioned Germany's role in World War II were generally more informed about European integration and better educated than were respondents who did not mention it (71% of those who mentioned this topic were very informed about European integration, in contrast with 28.6% of those who did not mention it; 72% of those who mentioned it had completed high school, in contrast with 28% of those who did not). They were also more likely to favor a Centralized Integration than a Decentralized Cooperation European integration project (67% of those who mentioned the topic favored a Centralized Integration model, in contrast with 33% among those who did not mention it).

A closer look at the comments made by respondents or discussed in newspaper op-ed pieces reveals two major classes of arguments, sometimes formulated jointly by a single respondent or in a single newspaper article. The first one rests on a particular vision of Germany and its obligations toward other countries. It includes comments about the respondents' concern that Germany may again represent a threat to peace and about the responsibility that Germany has toward countries that suffered from German aggression in World War II, and is connected with a long-standing debate on how to deal with and interpret the Nazi period. The second class of arguments rests on a particular perception of foreign images of and attitudes toward Germany. It includes comments about other countries' misgivings and negative stereotypes with respect to Germany and about the constraints these represent for German foreign policy, and is connected with foreign policy debates and with a broader preoccupation with Germany's image abroad. This second class of arguments clearly predominates over the first one in op-ed articles about European integration.

Dealing with and Understanding the Nazi Past

When examining the role of the Nazi past in Germany's national culture, it is worth making a distinction between two analytically different questions: Why did it happen? How have Germans dealt with the Nazi past? The distinction is useful because it corresponds to contrasting comments made by West German respondents when discussing European integration.

Why Did It Happen?

> With the past in mind, it is a good thing that Germany is part of a larger group.
> (110, Weststadt, 30 or younger, more than High School)

> Germany cannot go alone. The past has demonstrated how dangerous it is when Germany goes alone.
> (125, Weststadt, aged 31–50, representative of Deutscher Gewerkschaftsbund [German Unions Association])

> Germany must be a member of the EU so that Germans learn that their strength comes from being part of a community, rather than thinking that they must dominate other countries, as always.
> (111, Weststadt, 30 or younger, more than High School)

These three quotes reveal an image of Germany depicted as "aggressive," shaped by the memory of World War II. They also implicitly explain World War II as resulting from Germany's aggression, in turn due to the character of its population. Finally, they reflect skepticism about the extent to which Germany has changed. As far as this chapter is concerned, the quotes are a good illustration of how salient preoccupations in a particular society shape the arguments people develop to explain their attitudes or their behavior. German society has indeed struggled for more than fifty years to understand why the Nazis came to power. The following discussion describes the main explanations that have been provided and points out which ones have circulated more widely among the public.

The historiographic tradition that attaches an exceptional character to the Nazi period has tended to dominate the scholarly debate and schoolbook accounts in the post–World War II period. From 1945 to the mid-1960s, main representatives of West German historiography turned against the prevailing view among the Allies that there was something "wrong" with German culture and character (a view still present in contemporary accounts of German national identity by American scholars).[8] In contrast to the Allies, these historians tended to explain the Nazi period as resulting from a fatal combination of totalitarian trends common to the West, rooted in modernity and in the consequent advent of the masses; from the West's initial lack of resolve against Hitler; from specific national characteristics; from circumstantial factors (e.g., the Versailles Treaty, the 1929 world recession); and from Hitler's quasi-demonic character. More or less explicit in these accounts was the desire to partially exculpate the

German population and thus legitimize calls for the nationalization of the denazification and reeducation policies conducted by the Allies.[9]

In the late 1960s, a structural turn took place that challenged traditional views of the Nazi past as exceptional and emphasized instead the roles of economic and social factors.[10] What Kohn had already broadly outlined (in a book that was largely ignored in Germany, the weakness of the democratic and Western tradition in Germany, was thoroughly developed by Dahrendorf into the thesis of Germany's lack of a liberal-democratic tradition.[11] For more than a decade, the thesis of the failed liberal-democratic transformation remained unchallenged, and most efforts by historians were devoted to explaining why this transformation did not happen or happened only in a partial way.[12]

A new trend in German historiography about the Nazi period began in 1980 with the publication of Blackbourn and Eley's *Mythen Deutscher Geschichtsschreibung*, a neo-Marxist refutation of the German exceptionalism thesis defended by authors in the structural tradition.[13] In contrast with their predecessors, Blackbourn and Eley argued that German social and political developments in the late nineteenth century were not very unlike those in other European countries. Ironically, Blackbourn and Eley's leftist critique provided ammunition to more conservative historians who advocated an updated version of the discontinuity thesis of the Nazi period. In the context of Christian-Liberal political hegemony and governmental sympathy toward attempts to strengthen West German national consciousness, the revisionist thesis gained high public visibility in 1986 with the publication of an essay by Ernst Nolte and a book by Andreas Hillgruber.[14] These authors were representative of a new generation of historians who again relativized the singularity of the Nazi period, questioned the unique and original character of the Holocaust, attributed a defensive purpose to German aggression in World War II, and stressed the unique significance of personalities like Hitler in the unfolding of events that led to World War II and the Final Solution. The subsequent reaction to these views, spearheaded by Habermas, generated lively debate in Germany in the late 1980s.[15]

The question "Why did it happen?" remains a controversial one. As I completed my interviews in the summer of 1996, a new debate had just erupted around Daniel Goldhagen's bestseller, *Hitler's Willing Executioners*.[16] This time German historians were outraged not by theses deemed revisionist but rather by the thesis of an American scholar who moved in the opposite direction by proposing that the ultimate explanation of the Holocaust was the German population's underlying annihilating anti-Semitism. Goldhagen's thesis, by invoking character rather than depersonalized social and political structures, overstepped the boundaries of liberal understandings of the continuities in German history and of the normalcy of the Nazi period.

Goldhagen's thesis was not entirely revolutionary. In fact, it linked with an approach to the Nazi period that had been fashionable in the immediate postwar period. Prestigious scholars from Röpke to Adorno, as well as many publicists, had argued that the Nazi regime had a basis in the character of the German population (e.g., "militarism," "authoritarianism," "blind obedience"). In particular, Adorno and his co-investigators claimed the existence of an "authoritarian personality" underlying support for the Nazi regime.[17] Later on, in the 1960s, while liberal historians began examining the structural foundations of Nazi Germany and the role of authoritarian and militaristic legacies, social scientists focused on determining whether the German population's attitudes and values were shifting from authoritarian to democratic. Almond and Verba's influential 1963 study, *The Civic Culture*, for instance, showed that nondemocratic values were more prevalent among the West German population than among other publics.[18] Later studies, however, revealed a rapid transformation in those values, thus suggesting that West Germany's democracy stood on solid foundations, and reassuring those concerned about a potential reenactment of Nazi Germany.[19] These results are borne out by historical events, for neither support for far left or far right political parties nor acts of xenophobic violence have ever reached levels comparable to those of the Nazi period. Furthermore, empirical studies show that West Germany does not stand out on these issues relative to other nations.[20] This changed German reality explains Goldhagen's repeated assertions during the debate over his book that he by no means was suggesting that the political culture portrayed in *Hitler's Willing Executioners* could be used to describe modern Germany, an assertion that won him considerable public support despite the cold scholarly reception. However, notwithstanding the gradual emergence of a positive image of modern Germany, many still believe in the persistence of Germany's inner demons, as when Helmut Schmidt insisted in the early 1990s on the need to protect Germany from itself by binding it tightly to the European Union.[21]

Thus, West German historiography on the Nazi period has oscillated between explanations that have stressed continuities and distinctive factors in German history up to the Nazi regime, and explanations that have stressed the discontinuity represented by the Nazi regime and thus challenged the view of German history as departing in major ways from that of its neighbors. As I have also shown, this debate has run parallel to another one concerned with the continuities of culture and character underlying the Nazi period and the persistence of these in contemporary Germany. The intensity of these debates (e.g., the "Historikerstreit"), often portrayed in the quality press, cannot have failed to involve attentive segments of the population.

When one moves from the historiographic level to the interpretation of the Nazi past that has been portrayed in history textbooks and, therefore, become more accessible to the wider public, one notices that it only partially reflects the debates described above.[22] As one would expect, World War II figures prominently in German contemporary history textbooks for the *Realschule*.[23] But the way history has traditionally been presented in West German schoolbooks, with its focus on the sequential unfolding of events and its emphasis on politics and diplomacy, has from the outset ruled out a discussion of the continuity theses proposed by structural historians and by social scientists concerned with the role of psychosocial or political culture variables.[24] Thus, the discontinuity thesis dominates textbook representations of World War II.[25]

In his 1965 book, *Gesellschaft und Demokratie in Deutschland*, Dahrendorf provided a synthesis of the typical portrayal of World War II in West German schoolbooks:[26]

- The narrative begins with World War I: all participants found themselves forced into this war.
- No country bore special responsibility or guilt for World War I.
- Germany lost World War I.
- Germany had to accept very hard peace conditions.
- The Treaty of Versailles, with its war guilt thesis and its territorial, military, and economic implications, contradicted the idea that all participants were collectively responsible for the outbreak of war.
- The Treaty of Versailles was an overreaction, which explains all the overreactions that followed.
- The extreme conditions set by the Treaty of Versailles necessarily brought about a national movement against it, which took on a National Socialist character.
- Some additional, mostly economic, problems such as inflation and the economic crisis helped National Socialism into power.
- German history took a terrible turn, unpardonable in its character, but understandable in its causes.
- The political leaders and not the German people were responsible for the worst aberrations committed during the Nazi period.
- Although World War II was not ultimately Hitler's making, he bears the main responsibility for it.

Dahrendorf's synthesis is very close to the content of Ebeling's 1955 contemporary history textbook. This textbook decries the Treaty of Versailles for being particularly unjust, and portrays Wilhelmine Germany as a peace-seeking country that tried until the last minute to prevent World War I but was fatally trapped in the system of treaty obligations.[27] Furthermore, Ebeling's 1955 textbook frames Hitler's rise to power in an exculpatory way by including a leading section on dictatorships during the 1930s that relativizes the singularity of National Socialism. However, Dahrendorf's synthesis does not reflect so well the content of textbooks published in the late 1960s and afterwards, including later editions of the Ebeling text itself. Although the Treaty of Versailles remains part of the overall picture, Germany's responsibility for beginning World War I was no longer denied, and the treaty itself is no longer portrayed as especially unjust or burdensome.[28] Moreover, the economic crisis of the late 1920s is no longer presented as a German catastrophe but, rather, as part of a worldwide recession. Textbooks published since the late 1960s present both the Treaty of Versailles and the 1929 economic crisis as objects of manipulation by the National Socialists.[29] Thus, the responsibility for the Nazis' rise to power and World War II falls mostly on the conditions that had made dictatorial regimes possible in various European countries, and on Hitler himself.[30] They do not, however, question standard interpretations of the Nazi period transmitted to the German public that stress the Nazi period's discontinuity with previous and later German history and that relativizes its uniqueness.

How Have Germans Dealt with the Nazi Past?

> Germany bears the responsibility for two world wars.
> (126, Weststadt, older than 50, more than High School)

> I take it for extremely necessary that we, as Germans, engage ourselves strongly toward European unification. We are obligated, because of our history, toward Europeans. (128, Weststadt, older than 50, more than High School)

> We have an obligation to engage ourselves with other countries.
>
> [*Why?*]
>
> Perhaps because of our past. We lost the war and caused a lot of pain to other countries. I thus think that it is fair that Germany engage itself with other countries and even that it pay a little more than other countries.
> [113; Weststadt; 31–50; More than High School]

These three quotes convey the impact that the debate about Germany's confrontation with the Nazi past has had on thinking about the European Union. This debate, with ebbs and flows, has gone on uninterruptedly since the end of World War II. Thus, Hannah Arendt's assertion that the reality of the Nazi crimes, of the war and the defeat, whether confronted or repressed, still dominates the entire life of Germany, is as true in the 1990s as when first formulated.[31]

The debate about the Nazi past began immediately after the war, with a great deal of discussion on the topic of guilt and responsibility. It was initiated by the Allies and taken up by the German population itself around 1946. Jaspers's 1946 Heidelberg Lecture, in which he accepted the notion of collective political guilt but rejected the notion of collective moral guilt, set the tone for the way West Germany would approach World War II and the Holocaust in coming years.[32] Reuter says:

> Political guilt—in Jaspers' words, the liability of all citizens for the consequences of actions done by or in the name of Nazi Germany—collective and undifferentiated, but limited in terms of time and extent, was accepted and assimilated by the great majority of West Germans, whether eagerly or not. There were no fundamental public controversies among the political and societal elites about the responsibility for the war, about the responsibility for the extermination of European Jewry and other minorities, about the inhumane character of the National Socialist regime, about the political and territorial consequences Germany had to accept, or about the legitimacy of the victors to occupy, to punish, and to transform the German political system.[33]

Collective moral guilt was another matter. This is because it evoked, among other things, the discomforting idea of continuities in German history and the existence of an "evil" German character.[34] In the immediate postwar period, exiles and the SPD resolutely rejected the concept of collective moral guilt with the argument that they had stood against the Nazi regime, whereas the CDU, divided on the issue, tended to avoid any type of pronouncement.[35] Consequently, the emphasis tended to shift toward the recognition of individual moral guilt and, with respect to the younger generations, toward drawing the moral lessons of World War II and remembering.

In the early years of the FRG, public debate about World War II abated considerably. This was partly due to the FRG's concentration on economic recovery but also to public reaction against the denazification measures imposed by the Allies. Widespread repression of the past in the private sphere was indeed accompanied by public mobilization to resist the measures imposed by the Allies on those suspected of having collaborated in some form with the Nazi regime. In particular, pressure was directed toward the revocation of denazification measures, the release of war criminals, and the rehabilitation of civil servants. Parallel to this pressure, there was increasing support for neo-Nazi political organizations and involvement in anti-Semitic violence.[36] Some have described the 1950s as years of "renazification" and have accused the government and the opposition of giving in to public pressure in order to maintain electoral support. In his government address of 1949, for instance, Adenauer catered to his electorate through criticism of the denazification policies, demands for the rehabilitation of dismissed civil servants and soldiers, and lament over the situation of war prisoners.[37]

An examination of a typical contemporary history schoolbook of this period confirms the impression that large segments of West German society had not developed a sense of moral responsibility for the Nazi past.[38] The German population was innocent, according to the textbook, for it did not know about what went on and was skillfully manipulated by Hitler's propaganda.[39] Furthermore, one reads that the Nazi tragedy resulted from a chain of unfortunate circumstances and thus one cannot speak of collective responsibility.[40] Finally, says the book, the population fought not for Hitler's ideas but mainly against communism.[41]

In the late 1950s, public debate on the Nazi period took off again, less centered now on philosophical questions of guilt, which were left to intellectuals. TV programs, for instance, focused on practical issues such as scandals surrounding disclosures about the Nazi connections of prominent people or episodes of anti-Semitic violence. The latter, together with antidemocratic nationalist messages in the quality press, were in fact on the rise.[42] These disclosures and debates revealed a clear split in West German society, with significant segments of the population nostalgic for a prouder and more assertive Germany. In this context, a select group of intellectuals, the Group 47, became the moral conscience of the new Republic. Members of this prestigious literary group, such as Schroers, Grass, and Lenz, as well as other recipients of the prestigious Bremer Literaturpreis in the late 1950s and early 1960s, like Michelsen, addressed moral issues directly related to the Nazi period in their award-winning novels.[43]

In Schroers's novel, *In fremder Sache*, the reader encounters frequent sarcastic comments about Germany, targeted against a society that (in the author's view) contemplated with indifference the manner in which former Nazis had been allowed to take public positions shortly after World War II, a society where many former Hitler supporters pretended "not to have known" or washed their hands of crimes they let others commit ("He did not know that there are no innocent people, only a state of no indictment, which certainly, if one has luck and is careful, can be maintained over a lifetime"; "Under police custody, he will manage to get rid of this distracted look of the uninvolved and learn that without exception everyone is involved, regardless of how much one is aware of it. He has the innocence of Pilatus, and such people drive me through the roof.").[44]

Günter Grass, in his funny, bitter, and tragic chronicle of German history between 1924 and 1954, *Die Blechtrommel*, expresses through the penetrating eyes of a child who refuses to grow up, his feelings of revulsion toward a society in full decay. Challenging the official interpretation that sharply cuts off the Nazi period from the time preceding and following it (e.g., the myth of 1945 as "Hour zero"), Grass stresses instead the continuities in German history. He is particularly critical of the lack of opposition to the Nazi regime. Among the targets of the author's poisonous remarks are people pretending to belong to the Resistance (not even Social Democrats are left unscathed) or to have gone into "inward emigration," as in these reminiscences by the book's protagonist, Oskar Matzerath:

> That word "resistance" had become very fashionable. We hear of the "spirit of resistance," of "resistance circles." There is even talk of "inward resistance," a "psychic emigration." Not to mention those courageous and uncompromising souls who call themselves Resistance Fighters, men of the Resistance, because they were fined during the war for not blacking out their bedroom windows properly.... Yes, I did all that. But does that make me, as I lie in this mental hospital, a Resistance Fighter? I must answer in the negative, and I hope that you too, you who are not inmates in mental hospitals, will regard me as nothing more than an eccentric who, for private and what is more aesthetic reasons, though to be sure the advice of Bebra my mentor had something to do with it, rejected the cut and color of the uniforms, the rhythm and tone of the music normally played on rostrums, and therefore drummed up a bit of protest on an instrument that was a mere toy.[45]

Drama is particularly well suited to the discussion of moral dilemmas. It is thus not surprising that both Siegfried Lenz and Hans Gunter Michelsen used plays to shake up German society and try to force it to face its moral responsibility. In Lenz's *Zeit der Schuldlosen*, nine ordinary citizens, representing different social classes and generations, are put into a decisive situation: they have been arrested and told that they will only be freed when they convince or force a political prisoner, who has participated in a violent action, to reveal the names of his collaborators.[46] They try different strategies, but fail. Eventually, one of them kills the prisoner and they are all released. Some time later, the previous, repressive government has been toppled, the killed prisoner has been made into a martyr, and the nine ordinary citizens are arrested again. They now have to disclose who killed the prisoner. None of them wants to confess, until at the end of the play, one of the prisoners, the Consul, kills himself.

Lenz's play asks us to reflect on three moral questions that are relevant to the confrontation of the Nazi past. One question, developed in the first act, refers to the legitimacy of violence against a state perceived as lawless, even if this means putting at risk innocent lives ("What my friends do, they do for you too," says the political prisoner).[47] Another moral question is whether saving oneself justifies murder. The third question, developed in the second act, refers to the concept of guilt. Is it only the executioner who is guilty, or is it the group of people that lets things happen? The author brings to the fore the issue of collective guilt, the idea that we are guilty for those things that we let others do, much as does Sartre in his play *Les Mouches*.

Michelsen's play *Helm* touches on similar themes but is directed more against forgetting, against the illusion of the expiration of moral responsibility (as in the debates that took place in West Germany about the duration of the statutes of limitations on war crimes).[48] Twenty years after the war, five war veterans have been invited to a hunt by a former comrade, Fritz Helm, whom they had unjustly penalized by sending him on a suicide mission in which he was severely and permanently injured. Helm does not show up at their meeting point in the forest, however. Gradually, the veterans start getting nervous, suspecting that they have been tricked by him. Every time one goes somewhere apart from the group, a shot is heard and the person does not return. We do not know whether those who disappear are dead, nor whether Helm is responsible for the shots. What matters is that the situation forces each of the former soldiers to face the past. This confrontation with the past finds them reacting in different ways. Some pretend that they did not have anything to do with what happened to Helm; others recognize their mistake; one regrets not having killed Helm. There is no redemption, however, and they disappear, one by one. Michelsen addresses this play to bourgeoisified West Germany in which, intoxicated by the effects of the "economic miracle," individuals had all too easily forgotten what they did or did not do during World War II. Not unlike Schroers's, Michelsen's lesson is that none of us is entitled to forget, that we will all eventually be made accountable for our past deeds.

Whereas the early 1960s' debates on the Nazi past focused on the issue of responsibility, the late 1960s signaled the beginnings, but only the beginnings, of some public discussion about the Holocaust, until then a mostly ignored topic.[49] In 1960, in the wake of public commotion caused by the neo-Nazi profanation of the Cologne synagogue on Christmas Eve, the German parliament passed a law that penalized hate crimes targeted against specific "segments of the population."[50] Later on, the televised Eichmann trial in Israel and the Auschwitz trial in 1963 further reminded the German population about the Nazi genocide. The public remained rather indifferent, however, as evidenced by the low audience ratings for the televised Auschwitz trial.[51] Contemporary history textbooks themselves hardly contained more than a few lines on the persecution of the Jews and the Holocaust.[52]

Also in the late 1960s, the antibourgeois student movement reignited the debate about the Nazi period from a new perspective. The student revolts expressed intense generational conflict, rooted in the contrasting life experiences of those born around the end of World War II and their parents and grandparents. This generational conflict was portrayed in award-winning novels of that time, such as Herburger's *The Eroberung der Zi-*

tadelle and Born's *Die erdabgewandte Seite der Geschichte*, both recipients of the Bremer Literaturpreis.[53] Their central theme was no longer the moral responsibility of the war generations and the failure of these generations to face the past (these were taken for granted and often referred to); instead, they concentrated on the daily existence of young adults who faced the contradictions of their bourgeois existence, and who, out of mistrust of their parents and because of their parents' own incapacity to communicate, found themselves deprived of role models.[54]

The confrontation with the Nazi past proceeded unremittingly in the 1970s, 1980s, and 1990s, prompted by contemporary media and political events that gradually shifted the focus from World War II as a whole to the Holocaust. Attracting widespread public interest were such events as Brandt's 1970 visit to Warsaw's ghetto, the Holocaust television series in 1980, the awarding of the 1982 Goethe Prize for literature to Ernst Jünger, Kohl's 1985 visit to Bitburg cemetery, President Richard von Weizsäcker's praised and popular 1985 address, the 1986–87 "*Historikerstreit,*" the building of the history museums in Bonn and Berlin, the 1996 episodes of anti-immigrant violence, the 1996 publication of Goldhagen's book, the 1998 Walser-Bubis debate, and the debate on the Holocaust monument in Berlin. The granting of awards to novels about the Nazi period, including the persecution of the Jews, has reflected the will by segments of the elites to keep the past alive for younger generations. Thus, the 1980 Bremer Literaturpreis was awarded to a biographical novel by Christoph Meckel, *Blickwinkel*, a bitter and reproachful telling of the author's father's passive attitude toward the Nazi regime and of his repressing of the past thereafter.[55] The 1981 award went to Peter Weiss for his epic about the socialist and communist resistance against the Nazi regime, *Die Äesthetik des Widerstands*.[56] Finally, the 1995 Bremer Literaturpreis was awarded to George-Arthur Goldschmidt for *Der unterbrochene Wald*, an autobiographical book about the author's experience as a German Jewish boy; he was sent away to a rural region in France to keep him safe from the Nazi government, and had to move constantly from family to family to avoid being caught.[57] It is a highly introspective book that explores the child's traumatic and contradictory feelings about being both relatively safe and away from his family.[58]

Starting in the late 1960s, history textbooks for secondary schools both reflected and contributed to the changes in how the FRG dealt with its past. They no longer contained an explicit denial of collective guilt and did not justify support for Nazism in Germany by explicitly invoking the effect of propaganda or claiming that the German population did not share Hitler's plans. On the contrary, they expressed a willingness to carry the burden of world condemnation of Germany as a nation. The German population was still depicted as victim, however—victim of what Hitler had done in its name, and victim of what others had done to it: "Because of him the German name was burdened and shamed with the worst crime in the history of humanity. They cannot easily forget what was done in the name of the German people to millions of other people. We all carry this shame. Not even what we ourselves have suffered, what the others brought on us in terms of pain and injustice, makes it disappear. We must take this into account when we deal with others, no matter how bitter this may be for us."[59]

A radical departure in the treatment of the Nazi past was perceptible in the 1980s, when history textbooks began to devote significant space to the racist component of Nazi ideology and to the Holocaust. This discussion was contextualized, however, through references to the Exodus, to the discrimination of Jews throughout history, and to the racist theories of the nineteenth century.[60] A more significant change in these textbooks was the unusual harshness and sarcasm with which the German population was blamed for what the Nazi regime did:

> And how did German citizens stand with respect to the other, the true side? Certainly, they heard of this or that neighbor who had vanished. Concentration camps—these were two words that since 1933 had become more and more familiar. They were briefly given pause when news of the Reich's week of assassinations went through the country. They lamented that their family doctor had to close his office in 1936 because of being a Jew. They observed with some discomfort, how their city's synagogue went up in flames in 1938 while the firemen just stood there, doing nothing to put out the fire. And it made them shiver when in the summer of 1939 they began reading the word *War* with increasing frequency in the papers.
>
> At the beginning, however, these were only short moments of lucidity and reflection that they quickly overcame. "The Führer surely knows best," was their easy answer, which immediately freed them from any responsibility. And thus the majority of Germans fulfilled the small duties that some division of the Party machinery had assigned to them, suddenly considered themselves important, just because they wore a [brown] uniform or whatever badge, hung the flag with the swastika on their balcony whenever the Führer demanded it, and finally jubilated: "Führer, command us! We follow!"[61]

This quote stands in sharp contrast to the apologetic tone of textbooks from previous decades. It represents the end of a long and slow transformation in the content of secondary school history textbooks toward a growing acknowledgment of the responsibility the German population bore for the Nazi past.

In sum, the West German population, willingly or unwillingly, came to confront the Nazi past during the second half of the twentieth century. It is not surprising then that when people justify Germany's membership in the European Union, they draw on arguments that, directly or indirectly, refer to Germany's responsibility for World War II.

In Fear of Germany

At one point in Willhelm Genazino's 1989 travel novel *Der Fleck, Die Jacke, Die Zimmer, Der Schmerz*, about bourgeois loneliness in a colorful but absurd world, the narrator, a *flâneur*, remarks while sitting in a Paris café:

> There is again anxiety about Germany. The country does not realize it; it listens only to its self-praise, and since it becomes more irresistible year after year, it has always something about which to marvel.[62]

The author-narrator's observation interests us because it betrays the German population's sensitivity to other countries' fears of Germany even as it negates it. In fact, Germans do care, as in the following excerpts from my interviews on European integration:

> Germany should make it clear that the war ended fifty years ago and [other countries] should decide once and for all whether we are the old enemy or their partner.   (107, Weststadt, older than 50, more than High School)

> Germany, due to its past, still has this reputation that it looks after its interests and does not care very much about cooperation with other countries.... It is logical, since in both World Wars Germany was the main aggressor. It is thus not surprising that people in other countries still have the feeling that Germany still entertains some kind of plans.
> (116, Weststadt, 30 or younger, more than High School)

The FRG's limited autonomy in the conduct of foreign affairs and the West German population's perceived bad image abroad have been salient themes in West Germany's cultural landscape since the end of World War II. These two related topics deserve separate discussion.

The FRG's Conditional Sovereignty

In a national representative survey conducted in 1985, 63% of the respondents judged that the FRG's foreign policy was strongly or very strongly affected by the Third Reich and World War II.[63] This perception is consistent with the way West German foreign policy has been portrayed. The standard narrative about the history of the Federal Republic of Germany emphasizes the background of foreign constraints and mistrust that surrounded the FRG's patient and careful struggle to regain sovereignty and achieve German reunification. The story begins with the four years that followed German capitulation on May 1945. Germany was then an occupied territory whose political future was uncertain. In the midst of destruction and economic misery, the Allies imposed denazification and reeducation policies as well reparations and the dismantlement of large industrial sectors. They also conducted the Nüremberg trials, which, as emphasized in Ebeling's 1955 secondary school history textbook, initially excluded all German participation in the prosecution and the jury.[64] As shown in the previous sections, there was intense debate about the Allied policies in Germany, as well as about the question of Germany's collective guilt, an idea that was also promoted by the Allies. The literature on the years before the Bonn Republic does not fail to discuss the Allied policies and the population's angry and dismissive reaction to them.

The standard description of the FRG's political and diplomatic emancipation stresses that the creation of the FRG did not put an end to foreign dependence. It goes as follows: In 1949, months after Erhard's monetary reform, the Western Allies authorized and encouraged the formation of the Federal Republic of Germany. The FRG remained, however, a state under Allied supervision. The Occupation Statute, in particular, restricted the new state's sovereignty, both internally and externally.[65] German reunification and security with respect to the Soviet Union were the FRG's priorities, whose attainment, however, depended on international trust of a hypothetically reunified Germany and, increasingly, on the evolution of West–Soviet Union relations. Faced with lack of trust toward Germany, the constraints of the Cold War, and deeply mistrustful of the Soviet Union, Adenauer had few options but to give up immediate German reunification and decisively anchor the FRG in the West, which prompted irate criticism from the left.[66]

Upon implementation of the Paris Treaties in May 1955, the FRG was sovereign formally but not completely: the Allies still held emergency powers to guarantee the security of their troops in the FRG and the power to decide on issues pertaining to the FRG as a whole, including the issue of reunification and the signing of a peace treaty, and the government of Berlin. These formal constraints on the FRG's sovereignty served to back more informal ones concerning foreign policy toward Eastern Europe. It was indeed a source of concern for the West that the FRG, whether for security or reunification reasons, might decide to pursue an independent policy toward the Soviet Union; this would put at risk the balance of forces between East and West, along with NATO's strategic plans.[67] The West was thus uncomfortable with Adenauer's secret diplomacy with the Soviet Union in 1963, which evoked the specter of Rapallo (1922),[68] and with the plans for a Bonn visit by Khrushchev in 1964.[69]

Official accounts of West German foreign policy during this period thus emphasize its subordination to strategic decisions taken in Washington and Moscow, and the lack of weight of a relatively small state such as the FRG in global foreign policy matters. The new foreign policy of the 1966 CDU-SPD coalition government and the 1969 SPD government, and the end of the Allies' emergency rights in 1968, marked significant steps forward in the FRG's quest for sovereignty and equal international status. In the context of East-West détente, the FRG's abandonment of the politics of diplomatic isolation toward the GDR and the signing of treaties with the Soviet Union, the GDR, Poland, and Czechoslovakia (Ostpolitik) unlocked the diplomatic stalemate that had paralyzed both the FRG and the West's diplomacy for more than a decade.[70] Most significant was the FRG's recognition of the GDR as a state, which reassured the West and the Soviet Union and thus allowed the FRG more initiative in foreign policy. The hardening of East-West relations after 1979 and NATO's controversial decision to deploy middle-range nuclear missiles in Germany in the early 1980s demonstrated again that the FRG, because of its strategic geopolitical position, could not be fully sovereign.[71] Only the fall of communism and the end of the Cold War in the late 1980s made possible German reunification and a peace treaty with the four powers, and thus the restoration of normality in German foreign policy.

Over the years, standard accounts of West German foreign policy since World War II have thus conveyed a strong sense of dependence with respect to other countries' plans and international mistrust of the FRG. This sense of dependence and foreign mistrust, unusual in the history of alliances,[72] has been underlined in the typical narrative through frequent use of words like fear, anxiety, worry, mistrust, or discomfort.[73] German foreign policy analysts have mentioned these fears whenever the FRG or reunited Germany showed some assertiveness, especially during the period of the Bahr-Brandt Ostpolitik[74] and around the time of German reunification.[75] The public was told, for instance, about other countries' fears that the Ostpolitik would lead to another Rapallo; later, during the German reunification process, the public learned about international distress caused by talk of Germany's middle position in Europe and its plans to become the catalyst of a new peace order, which evoked memories of the Nazi past; finally, both in the 1970s and during German reunification, the German public was told that the world worried about a too powerful Germany (e.g., when Germany unilaterally recognized Slovenia and Croatia).

German political leaders have been effective transmitters of and have agreed with other countries' misgivings about Germany. Repeatedly in the history of the FRG, German chancellors and presidents have stressed, for instance, Germany's need to protect itself from itself by joining larger international organizations such as the EU. On other occasions, while reassuring other countries about the FRG, they have listed the precise reasons why other countries feared Germany. Thus, in his 1961–62 New Year's address President Lübke said: "May the world realize that there is nothing that the German people wishes more than the attainment of peace and the realization of its right to self-determination." He then continued, however, with the following apology: "We, today's Germans, are not moved by any will to power, any desire for revenge."[76] Similarly, in a 1971 article Willy Brandt asked other countries not to be afraid of a more powerful Germany, but then, a few lines below, suggested that this fear might have some justification: "we must again find the right measure, which historically has often seemed too difficult."[77] In the 1990s, Helmut Schmidt and Helmut Kohl made similar comments when discussing foreign anxiety about a powerful reunited Germany.[78]

Besides reports on German foreign policy or addresses by political leaders, an effective vehicle to transmit other countries' fears of Germany has been journal or newspaper contributions by foreign analysts about the images that other countries have of Germany.[79] Such contributions were very frequent around the time of German reunification, and although they usually concluded that Germany enjoyed the trust of other nations, they did not fail to methodically lay out the often injurious prejudices foreign political leaders, media analysts, and ordinary citizens held toward Germany. Thus, Richard Davy, for instance, does not fail to cites Thatcher's critical views on German reunification and an article by Connor Cruise O'Brien's published in *The Times* (October 31, 1990), which predicts the emergence of the Fourth Reich, the rehabilitation of racist theories, and the appearance of monuments to Hitler everywhere, before concluding that British public opinion makers are nonetheless generally optimistic about a reunified Germany![80]

Germany's Image Abroad

Over the past several decades the West German population has become conscious of the fact that other countries' fears of Germany have constrained their country's foreign policy. My in-depth interviews with Weststadt respondents revealed that this consciousness of other countries' fears not only follows them when they travel abroad, but has also at times been nourished by these travel experiences. One example is the anecdote told to me by a twenty-year-old student, about her experience as an exchange student living with a family in Poland. Although everything went very well with the family and she thoroughly enjoyed her time in Poland, she once felt very uncomfortable when the father of the host family began to discuss the Nazi period and insisted on her reading a book that contained abundant photographic material about the Holocaust. My respondent brought this story into the conversation to illustrate a point she was trying to make about the negative images that people in other countries hold about Germany. While she thought that these negative images justify Germany's efforts to contribute to European integration, she also felt that they represent a distorted view of Germany and saw no reason to apologize for events that not even her parents had lived through.

The perception that Germany is disliked or feared abroad has been a distinctive feature of West German culture since the end of World War II. This has been conveyed through numerous surveys conducted since the mid-1950s. In fact, these surveys tell us as much about the cultural presuppositions of those organizing the surveys, representatives of the well-educated segments in West German society, as about the population itself. One very clear example is the following question, part of a survey conducted by the prestigious Allensbach Institut für Demoskopie: "One often hears that Germans are disliked around the world. How do you explain this?" The wording of this question, asked at least in 1955, 1969, 1975, and 1980, violates a basic rule in question writing: do not assume that everyone accepts the premise on which a question is based, in this case, that "Germans are disliked around the world."[81] In fact, the *Allensbacher Jahrbuch* has reported another, more academically sound, version of the question, for the year 1952 and then for 1975 and several years after: "Do you believe that Germans are liked or disliked around the world?" It would appear then that the first version of the question reflected a strong conviction on the part of those who wrote the questionnaire that most, if not all, Germans perceived that they were disliked around the world.

The distribution of answers to the second version of the question shows that the assumption implicit in the first version is not justified: in the years 1952, 1975, 1987, and 1997, the respondents who said that Germans are disliked around the world represented respectively 34%, 22%, 25%, and 38% of the sample, whereas the respondents who said that Germans are liked represented 38%, 54%, 57%, and 39%.[82] West Germans therefore have tended to perceive themselves more as liked than disliked. The high percentages of respondents who, especially in 1952 and 1997, perceived themselves as disliked are indicative, however, of a salient feature in West German culture. In fact, when the loaded version of the question was asked, the respondents who voluntarily answered "we are not disliked" represented only 14% (1955), 9% (1969), 7% (1975), and 9% (1980) of the samples.

The reasons that West German respondents gave to explain why Germans are not liked around the world are consistent with some of the themes developed in this chapter, that is, the importance of the Nazi past in West Germany's collective memory and the belief in the pernicious role that some negative character traits have played in German history. Thus, although respondents mentioned a variety of reasons, among the most frequently cited were those related to World War II and the Third Reich and those related to German feelings of superiority and self-righteous attitudes. World War II and the Third Reich, in particular, were mentioned by 13%, 38%, 32%, 27%, and 36% of the respondents in the years 1955, 1969, 1975, and 1980 respectively, with the loaded version of the question, and by 14% in 1997 with the balanced version. Except in 1955 when the most frequent explanation was the German population's work ethic (20%), World War II and the Third Reich have been the reasons most often mentioned.

As reflected in some of the comments made during the in-depth interviews, Germans on the whole do not, however, think that the dislike and fear other countries feel toward Germany are justified. A national survey conducted in 1993 showed, for instance, that 60% of the West German respondents thought that international anxiety about Germany playing a bigger role in world politics after reunification was unjustified. The percentage was even higher when the question was asked of a sample of social leaders (78%).[83] The feeling that the memory of World War II is actually instrumentalized by other countries in their relations with Germany is in fact widespread. The inclusion of a question on this issue in a survey conducted in 1991 is in itself indicative of the prevalence of this view in German society, and the answers confirmed this assumption. When asked to express their degree of agreement with a statement that said "The responsibility of the Germans for the war is used by many abroad to exert pressure in order to obtain compensation payments," respondents on the average agreed: on a scale from 1 to 6, where 6 meant full agreement, the average value obtained was 4.5.[84]

When West German individuals reflect upon European integration, they do not do so in a vacuum. The way they interpret information concerning the functioning and projects of the European Union is mediated, whether consciously or not, by the culture in which they live, ranging from direct personal experience to the knowledge they acquired while going to school many years earlier. Chapters 2, 3, and 4 showed what aspects of the German national culture differentiate the West German respondents' approach to European integration from those of the Spanish and British respondents. These aspects are all related to the West German respondents' interpretation of Germany's role in World War II and how it impacted the life of the FRG. They are (1) the respondents' belief in the existence and persistence in Germany of dangerous traits of character such as the will to dominate other peoples; (2) the sense of responsibility for other countries, rooted in the acceptance of collective responsibility for World War II; and, finally, a pragmatic desire to reassure other countries about Germany's ambitions so as (3) not to feed their fears or (4) their negative images of Germany.

Media discussions of European integration have surely contributed to connecting these aspects of German national culture to the discourse of ordinary people about this process. But the picture is not complete unless one explains why those cultural aspects and not others, and why public opinion makers acting through the media are successful in transmitting their way of framing European integration. Furthermore, one needs to explain why ordinary citizens have connected European integration to aspects of German national culture that were rarely emphasized in the editorials and opinion pieces discussed in chapter 4, such as the first, second, and fourth aspects listed in the previous paragraph.

The discussion in this chapter has demonstrated that the answer to these questions lies in the centrality of these issues in Germany's national culture. Emphasis on the negative aspects of German character ties in with the debate on the continuities of German history, emphasis on the sense of responsibility for other countries ties in with the debate on German collective guilt for the Nazi past, emphasis on other countries' fears ties in with the debate about German foreign policy, and emphasis on the poor image that other countries have of Germany ties in with the experiences German citizens have had in other countries and their access to what citizens in other countries think. The best way to demonstrate the validity of these conclusions is to compare West and East German views on European integration.

Seven

East Germany: A Different Past, a Different Memory

Two OSTSTADT respondents referred to Germany's role in World War II when discussing European integration. The two, informed advocates of a political integration model of European integration, provided familiar arguments, already made by Weststadt respondents. The first one, a cosmopolitan agricultural engineer who now owns a restaurant, repeated arguments formulated by Schmidt and Kohl at the time of German reunification when he said:

> It should do it [be part of the European Union] for self-protection, because Germany always has this tendency toward hegemony, which rests in its economic power. Germans are hard-working and powerful, and this makes them prone to lead. (65, Oststadt, 31–50, more than High School)

The second respondent, a CDU representative, repeated the argument that Germany needs to be part of the EU to maintain the trust of other nations. Germany, according to him, must be, and has learnt to be, very careful not to be too assertive, because of what he perceives as a long foreign occupation:

> Germany was occupied by foreign powers for more than forty years. This has left its mark, it has led to a special reluctance, at least in the public sphere, to express national feelings, and this is mirrored in Germany's foreign policy.
> (55, Oststadt, CDU)

It is puzzling that these arguments were not made more often among Oststadt respondents, in view of the fact that they were often discussed in the German press at the time of reunification. In this chapter, I demonstrate that the concept of frame alignment helps to solve this puzzle for it points toward the examination of the fit between arguments used in the debate about European integration and broader preoccupations in the culture in which they are formulated. There is substantial evidence to support the hypothesis that one reason why Oststadt respondents did not refer to Germany's role in World War II when discussing European integration is that it is a theme that plays a marginal role in post-reunification eastern Germany.

The results of my interviews in Oststadt made quite clear that East Germany's current cultural anchoring points are not the Nazi past as in West Germany but German reunification, with all its concomitant adjustment problems, and the Communist past. Whereas twenty Weststadt respondents spontaneously mentioned World War II or the Nazi period, only thirteen Oststadt respondents did so; meanwhile, whereas only four Weststadt respondents mentioned German reunification during the interviews, thirteen Oststadt respondents did so. A survey conducted by the Allensbach Institut für Demoskopie in 1997 demonstrates that this contrast between my Weststadt and Oststadt respondents was not haphazard. When asked about the historical events that make German history different from the history of other countries, 44% of West German respondents in the Allensbach survey mentioned the Third Reich, National Socialism, and Hitler, compared with 13% of East German respondents. Furthermore, 20% of West German respondents mentioned Nazi crimes, compared with 4% of East German respondents. The percentages of West and East German respondents who mentioned World War II were very similar, 29% and 33% respectively; a smaller proportion of the former (5% versus 18%) mentioned that Germany has started wars. Finally, 20% of West German respondents mentioned German reunification, compared with 40% of East German respondents.[1]

Shifting Collective Memory

Semi-structured in-depth interviews are a good gauge of the problems that concern a community at a particular point in time. My experience in Weststadt and Oststadt could not have offered clearer contrasts. Whereas my Weststadt respondents expressed interest in and preoccupation with a variety of topics—xenophobia, BSE ("mad cow disease"), the environment, unemployment, youth crime, drugs, and so on—my Oststadt respondents had one problem foremost in their minds, which was how to adjust to the identity, social, and economic problems of reunification. As an editor of Oststadt's local paper, the *Oststadt Zeitung*, put it,

> In East Germany, the majority of the population are busy with defining their own status and position in society: Who are they? Are they German, are they Oststadtan, Anhaltan? And Europe simply complicates things, not least because of how distant it is perceived to be.   (54, Oststadt, *Oststadt Zeitung*)

The respondents' comments and stories referred to local and personal problems alike. Many were frustrated because of the brutal economic liberalization and restructuring that had taken place in a very short time.

One example that they often mentioned concerned the old beer factory, a source of pride for the population of Oststadt, that had been bought by a concern from Bavaria only to be closed just a few months later. More generally, a retired electrical engineer argued that

> The main problem is that, because of having been linked to the Eastern Bloc, East Germany does not fit in the Western market, does not have something to offer. The process was not well prepared. Kohl did not have good advisors and one of the consequences of this error is that East Germany has been sacked by speculators, who have bought cheap and sold expensive.
> (95, Oststadt, older than 50, more than High School)

Another example relates to the problems created by the liberalization of the economy. One of my respondents (105, Oststadt, aged 31–50, less than High School), a married man with two unemployed children, told me that before reunification he and his wife earned 1500 DM and paid 100 DM for rent, whereas now they earn 1700 DM and pay 600 DM for the same apartment.

Some respondents directed their anger at Helmut Kohl, whose promises of "blooming landscapes" had remained unfulfilled:

> You see, I don't trust politicians. When I think about Helmut Kohl, for instance, who before the transition had promised us a Golden Age, and who has not achieved what he promised, I can only conclude that these people only look upon their own interests.... The big economic actors will surely benefit from it [European integration]; as for the little people, that is not so clear, for the same reason that the reunification has been very beneficial to big business, but very disadvantageous to the common people.... You see, the capitalist system has rolled us over, we, a people with a totally different upbringing, and the same could happen through [European] unification to many poorer countries, that is, they could be rolled over by German capital.
> (96, Oststadt, older than 50, more than High School)

In general, I often got the impression that respondents welcomed the opportunity offered by the interview to discuss their problems and vent their frustrations, as when I interviewed two friendly representatives of the local association for the unemployed, who halfway into the interview got carried away and became extremely angry as they spoke about the lack of programs for the unemployed and about competition from workers from Eastern Europe:

> Oststadt was a city specialized in machine industry, electrotechnical industry, chemical industry. Everything has been destroyed, and this has affected academics, workers in their 40s, and women. The latter try to persevere through continuing education and training, but they receive low priority in the labor

market. For young people, the problem is less important, because they can always emigrate. (59, Oststadt, Unemployment Association)

Similar problems were brought up in a later conversation with members of a local women's association who told me about how disproportionately they had been affected by laying-off measures, and the efforts they were making to obtain the needed qualifications to reenter the labor force.

Finally, there was the problem of identity, already mentioned in the quote from the editor of the *Oststadt Zeitung*. Respondents were frustrated because of the prejudice shown by "Wessies" toward "Ossies." According to an employee at Oststadt's Welfare Association,

> Government officials had this idea that we lived in the jungle, that we did not know how to work, that we could not eat with knife and fork. In fact, we had a good school system, we have all received a good education, and these skills have been ignored. This does not mean that people want the DDR back. It is impossible because the industry has been destroyed. What this means is that an all-German identity has not developed. People still see themselves as "Ossies" and assert East German values that they consider better than the "Wessies'." The "Ossies" and the "Wessies" don't get along very well because the "Ossies" have a totally different mentality from that of the "Wessies"; this is due to different upbringing, to different living conditions. For the "Wessies," the educational system emphasizes the principle of maximum efficiency; while with us the emphasis was more on community values, on the idea of collective work. Thus, in the end, many who at the beginning screamed "We are a People" are now back to reality and say "How nice it used to be here."
>
> (60, Oststadt, Welfare Association)

The rapid and dramatic transformations experienced in the new *Länder* have thus meant a shift in the historical reference points of East German national culture from the Nazi period and World War II to Communism and German reunification. Oststadt respondents demonstrated, however, that despite being preoccupied with the consequences of reunification, they had internalized quite thoroughly the cognitive frame on European integration prevailing in West Germany. Also, the survey information provided above shows that when asked about events that differentiate the history of Germany from that of other countries, East Germans mentioned World War II as often as did West Germans and even mentioned more often than did West Germans that Germany had initiated wars.

Despite the aforementioned similarities, East German respondents were much less likely to mention everything related to the Nazi past. To understand this and thus round out the explanation of the contrasts between West and East Germans in how frequently they mention German responsibility in World War II and the Nazi past when discussing European integration, we must now turn to the role of the Nazi past in East German culture and to East German perceptions of how World War II has impacted Germany's image abroad.

Dealing with the Past in East Germany

The main contrast between the way West and East Germans confronted the Nazi past is that in the FRG there was public debate between radically different views, whereas in the GDR a similar debate took place within much narrower margins. When West German respondents said that Germany must contribute to efforts to European integration for self-protection, they were echoing an argument about the continuity of pernicious cultural or psychological aspects of German culture that, as I have suggested above, has been brought up often enough for over forty years to be part of the cultural repertoire available to the West German population.

The dominant view in the GDR's historiography expressed a Marxist-Leninist approach to historical evolution, following which the Nazi period and World War II were just a phase in the intensification of class contradictions on the road to socialism. Furthermore, this view distinguishes between a good, progressive tradition and a bad, regressive tradition, in German history.[2] The conception of German history and culture as consisting of positive and negative aspects is also evident in historiographical discussions in West Germany. The difference between the West German and East German discussions was, first of all, conceptual, since the East German distinction between progressive and regressive aspects was made with respect to their contribution to socialist human emancipation, while the West German distinction was made with respect to a more heterogeneous set of political, moral, and ideal values. Furthermore, at least until the 1970s, the East German distinction between progressive and regressive aspects of German history overlapped with the distinction between oppressed and oppressing classes, whereas there is no class referent in the West German distinction between positive and negative aspects of German culture. In the 1970s and thereafter, efforts by the East German state to develop a strong national consciousness led to a loosening of the link between the progressive/repressive and the oppressed/oppressor dichotomies. From then on, members of or actions by oppressing classes were considered to belong to the progressive tradition to the extent that they had contributed to the long-term attainment of socialism. This change of approach allowed the GDR to rehabilitate previously condemned figures such as Luther, Frederick the Great, and Bismarck and to include some aspects of their legacies within the progressive tradition.[3]

Finally and most crucially, East German historiography stressed the bifurcation of the progressive and regressive traditions with the division of Germany into the GDR and the FRG. Accordingly, militarism and authoritarianism were seen as regressive characteristics that applied to the FRG but not to the GDR. Citizens of the GDR thus did not grow up in a society that debated the need to protect itself against inner demons.

West German respondents also referred to Germany's moral responsibility to contribute to the European unification effort because of the suffering it inflicted on other countries and peoples during World War II. I have shown that despite the great amount of individual memory repression and active denial of collective responsibility in the FRG, there was an intense debate about guilt and responsibility for the Nazi past for most of the postwar era, in which the voices of those acknowledging German responsibility and admonishing the population against forgetting were heard loudly and with increasing frequency over time. The same cannot be said about the GDR.

In the GDR, one can speak of phases in the confrontation with the Nazi past rather than the existence of a public debate on the issue. With the exception of the early, pre-GDR, period, during which some German Communist leaders acknowledged German responsibility for the Nazi period, one had to wait for the celebration of the 35th anniversary of the GDR to hear a public admission of responsibility for the Nazi past by an East German leader.[4] The GDR's official version of the 1933–45 period exculpated the nation and the East German population through two mechanisms: first, by concentrating responsibility for the war and war crimes on the Nazi leaders and on the imperialist and militarist monopoly capitalists who allegedly controlled them, and second, by making antifascism into a main element of the Communist regime's legitimizing ideology.

The exculpation of the population followed familiar lines already discussed for the FRG, with small variations due to the narrative's Marxist overtones. This becomes apparent when one examines secondary school history textbooks for the years 1952, 1962–64, and 1984–86 (see appendix 4), and award-winning novels for the entire period.[5] The storyline includes the following points:

- German imperialists were responsible for World War I.
- Germany lost World War I.
- Germany had to accept very difficult peace conditions, which mostly affected the workers; Versailles was a plot by Western monopoly capital to turn Germany against the Soviet Union. The anger and frustration it created among the population prepared the ground for Hitler's demagoguery.
- Some additional problems, mostly economic, such as inflation and the economic crisis, helped National Socialism into power.

- World War II, like World War I, was a logical manifestation of the increasing contradictions of capitalism; it belongs in the logic of the history; World War II manifested these contradictions in the form of an aggression of Western imperialism against the Soviet Union.
- The political leaders and the imperialist and militarist groups for which they worked were responsible for the worst aberrations. The German population was not responsible.

I have purposely borrowed the structure of Dahrendorf's outline of the major features of the FRG's explanation for World War II, which (as I showed above) corresponded more to textbooks from the 1950s than to textbooks from later periods, simply to emphasize the similarities between the two. In addition to these similarities, the GDR's narrative, like the FRG's, contextualized and relativized the Nazi period and the Nazi crimes. It did so by including National Socialism as part of the dictatorial wave of the 1920s and 1930s and by explaining it as a result of the growing contradictions of world capitalism. However, the GDR textbooks did not have the exculpatory tone of the FRG's 1950s textbooks; they devoted more space to discussing the persecution of the Jews and other ethnic and national groups than did all the FRG textbooks examined here; and, unlike the FRG textbooks, they emphasized that the Jews were only one among many persecuted groups. In fact, they reiterated that the Slavs suffered more under Nazi persecution than did the Jews.[6]

The GDR textbooks failed to move toward admission of the population's responsibility as much as did FRG textbooks from the 1980s and the 1990s. Although the 1986 textbook timidly conceded that aside from some antifascist resistance "the bulk of the German people continued to follow Hitler's fatal path,"[7] it did so while simultaneously stressing the manipulation to which the masses were made subject. Moreover, the 1984 GDR textbook, like a 1969 FRG textbook, portrayed the German population more as victim than as perpetrator:

> Throughout the world, its name [Germany's] was tainted by scorn and shame, for cruel crimes against peace and humanity were indeed committed in the name of the German people. Millions of Germans had to pay with their lives for the power and conquest ambitions of monopoly capital, the big landowners, and the militarists.[8]

For their part, 1950s literary accounts of the war devoted much less space to the early phases of World War II than to the last years, when Germany was on the defensive and the bombing of German cities began, as if to stress the suffering Germans themselves experienced. Furthermore, while allowing for differences of character and attitudes among the population, they emphasized the goodness and gullibility of the German population. One good example of this is Gotthold Gloger's novel, *Philomena Kleespiess trug die Fahne*, for which the author received the Heinrich Mann Nationalpreis der DDR. The book narrates the history of Germany from 1910 to the early 1950s, as experienced in a small rural region near Frankfurt, upon which war and human destruction falls like an uncontrollable force of nature. The thread that carries through the entire book is the opposition between Wealth-Militarism and Poverty-Pacifism. Throughout the book, the village's inhabitants are portrayed as victims of forces that they cannot control; only at the end, under Communist guidance, do they draw the lesson that they have to take their lives into their own hands, a message that also pervades the GDR history textbooks. The embodiment of the region's spirit and the main character in this sentimental saga is Philomena Kleespiess, a poor, very naive, devout, good woman, who loses her fiancée in World War I and remains single for the rest of her life. The following excerpt tells about her naiveté and that of many of her co-villagers:

> [*Mela meets a group of members of a Nazi organization for young people, who want to sell her eggs.*] "We stand by the Führer and are his faithful followers. Under Adolf Hitler the Reich will finally attain the position in the world to which it is entitled." Mela listened to everything. "That's fine," she said, and was happy to see young people march into the future with such determined optimism.... Mela was really excited about her encounter with the Jungvolk [*Young People—name of the organization.*] "Life is certainly worth it for them," she thought. "They believe in something new." Philomena had always waited for something like this. She had saved herself for this. Because of dreams she had lived an unfulfilled life, always waiting for the better that had to come.[9]

Dieter Noll's very successful book, *Die Abenteuer des Werner Holt*, conveyed the same message, that is, that the German people were simply taken in by Nazi propaganda. The book describes the gradual transformation of Werner Holt, a German teenager who volunteers to the army in the last two years of World War II and then turns from a blind and proud supporter of the war and of Germany's goals, moved by the desire of adventure, into a horrified, anomic, detached person, who simply wants the war to end. Werner Holt's revered best friend, Wolzow, a person totally and crazily imbued with a militaristic and nationalistic ethos inherited from his family, stands for the manipulative capacity of National Socialism. Thus, at the end of the book:

> "But what is Wolzow for them, for me?" A thought came to Holt, thickened, and turned into a certainty. It took his breath away. The shutters fell from his eyes, the dark room turned full of light. *He* was their fate.... *Fate*, he thought, my fate has a name, *Wolzow*. What have I done with my eyes, my understanding? My *fate* is a human being, a living human being with body and brains and beating heart, who accumulates power over life and death, he or another, here

in this cellar, the same everywhere, across the entire country.... And now he realized: That which remains anonymous, the system, organized in ranks and uniforms, a hierarchy of violence, is our *fate*! Lies, it was all deceit,... it was not the power of fate over powerless people, not predestination over a predetermined path, not God over people of the earth, over mortals, but instead human beings over human beings, the holders of power over those without power, and always mortals over mortals![10]

It would be a misrepresentation to say that these books totally exculpate the population. In Noll's book, for instance, Werner Holt ends by confessing to himself: "I have been an accomplice in everything. I have kept silence and watched. Some of it was also in me. And now I am guilty."[11] Nonetheless, an occasional expression of contrition like this pales in comparison with the message of essential innocence that pervades the rest of the narrative. One needs to wait until the 1970s, with the publication of Christa Wolf's *Kindheitsmuster* and Franz Fühmann's *22 Tage oder die Hälfte des Lebens*, for more critical approaches to the German population's behavior during the Nazi period,[12] and then, to the 1980s, when Helga Schubert received the Heinrich Mann Nationalpreis der DDR for her intimate autobiographical novel *Blickwinkel*, in which she openly discussed the question of guilt:

> Our strange feeling of guilt. Always misplaced. We felt shame for things other than those for which we should feel ashamed. We felt shame for being German. On tiptoes we went to the formerly German or German-occupied countries, to their cities. But not to be recognized as German.
>
> We were not supposed to feel collective guilt. We were supposed to direct our attention to the revolutionary traditions in Germany, memorize them, be proud of them, continue them. The fact that Hitler won power and also admiration surely was due, we learned, not to the nature of the German people, but to a particular stage of capitalism. It did not have anything to do with us.
>
> And yet we let ourselves be driven into a senseless self-defense. To calm ourselves, we kept on counting down the beads of our rosary in prayer: We are not so bad, surely not, we Germans. Only occasionally do we secretly feel proud to belong to this people, which splits and reunites and fights and hates itself, arrogant and pedantic and sentimental, simple and parochial. And for all the admiration we may also show for languages that sound different and for all the contempt that we may have for ourselves, we feel secretly at ease with our origins. But this is something we would never admit. Never.
>
> Don't you see that the thoughts you are expressing are dangerous?
>
> Dangerous because they can be misunderstood. Think of the Polish teacher, who became outraged and filled with anxiety. Never, she said, should a German

doubt his guilt, yes, even if he was not born yet at the time. Our children and grandchildren have had to grow up with this guilt.[13]

In these paragraphs Schubert certainly questions the notion of collective guilt, but the honesty of her reflections, the distance she expresses toward official discourse, and the admission of negative character traits in the German population, signal a definite evolution in the way East German literature approached the topic of German responsibility. Furthermore, it suggests that despite official exculpation, many East Germans had developed a sense of guilt for World War II and that East Germans faced in other Eastern European countries reproaches identical to those felt by West Germans in the West.

One thus cannot say that East Germans did not deal at all with the Nazi past or did not develop a sense of responsibility or guilt, especially in the later 1970s and early 1980s. Indeed, this discussion shows some parallel evolution with that of the FRG. Compared with the FRG, however, the voices advocating a serious confrontation with the past were heard less often and less openly. This can be explained in part with reference to the GDR's official antifascist ideology.

The GDR's official discourse presented the end of World War II as a moment of liberation, in which German imperialists were defeated by the Soviet army, helped by members of the German Communist resistance. With the development of an antifascist bloc early in the history of the GDR, the Communists began to present the German territory as divided between an antifascist GDR and an FRG still ruled by fascist representatives of monopoly capitalism. The mythification of the antifascist character of the GDR, consistent with the interpretation of German history described above as bifurcating after World War II into a regressive FRG and a progressive DDR, allowed the government to push aside debate about collective responsibility for the Nazi past.

The antifascist legitimating message was backed by claims, which the historical record seems to confirm,[14] that the denazification process had been more rapid and thorough in East Germany than in West Germany. When West Germans countered by saying that many former Nazis continued to occupy official posts in the GDR, the GDR government argued that it was legitimate to rehabilitate former Nazi sympathizers as long as they were not war criminals and were willing to contribute to the development of socialism. Thus, in Heiner and Inge Müller's play, *Die Korrektur*, the leader of a brigade who has accused an engineer of being a former Nazi is reprimanded by the party secretary, who says: "In the past I thought: We must cut off every hand that ever moved for Hitler. Today, I see that Socialism must also be built with these hands."[15] Meanwhile, the West Germans were accused of having protected the big criminals and penalized the less important ones: "In West Germany, it is well known that they have formally ground millions of small-time Nazis through the denazification mill, so that the big criminals could hide away."[16]

The Role of Germany's Image Abroad in the GDR's Foreign Policy

As shown in this chapter, the Weststadt respondents' emphasis on the need for Germany to support and be involved in the effort of European integration in order to calm other countries' fears tied in with a frequently discussed long-lasting concern by politicians and public intellectuals in the former FRG for Germany's image abroad. In order to explain why Oststadt respondents mentioned other countries' fears of Germany so seldom when discussing European integration, one may examine the nature of the GDR's foreign policy. The GDR's foreign policy shared the same priorities as the FRG's—security and regaining full sovereignty—and followed a very similar historical development: (1) the Occupation Statute until the attainment of statehood in 1949, (2) negligible diplomatic activity with the other side of the Iron Curtain until 1972, because of the FRG's reliance on the Hallstein doctrine that prevented other countries from maintaining diplomatic relations with the GDR, and (3) relative autonomy in foreign policy after the signing of the Basic Treaty with the FRG in 1972. Also, whereas the FRG's foreign policy was subordinated to the NATO plans, the GDR's was subordinated to the Warsaw Pact's. Beyond these similarities, the GDR, a sovereign state since 1955, had to wait not until 1955, like the FRG, but until the signing of the Basic Treaty with the FRG in 1972 to become a relatively autonomous international actor with the right to foreign diplomatic representation.[17] Even then, its degree of internal and external autonomy with respect to the Warsaw Pact and, more specifically, to the Soviet Union was much less than the FRG's with respect to NATO and the United States; in fact, its sovereignty was more constrained by the Soviet Union than was that of other Eastern European countries like Poland and Hungary.[18]

Conflicts between the GDR and other countries in the Eastern bloc did not translate into open reminders of Germany's role in World War II or into discussion of alleged negative German traits. This would have been tantamount to questioning the legitimacy of the antifascist rhetoric of the GDR's socialist regime, a source of instability that would not have been in the Soviet Union's interest. Furthermore, the structure of power in the Eastern bloc, with the Soviet Union taking almost unilaterally most significant foreign policy decisions, prevented the type of debate between Communist countries that would have led to the expression of mistrust of the

GDR. Finally, the GDR mitigated the resentment that Poland and Czechoslovakia may have felt toward Germany immediately after the war through a tactful diplomatic policy that included an early recognition of the Oder-Neisse border between the GDR and Poland.[19]

Schubert's reference to persistent resentment toward Germany by the Poles and the anecdote told by one of my Weststadt respondents about her visit to Poland show that the memory of Germany's role in World War II has persisted in the Eastern bloc as it has in the Western bloc. Survey data collected in the years after reunification partly confirm this, by showing that equal proportions of West and East Germans believe that Germans are not liked abroad. Nonetheless, the explanations that East and West Germans provided for this dislike show slight contrasts. In 1997, 14% of West German respondents attributed this dislike to World War II, compared with 9% among East German respondents. Also, it is not obvious that East Germans would transpose their perceptions of mistrust and resentment in Eastern Europe to Western Europe, with which they had had limited contact, and then rely on these perceptions to justify Germany's active involvement in the process of European integration.[20]

The comparison between the ways of conceiving European integration in Weststadt (West Germany) and Oststadt (East Germany) in the last two chapters represents a unique opportunity to examine the role of culture or, more specifically, cultural repertoires. After only seventy-eight years of common statehood and two world wars initiated by Germany, West Germans and East Germans were forced to part ways and live under radically different political structures and institutions as members of the Western and Eastern blocs. Defeat in World War II, economic destruction, and partition put an end to supranational identity projects, like Mitteleuropa, and facilitated the development of a Western European identity in the FRG and a socialist identity in the GDR. Thus, from the perspective of the adoption of a European identity above national and regional identities, West Germans became better prepared to accept European unification than were East Germans.

Other processes contributed to distinguish West Germans and East Germans in their approach to European unification. The almost fifty years during which they lived in separate states coincided with the project of European unification, a Western by-product of World War II, motivated among other reasons by the Allies' desire to firmly anchor the FRG in the West. The way West Germans understood and justified European integration and membership in the emerging common European structures was deeply influenced by the political culture that developed in the FRG during those years, itself not wholly unaffected by debates concerning European integration. The new political culture emerged within a democratic political framework that allowed for the expression and debate of multiple views, and in an international system in which the FRG was a subordinated but increasingly autonomous player. Among the most important debates in the post–World War II West German political sphere were debates about the origins of National Socialism and World War II and about German responsibility for World War II. The views that reached the wider public were that the Nazi period was a rather exceptional event in German history and that although Germany was politically responsible for World War II and many Germans were individually responsible, the German population was not collectively responsible. Nonetheless, less widespread views, such as the belief in the existence and persistence of dangerous psychological and cultural traits in Germany and the conviction that Germany had a moral responsibility toward other countries, were openly discussed in the public sphere. These less widespread views have been used by members of the better educated and more informed segments of the old Länder to justify European integration and Germany's contribution to its attainment.

Aside from the debates described above, the dynamics of the FRG's foreign policy, the controversies surrounding the FRG's relations with other countries, and the centrality of foreign policy and security in FRG politics also contributed to the salience of a specific view of Germany's autonomy in the international system that had a significant impact on the way people interpreted European integration and Germany's role in it. This view, cemented by the experiences FRG citizens had while traveling or on business in neighboring Western countries, was that there was mistrust and resentment toward Germany because of World War II and that Germans needed to take these feelings into account when conducting foreign policy. One way of reassuring the West about German intentions was to contribute toward the European integration effort without appearing too assertive.

The East Germans' approach to European integration was also shaped by the GDR's political culture and by the circumstances of reunification. The GDR, as part of the Eastern bloc, did not participate in the development of the Common Market and other European structures and institutions. Most East Germans thus probably first heard of the European Communities upon reunification and had to rapidly develop a basic understanding of the goals and purposes of European integration and what it meant for Germany. But the circumstances of reunification and the GDR's political culture predisposed East Germans little to adopt a discourse on European integration rooted in the collective memory of World War II—first, because the trauma associated with reunification in East

Germany rapidly shifted the historical center or anchoring point of East German culture from National Socialism and World War II to communism and reunification, and second, because the GDR's political culture and collective memory contrasted sharply with the FRG's.

The GDR was a highly centralized socialist country with a very narrow margin for the expression and debate of ideas. Furthermore, as part of the Eastern bloc it enjoyed very little autonomy in foreign affairs. The dominant interpretation of the Nazi period and World War II was that they represented an advanced stage in the history of class struggles and an expression of the increasing contradictions of capitalism in its imperialist phase. German history consisted in the conflict between progressive and regressive forces that, at the end of World War II, bifurcated and led to the emergence of a militaristic, fascist state, the FRG, and a peace-oriented, socialist state, the GDR. This interpretation excluded debate about the persistence in the GDR of negative psychological or cultural traits, such as authoritarianism or militarism, which were in fact ascribed to the FRG. For the most part it also excluded the notion of collective guilt and thus the GDR's moral responsibility toward other countries.

The third justification for supporting European integration heard in West Germany, the need to reassure other countries about Germany's intentions, was also alien to the GDR's political culture. While mistrust toward the GDR rooted in World War II subsisted at the popular level, it was never part of foreign policy discourse within the Eastern bloc, partly because of the GDR's very limited autonomy in foreign affairs with respect to the Soviet Union and partly because it would have eroded the legitimacy of the GDR as an antifascist state.

In sum, the different ways reunification was experienced in East Germany and West Germany and the contrast between the FRG's and GDR's political cultures explain why Weststadt respondents invoked the Nazi past and World War II as part of their justifications for Germany's support of European integration whereas Oststadt respondents did not.

Eight

The United Kingdom: Reluctant Europeans

WE HAVE seen in chapters 2, 3, and 4 that British discourse on European integration contrasts with Spanish and German discourses by its emphasis on the effects of EU membership on sovereignty and identity. Concern about the impact of European integration on British identity and sovereignty was slightly greater among less informed than among more informed British respondents, although this difference is not statistically significant. There were also no differences in the way Engleton and Scotsburg respondents visualized the European Union: both conceived it as a sort of superstate gobbling up British sovereignty and identity.

These preoccupations are related to the most salient theme in British post–World War II national culture: the United Kingdom's satisfaction with its cultural and historical singularity.

Comfortably Different

In the preface to his path-breaking and provocative book, *The Rise of English Nationalism: A Cultural History, 1740–1830*, Gerald Newman criticizes the English historian Alan McFarlane for exaggerating a "common view when he says that England historically was a 'society in which almost every aspect of the culture was diametrically opposed to that of the surrounding nations.'" He then goes on to say: "What if this is just stuff and nonsense? What if it is just the reflection of a myth—one of the central myths, perhaps, of English nationalism?"[1]

The comments Scotsburg and Engleton respondents made when justifying their views on European integration testify to the strength of this myth of difference. Their respondents distinguished themselves from Spanish and German respondents by the frequency with which they brought the issues of national identity and sovereignty into the discussion of European integration. They justified this comment by emphasizing that British culture is singular and radically different from the cultures of other European countries. Thus, Scotsburg's conservative City Council representative remarked: "You know, it is an impression, perhaps a wrong one, perhaps we have the wrong impression. But we feel that the Europeans are so different from us" (49, Scotsburg). Scotsburg's National Women's

Register's representative also expressed the feeling that Britain does not have a lot in common with Continental Europe:

> We don't share land borders. I do not think that any of their cultures have rubbed off on us.... I do not think that many people who live in this area have anything in common with anybody in the Continent, in France, in Germany, in Spain. And the whole outlook!
>
> *What do you mean by outlook?*
>
> Yes, it is hard to say what exactly that is, but there is a sense that there is a difference. (33, Scotsburg)

In all, of the 18 respondents who mentioned the threat to identity and sovereignty while discussing European integration, 10 stressed the singularity of British culture or the stark differences between British and other European cultures. Yet, respondents could not identify distinguishing features, and when pressed, sometimes volunteered strange ones, unlikely to be the actual force behind skepticism toward European integration. "It is hard to say," said a respondent, "but it seems that we, in this country, we work excessive hours and that is unpaid." Another respondent referred to the " 'slightly' different way of looking at things; faced with the same problem, they come up with different answers, a different thinking process" (48, Scotsburg, aged 31–50, more than High School). A third respondent referred to national holidays and the ways people work in the workplace "and things like that" (9, Engleton, Less than 30, More than High School).

Although the idea of difference is central to all national identities, in the British case it plays a comparatively greater role. According to Gerald Newman, English national identity, a late eighteenth-century product, was forged in direct contraposition to European, mainly French, culture by intellectuals deeply resentful of a caste-like cosmopolitan British political elite. Colley reaches the same conclusion about the role of anti-French sentiment at the root of British national identity, but stresses the role of war.[2] In this, however, the British did not differentiate themselves very much from the Spaniards or the Germans, for whom contrasts with France, especially in the period around the French Revolution, also played a significant role in the development of a national identity.[3] The comparative strength of the Britons' belief in their being different from other cultures in general, and from other European cultures in particular, conveys instead the effects of the British Empire on British identity and of the survival after World War II of the competing non-European identities that resulted from it. The consequential contrast between the United Kingdom and Spain or Germany is thus that the United Kingdom succeeded in realizing a supranational project, politically and ideologically, whereas Spain and Germany failed to achieve their respective Hispanidad and Mitteleuropa projects. The British Empire not only conferred on the United Kingdom unquestionable Great Power status, it also led to the emergence of an imperial supranational identity that, conceived in various ways, competed for primacy with more local forms of British national identity centered in the British Isles and, after World War II, with the development of a European identity and support for European integration.

As in Germany, where ever more geographically extensive and culture-encompassing supranational projects were advocated in the period preceding World War II, we find in turn-of-the-century Britain different supranational political projects, formulated by writers and politicians alike, ranging from Anglo-Saxon (Seeley, Rosebury) and Imperial (Carzon, Joseph Chamberlain), to what one could label Pan-British (Rhodes).[4] British world hegemony at this time also favored the formulation and popularizing of Anglo-Saxonism, an elaboration of an old myth going back to sixteenth-century England, inspired by the belief in the superiority of the Anglo-Saxon race and a Darwinian conception of international relations.[5] The Imperial supranational project was actively promoted in the British state before and after World War II. The Empire Marketing Board, Imperial Propaganda, the celebration of Imperial Day, and the BBC's Christmas Day Program, centered on the Royal Address to the Imperial subjects and, after the loss of Empire, to the members of the British Commonwealth, are examples of the continuous efforts undertaken by the British state before and after World War II to strengthen the economic, political, and emotional bonds linking the United Kingdom and the countries that formed the British Empire and then the British Commonwealth.[6]

After World War II, efforts to preserve the ties to the Commonwealth and to maintain the special relationship with the United States and the persistent invocation of the Imperial past in politics, history textbooks, and the arts both expressed the enduring character of the non-European supranational identity projects and contributed to their persistence in the popular imagination. The relative success of the United Kingdom's efforts to maintain close ties with both the United States and the countries of its former empire and the persistent evocative power of Imperial images reflect the fact that, unlike Spain and Germany, the United Kingdom emerged from World War II battered but victorious. Moreover, its subsequent economic and political decline was orderly enough to prevent the onset of a radical reorientation of British identity.[7] Thus, as Wallace says, "British political and intellectual elites have found it difficult to return to the European identity which eighteenth century Britain took for granted, and nineteenth century Britain progressively abandoned as the empire expanded and as German industry pushed British goods out of continental markets."[8]

A direct consequence of the British Empire and its correlate, the development of an imperial supranational project, were the articulation of "Little England" identity projects and the obsession with British singularity. As Grainger reminds us, "The Pall Mall Gazette, apparently the first to use the term 'Little Englander', applied it 'to those public persons in this country who disagree with "Imperialism" and are usually found in opposition when the Government is engaged in the disputes and wars that of necessity frequently occur in managing the affairs of an Empire whose interests are so varied and whose frontiers are so long'."[9]

Some of the early Little Englanders, of liberal persuasion, clung to a British identity centered in the Isles and defined by Protestantism and Parliamentarism (Hobhouse, Hobson, Robertson, Hammond), whereas more conservative ones, in ways reminiscent of the *Generación del 98*'s reflections on the essence of Spain, located the sources and defining characteristics of British identity in a historically distant past that predated the Norman invasion, Protestantism, and Parliamentarism (Belloc, Chesterton).[10] What they all shared in common, however, was a general dislike of foreign entanglements: "No casus federalis could ever be acceptable, no binding military commitment could ever be entered into; the island must for ever remain unpledged and unfated—and perfidious.... Little Englanders were renowned mainly not for the assertion of a patria but for their negation of other patriae."[11] According to Samuel, "Little Englandism" was pervasive before World War II, "when Czechoslovakia could be seen by politicians as that faraway country of which we know little" and Hitler could be thought of as *absurd*.[12] He also notes that late in the twentieth century it ceased to be a predominantly liberal project and became a mostly right-wing phenomenon.

The Little England phenomenon became closely linked to the British obsession with its singularity, with the peculiarities of British history and character that differentiate the United Kingdom and its people from other countries and peoples. Numerous authors have commented on the British population's propensity to distinguish the United Kingdom's culture from other European cultures and on the presumed British dislike of foreigners, which, as we saw in chapter 2, was referred to by many Scotsburg and Engleton respondents. Orwell, for instance, thought that xenophobia was one of the major flaws of the English character and—questionably—attributed it to factors such as different eating habits and the relative simplicity of English grammar compared to the grammar of other European languages.[13] Robbins notes that rejection of foreigners has traditionally been based on the conception that they are "too different," thus connecting the two cultural strands discussed here, the belief in British singularity and anti-foreigner attitudes.[14] Yet another author, Samuel, in his beautifully written and insightful essay "Exciting to Be English," stresses the centrality in British culture of the conviction that the United Kingdom is different, and the mixture of indifference, misunderstanding, and suspicion with which foreigners and foreign cultural products have traditionally been evaluated.[15] This conviction manifests itself in a cult of the local and a rejection of the foreign—generally French—in the sciences (e.g., empiricism versus rationalist theorizing) as well as the arts.[16] Furthermore, Samuel notes how "foreign influences are still routinely blamed when the nation is in moral difficulties or when there are threats to the public health.... In science fiction, foreigners are dark creatures inhabiting outer space; in spy stories, which emerged in the 1950s as a major form of popular fiction, they are sinister agents; on the box, like Stavros, the 'loadsamoney' Greek, they are figures of fun."[17] Within this framework of continuity, Samuel detects a trend in British self-images, from a sense of superiority during and immediately after World War II to a growing sense of vulnerability expressed in fears and rejection of anything foreign. According to him, this trend has resulted from economic and imperial decline, immigration, peripheral nationalism, and the active mobilization of mostly right-wing ideologues and politicians.[18]

The obsession with British singularity was a consequence of Empire, for Empire involved a high level of contact, both institutional and physical, with highly diverse cultural groupings, which countries that failed to maintain or develop an empire in the age of nationalism, such as Spain and Germany, did not experience. Thus, the overseas regions that formed the Empire and its inhabitants became the "Other" against which British identity defined itself. According to Gikandi, "this other was a constitutive element in the invention of Britishness; ... it was in writing about it that the metropolis could be drawn into the sites of what it assumed to be colonial difference and turn them into indispensable spaces of self-reflection."[19] In a similar vein, Paul Scott writes that "in India the English stopped being unconsciously English and became consciously English."[20] And yet again, Colley states that the African and Asian imperial territories came "to embody an essential quality of difference against which Britishness could emerge with far greater clarity."[21] It was indeed this quality of difference that helped to unify into a single identity the various cultures that coexisted in the United Kingdom, through a rhetoric of disaffirmation.[22] More than the imperial supranational project, which greatly shaped British identity and motivated its articulation in the first place, the Little England phenomenon and the British obsession with difference were in the end the major obstacles to the development of a feeling of identification with Europe, which in turn contributed to a relatively low level of support for European integration. As Grainger points out, "It was this peculiar patriotism, strained, diluted, 'hypochondrically' tender of conscience and above suspicion that, like the pale Galilean, would conquer and possess the English mind long after patriae had been forgotten or discredited."[23] Similarly, Gorra notes that "fascination with the English condition has, of course, only increased as empire recedes into the past."[24]

Besides scholarly analyses of British national identity, literature provides a good source of information on how the British have seen themselves in the second half of the twentieth century. This information supports the view of British society as obsessed with its singularity and not particularly interested in or sympathetic to foreign, and more particularly continental, European cultures. Thus, Taylor, in his analysis of British post–World War II fiction, remarks that "with minor exceptions the attitude to foreign countries, their customs, landscape and representatives, is deeply insular—an ingrained suspicion that frequently borders on outright hostility," and that "detachment from European culture and anything that might amount to European statehood is a feature of the protagonists of the average postwar English novel."[25] Similarly, Gindin stresses the high frequency with which the arty and the foreign are satirized in postwar British fiction.[26]

Analyses of award-winning novels in the United Kingdom from the late 1940s to the early 1990s support Taylor's and Gindin's assessments. Many of the characters in these novels observe, think about, discuss, and deal with foreigners, including Europeans, as if they were different, weird, and opaque beings, with whom one must inevitably come into contact but whom one does not much care to understand or become intimate with. In "Goose-Down," for instance, a short story about the anxiety experienced by the inhabitants of a small English village shortly before World War II (included in Barker's 1948 book *Innocents: Variations on a Theme*), one of characters, Mr. Minnenick, reflects as follows about the possibility of air-raids:

> Air-raids were sobering things. There was no funny side—as far as Mr. Minnenick could see—to an air raid. And they had a peculiarly foreign horror. When they happened in Spain or China they were a dreadful consequence of being Spanish or Chinese. If they happened in England, in the unlikely neighborhood of Mr. Minnenick and the Misses Pewsey, they would be out of context, they would be monstrously wrong, for here justice was balanced with virtue, there were no dreadful consequences of being English.[27]

The characters in Barker's short story exemplify the innocence of village folk, immersed in a self-contained world of daily routines and only small disturbances, and caught unprepared by external and incomprehensible forces that threaten to disturb the prevailing calm. These villagers, for all their parochialism, have a distinct and clear idea of what it means to be English. One of its distinctive elements is, as Orwell remarks and Mr. Minnenick echoes, "the habit of not killing one another."[28] Mr. Minnenick actually goes further than Orwell in attributing the lack of violence in England not to ingrained cultural attributes, but rather to some kind of providential design that marks the English as a chosen people: violence in other parts of the world "happened" or was "a consequence of" rather than "was an attribute or characteristic of."

Barker's Mr. Minnenick also displays a deeply internalized habit of thinking in national categories and a tendency not to be so discerning when it comes to describing nationals from other countries. Mr. Minnenick does not seem to see Spain as very different from China. Or, better said, in his mental landscape Spain is as distant as China. He is not alone. British postwar novels contain numerous characters for which Continental Europe is a strange and distant location. As one moves up the social scale and forward in time, however, a split becomes discernable between "Little Englanders" and alleged "Europhiles." In Kingsley Amis's *Lucky Jim*, for instance, that quintessential British postwar novel, Prof. Welch, the main character's senior colleague, laments what he sees as his wife's "Continental way of looking at things, almost Gallic," which contrasts with his interest in the English tradition and his belief that English culture is not just "a sort of aspect of the development of Western European culture."[29] What is important here is that the wife is portrayed as "Continental" not because of her professed admiration for things European but because of what Welch considers her modern outlook on social problems affecting the United Kingdom. She "is a Western European first and an Englishwoman second" by Welch's attribution rather than by her own decision. "Continental" thus stands for modernity, much as forward-looking Spaniards in the nineteenth century were called "Afrancesados" (people imbued with French ideas) and in the early twentieth century "Europeizantes" or "Europeístas." The contrast between Spain and the United Kingdom is that in the late 1950s a Europeanist outlook, even if differently interpreted by supporters and opponents of the dictatorship, was becoming hegemonic in Spain, whereas it remained something eccentric in the United Kingdom.

Anyone familiar with theories of group identity knows that identities fulfill a double function of inclusion and differentiation.[30] Contrasts with the "Other" are thus fundamental in the process of identity creation and sustenance and entail a tendency toward emphasizing in-group homogeneity and out-group differentiation.[31] What distinguishes the characters of British novels is not so much their stereotyping bent but, rather, their taxonomic obsession, whether with respect to class or national origin, with accent serving as the main distinctive marker, a marker that serves to immediately identify most, if not all, foreigners as of lower status. Nowhere is this more evident than in novels or episodes in an imperial location. P. H.

Newby's *Something to Answer For* provides a perfect illustration of this exaggerated classificatory tendency.[32] The novel tells the story of Townrow, Irish-born but educated in England, who travels to Egypt to help a friend's widow, Mrs. K., to repatriate the inheritance she has received from her late husband. The story takes place around the time of the Suez crisis. Mrs. K. is a caricaturized version of the racially conscious and condescending colonialist. This is how she describes her husband:

> I'd never have married him if he'd been a Jew or an Arab no matter how much money he'd got, but Lebanese is different, they are almost European in a way and Elie is Christian, of course, which makes a difference even though he's R.C. My mother was strong Baptist and she would not have liked me marrying a R.C. His English is as good as mine, if not better.[33]
>
> He was a foreigner, though, and foreigners don't really think like us. They know right from wrong but they can't act on it.[34]

The main characters in *Nothing to Answer For*, Townrow and Mrs. K. are always defining themselves in national terms, and although their presence in Egypt makes them feel quasi-European in contrast to the Arabs or the Jews, they still feel they are, for right or wrong, definitely distinct from Europeans.

In contrast to Mrs. K., Townrow is not imbued with Mrs. K.'s colonialist culture. He represents the homegrown, inward-looking Briton, completely lost amidst people of so many national origins. Some of the unreal, half-comic episodes he experiences allow the author to describe Townrow's lack of understanding of the foreign and his parochial national identity. Early in the novel, for instance, an Israeli who accuses the British of not having prevented the Holocaust confronts a puzzled Townrow. " 'Why did your government not warn us about going on those trains?... .This was British Government policy. What other explanation could there be? The British Government connived. What are the Jews of Europe to the British?' "[35] To this criticism, a perplexed Townrow is incapable of reacting. The author tells us about his thoughts: "March 1942 was a time Townrow could remember because it was in the Easter of that year that he was slung out of college and went into the army. But he just could not remember what was generally known about the concentration camps at that time. If there were stories in the papers people may have written them off as propaganda."

A Greek travel agent then joins the Israeli and Townrow. He sides with the Israeli and picks up his criticism of the British:

> I was two years at school in England. I understand the English. You sir, and I ... know that all governments are bad.... Any Frenchman will tell you. Americans, Russians, Venezuelans ... will say they have crooked governments.

... The Englishman is not like this. He thinks he is good and sincere himself and he believes he has a government that is good and sincere too.... This is what he understands about life. Every Englishman, when he is abroad, feels he can speak authoritatively for Whitehall. An illusion. They think, in Britain, that private life and public policy is one seamless garment. Every country has its special illusion. This is the British illusion.[36]

Townrow replies: "I don't know Greece.... Maybe you have got crooked government there. Maybe the French have too. And all the others. I don't think they're all honest men in Westminster, either." In fact, Townrow does not know how to react; his worldview is much simpler. At this particular moment, he is only capable of noticing how good the Greek's English accent is. Only much later in the novel will he reflect back on this discussion and conclude:

> You couldn't see Churchill and Attlee and Eden and Macmillan and that lot turning a blind eye to the Jews being massacred. All governments stink a bit. The Greek had been right about that.... But the British system was too open for anything really shameful. They shot the Irish martyrs but the ghosts walked. Ireland was the exception. It was the dark stain, forty years ago, but the British had no stomach for it now.[37]

Townrow reflects on the British on repeated occasions throughout the book. In these reflections one recognizes familiar themes in British culture such as the myth of the British abhorrence of war ("People who start wars and invasions and commit acts of aggression are just Bad Men. The English have become very priggish about this"[38]) or the dislike of the French ("The French were an unscrupulous lot. He'd never liked them"[39]). The French, who according to Colley and Newman have played such a crucial role in the development of English and British identities, in fact appear in British postwar fiction as the embodiment of the European character: "modern" in Amis's *Lucky Jim*, "unscrupulous" in Newby's *Something to Answer For*, or "xenophobe"—as opposed to "racially complacent" like the British—in Lively's *Moon Tiger*.[40] In my interviews in Scotsburg and Engleton, this dislike of the French, who were often referred to as "Frogs," was frequently mentioned. For example, the fencing teacher from Scotsburg, while stressing the traditional friendship between the Scots and the French, said:

> France and England, they hate each other. You know, they really do, and these things aren't going to go away. If you look at the last thirty, forty years, you only see rivalry between the two. Why does Britain have an atomic bomb? Is it because the Russians have an atomic bomb? Is it because the Americans have an atomic bomb? It's because the French have an atomic bomb: "If the French

have an atomic bomb, we are having an atomic bomb".... Look at the past 1000 years. In the past 1000 years we've spent most of the time fighting the French. [*Laughter*] (48, Scotsburg, 31–50, more than High School)[41]

Many of the characters of the award-winning postwar British novels examined here thus confirm the cultural analysts' descriptions of the British as obsessed with their own singularity and as uninformed about, uninterested in, and generally mistrustful of things European. The lands of the former empire are, in fact, featured as frequently as or more often than Continental European settings in the award-winning novels on which I base this analysis: three novels take place in Continental Europe and three in former imperial locations; moreover, nine novels refer at some point to episodes taking place in the former colonies, compared to six in Continental Europe. The examination of contemporary history textbooks and curricula and Christmas addresses by the heads of the British Royal House since the end of World War II help to complete the picture sketched so far. The textbooks do not particularly shock for concentrating on the United Kingdom. In fact, their coverage of non-national historical events is greater than that of Spanish contemporary history textbooks, at least until the death of Franco, and similar to or greater than that observed for both Germanies before 1989 and reunited Germany thereafter. What differentiates British from Spanish and German textbooks is the greater attention paid to the world outside Europe, the world corresponding to the former British Empire. As a result, the hierarchy of proximity that one finds in Spanish and German contemporary history textbooks—Nation, Europe, Rest of the world—is not so clearly delineated in British contemporary history textbooks.

One illustration of this is provided by the *1990 Final Report by the National Curriculum History Working Group Set Up by the Secretaries of State for Education and Science and for Wales.*[42] The goal of the report was to make recommendations on attainment targets and programs of study for history within the National Curriculum. One of the recommendations was to allocate the teaching of contemporary history to what was labeled Stage 4, corresponding to ages 14 to 16. The report proposed to include two Core History Study Units, which were *Britain in the Twentieth Century* and *The Era of the Second World War: 1933–1948*. Beyond this, the report recommended a choice of one course from each of two lists, labeled A and B.

List A was composed of the following courses:

1. *East and West: Europe 1948 to the present day*
2. *Russia and the USSR: 1905 to the present day*
3. *The United States of America: 1917 to the present day*

List B included the following courses:

1. *India and Pakistan: 1930 to 1964*
2. *Africa south of the Sahara since 1945*
3. *Japan: 1868 to the present day*
4. *China: 1937 to the present day*

There is thus no question that European history gets its due. On the other hand, the teaching of European history is not privileged with respect to the teaching of the history of former imperial possessions.

The examination of the Christmas addresses by King George between 1948 and 1951 and Queen Elizabeth from 1952 onwards further confirms Europe's lack of a central position in British culture.[43] The geographical scope of the annual address distinguishes it from the Spanish and German equivalents. The Royal Christmas address is directed not to the population of the United Kingdom but to the population of all the members of the Commonwealth. This constrains from the outset what can be said, for it would be strange for the speech to contain frequent and positive references to Continental Europe. It is nonetheless surprising that Europe is mentioned directly only once in all the Christmas addresses delivered before 1996. This single mention occurred in 1972, on the occasion of the United Kingdom's entry into the EEC. The queen's words left no doubt about the different meaning that the British monarchy attached to Europe versus the Commonwealth. Whereas the Commonwealth in this, as in the majority of addresses, is described as a family, the European Community is presented as a partnership between neighbors who, on balance, see more benefits than disadvantages is coming together.

> Britain is about to join her neighbors in the European Community and you may well ask how this will affect the Commonwealth. The new links with Europe will not replace those with the Commonwealth. They cannot alter our historical and personal attachments with kinsmen and friends overseas. Old friends will not be lost: Britain will take her Commonwealth links with her....
>
> ... Britain and these other European countries see in the Community a new opportunity for the future. They believe that the things they have in common are more important than the things which divide them, and that if they work together not only they but the whole world will benefit.

The feeling of distinctiveness and separateness with respect to the rest of Europe that pervades British culture becomes most evident when one examines survey data like those provided by the 1995 International Social Survey Program (ISSP) on social identity. One of the first items in this questionnaire asked respondents how close they felt to their continent. The comparison of the United Kingdom with Spain and both West and

East Germany is telling. In West Germany, East Germany, and Spain, the percentages of respondents (of those providing valid answers) who said that they felt close or very close were 58%, 59%, and 62% respectively. In the United Kingdom, the percentage was only 21%.[44] According to Deutsch, political union is only possible when a we-feeling develops.[45] Hechter and Gellner invoke a feeling of cultural distinctiveness as a major factor explaining peripheral nationalist movements in plurinational states.[46] The discussion above and these survey data leave little doubt about the British feeling of cultural distinctiveness. At the same time, they explain the concern about national identity and sovereignty among British respondents when discussing European integration and their relative skepticism toward this political process.

The fact that many people in the United Kingdom see themselves as different from the rest of Europe does not, however, fully explain why they want to hang on to their distinctiveness. The examination of cultural developments in Spain and Germany has shown after all that many Spaniards and Germans wanted to break with major aspects of their identity and "Europeanize," whether culturally, politically, or both. Underlying the passion with which many respondents in this study clung to a national identity that they often could not define was a fundamental satisfaction with British culture and history.

Satisfied with Being British

Despite feeling different, my Engleton and Scotsburg respondents rarely expressed a feeling of superiority over foreigners. The nationalism that emerged through the interviews was not, as Gindin says, "the nationalism of fifes and drums along the Irrawaddy in the Kipling tradition, but that of someone sticking to what he knows and feels comfortable about."[47] Numerous authors who directly or indirectly have analyzed British culture and British identity have conveyed this satisfaction with the idea of being British. According to these authors, the British see themselves mostly in positive or neutral terms. Here is a list of self-ascribed attributes that one finds in the literature: loyal, considerate, patient, fair, decent, set on compromise, consensus-seeking, keen on liberty, adventurous, truthful, logical, generous, humane, hardworking, practical, independent, morally impeccable.[48] The authors themselves are more critical of the British character. While Orwell ascribes to the British positive qualities such as those of being gentle and respectful of legality, he also criticizes them for being xenophobic, parochial, self-satisfied, artistically insensitive, hypocritical, and politically ignorant. Of all these negative traits, the one most frequently mentioned in the literature is that of being xenophobic.[49] It is also one of the characteristics most often mentioned by the respondents, as I showed in chapter 2.

British fiction has undoubtedly contributed to creating the feeling of pride in being different, even as it has made fun of it. Firstly, this has occurred because an unmistakable "Little Englandism" predominates in characters with whom readers are supposed to identify. For instance, Jim Dixon in *Lucky Jim*, in his "Merry England" address near the end of the story, calls for the defense of the native tradition and the common heritage, and, as he says, "for what we once had and may, some day, have again—Merrie England."[50] Secondly, for all the criticism of British parochialism and xenophobia in many novels, the lightness of the narrative and the reliance on a half-humoristic, half-satirical style deters from the effect this criticism may have on the reader. It is difficult to feel intense dislike toward characters like Mrs. K. in Newby's novel, for all her racist views, or draw moral lessons from Townrow's reactions to the Israeli's accusations at the airport. One gets the impression that accusations of parochialism and xenophobia, like persistent economic and political decline, are features of British life that many may well be willing to put up with as part of the effort to preserve tradition. While these features are almost absent in the post-1975 award-winning novels that I have analyzed, there is no alternative and uniform discourse to replace them.

Respondents, like the essayists writers quoted above, were sometimes critical of what they saw as the British character. Nonetheless, there was no sense of trauma in the way they talked about their society and culture. Nor is there a sense of trauma that has had to be addressed and overcome in novels, history textbooks, and Royal Christmas addresses. In Spanish contemporary history textbooks, a significant proportion of the content, until the most recent years, is devoted to explaining the Civil War and Franco's dictatorship. In Germany, the narrative is organized around the explanation of World War II and the way Germany has confronted its Nazi past and transformed itself into a democratic society. In the United Kingdom, the only discernable storyline concerns British decline, but this story, as I show below, is told in ways that smooth out its rough edges and make it appear as a nondramatic event. British contemporary history textbooks just consist of a methodical telling of the main socioeconomic and political developments in British and world history since World War I. In sum, most of what one hears or reads seems to confirm Engleton's Conservative representative's comment that "what is happening is that the UK system has generally developed over centuries and it is one with which the large majority of the people are very happy" (7, Engleton).

Two of the main sources of national identity for Engleton and Scotsburg respondents, considered worth defending against the onslaught of European integration, were the monarchy and the British traditions and way of life. "I mean, we've got our royal family, who we revere," said the Conservative City Council member from Scotsburg. "There are people who are anti-royalist, of course, but the vast majority, you know, they worship the Queen and the royal family. Despite all the wrong-doings that have been going on recently" (49, Scotsburg). Another respondent, this time from Engleton, felt completely torn about the United Kingdom giving up the pound. While her head told her that the euro might be a positive development, her emotions opposed the move on grounds that "it sort of takes away from your identity." For her, this change would be tantamount to giving up the monarchy or "being told that our Prime Minister is no longer our figure-head [*sic*]" (Engleton, 16, 31–50, more than High School). Yet other respondents expressed their desire to preserve the "heritage of Britain" (9, Engleton, 30 or younger, more than High School) or opposed the euro because "it would be weird not to see the Queen's face in the coin" (20, Engleton, 30 or younger, more than High School).

In the respondents' preoccupation with monarchy, simple traditions, and Britain's heritage, we see an example of what Samuel has labeled the "cult of the ordinary" and the "enlarged sense of the national past" in British contemporary society[51] and of what Nairn calls "the glamour of backwardness."[52] The monarchy, or more precisely, "the Royals"—as personification of the monarchy—have come in fact to embody both the "ordinariness" and the "national past" that many British people revere. Nowhere are these traits of British society better analyzed than in Samuel's essay already cited in this section, and in Nairn's satirical analysis of the importance of the monarchy in the United Kingdom, *The Enchanted Glass*. Like Colley and Newman, Nairn traces the transformation of the monarchical institution into a revered institution to George III's reign and especially to the period coinciding with the late eighteenth-century wars against revolutionary France. While Newman stresses the role played by the king's sponsoring of local art, his anti-French stance, and his opposition to elite corruption, Colley and Nairn focus on the role that George III's ordinary appearance and vulnerability played in appealing to the population. This "ordinariness," cultivated especially in the second half of the twentieth century and combined with carefully staged periodic celebrations over the past two hundred years, is, according to Nairn, the key to understanding the British monarchy's enduring popularity. It explains why it is presented in public discourse as representing "everything decent in British culture," as "symbolizing an elderly nation apologetically yet triumphantly set in its ways."[53]

For Nairn, Ukania ("the Geist or informing spirit of the UK") is a family, not a modern state.[54] This is quite evident in the Christmas addresses. Whereas Germany's heads of state (East and West) speak of Germany as "community" (Volk) or "society," Franco literally presents himself as the captain of a ship, and the Spanish king speaks of Spain as a "society" or "people," Queen Elizabeth portrays the United Kingdom as a family. Queen Elizabeth's Christmas addresses (and the late King George's) are always an occasion to discuss the year's royal family events: weddings, births, illnesses, anniversaries, coronations, and family troubles.[55] They are also an occasion to discuss the royal family's travels during the year, usually to far away countries belonging to the Commonwealth.[56] The Commonwealth itself is presented as a family.[57] If by any chance there has been conflict within the Commonwealth in a given year, the queen's address makes the analogy with tensions in a family, which, as in a family, ought to be solved with love, comradeship, and tolerance.[58]

The queen's Christmas addresses also provide an opportunity to celebrate British history and traditions. The United Kingdom appears in them as an "Old" people, an "Old" country, with a history of "past achievements." The message is familiar: the United Kingdom is the cradle of parliamentary democracy and a model of democratic government and rule of law; the people are adventurous, courageous, and freedom loving. There are no major defeats to remember; mostly acts of "genius," "courage," and "heroic resistance," such as the defeat of the Armada, Trafalgar, Waterloo, Dunkirk, the Battle of Britain, D day, the Falklands, and the Gulf War, populate the collective memory structured by these addresses.[59] The British Empire crumbles in the meantime, but the listener of these Christmas addresses only hear of occasional "disputes" and "happy" events, such as Nigeria's decision to be part of the Commonwealth after gaining independence.[60]

There are no black spots in the history constructed by the queen's Christmas addresses except, perhaps, the Northern Ireland problem, which appears on at least three occasions in the last fifty-some years. This almost pristine narrative also predominates in contemporary history books intended for use in secondary school. Sensitive events such as those involving imperialism and decolonization, which could have been constructed in negative terms (e.g., as exploitation and defeat), appear in a generally positive light, with positive comments invariably following any negative ones. In a 1952 history textbook we read the following about the expansion of the British Empire:

> When the British first took over parts of the world overseas they, like other European Powers, thought only of how their rule would benefit their own country. But later they began to think of how it would benefit the native inhabitants. Gradually there arose the idea that Britain was a trustee for the welfare of these native inhabitants, who for some reason or another were not governing themselves, and that Britain would give up her position as trustee when these people became self-governing.[61]

In another quote, this time from a 1966 textbook, the author criticizes Joseph Chamberlain's feeling of racial superiority, only to immediately qualify it by saying, "But this arrogant racialism was accompanied by a sense of obligation towards the native peoples."[62] Similarly, a 1977 textbook says about the colonization of India that

> If the British had begun by plundering India, they were soon concerned to improve it, though still largely in their own interest.... They administered their great possessions without corruption and generally with justice. However, their administration was always alien;... And the very success of British rule created an influential opposition. It led to the growth of a prosperous middle class who learned about the British parliamentary system and absorbed the democratic ideals behind it.[63]

In sum, we certainly read about mistakes, but even more often about the fine intentions and beneficial net outcomes of imperialism. One could also illustrate at length the way in which British history textbooks turn almost every defeat into a victory, and how the United Kingdom always seems to be in control. The retreat at Dunkirk thus becomes a heroic feat,[64] decolonization results from the British Labour Party's and its Conservative successor's farsightedness, the movement toward European integration gets its earliest and most decisive impulse from Churchill's speech in Switzerland, and the list goes on. It is thus not surprising that the British population is proud of its past and that Scotsburg and Engleton respondents want to preserve their heritage against the European Union's intrusion. The 1995 ISSP survey on national identity bears this out quite convincingly. When asked how proud they were of their history, 8%, 10%, and 26% of the West German, East German, and Spanish respondents respectively said that they were very proud. The corresponding figure for the United Kingdom was 50%.[65]

British Decline and the Defense of Identity and Sovereignty

The desire to preserve British distinctiveness and heritage is so strong, the "glamour of backwardness" so great, to use again Nairn's formula, that some respondents consciously attached more priority to the defense of identity and sovereignty than to commitment to European integration, which they saw as more economically and politically rational:

> Well, various people have explained it to me, 'cause it is to our advantage if we have one currency, but from a nationalistic point of view [she laughs embarrassedly] I don't like it. When you come from a country, really, you know you get your identity in many ways from being part of that culture. I mean, it sounds

silly, but I mean, the currency, I suppose I just always thought of it as one of those things that make up our identity.
> (16, Engleton, 31–50, more than High School)

Others expressed concern about the loss of identity and sovereignty and thus resisted further steps toward European integration precisely because they were aware of the United Kingdom's diminished world status:

> I'm quite sure that national interests would find their way into just any debate of any significance, leaving us with a Europe dominated by perhaps a couple of powers, with the smaller areas being less well represented.
> (45, Scotsburg, Scottish Nationalist Party)

Yet others struggled to reconcile the fact that they were aware of British decline but did not want to renounce their cultural specificity. A teacher from Scotsburg, for instance, conceded that the United Kingdom needed to be involved in efforts toward European integration because "The position of Britain in the world today is not the major world power it was a hundred years ago," but still firmly opposed a divestment of power that would jeopardize national identities (Scotsburg, 38, 31–50, more than High School). A similar comment was made by a college student from Engleton, who after saying that "We are not the industrial Empire we used to be.... People always want to see us as the British Empire, you know, and starting the Industrial Revolution, etc.... It is not that anymore. It does not have all those industries," said that she supported the pound because "It is what we are used to" (27, Engleton, 30 or younger, more than HS education).

In total, 5 out of 18 respondents who expressed concern about losing identity and sovereignty explicitly mentioned British decline. Some among the rest did not mention British decline explicitly but made it clear that they were conscious of it. For instance, one respondent said that the British are used to dominating instead of having to seek compromise, as they must in the European Union (thus implying that the United Kingdom's views do not necessarily prevail).

The frequent references to the United Kingdom's decline are congruous with the great salience that this topic has acquired in the public sphere, in scholarly debates, and in the culture at large. This decline has in fact become a flexible issue that can be used to support all sorts of, even contradictory, arguments. For instance, it can be used against more involvement in the European Union on grounds that the United Kingdom cannot afford to be isolationist, and it can be used to argue for caution regarding this involvement on grounds that decline makes the national identity even more vulnerable. As I have shown when discussing Spain, Germany, and the topics of British distinctiveness and the United Kingdom's glorious heritage, this is another example of how the arguments that people invoke when discussing European integration correspond to salient preoccupations in the broader national cultures. It is this alignment between specific arguments and the broader national cultures in which they are formulated that makes the arguments credible both for those who make them and for those who receive them.

Although consciousness of the United Kingdom's decline dates back to the late nineteenth century, it only became a widely accepted fact and the object of intellectual discussion in the post-Suez period or later.[66] When reviewing op-ed articles in *The Economist* and *The New Statesman*, I pointed out, for example, that acknowledgment of the United Kingdom's decline in the context of discussions about European integration took place only in the mid-1960s in *The Economist* and in the 1980s in *The New Statesman*. Samuel, meanwhile, claims that the "eclipse of British power could hardly be said to have registered itself on the public mind before the 1970s."[67] Since the mid-1960s, however, the explanation of British decline has been a major topic in scholarly research and more popular forms of intellectual discussion. Scholars have debated about the timing of decline and about its causes. Some authors have emphasized economic factors (e.g., investment abroad),[68] while others have emphasized cultural ones (loss of entrepreneurial spirit)[69] and political ones (e.g., lack of investment in education).[70] Some authors have located the roots of the crisis in the British Isles, whereas others have focused on the burden and mentality-transforming effects of Empire.[71] Finally, ambitious scholars like Anderson and Nairn have developed a metahistorical explanation that ties all of the abovementioned factors into a grand narrative in which the main culprit for the United Kingdom's decline is the oligarchy that has ruled the country since the 1688 Revolution, an originally aristocratic-mercantile class alliance progressively centered in the City of London and focused first on the empire and then on the global markets.[72] The cult of British distinctiveness, of monarchy, and of the past that I have outlined in this section fits quite well within this metanarrative, aspects of which have been passionately disputed.

Contemporary history textbooks have also concentrated on British economic and political decline, to the point where this decline constitutes perhaps the only storyline one can detect in them with respect to the United Kingdom. The version of this decline is certainly a sanitized one, in which (1) description predominates over explanation, (2) the drama of long-term decline is diffused through an emphasis on periodic recoveries (e.g., rise in standards of living in the 1950s) and the United Kingdom's persistent great power status, (3) raw economic explanatory factors, mostly exogenous (e.g., enhanced foreign competition; other countries' protectionism), dominate over social and political ones,[73] and (4) Europe's general decline and the United States' rise to dominance provide the main context for the exposition.[74] Anderson's and Nairn's radical republican theses are nowhere to be found; nor is, for instance, Saunders's stark analysis of British decline after World War II.[75] Nonetheless, the textbooks' descriptions convey the sense of decline all the same.

Post-World War II British fiction has also emphasized and been imbued with the spirit of decline. The predominantly "realist" novels of this period tend to be very critical of contemporary social and moral conditions. Referring to British fiction between 1945 and 1975, Taylor writes that "A diminished international status; a venal and self-interested executive; a populace animated by fussy social judgements, repressed, insecure, and inward-looking—of such, at least according to the novelists, does 'Englishness' in the third quarter of the twentieth century consist."[76] The content of British award-winning novels since the late 1940s confirms this assessment. Neither the sentiment of national pride that accompanied victory in World War II nor the rise in standards of living during the 1950s is featured in these novels. Instead, a good number among them deal with limited opportunities for intellectuals (*Scamp, Hear and Forgive, Lucky Jim*), working-class hardship (*The Loneliness of the Long Distance Runner, Saville, How Late it Was, How Late*), and alienated rural and urban dwellers (*Innocents, The Elected Member, Last Orders*).[77] With few exceptions, the main characters are unglamorous losers, whose life horizons do not extend beyond the local and the search for some small emotional gratification. This anti-heroic mood reflects, according to Phelps, the "withering away of Britain's imperial world."[78] In contrast with these depressing social and historical landscapes, the imperial past in novels of this period seems brighter, not because of the storylines, which do not necessarily portray the glamorous aspects of imperial administration, but rather because of the higher social status of their characters and because we are reminded that the United Kingdom once presided over this vast empire (*The Sun Doctor, Something to Answer For, Rites of Passage*).

In sum, few themes in British postwar culture have been so salient as that of economic and political decline. This explains why some respondents justify their reservations about the European Union by pointing to the United Kingdom's lack of leverage, while others feel like they have to apologize for holding Eurosceptical positions in the face of their awareness of the United Kingdom's decline.

Chapters 2 and 3 showed that the British respondents' concern with the loss of national identity and sovereignty was rooted in a strong feeling of distinctiveness and a profound satisfaction with the United Kingdom and its past. Both the feeling of distinctiveness and the satisfaction Scotsburg and Engleton respondents expressed in the interviews resonate with salient features of British postwar society that have been analyzed by scholars and satirized by writers, and that are reproduced institutionally through the educational system (history textbooks) and rituals of power (Christmas addresses). Moreover, as this chapter has emphasized, the feeling of distinctiveness and the satisfaction with the United Kingdom that the respondents expressed were not primarily grounded, at the popular level, on overt feelings of superiority, especially with respect to the rest of Europe. On the contrary, the respondents were concerned that their clinging to British identity and sovereignty might be perceived as odd, in view of the United Kingdom's diminished world status. Their resistance to Europe was therefore one based on emotion, on love for the local, rather than on reason. I have argued in this chapter that the British feelings of distinctiveness are heirs to the British Empire and its sequel, the Commonwealth. Unlike Spain and Germany, the United Kingdom succeeded in building an empire and in maintaining strong links with its former colonies in the post–World War II period. The British Empire favored the development of non-European supranational identities that competed with the European identity after World War II and induced an intense process of self-reflection about British identity that rested on comparisons with the different societies that constituted it. Thus, in the immediate aftermath of World War II, there was little need for the British population's imagination to turn to Europe; at the same time, large segments of the British population were too obsessed with their own singularity to be able to identify with Europe and thus feel that European integration had something to do with them. In the decades that followed World War II, the political payoffs of victory in the war, gradual rather than sudden economic and political decline, and the resistance of significant social sectors to acknowledging this decline, facilitated the persistence in the United Kingdom of supranational identities in competition with Europe and of the belief in British distinctiveness with respect to Europe, which weakened the United Kingdom's degree of commitment to the process of European integration.

This chapter has also uncovered a significant contrast between the roles of culture in the United Kingdom, Spain, and the two Germanies in providing interpretive tools for thinking European integration. Whereas in Spain and Germany respondents invoked arguments about European integration that had been developed jointly by dominant factions of the intelligentsia and by the political elites, in the United Kingdom respondents invoked arguments that were only unsystematically articulated by elites. Spain's modernization and its "Europeanization" were part of an explicit political program; Germany's "dealing with the Nazi past" and its reassuring foreign policy were part of an explicit political program; there is no program, however, whose overt goals have been to make the British feel and remain distinctive and satisfied with themselves. The only articulate program put forward by the intelligentsia has been that of the Republican and Marxist left, expressed through journals such as *Past and Present* or *New Left Review*. This program, almost as critical of the Labour Party as of the Conservative Party, rests to a large extent on Anderson's and Nairn's cultural and political interpretation of the modern history of the United Kingdom, and strongly criticizes the features of British society that I have analyzed in this chapter. Judging from the respondents' comments, however, and from pronouncements by political leaders, this program has not been very influential beyond academia.

The absence of an explicit and systematic political or intellectual program promoting a feeling of distinctiveness and pride in British history and institutions does not mean that British elites have not participated in this British worldview and contributed to reproducing it. A ritual such as the Royal Christmas Day address to the members of the Commonwealth is just one example of how the dominant elites have kept alternative identities alive. Furthermore, chapter 4 showed how pro-Labour commentators such as the historian Paul Johnson devoted major opinion articles to celebrating British distinctiveness and achievements in the context of the debate about British entry in the Common Market.[79] At the other end of the political spectrum, politicians like Enoch Powell and Margaret Thatcher have also contributed to cementing pride in distinctiveness through racist discourse (in Powell's case)[80] and nostalgia for the aesthetics and moral standards of an imperial past (in Thatcher's case).[81] Barnett's detailed examination of parliamentary debates during the Falklands War has also shown how in a crisis situation, left and right have reacted as one to affirm British political traditions and heritage.[82] Finally, the contrast between the very close alignment to the United States of the United Kingdom and the old Dominions in CNN-broadcasted world military crises since the 1990s on the one hand and the more distant attitude of other European countries on the other cannot help but remind the British population of the United Kingdom's separate standing with respect to other European countries.

In sum, the comparisons in the chapters 5 through 8 have demonstrated that the themes and interpretation schemes in the broader national cultures that have shaped popular understandings of European integration in Germany, the United Kingdom, and Spain, are themes that were broadly shared at the political level and variously institutionalized. At the more substantive level, they have showed that the greater sensitivity of the British toward the EU's potential threat to national identity and culture results from the fact that the British have generally felt less part of Europe than have Spaniards and Germans. These chapters have also demonstrated that the modernization and Europeanization drives in the case of Spain and a desire to improve other countries' trust in the case of West Germany have been powerful factors in inspiring the arguments people use when discussing European integration in these countries. The next chapter summarizes the argument developed in this book, and validates quantitatively its most important propositions.

Nine

Frames and Attitudes toward European Integration: A Statistical Validation

PREVIOUS CHAPTERS have argued for the role of frames in explaining attitudes toward European integration and in providing clues about the cultural, historical, and structural forces responsible for international contrasts. Through an inductive approach that is heuristically guided by the literature on frames, I have developed an interpretation for why the United Kingdom population expresses greater skepticism about membership in the European Union and European integration than do the Spanish and German populations. According to this interpretation, the root cause of the contrast is the Spanish and German failure to carry out their supranational projects outside or at the margins of Europe and thus to be able to compete with the great European and non-European world powers. This failure was definitive by the end of World War II. Unlike Spain and Germany, the United Kingdom had created an extra-European empire in the nineteenth century that remained almost intact at the end of World War II. Consequently, when plans for European integration were put forward, the British population split between those favoring them and those who identified more with the United Kingdom's extra-European engagements. Also, in contrast to Germans and Spaniards, whose horizons had remained European, Britons had developed a strong sense of singularity, of being different from other peoples, through contact with the diverse cultures that formed the British Empire. This sense of singularity was then extended to comparisons with the rest of Europe, which led the British population to identify less with Europe than did the Spanish and German populations. Thus, Britons found the idea of European integration less attractive and feared more that European integration would erode their national identity and culture than did the Spanish and German populations.

Some of the arguments developed in this book through the systematic application of qualitative and historical-comparative methods gain further credibility when one examines the results of statistical analyses of survey data based on national representative samples of respondents. The analysis that follows draws on survey results from the *Eurobarometer Study 51.0* conducted in 1999 in the countries that form the European Union. I first focus on the roles that the perception of the effects on national identity of membership in the European Union and the degree of identification with Europe play in explaining support for European integration. Then, I examine the plausibility of the explanation provided in this book for the contrasts in support for the European Union between the United Kingdom and both Germany and Spain. I end the chapter with a reflection on the general factors explaining international contrasts in support for European integration and with proposals for further comparative work, all of these based on the results of the statistical analysis reported here.

Frames, European Identity, and Support for Membership in the European Union

From an analytical standpoint, the main claim made in this book is that attitudes toward European integration and the European Union depend on people's social representations. People who ascribe to the European integration process or the European Union qualities or goals with which they disagree or that they do not like should develop more negative attitudes than those who ascribe to them qualities or goals with which they agree or that they like. The Eurobarometer Study 51.0 includes a series of items to tap into people's specific fears about the implications of the European Union. One of these indicators refers to the fear of losing the national identity and culture, which, based on in-depth interviews, serves to distinguish British from Spanish and German respondents. This item is measured as a dichotomous variable (1 = Yes; 0 = No). In addition, the Eurobarometer 51.0 includes an item that measures the degree of attachment to Europe, which also plays a central role in this book's explanation of attitudes toward European integration and the European Union. The degree of attachment to Europe is measured as a four-value scale, with 4 meaning "Very attached" and 1 meaning "Not at all attached."[1] Based on the discussion in previous chapters, the expectation is that respondents who harbor fears of losing their national identity and who do not feel close to Europe are more opposed to membership in the European Union than are those who do not harbor fears of losing their national identity and who feel close to Europe.

Table 11 presents the results of estimating various regression and logit regression models to test these hypotheses. There are two dependent variables. The first dependent variable measures whether respondents feel that membership in the European Union is a good (coded 1) or a bad thing (coded 0). This is the most frequently used indicator of support for the European Union in the literature. It is assumed to tap into the utilitarian dimension of support.[2] Despite its shortcomings, which I discuss in chapter 3, the use of this variable allows me to contrast my findings with those of previously published studies. The second dependent variable focuses

TABLE 11
The Effects of Fearing that the EU will Harm National Identity and the Degree of Closeness to European Union on International Contrasts in Support for Membership in the EU and the Degree of Preference for an Integrative Model of Integration

Independent Variable	Effect on Log-Odds of Thinking that Membership in the European Union is a 'Good Thing' rather than a 'Bad Thing'		Effect on Degree of Support for Integrative Model of Integration	
Fear of Losing National Identity		−1.20*		−0.40*
Degree of Closeness to Europe		0.95*		0.35*
N. Ireland[a]	9.86*	11.40*	0.61*	0.58*
W. Germany[a]	3.32*	1.95*	0.88*	0.62*
E. Germany[a]	3.18*	1.76*	0.77*	0.50*
Spain[a]	13.58*	5.56*	1.32*	0.90*
Italy[a]	12.83*	6.49*	1.53*	1.18*
Portugal[a]	13.10*	7.79*	1.11*	0.81*
Greece[a]	4.31*	4.55*	0.96*	0.88*
Belgium[a]	5.66*	3.28*	1.30*	1.01*
Luxembourg[a]	18.30*	9.16*	1.36*	1.00*
France[a]	2.94*	2.06*	1.11*	0.91*
Netherlands[a]	9.68*	8.29*	1.05*	0.89*
Austria[a]	1.44*	0.60*	0.70*	0.39*
Sweden[a]	0.62*	0.24*	−0.25*	−0.55*
Finland[a]	1.58*	0.79	0.12	−0.14*
Denmark[a]	1.25	0.57*	−0.02	−0.09
Ireland[a]	22.65*	21.72*	0.86*	0.70*
R-square			16.3%	23.7%
Cox-Snell pseudo R-square	15.3%	25.2%		
N = 9995				

Range of dependent variable "Support for Integrative Model of Integration": 0–4
Range of independent variable "Degree of Closeness to Europe": 1–4
Range of independent variable "Fear of Losing National Identity": 0–1
[Country][a]: The country-specific log-adds coefficients have been transformed into odds-ratios
*Significant at 0.05 level, two-tailed.
Omitted country category: Great Britain
Source: Eurobarometer 51.0 (1999).

more on support for the transfer of competences and sovereignty. I constructed this variable by adding the answer values corresponding to two questions in which respondents were asked whether they were (1) for the creation of a single currency and (2) for the creation of a common defense and security policy.

The upper part of table 11 contains logit and regression estimates of the effects of the fear of losing one's national identity and of how close one feels to Europe on the two dependent variables. The statistical analysis holds constant the country of residence and a series of socioeconomic, cognitive, and political variables that have frequently been invoked as determinants of support for membership in the European Union.[3]

The estimates for these statistical models indicate that respondents who fear losing their national identity as part of the European Union are less supportive of both membership in and transfers of sovereignty and competences to the European Union than are the rest of the respondents.[4] Furthermore, the estimates indicate that respondents who feel closer to Europe are also more supportive of membership in the European Union and of transfers of sovereignty and competences to the European Union than are the rest of the respondents.[5] These results thus support the hypotheses developed in this book concerning the roles of frames and the degree of identification with Europe in explaining variation in support for European integration.

Identification with Europe and Contrasts in Support for European Integration between the United Kingdom and Other Countries

The findings above are revealing from a descriptive viewpoint. This book's focus on frames, however, is less guided by a desire to examine the role of frames on support for membership in the European Union or European integration than by a search for clues about the identity and structural factors that inspire the emergence of such frames. The Eurobarometer does not allow a full test of the argument developed in previous chapters. Nonetheless, one can use Eurobarometer data to test the hypothesis that the British are less supportive of membership in the European Union than the Spaniards and the Germans because they feel less attached to Europe and are thus more afraid of losing their national identity as part of the European Union.

The lower segment of table 11 presents country contrasts in support for membership in the European Union and support for the transfer of sovereignty and competences to the European Union, before (columns 1 and 3) and after (columns 2 and 4) holding constant how close respondents feel to Europe and whether they fear losing their national identity as part of the European Union. Because of how the Eurobarometer Study 51.0 was conducted, the country comparison distinguishes between West and East Germany and between Great Britain and Northern Ireland. The logic of the statistical analysis is quite simple. If closeness to Europe and fear of losing national identity account for part of the contrasts between the

United Kingdom and other countries, these contrasts should become smaller when the two independent variables are held constant.

Column 1 shows that after holding a series of individual level variables constant, respondents in all European Union countries except Sweden express on average greater support for membership in the European Union than do those in Great Britain. The statistical results also show that the odds of thinking that membership is a good thing rather than a bad thing are 9.86 times higher in Northern Ireland than they are in the rest of the United Kingdom. Furthermore, column 3 shows that respondents in all countries except for Sweden and Denmark are on average more supportive of transfers of sovereignty and competences to the European Union than are those in Great Britain. Again, support is greater in Northern Ireland than it is in the rest of the United Kingdom. In sum, the results above, which adjust for the composition of the country samples by sociodemographic and other individual characteristics, confirm British "Euroscepticism." The question now is to see whether differences in the perception that membership in the European Union will erode national identity and in the degree of closeness people feel to Europe explain these contrasts in support for European integration.

Columns 2 and 4 report the contrasts between Great Britain and the rest of the countries after holding the above-mentioned independent variables constant. In the majority of the European Union countries, support for membership in the European Union (column 2) remains higher than in Great Britain. The exceptions are Sweden, as before, and Austria, Denmark, and Finland. In these countries support is now the same—Finland—or lower. The same conclusions apply when one examines the degree of support for a transfer of sovereignty and competences to the European Union (column 4). The comparison between columns 1 and 2 and between columns 3 and 4 shows, however, that the contrasts with Great Britain diminish, and in some cases considerably. In Spain, for instance, the odds of thinking that membership in the European Union is a good thing rather than a bad thing change from being about 14 times (13.58) higher than in Great Britain to being about 6 times higher (6.49). Also consistent with expectations is the finding that holding constant the respondents' fears of losing the national identity and how close respondents feel to Europe does not affect the contrasts between Northern Ireland and Great Britain at all, nor, for that matter, does it affect the contrasts between Ireland and the United Kingdom. Other reasons explain why respondents in Ireland and Northern Ireland are more supportive of European integration than are respondents in Great Britain.

These statistical results are consistent with the book's argument about the role of Empire as the root cause of the British heightened sense of "difference" and, partly because of this and related fears of losing the national identity, as the cause of less support for efforts toward European integration. The large number of control variables in the analysis and the good fit of the models in columns 2 and 4 (Cox-Snell pseudo-R square = 25.2% and R-square = 23.7%) reinforce the validity of these conclusions.

Beyond European Identity: Support for Membership in Spain, Germany, and the United Kingdom

The focus of this book is on those factors that explain differences in support for European integration between the United Kingdom and both Germany and Spain. The preceding section has demonstrated that international contrasts in the perceived threat of the European Union to national identities and in how close people feel to Europe go a long way toward explaining differences in support for European integration. After holding these variables constant, however, German and Spanish respondents remain more supportive of European integration than do the British respondents. To explain these remaining contrasts, one can examine the roles of other factors that, based on the discussion in previous chapters, may have contributed to higher levels of support for European integration in Spain and Germany relative to the United Kingdom and other countries. These are the desire to modernize the country and break with a centuries-old tradition of isolationism in the case of Spain, and the pragmatic desire to improve the country's reputation after World War II in the case of Germany. The Eurobarometer Study 51.0 does not include variables that would allow for a direct test of these hypotheses. Nevertheless, one can proceed by exclusion, that is, by showing that alternative potential explanations fail to account for the levels of support for European integration in these countries.

In what follows, I estimate first a 3-level hierarchical linear model to explain attitudes toward the transfer of sovereignty and competences to the European Union as measured by the same dependent variable as in the previous statistical analysis.[6] The model includes variables measured at the individual, regional, and country levels of aggregation. The regional- and country-level variables are the focus of this analysis, for they are meant to control for various explanatory factors of the greater support for transfers of sovereignty and competences observed in Germany and Spain, when compared to the United Kingdom and other European Union countries.

Some of the aggregate-level variables in the statistical analysis have been used by Gabel and by Eichenberg and Dalton in their statistical models. These variables measure macroeconomic processes (i.e., the level of economic growth and the level of inflation), exchange (i.e., the percentages of overall trade conducted with members of the European Union and residence in regions that border on another European Union country), and the impact of World War II (i.e., the number of casualties per capita). The predictions made by the authors above are that support for membership in the European Union increases with rates of economic growth, trade interdependence, residence in a border region, and the number of casualties per capita in World War II. They also predict that support decreases with rates of inflation, because inflation is an indicator of poor economic performance that indirectly reflects on people's evaluations of the economic benefits of membership in the European Union.

Other aggregate-level variables included in the analysis here either have not been tested before or have been tested with other indicators. To the former category correspond a measure of whether respondents live in a predominantly Catholic country, a measure of the distance between the region where respondents live and Brussels, and a measure of whether respondents live in a country that has only recently become a democracy. To the latter category corresponds a measure of whether respondents live in a region targeted by the main package of structural funds provided by the European Commission to reduce regional inequalities in Europe (Objective 1 regions).[7]

The key part of the statistical analysis performed in this section is the examination of average country residuals for this model. If the model perfectly explains the average level of support for transfers of sovereignty and competences to the European Union in a particular country, the average value for this country's residuals should be zero; otherwise, the average value for the residuals will deviate from zero. Based on the variables included in the model and the argument developed in this book, one would expect the average residual for Spain to be close to zero. Indeed, the model includes indicators of people's fear of losing their national identity and of the degree to which they feel close to Europe, which, as demonstrated above, affect the Spaniards' degree of support for European integration. Moreover, it includes two aggregate variables, Objective 1 Region and New Democracy, that tap into the main factors Spanish respondents referred to when invoking the topic of modernization in discussions of Spain's membership in the European Union (e.g., Structural Funds, democratic consolidation). The two aggregate variables can be treated as indirect measures of the presence or absence of the modernization frame among the population. This only requires the tenable assumption that the European Union's Structural Funds and its democratic principles have favored the development among Spaniards of the expectation that the European Union will contribute to the country's economic and political modernization.

Whereas some of the variables included in the statistical model can be seen as indirect measures of the frames on the European Union that distinguish Spaniards from Britons and Germans, none of the variables in the statistical model taps on the West German respondents' distinct concern for other countries' fears of Germany. Variables such as the number of casualties in World War II, residence in Objective 1 regions, how far respondents live from Brussels, and residence in a Catholic country should all contribute to explaining West and East German levels of support for European integration, but if the argument developed in this book is correct, they should be insufficient. As long as the statistical model is well specified, that is, as long as it contributes to explain a large percentage of variation in support for European integration, one would expect the average country residuals for Germany to be greater than zero. Moreover, one would also expect these residuals to be bigger in West Germany than in East Germany, since I have shown that concerns about reassuring other countries are absent from the East German's frame on European integration.

Table 12 reports the statistical coefficients for the most relevant variables included in the estimated hierarchical linear model. I comment on these coefficients in the section below. At this point, let us just observe

TABLE 12
The Effects of Economic, Social, and Other Variables on Preference for an Integrative Model

	Multiple Regression Coefficients[1]
Inflation 97–98	0.27*
Growth 96–98	−0.01
% share trade with EU	−2.53
Ln. deaths in WWII	0.01†
Catholic country	0.89*
new democracy	0.28
lives in border region with another EU country	0.10*
Ln. distance to Brussels	−0.16*
Objective 1 region	0.13†
fear of losing national identity	−0.40*
degree of closeness to Europe	0.34*
Proportion of total variance explained (%)	20.7%.
Proportion of country variance explained (%)	80.4%.
Proportion of regional variance explained (%)	36.0%.
Proportion of individual variance explained (%)	11.0%.

* Significant at 0.05 level, two-tailed.
† Significant at 0.05 level, one-tailed.
N = 9995
[1]controlling for household income, occupational group, gender, age, frequency with which respondents discuss politics, support of party in power, support of bourgeois political parties, and support of working-class political parties. Results for these control variables available upon request.
Source: Eurobarometer Study 51.0.

that it is a relatively well specified model by social science standards. The variables in the model explain about 21% of the total variance and, what is most important, as much as 80% of the international variance. Figure 9.1 is a bar chart that reports the average country residuals based on the model. These country residuals tell us about the plausibility of the arguments developed in this book concerning the roles that the desire to modernize, the desire to break with isolation, the desire to reassure other countries, fears of losing the national identity, and feelings of closeness to Europe, play in explaining support for European integration in Spain, Germany, and the United Kingdom. The average residuals are positive in West Germany, Northern Ireland, and East Germany, and negative in Spain and Great Britain. Of these, the biggest residuals, that is those that indicate the poorest fit, correspond to West Germany (0.295) and Great Britain (−0.321). What this means is that the variables included in the model are more or less sufficient to account for Spain's, Northern Ire-

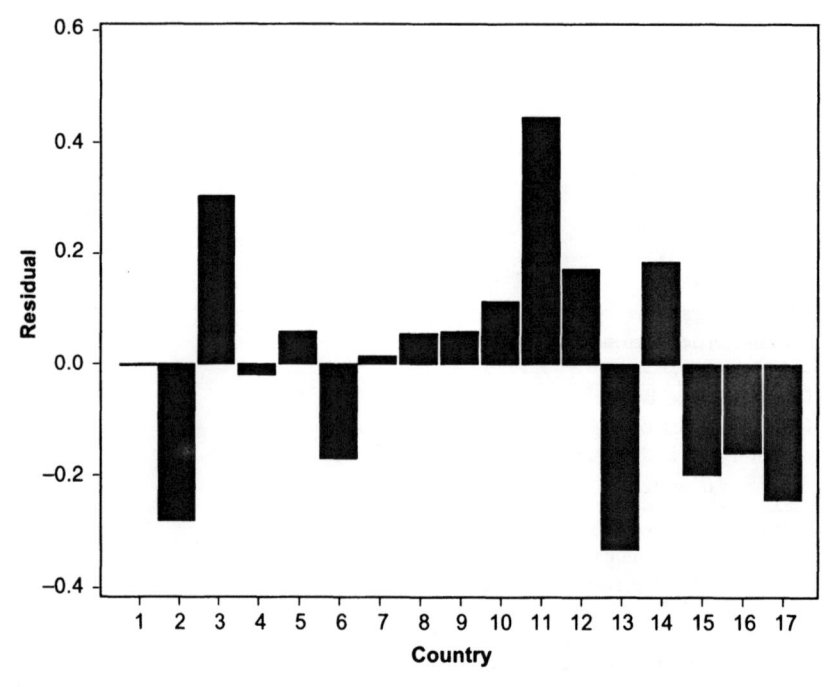

Figure 9.1 Average empirical Bayes residuals by country, obtained after estimating hierarchical linear model in table 12. 1. Belgium; 2. Denmark; 3. West Germany; 4. Greece; 5. Italy; 6. Spain; 7. France; 8. Ireland; 9. Northern Ireland; 10. Luxembourg; 11. Netherlands; 12. Portugal; 13. Great Britain; 14. East Germany; 15. Finland; 16. Sweden; 17. Austria.

land's, and East Germany's levels of support for transfers of sovereignty and competences to the European Union, but relatively insufficient to account for those in West Germany and Great Britain.

For Spain, the results above mean that support for European integration is due to a very large extent to the combined effect of the variables in the model. Nonetheless, since living in a newly democratic country has no statistically significant effect ($p < .05$) on support for European integration, one must infer that the modernization frame contributes somewhat less to raising levels of support for European integration relative to other countries than do the strong confidence in the survival of Spain's national identity and the strong feelings of closeness to Europe. The negative value for the residual means that support for European integration in Spain is lower than one would expect based on the variables included in the model.

For Great Britain, the results mean that fears of losing national identity and relatively weak feelings of closeness to Europe, as well as the other factors included in the model, important as they are in explaining lower levels of support for European integration compared to other countries,[8] do not fully account for the population's "Euroscepticism." One sees, however, that the aggregate variables included in the model do explain the levels of support for European integration in Northern Ireland and the Republic of Ireland.

For West Germany, the statistical results mean that potential explanatory factors for the population's level of support for European integration, such as the high number of casualties in World War II, to name one relevant example, do not completely account for the population's degree of support for European integration. By exclusion, this finding and the observation that the positive residual for East Germany is about half the size of that for West Germany, adds plausibility to the argument that a concern to reassure other countries about a too strong Germany plays a significant role in explaining West Germany's support for European integration. Nonetheless, the indirect nature of this reasoning makes the conclusions provisional until better data become available to conduct a direct test of this hypothesis.

Beyond Spain, Germany, and the United Kingdom

The statistical results above tell us much about the factors underlying variation in support for European integration. Previous work has focused on the roles of individual characteristics when explaining support for European integration. Thanks to the efforts of researchers such as Matthew Gabel, we now have a much clearer understanding of the factors explaining individual variation in support for European integration. Gabel's theoretical approach, focused on the applicability of microeconomic theory to the study of European integration, has, however, limited his ability to account for the role of country of residence. Only by departing from microeconomic theory has he been able to unveil some of the factors explaining international contrasts. Examples of this are his consideration of the death toll in World War II and of macroeconomic variables such as economic well-being, inflation, and trade interdependence, also considered by Eichenberg and Dalton. The model estimated in table 9.2 moves further in this direction, by expanding Gabel's and Eichenberg and Dalton's lists of aggregate-level variables.

The results presented in table 12 allow for an evaluation of the contribution of aggregate-level variables cited in the literature or suggested by a consideration of the history of European integration and of theories to explain related phenomena, like state- and nation-building. Of the nine aggregate-level variables, six have effects that are statistically significant at the .05 level: the level of inflation, whether the country is Catholic, the distance to Brussels from the regions where respondents live, whether respondents live in regions that border on some other EU country, whether respondents live in Objective 1 regions, and the number of casualties per capita in World War II.

The effect of inflation rates is contrary to expectations, since it is positive rather than negative, whereas the other statistically significant effects are consistent with expectations. According to the results reported in table 12, the greater the distance from Brussels, the lower the level of support for transfers of sovereignty and competences to the European Union. The coefficient -0.16 for the effect of the natural logarithm of the distance indicates, for instance, that holding other variables constant, the level of support for transfers of sovereignty and competences to the European Union among people who reside on average about 394 km from Brussels (the first quartile of the distribution) is 0.17 units lower than for that among people who live on average about 1214 km away from Brussels (the third quartile of the distribution). Table 12 also shows that people who live in Catholic regions are more supportive of European integration than are people who do not live in Catholic regions. The coefficient 0.89 means that, holding other variables constant, the former are 0.89 units more supportive of transfers of sovereignty and competences than are the latter. Table 12 further shows that people who live in regions that border with another EU state are more supportive of European integration than are people who do not live in border regions; the coefficient 0.10 means that, holding other variables constant, they are 0.10 units more supportive of transfers of sovereignty and competences than are the latter. Another relevant result in this statistical analysis is that respondents who live in Objective 1 regions are, as expected, more supportive of transfers of sovereignty and competences than are those who do not live in these regions. The coefficient 0.13 means that, holding other variables constant, the former respondents are on average 0.13 units more supportive of transfers of sovereignty and competences than are the latter. Finally, the statistical results in table 12 show that support for transfers of sovereignty and competences to the European Union increases, but very slowly, with the number of World War II casualties per capita in the countries where respondents live. For example, holding other variables constant, in countries where the number of casualties per capita was about 1 per thousand (25% percentile of the country distribution—e.g., Denmark), the predicted level of support for the transfer of sovereignty and competences is 0.04 units lower than in those where the number of casualties per capita was about 41 per thousand (75% percentile—e.g., more than the Netherlands but fewer than Greece). Although some of the effects described above are small, taken together they play a very important role, not only in explaining support for membership in the European Union but also in explaining international variability.

In sum, the statistical analysis in this chapter confirms or strongly supports the analytical and theoretical arguments developed in this book and paves the way for further research. It has demonstrated that fear of losing one's national identity as part of the European Union and the closeness one feels to Europe matter in explaining the degree to which one supports membership in the European Union. It has also shown that British skepticism is rooted in a comparatively low degree of identification with Europe and a fear of losing national identity. Finally, it is consistent with the arguments that a desire to modernize and to break with isolation in the case of Spain and a desire to regain the trust of other countries after World War II in the case of West Germany are factors behind their support for European integration.

Beyond validating this book's arguments, the above statistical analysis points toward topics that ought to be explored more systematically and case studies that would shed more light on our understanding of attitudes toward European integration. The finding that respondents who live in Catholic countries express more support for European integration than do other respondents is consistent with predictions in the literature. The finding further testifies to the enduring power of religion as one of the key articulating sociological factors of the culture and politics of contemporary Europe, long after its loss of ascendancy over the souls of a largely secularized society. To demonstrate, however, that religion indeed plays a significant role and does not just mask the effects of other variables, one must further specify the causal mechanisms through which it operates. This will require moving away from the focus on social representations that constitutes this book's analytical framework. There is indeed no empirical evidence that religious beliefs themselves are the underlying factor behind variation in support for European integration. Catholicism most likely works at other levels, through networks of cultural affinity and networks of political communication and cooperation across Europe.

The analysis of average country residuals for the statistical model in table 12 has highlighted countries whose support for European integration exceeds or fails to reach the level one would expect based on the variables included in the model. This information is very valuable, for it points to where research on attitudes toward European integration can result in a greater substantive payoff. The finding that Austria shows less support for transfers of sovereignty and competences to the European Union than expected, combined with ultra-rightist Jörg Haider's recent notoriety, cannot help but conjure up the image of a country that did not draw the same lessons from World War II as West Germany. A study similar to this one, analyzing people's frames of European unification, linking them to the country's post–World War II political cultures, and drawing comparisons with East Germany and West Germany, could both explain Austria's relatively low level of support for European integration and buttress this book's explanation for West Germany's stance on European integration. Another possible interpretation of Austria's relatively low level of support for EU membership is that a decades-old tradition of neutrality has made its population wary of international engagements. Here, a comparison with Sweden, whose levels of support for membership in the European Union are also relatively low, and lower than expected with the model in table 12, and perhaps with Switzerland, which has until now declined membership in the European Union, could be fruitful. Finally, the comparison between the Netherlands and Belgium could also offer relevant insights on the forces shaping support for membership in the European Union and of European integration. Both countries are net supporters of membership in the European Union (see Chapter 1). It is paradoxical that after holding all variables in table 12 constant, the population of the Netherlands is more supportive of membership in the European Union than one would expect. Since they are neighboring countries, located at the center of Europe, and are both small, highly developed economically, and tied by strong historical, cultural, and economic links, they present a promising controlled comparison. The comparison becomes even more interesting when one considers that one of their differentiating characteristics is that Belgium is predominantly Catholic, whereas the Netherlands is not. This runs counter to the predictions drawn from the statistical analysis and calls for further study, not only to better understand support for membership in the European Union but also to understand the precise role of Catholicism in furthering support for that membership.

Ten

Conclusions

RATHER THAN follow standard practice and draw explanations of international variation in support for European integration from extant theories or plain observation, I have approached this topic through examination of popular social representations of the European Union. I have also examined the translation of these social representations into justifications for or against membership in the European Union and for or against different models of European integration. Underlying my approach is the realization that attitudes toward the EU and toward European integration do not simply reflect the values, identities, and interests of individuals faced with an objective and uniformly understood reality. What individuals confront is the distorted image of this reality as it is filtered by national or subnational cultures. These cultures act like differently shaped curved mirrors that exaggerate or shrink the dimensions of the object that they are reflecting. Therefore, some aspects of the European Union and European integration are perceived similarly everywhere, whereas other aspects acquire more salience in some countries or regions than others.

The first part of the book has focused on how people conceive of European integration. It has shown that despite low degrees of interest and information about the European Union, a shared image of what it is has gradually developed among the German, British, and Spanish publics. This shared image is, if we follow theories of nationalism, a precondition for the development of a feeling of belonging to an imagined community such as Europe.[1] On the positive side, citizens see a very big market that will benefit all member states, the opportunity of building a strong bloc that will compete politically and economically with the United States and Japan, and a geographical space in which barriers for the movement of people have disappeared. On the negative side, they see an inefficient, overbureaucratized, unaccountable, overzealous, and often corrupt organization. Beyond the similarities, citizens of the United Kingdom, Spain, and Germany have developed particular ways of seeing European integration that reflect, as shown in interviews, their respective national self-perceptions, collective memories, and current preoccupations. Thus, Germans criticize the EU's democratic deficit and worry about competition in the labor market by foreign workers, Britons worry about losing their national identity, and Spaniards see the European Union as an opportunity to modernize and break with a long isolationist tradition. In one country, Germany, I have demonstrated that images of the European Union differ between regions. Thus, in West Germany people conceive of European integration as an opportunity for Germany to regain the trust of the international community after the horrors of World War II, as an insurance against a revival of far-right nationalism in Germany, and as an opportunity to do something for countries that suffered under Germany in World War II. In East Germany, this conceptualization of the process of European integration is entirely missing. This is fortunate from a theoretical point of view, for it has allowed me to demonstrate the role of cultural resonance in promoting the development and diffusion of particular frames on European integration.

The analysis of frames is useful as a heuristic because it contributes to tracing the deeper cultural and structural causes of variation in support of European integration and the European Union. Frames are also, however, the most immediate causal link in the explanation of this variance. After all, people's attitudes toward European integration and the European Union are not unconscious and automatic processes; instead, they are preceded by some sort of reflection and are justified through "good reasons," as I explain in chapter 3. These good reasons are the vehicle for the expression of people's frames. Therefore, in chapter 3 I explore the relationships between frames on the European Union and European integration and attitudes toward these objects of evaluation. This gives me an opportunity to refine the concept of support, by differentiating between models of European integration. Thus, I begin by focusing on the cleavage between supporters and nonsupporters and show that supporters stand out for their greater emphasis on the economic advantages of a single market and on the European Union's expected contribution to peace and a better understanding between peoples. Meanwhile, nonsupporters emphasize more than do supporters the threat of European integration to national identity and sovereignty. As with frames in general, in-depth interviews with German, British, and Spanish citizens also reveal national peculiarities in the themes that distinguish supporters from nonsupporters. In Germany, for instance, fears of foreign labor competition also distinguish the two groups; in the United Kingdom, it is the impression that the country's voice is not heard in the European institutions; finally, in Spain, it is the degree of optimism with respect to the EU's economic consequences.

I follow the analysis of contrasts between supporters and nonsupporters of European integration and the European Union with a finer distinction between projects of European integration and a comparison between the frames of the most popular ones. To be sure, while most people can be classified as supporters or nonsupporters of European integration, an important segment of the population lack a clear idea of how they want Europe to be organized politically. Among my respondents, this segment included more than one fourth of the sample. My classification of models of European integration differentiates between two dimensions of integration: the transfer of competences and the transfer of sovereignty. Although the transfer of competences is already a form of transfer of sovereignty, because a state can no longer decide alone on issues that concern it, this dimension refers essentially to how one governs, whereas the sovereignty dimension refers more to who holds the ultimate power over a state's own affairs. The former dimension distinguishes between "Centralizers" and "Decentralizers," the latter between "Supporters of Integration" and "Supporters of Cooperation." By combining the two dimensions, I obtain four models of integration: Centralized Integration, Decentralized Integration, Centralized Cooperation, and Decentralized Cooperation. Through in-depth interviews with ordinary citizens and local elites in Germany, the United Kingdom, and Spain, I conclude that the Centralized Integration and Decentralized Cooperation models are the two most popular ones. Except for the United Kingdom, local elites and respondents with more formal education side in slightly higher proportions with the former than with the latter model. Supporters of the Centralized Integration model also tend to be more progressive politically. I point out, however, that supporters of the Centralized Integration model are not strong "Centralists." While favorable to the transfer of important functions to the European institutions, they are by and large favorable to a generous application of the subsidiarity principle.

Like supporters and nonsupporters of European integration, supporters of the Centralized Integration and Decentralized Cooperation models distinguish themselves by conceptualizing European integration and the European Union in specific ways. Thus, those who support the Centralized Integration model emphasize transnational problems, the need to defend a social market economy, their wish to witness the development of a strong bloc that competes against the United States and Japan, and their belief that the European Union will contribute to maintaining peace in Europe. Meanwhile, respondents who support the Decentralized Cooperation model stress their desire to defend the states' national identity, point out the sharp contrasts between the EU members, emphasize the EU's governance problems, and indicate how highly they value the defense of the national interest and state sovereignty. These contrasts are useful per se, but also because they offer clues to the causes for the different levels of support of European integration in the United Kingdom, Spain, and Germany. The comparison between the frames on European integration among supporters of the Centralized Integration and Decentralized Cooperation models leads to the conclusion that differences in how much people fear losing their country's identity and culture are the most likely explanation for the contrasts in support of European integration between the United Kingdom, Spain, and Germany.

The elements that distinguish German, British, and Spanish frames on European integration have a long history, which suggests that long-standing cultural factors underlie them. Chapter 4 demonstrates the stability of frames on European integration in the United Kingdom, Germany, and Spain, through content analysis of editorials and opinion pieces published in quality newspapers in these countries since the early reconstruction efforts that followed World War II. This content analysis shows that in the United Kingdom the European unification process has traditionally been portrayed in more negative terms, and calls for transfers of sovereignty to European institutions have been less frequent, than in West Germany. Meanwhile, while closer to the West German than to the British quality press's approach to European integration, the Spanish press's approach has been more factual and less descriptive. Moreover, it has been split between a center-left position favorable to a Centralized Integration model of European integration and a conservative position favorable to a Decentralized Cooperation model.

The images of European integration that newspaper editorials and opinion pieces project mirror that of the population I interviewed between 1996 and 1997 and remain pretty much constant for the four and a half decades that I have analyzed. They are also closer to those of local elites and more educated respondents than to those of ordinary citizens, as one would expect, given the more similar social background of their authors. Thus, for instance, ordinary citizens pay more attention than do journalists, who are members of the more educated segments of German, British, and Spanish societies, to aspects of European integration that touch them more directly, like the Common Agricultural Policy, the Structural Funds, the removal of barriers to movement across the borders of the European Community, and competition by foreign workers. The strong similarity between the newspapers' frames and those of the interview respondents means that the contrasts between British, Spanish, and German views presented in chapters 2 and 3 are reproduced in chapter 4. Thus, the British emphasis on sovereignty, the West German emphasis on regaining the trust of other nations, and the Spanish thrust to break with isolation, to modernize, and to improve Spain's status in the international community are again main distinguishing features of the frames in the countries under investigation.

Through qualitative analysis of the evolution in the content of editorials and opinion pieces, one begins to unravel the historical, cultural, and structural puzzle constituted by the different frames and the contrasting approaches to European integration in the United Kingdom, Spain, and Germany. The clues offered by this analysis acquire full expression when one examines the main preoccupations that have characterized these countries' political cultures in the post–World War II era, as in chapters 5 to 8. In turn, chapter 9 corroborates through quantitative analysis the interpretation for the contrasts between British, German, and Spanish attitudes toward European integration developed in the preceding four chapters.

In view of the long list of arguments that has been offered to explain attitudes toward European integration in Spain, Germany, and Great Britain, and contrasts between each of these countries and the rest of the members of the European Union, it should come as no surprise that some of these arguments receive empirical support in the book. The comparison between the three countries confirms, for instance, the views of those who stress the significance that Spaniards attach to the EU's modernization promise and the symbolic dimension underlying their majority support for membership in the EU: the craving for Spain's recognition as a major international actor and the assertion of Spain's Europeanness.[2] It also confirms the views of those who emphasize the West Germans' pragmatic support for European integration as a means to reassure the world about Germany's non-hegemonic designs.[3] Finally, it proves right those who point out that Britons are more concerned about protecting their national identity than are other Europeans.[4]

The previous chapters cast doubt, however, on the significance of other factors mentioned in the literature as explanations for the different levels of support for European integration found in Germany, Great Britain, and Spain. A desire to consolidate and protect Spain's new democratic system may have played a role in the political elites' efforts to negotiate Spain's membership in the European Union, but it was not the primary motivation behind these efforts. Also, democratic consolidation is not a significant factor underlying the Spanish citizens' justifications for their support of EU membership and European integration.[5] Equally lacking in empirical backing are abstract psychological arguments about the role that European integration has played in providing a substitute identity for West Germans, as they processed and overcame the trauma of Germany's post-1945 division.[6] West Germans certainly displayed a lower degree of national consciousness than did the citizens of other EU member states during the period in which there were two German states. But the relative degree of national consciousness has not changed very much since reunification, nor did a craving for a substitute identity figure prominently in public debate about European integration in the 1945–90 period.

Finally, collective psychology is also a poor candidate to explain the relative lack of support for European integration in the United Kingdom. Leaving aside the obvious contradiction of positing both that initial opposition to membership rested on British self-assuredness after victory in 1945 and that later opposition to membership and efforts toward European unification rested on British lack of self-assuredness in the face of decline, the empirical evidence collected in this book does not support the argument that British citizens oppose European integration in order to boost their identity in the face of decline.[7] To be sure, much more than Spaniards and Germans, Britons are concerned about the negative implications that European integration may have on their national identity. But there is no empirical evidence to sustain the claim that this greater concern reflects confusion or despair in the face of British decline. As revealed in comments from interviews discussed in previous chapters, decline is something of which many Britons are painfully aware, but no one related decline to a crisis of identity. What we have seen instead is that some people concede that full engagement in the European integration process would help to stave off this decline, but still prefer to sacrifice optimal economic rationality in order to preserve traditions and institutions that they cherish.

The focus on the images of European integration people rely on when justifying support for membership in the European Union or efforts toward European unification allows us to move from the context of individual contrasts to the context of national contrasts. More precisely, it allows us to make the transition from individual interests, values, and identities to national culture. Among the materials that constitute a national culture, I have focused on long-lasting and highly salient debates or publicly expressed and taken-for-granted diagnostics about the nation (its history, its present conditions, its tasks ahead) and the nation's relations with other nations. These have been the primary constitutive materials for people's reflection on issues of European integration, and the filtering tools relied upon by them when interpreting messages transmitted by the media about European integration.

Briefly stated, the storyline goes as follows: Before World War II, there were nationalist and supranational identity projects in Germany, the United Kingdom, and Spain that competed with a sense of affinity with Europe, as in the United Kingdom, or competed and were incompatible with both a sense of affinity with Europe and the democratic values it represented, as in Spain and Germany. The pursuit of such supranational projects in these and other countries corresponded to a view of the geopolitical European space as a gameboard for competition between the different European powers. The alternative projects in the countries I examine in this book were Little Englandism, Empire, and the Anglo-Saxon community in the United Kingdom, anti-parliamentarism, isolationism ("Casticismo"), and the Hispanidad in Spain, and anti-parliamentarism and a Central European identity in Germany. The high intensity of conflict between alternative identity and political projects in Spain and Germany eventually led to the Spanish Civil War and World War II. At the end of World War I and more clearly so, at the end of World War II, Western European powers gave up their hegemonical ambitions within Europe and considered seriously for the first time the idea of cooperative arrangements toward the unification of Europe. In this context, countries such as Spain and Germany, defeated, diplomatically isolated, and economically bankrupt, were also forced to abandon their non–Western European projects. Meanwhile, a victorious United Kingdom remained torn between its commitment to Europe and its commitment to alternative identities. The resulting persistence of a strong sense of being different with respect to Europe among sizable segments of the British population, after the British Empire itself had dissolved, largely explains why there has traditionally been less support for European integration and the European Union in the United Kingdom than in Spain or Germany. This relative lack of identification with Europe, along with the way European integration has been framed in British public debate, has created among the British population a strong sense that their national identity and culture are threatened by membership in the European Union.

The British fear of losing the national identity and culture are largely absent in Spain and Germany. No longer divided about their European identity, Spaniards and Germans have been more receptive to efforts toward European integration. Additional factors have served to translate this receptiveness into active support. In Spain, as the analysis of editorials and opinion pieces in newspapers shows, membership in the Common Market was from early on perceived as the only viable strategy toward closing the economic development gap between Spain and its European neighbors. Nowadays, the expected economic benefits of membership in the European Union, in the form of a stimulus to change old mentalities and obsolete production structures and the reception of structural funds from the European Union, ensure sustained support for European integration and the European Union among Spaniards.

When it comes to Germany, one needs to distinguish between its Western and Eastern parts. The Federal Republic of Germany, formally sovereign since 1955, was constrained into practicing restraint in foreign relations in order to earn the trust of its Western allies and thus keep the door to German reunification open. An obsession with the FRG's image abroad thus presided over post–World War II West German culture and resulted in a pragmatic form of support for European integration. In addition, the highly publicized and persistent postwar debates about the German people's responsibility for World War II and about the German character inspired among small segments of West German society the desire to anchor the FRG in the European Communities. The political culture in the German Democratic Republic was very different from the FRG's, and less receptive to the justifications for supporting European integration that developed among West Germans and to which East Germans were exposed through the West German press after German reunification. Practically deprived of an autonomous foreign policy, and participant in a highly hierarchical and centralized Soviet bloc that silenced internal conflict by emphasizing the "brotherhood" between Socialist nations, the GDR did not participate in the FRG's obsession with its image abroad. There was also no public debate in the GDR about the government's need to be sensitive to its neighbors' feelings. Moreover, the GDR government's emphasis on the distinction between good and bad Germans—the former Socialist, the latter Fascist—and the conceptualization of World War II as a victory in the GDR's territory of the good Germans over the bad Germans, precluded the development among East Germans of a feeling of responsibility toward other Europeans or of self-doubt concerning the German character. Therefore, East Germans have not developed and have not been sensitive to justifications of support for European integration that emphasize pragmatic reasons, a feeling of responsibility toward other nations, and the need to protect Germany against itself. Consequently, economic justifications almost exclusively determine East Germans' attitudes toward European integration.

Note that the focus of this book has been on public opinion toward European integration rather than on the elites' attitudes and behavior. Furthermore, I have provided an explanation for the population's different attitudes that emphasizes the role of cultural and historical factors. One could argue that public opinion plays a secondary role in explaining the course of European integration and that the justifications people provide for their support for or opposition to European integration are weak rationalizations for positions that are simply guided by the degree of support provided for European integration by the elites. My focus on the population rather than on the political elites reflects the demonstrated existence of a reciprocal influence between the elites' and the population's attitudes and behavior with respect to European integration. Furthermore, it rests on the grounded assumption that elites participate to a large extent in the same non-instrumental preoccupations as the rest of the population. Although I do not discuss it in the text, for lack of comparable data for other countries, I was able to verify this through interviews with members of the Spanish elites in 1993,[8] which revealed that the triad formed by the topics of modernization, breaking with isolation, and Spain's prestige was as prominent among them as among ordinary citizens and local elites.[9]

The fact that the political elites are part of the same national culture as the rest of the citizens justifies a shift from elites to the general population when examining the effect of national cultures on attitudes toward European integration. Even if it were true that members of the elite always initiate the framing of a particular problem in a particular way, the frames they use would necessarily reflect cultural themes they by and large share with the rest of the population. Thus, a focus on how elites frame problems would tell us something about the mechanics of transmission of ideas but not very much about the underlying sources of these ideas and for their acceptance by the population. Furthermore, like Mary Shelley's Frankenstein, the "monster" that elites help to create, that is, both the attitudes toward European integration and the arguments that underpin them, often gets out of control and comes to dominate the elite's political choices, as recent referenda in Denmark, France, and Ireland, and the Blair government's hesitations on the United Kingdom's adoption of the euro have shown.

The results of this investigation help us to better understand how collective identities are constructed and the impact of these identities and other factors on loyalty to politico-administrative territorial units. They thus have implications both for the study of nationalism and the study of European integration. The road toward European unification, despite its uniqueness, bears analytical resemblance to processes of state-building. Unfortunately, the literature has been so blinded by the singularity of the European integration process that it has fully ignored the similarities between it and state-building and thus failed to take advantage of the theoretical and analytical contributions of the literature on nationalism. One of the significant contributions of this literature has been its emphasis on the constructed character of national identities.[10] Just as peripheral nationalist movements get their impetus from a deep-seated feeling of difference, sometimes colored with a sense of superiority, the United Kingdom's reluctance to contribute to efforts toward European integration is grounded on a feeling that British culture is too different from other European cultures. Also, just as the feeling of difference that underlies support for peripheral nationalist movements is socially constructed, the British sense of difference is a perplexing social construction. As I conducted this research project, I lived in Spain, Germany, France, and the United Kingdom. This forced me to get used to different eating schedules, different telephone connections, different ways of settling rent payments, different ways of interacting and expressing emotions. Beyond these little things, which made life more interesting anyway, I never had a sense of being lost in a culture that I did not understand. I did not have to adapt my behavior more in one society than in another. Everything seemed in some ways familiar. Thus I was baffled by my British respondents' constant references to "how different Britain is" and "how different European cultures are." "Where's the difference?" I would ask. And indeed, the respondents had little to offer as a reply but vague expressions such as "Our way of life." The truth is, this singularity of British culture is a myth. It is a myth, however, that has had a tremendous impact on the process of European construction. While one may attribute the early British hesitations regarding membership in the emerging European institutions to the UK's imperial status in the early post–World War II period, the persistence of these hesitations in the mid-1950s and later, as the empire was unraveling and British trade patterns were shifting toward continental Europe, is essentially explained by the enduring power of this myth of difference.

What is interesting about the effects of the myth of British distinctiveness on popular skepticism toward European integration is that, unlike the myths of difference that legitimize peripheral nationalist movements, its creation predates and is therefore independent of the movement of resistance to European integration. As the literature cited above has shown, it is a myth that essentially developed as the United Kingdom defined itself with respect to the lands and peoples of the British Empire, not with respect to Europe. As a clear illustration of the relative autonomy of culture, however, the myth of British singularity then went on to shape frames on European integration in the United Kingdom. In sum, the constructed character of identities does not detract from the autonomous role that they can play in the political process, and should not always be reduced to underlying structural forces.

The book's findings also bear on another contribution of the literature on nationalism, which is the hypothesis that other things being equal, the intensity of peripheral nationalism is greater in regions that are more developed than the political core than in other regions. I mentioned in chapter 1 that relatively high support for European integration in Italy, Germany, France, and perhaps Spain at first sight contradicts the "Overdevelopment" thesis. This book shows that the Spanish case is actually quite consistent with the theory. Despite being one of the largest European economies, Spain is less economically developed than is the average member state in the European Union. Furthermore, its population's positive approach to Europe, its framing of European integration in terms of the country's modernization, bears the imprint of Spain's past economic backwardness. At the EU level, the finding that the population of Objective 1 regions supports membership in the European Union more than does the population of other regions also lends validity to the Overdevelopment theory. In fact, the multivariate analysis in chapter 9 leaves Germany as the most obvious case that does not conform to the theory's predictions. As discussed in this book, the German case illustrates the independent role of political and military considerations in the readiness by a wealthy region or state to surrender sovereignty. Germany gave up part of its formal state sovereignty in order to buy actual sovereignty and eventually achieve the goal of German reunification. It was forced into accepting this compromise because of pressure by the international community and the reality of the Cold War. Such an historical scenario resulted from an exceptional combination of circumstances and can thus be seen as confirming rather than invalidating the Overdevelopment theory. Nonetheless, it highlights the potential role of geopolitical factors in the explanation of both peripheral nationalism and support for European integration.

The Future of European Integration

While it is true that the United Kingdom's political and journalistic elites have historically shown little interest in pursuing a centralized model of integration,[11] this book shows that their attitudes may be more closely aligned to the attitudes of their national audience and even of the European publics in general, as described in chapter 3, than have the attitudes of other EU countries' elites. It also demonstrates that British attitudes toward European integration are not as anomalous as one tends to think. The British political elites' support of a Decentralized Cooperative model or at most a Decentralized Integration model of European unification reflects European public opinion rather well, as expressed by my German, British, and Spanish respondents and revealed by survey results that show a steady decline in support for further integration efforts during the 1990s. British attitudes toward European integration are those of a highly developed country that was simply spared the worst atrocities of and defeat in World War II and that, because of this, has retained a strong sense of being unique and the ambivalence toward Europe that was typical of prewar national states. States such as Germany and Spain required the shocks of a Civil War and World War II to move beyond the nationalist mentality of nineteenth-century European states. One may bemoan that British politicians and public opinion have not reassessed their views in the face of decline or have done so slowly and reluctantly, but it takes major upheavals to alter central aspects of a country's culture.[12] Just as the big debate between Europeanizers and "Casticistas" or proponents of the "Hispanidad" project in Spain began only after the military defeat in Cuba and the Philippines in 1898, despite more than 200 years of gradual economic and political decline, the British began to reassess their national identity only after the Suez fiasco. But just as in Spain military defeat in Cuba failed to tilt the balance in favor of the Europeanizing program, Suez failed to trigger a revolution in the United Kingdom's self-definition and approach to Europe. Cultures have a habit of lasting more than the structural conditions that contributed to produce them, unless a sudden shock realigns them, if only momentarily. The study of attitudes toward European integration in Germany, the United Kingdom, and Spain is no exception. World War II and the Spanish Civil War led to the development of cultural configurations that could easily survive even when the political and economic conditions that produced them ceased to be. Only a major cataclysm such as the economic and demographic destruction caused by the civil war and the defeat of the Axis forces in World War II could thus put an end to the debate over Europe in Spain, and in all likelihood only a similar event would induce a drastic change in the British approach to European culture and the European project.

Germany (especially West Germany), rather than the United Kingdom, is the real anomaly, for its relative high support for European integration reflects the impact of a military defeat. The fact that nine years after reunification Germans still support European integration more than expected reveals again the slowness with which culture changes under normal conditions. But the tendency in the last decade, despite the German foreign affairs minister's pro-federalist pronouncements in 2001, has been for German public opinion to become less supportive of European integration. This was to be expected, for I have shown that West German support for European integration has a strong pragmatic component, aimed as it is at reassuring other countries regarding Germany's use of its economic and political strength. This pragmatic approach developed at a time when Germany was divided and vulnerable. Reunification and the end of communism have removed two good reasons for self-restraint, and this has gradually manifested itself in a new assertiveness and growing resistance to further European integration. The decline in commitment to European integration among the German population suggests that one major player in past efforts toward unification may gradually abdicate this role.

Germany's relinquishing of a leading role in the path toward greater European unification is one of several signs that the process of integration may have reached a plateau, despite the momentary euphoria caused by the implementation of the euro. The analysis of the German, British, and Spanish quality press has revealed, for instance, a growing split between center-left and conservative approaches toward European integration. Only the center-left, represented mostly by newspapers like *El País* and *Die Zeit*, seems at this point willing to move beyond the current level of integration, by stressing the need to strengthen the European Union's political dimension in order to form a political bloc that could balance U.S. world hegemony. Meanwhile, the British press and German and Spanish conservative newspapers, such as *Frankfurter Allgemeine Zeitung* and *Abc*, side more with a decentralized model of cooperation that emphasizes national interest and does not include much more than the internal market and the common currency. The loss of enthusiasm for further progress toward European integration among the German population, the current split among public intellectuals about the desired model of

European unification, and the greater heterogeneity of opinions that will be created by the admission of new members in the European Union suggest that major steps toward European unification beyond monetary unification are unlikely in the near future unless a major economic or political crisis creates new, unexpected opportunities.[13]

Until a new crisis arrives that pushes European unification to a new level, chapter 9 has suggested potentially fruitful new lines of research. One of these would consist of designing case or comparative studies around countries whose levels of support of European integration are not well explained by factors such as those examined in chapter 9. Denmark and Austria are examples of countries whose levels of support are less than what one would expect, while the Netherlands is a country in which support of European integration is greater than expected. The literature on European integration would be enriched by studies that focus on these countries. Equally promising would be further inquiry into the factors that explain the significant role of Catholic culture in the explanation of international variation in support of European integration, as shown in chapter 9. Such work would not only contribute to a better understanding of attitudes toward European integration but would also illuminate the role that religion continues to play in our highly secularized societies. Catholicism, along with World War II and Empire, are some examples of how the shadow of the past looms large over our lives.

Appendix 1

Selection and Distribution of Respondents, and the Interviewing Process

To SELECT respondents for the in-depth interviews, I relied on systematic sampling of entries in the cities' telephone books. My target sample consisted of approximately 18 respondents. Constrained as I was to working with small samples because of the ethnographic character of my project, I consciously sacrificed representativeness in order to ensure that compositional factors such as age and education did not affect the inter-city and international comparisons. This sample selection procedure also made intra-city comparisons between respondents in different age and education groups possible. I aimed to interview an equal number of respondents for different age-education combinations (see table 13). I defined three age groups (30 and under, 31 to 50, and More than 50) and two education groups (less than High School, more than High School). In the end, the random selection process that I followed made it very difficult to obtain an equal number of interviews per age-education combination. Nonetheless, the imbalances are not very great, especially when one moves to the country level.

As part of my fieldwork in each of the six cities, I also conducted interviews with members of the local elites. The selection was guided by an attempt to represent all groups likely to influence public opinion on the topic of European integration. The respondents included leading members of the local branches of the main political parties in the region where the interviews took place, the editor of the local paper, and representatives of the local chamber of commerce and industry, of the main workers' union, and of one of the town's housewives' or women's associations. In Oststadt, I also interviewed members of the local association for the unemployed.

Each interview was taped and lasted for about an hour. The questionnaire was based on a series of general closed and open-ended questions related to attitudes toward European integration, preceded by warm-up questions concerning the respondents' degree of interest in politics, degree of media exposure, and perception of the main problems affecting the country. I always asked respondents to justify their answers, and asked them whether they had heard other people or institutions make similar arguments. I personally transcribed, translated, coded, and analyzed the interviews.

TABLE 13
Distribution of Field Interviews to Ordinary Citizens by Age, Education, and City of Residence

Place of Interview	Age	Level of Education		Total
		Less than High School	More than High School	
Weststadt	30 or under	1	5	6
	31 to 50	2	4	6
	More than 50	3	3	6
	Total	6	12	18
Oststadt	30 or under	2	4	6
	31 to 50	3	2	5
	More than 50	4	3	7
	Total	9	9	18
Quijotón	30 or under	3	4	7
	31 to 50	2	3	5
	More than 50	3	2	5
	Total	8	9	17
Catadell	30 or under	1	3	4
	31 to 50	2	4	6
	More than 50	4	1	5
	Total	7	8	15
Engleton	30 or under	0	3	3
	31 to 50	2	5	7
	More than 50	3	3	6
	Total	5	11	16
Scotsburg	30 or under	2	1	3
	31 to 50	5	5	10
	More than 50	3	1	4
	Total	10	7	17

Although the results have been obtained from small samples that were not fully representative, from a statistical viewpoint, of the British, German, and Spanish populations, they can be taken as an adequate reflection of the main contrasts between the Spanish, British, and German frames on European integration. The number of interviews that I conducted in each of the cities—between 24 and 29—allowed me to attain closure in terms of the list of arguments respondents use to justify their views of European integration and the European Union. It is highly unlikely that topics that were not mentioned or were seldom mentioned in a particular city would have been mentioned or mentioned much more often with larger or more representative city samples. Thus, while it would certainly be risky to make precise population inferences about the relative salience of the various themes discussed above, it is safe to make inferences about the themes that distinguish British, German, and Spanish frames on European integration from each other. One can confidently rule out, for instance, that arguments about the lessons drawn from World War II would have been expressed in Great Britain or Spain with a larger or a different type of sample in these two countries. Meanwhile, the theme of national identity was clearly concentrated in the United Kingdom, whereas the themes of modernization and isolation were clearly concentrated in Spain. The fact that these distinguishing British and Spanish frames were formulated with similar frequencies in the two cities of each of these countries strengthens the conclusion that they are indeed frames that serve to distinguish British, German, and Spanish views of European integration.

Alternative sources of information further buttress the conclusion that World War II, national identity, modernization, and isolation are indeed themes that distinguish German, British, and Spanish frames on European integration and that can thus be used to account for contrasts in support of European integration between these three countries. The salience of modernization and isolation in the Spanish population's frames, for instance, is confirmed through data from a national representative survey conducted in March 1999 by ASEP, a Spanish survey research institute. In open-ended questions, the respondents were asked to justify their attitudes toward European integration and Spain's membership in the European Union and to list the aspects they most liked and disliked about the European Union. The rank-order correlation between the frequencies with which the twenty different themes in table 1 were mentioned in this national representative survey and those corresponding to my city samples is 0.6. Furthermore, expectations that European integration and the European Union will contribute to Spain's modernization was the sixth most mentioned topic (21.2% of the respondents mentioned it), and the desire to break with Spain's traditional isolation was the ninth most mentioned topic (5.1% of the respondents mentioned it). These results mimic those obtained in my Spanish city samples, where modernization and isolation were the seventh and ninth most mentioned themes. Also, the fear of losing the country's national identity and sovereignty was hardly mentioned by participants in the Spanish survey. Only 0.7% of the sample mentioned it, which confirms that fear of losing the national identity, a major component of the British frame, is not a salient feature of the Spanish one.

The fear of losing the national identity because of membership in the European Union is indeed a unique and distinguishing feature of the British approach to European integration. The 1999 Eurobarometer 51.0 asked respondents in a direct, closed-ended, question whether they were afraid of losing their national identity and culture as a consequence of the European Union. It should come as no surprise that the country percentages of respondents who express this fear are higher than they are in my city samples or in the 1999 Spanish survey, in which they were obtained through open-ended questions that were asked as follow-up to general questions about European integration. Nonetheless, the survey results show that whereas 64% of the British respondents expressed such fears, only 44%, 42%, and 35% in West Germany, East Germany, and Spain respectively did so.

Appendix 2

Newspaper Selection, Sampling, and Coding Procedures for Editorials and Opinion Pieces

IN GREAT BRITAIN, I selected *The Economist* and *The New Statesman*. The former is a pro-market, pro–free-trade weekly whose political views have generally been close to those of the Conservative Party. *The Economist*'s approach to European integration and the images of European integration that this newspaper conveys do not differ significantly from *The Times*'s (despite *The Economist*'s more international outlook). To make this comparison, I collected all op-ed articles on European integration published in *The Times* from 1946 to 1995. I then selected a random sample of 89 such articles, which I analyzed in the same way that I analyzed the rest of the newspapers. The results confirm the findings below regarding the frames that distinguish British from German and Spanish journalistic views of European integration. Furthermore, statistical analysis shows that the images of European integration transmitted by *The Times* are, as expected, closer to those of *The Economist* than to those of *The New Statesman*. In particular, *The Times* has historically criticized less than has *The New Statesman*, but more than have Spanish and German newspapers, the transfer of sovereignty to European institutions. *The New Statesman*, also a weekly, has closely followed the evolution of the Labour Party, from leftist to center-left "Third Way" political views.

In Germany, the selection was made difficult because of the division between West and East Germany for most of the period, and because of the absence of freedom of the press in socialist East Germany. I chose to analyze the conservative-liberal *Frankfurter Allgemeine Zeitung* (FAZ), whose views are seen as close to the Christian Democratic Union (CDU), and the liberal *Die Zeit*. For *Die Zeit* I examined odd years only, and for the *Frankfurter Allgemeine Zeitung*, I examined even years only. *Die Zeit*'s approach to European integration and the images of European integration that it conveys do not differ significantly from those of a more overtly leftist newspaper, such as the regional *Frankfurter Rundschau*. I verified this through examination of a sample of 90 editorials and opinion pieces published in the *Frankfurter Rundschau* between 1950 and 1995. This similarity exists so even in the early 1950s, when the leader of the Sozialdemokratische Partei Deutschlands (SPD), Schumacher, opposed some aspects of the European integration program defended by the

FRG's chancellor, Adenauer. The *Frankfurter Rundschau*, despite its criticism of Adenauer in this period, distanced itself quite clearly from Schumacher's views and resolutely advocated both the FRG's anchoring in the West and a federal Europe, just as did *Die Zeit*. I have examined *Die Zeit* rather than the *Frankfurter Rundschau* because *Die Zeit* is a national newspaper whereas the *Frankfurter Rundschau* is a regional one, and because *Die Zeit* represents better than does the *Frankfurter Rundschau* the center-left views that have traditionally predominated among SPD supporters. To examine the views on European integration expressed in East Germany before reunification, I examined the state-controlled national newspaper *Neues Deutschland*.

In Spain, the main complication in the selection process resulted from the dictatorship of General Franco (1939–75). I chose to examine the privately owned newspaper *Abc* for two main reasons. Firstly, it was the quality newspaper with the highest sales and with the most heterogeneous political profile during Franco's dictatorship. Unlike more conservative and less popular newspapers such as *Arriba*, it was open to both very conservative and more liberal contributors during a period in which there was hardly any progressive newspaper with a sufficiently long publication record. Secondly, it became the quintessential conservative newspaper once democracy was restored. For the period between 1971 and 1975, I complemented the analysis of *Abc* with the analysis of the weekly *Cambio16*, a center-left newspaper that became the most important vehicle of public dissent in the last years of the Franco regime. For the years after 1976, I examined *El País*, a center-left, pro–Socialist Party (PSOE) newspaper that revolutionized journalism in post-Franco Spain and is the most widely read newspaper in the country.

To perform the content analysis of the elite journalists' views, I collected all op-ed articles published in the selected newspapers between 1946 and 1997 (for German newspapers, alternate years). From this body of articles I then used systematic and stratified sampling to select the articles used in this analysis. All the articles were coded twice: once by research assistants and once by myself. I applied the questionnaire to each article, to determine what themes among those mentioned by respondents in the in-depth interviews were reflected in the articles. Expressions for or against European integration, for or against membership in European institutions, and for or against transfers of sovereignty were also coded. Expressions for or against European integration include general statements of support or opposition, as well as statements for or against the European Coal and Steel Community (ECSC), the European Defense Community (EDC), the European Economic Community, EURATOM, the Maastricht Treaty, and economic monetary union (EMU). Expressions for or against membership in European institutions include general statements of sup-port for or opposition to membership in these institutions, as well as statements for or against membership in the ECSC, the EDC, or the EEC. Expressions for or against transfers of sovereignty include general statements of support for or opposition to transfers of sovereignty, as well as statements for or against federalist arrangements, the High Authority of the ECSC, majority voting within the Council of Ministers of the EEC/EC/EU, the constitution or existence of a directly elected European Parliament, the empowerment of the European Parliament, the Maastricht Treaty, or economic and monetary union.

Although the views on European unification of elite journalists, as expressed in op-ed newspaper articles, are more articulate than those expressed by ordinary citizens and local elites in structured in-depth interviews, the researcher has less control over the type of information obtained. The information contained in newspaper articles is determined by the journalist, whereas the information contained in the structured in-depth interviews is elicited to some extent by the interviewer; all respondents have to address the same issues. For this reason, the quantitative information offered in this book must be seen as representing the explicit messages of elite journalists rather than as a full reflection of their views. For instance, the number of articles that explicitly reject the United Kingdom's membership in the European Economic Community does not accurately reflect the number of articles in which the journalist was against the United Kingdom's membership. Writers who may have been against it may have chosen not to make this opposition explicit in the article, either because they took for granted that this was how they would be understood, or because they did not feel like expressing these views.

Appendix 3

Frames on European Integration: A Discriminant Analysis, by City

THE TABLE below presents pooled within-group correlations between different frames (discriminant variables) and the standardized canonical discrimination functions. These discriminant functions are the basis on which figure 2.1 in chapter 2 is constructed.

TABLE 14
Standardized Canonical Discriminant Function Coefficients
Pooled within-group correlations between discriminant variables and standardized canonical discriminant functions are shown in parentheses.

	Function 1	*Function 2*
Common Market	−0.048 (0.028)	−0.160 (−0.084)
states too small	0.000 (−0.049)	−0.078 (0.137)
removal of barriers	0.035 (0.033)	−0.166 (−0.084)
governance	0.077 (0.003)	−0.486 (−0.206)
free movement and competition	0.464 (0.337)	0.171 (−0.206)
democratic deficit	0.327 (0.221)	0.208 (−0.003)
lessons from Word War II	0.743 (0.664)	0.353 (0.262)
peace	0.062 (0.150)	−0.449 (−0.217)
understanding	0.158 (0.141)	−0.076 (0.037)
modernize the country	−0.188 (−0.199)	0.506 (0.284)
CAP	−0.311 (−0.264)	0.288 (0.212)
Structural/Regional Funds	−0.172 (−0.246)	0.233 (0.121)
against isolation	−0.202 (−0.166)	0.328 (0.304)
lack of voice	−0.246 (−0.171)	0.329 (0.149)
sovereignty and identity	0.000 (−0.078)	−0.705 (−0.395)
social benefits	−0.066 (−0.177)	−0.182 (−0.157)

Appendix 4

Sources for Part II: Novels, History Textbooks, and Head of State Addresses

IN CHAPTERS 5 through 8 I analyze prize-winning novels written by nationals or long-term residents of the country in which the prize was awarded. My focus on nationals or long-term residents reflects my interest in national rather than foreign visions of the nation. In the FRG, I have chosen the Bremer Literaturpreis, one of the most prestigious and oldest German literature prizes awarded to literary publications.[1] In the GDR, I have chosen the Heinrich Mann Literaturpreis der DDR, the most prestigious literature prize in the former socialist republic. Although it was awarded to authors rather than novels, research and consultation with employees at the Culture Department of the Berlin Senate reassured me that it was made to coincide with the publication of major novels by the prize recipients.[2] In Spain, I have chosen the Premio Nacional de Literatura, which has been awarded since the late 1940s. The British case has proven to be more difficult, because there is no state-sponsored award like, for example, the Prix Goncourt in France or the Premio Nacional de Literatura in Spain. Furthermore, the most prestigious award for novels is the Booker Prize, which was not awarded until 1969. For the period before 1969, I have selected novels among the recipients of the Hawthornden Prize (the oldest of the well-known British literary prizes) and the Somerset Maugham Award. From 1969 on, I have selected novels from among the winners of the Booker Prize and the Whitbread Prize.[3] In examining all the novels I focused on subject matter, geographical and historical settings, and national self-images.

The second primary source that I use in these chapters is secondary school contemporary history textbooks. In the FRG, the Council of Secretaries of Culture of the different Länder decides on the content of school textbooks, which remains unchanged for several years. The different Länder can slightly modify this content by adding information of local interest. Based on this information, I have collected one textbook for each decade between the 1950s and the 1990s, corresponding to the 9th and 10th grades in the Realschule (the Realschule lies between the vocational-oriented Hauptschule and the university-oriented Gymnasium, and is the most attended type of secondary school). To ensure comparability, I have focused on one important textbook publisher that has been active since the 1950s. The study of textbooks is even easier in the GDR, since the content and format was directly decided by the state. Again, I have focused on the 9th and 10th grades (except for 1952, when contemporary history was taught in 8th grade), and selected one textbook per decade.

In Spain, the Secretary of Education and Culture has traditionally decided on the content of textbooks. This was especially the case during the Franco dictatorship. Since the granting of autonomy to the regions of Spain in the early 1980s, much of the content of these textbooks has been decided by the autonomous governments. I consulted both Catalan and Spanish history textbooks from the 1990s but did not find significant contrasts in the way the major events here were portrayed. Therefore, my analysis relies only on the Spanish textbooks. One peculiarity of the way history is taught in Spain, when compared with Germany and the United Kingdom, is that since the 1980s, Spanish and world history have been taught in consecutive years. Because of this, for the 1980s and 1990s I have selected both Spanish history and world history textbooks.

Of the three countries, the United Kingdom presents the greatest problems because there is no textbook tradition. I have bypassed this problem by collecting information on the British and world contemporary history requirements, as specified in the O Level examination and the more modern GCSE examination. In addition to this, I have selected general books on contemporary British and world history that were meant for and used in British secondary education and that adhered to O Level and GCSE examination guidelines.

Finally, I examine Christmas or New Year's addresses—depending on the country—by each country's head of state, delivered between 1946 and 1996.

The lists below include the novels and secondary school history textbooks I have used for my analysis of cultural themes and counterthemes in the United Kingdom, the FRG, the GDR, and Spain.

Novels

United Kingdom

1944. Martyn Skinner. *Letters to Malaya* (Hawthornden Prize).
1947. A. L. Barker. *Innocents* (Somerset Maugham Award).
1951. Roland Camberton. *Scamp* (Somerset Maugham Award).
1953. Emyr Humphreys. *Hear and Forgive* (Somerset Maugham Award).
1955. Kingsley Amis. *Lucky Jim* (Somerset Maugham Award).
1960. Alan Sillitoe. *The Loneliness of the Long Distance Runner* (Hawthornden Prize).

SOURCES: NOVELS AND HISTORY TEXTBOOKS 273

1962. Robert Shaw. *The Sun Doctor* (Hawthornden Prize).
1965. William Trevor. *The Old Boys* (Hawthornden Prize).
1967. Michael Frayn. *The Russian Interpreter* (Hawthornden Prize).
1969. P. H. Newby. *Something to Answer For* (Booker Prize).
1970. Bernice Rubens. *The Elected Member* (Booker Prize).
1972. John Berger. *G* (Booker Prize).
1974. Iris Murdoch. *The Sacred and Profane Love Machine* (Whitbread Prize).
1976. David Storey. *Saville* (Booker Prize).
1980. William Golding. *Rites of Passage* (Booker Prize).
1982. John Wain. *Young Shoulders* (Whitbread Prize).
1984. Anita Brookner. *Hotel du Lac* (Booker Prize).
1986. Kazuo Ishiguro. *An Artist of the Floating World* (Whitbread Prize).
1987. Penelope Lively. *Moon Tiger* (Booker Prize).
1989. Lindsay Clarke. *The Chymical Wedding* (Whitbread Prize).
1994. James Kelman. *How Late It Was, How Late* (Booker Prize).
1996. Graham Swift. *Last Orders* (Booker Prize).

Federal Republic of Germany (Bremer Literaturpreis).

1950. Heinrich Schmidt-Barrien. *Tanzgeschichten.*
1955. Ernst Jünger. *Am Sarazenenturm.*
1957. Rolf Schroers. *In Fremder Sache.*
1959. Günter Grass. *Die Blechtrommel.*
1961. Siegfried Lenz. *Zeit der Schuldlosen.*
1963. Hans Günter Michelsen. *Helm.*
1966. Wolfgang Hildesmeier. *Tynset.*
1968. Christian Enzensberger. *Grösserer Versuch über den Schmutz.*
1970. Gabrielle Wohmann. *Ernste Absicht.*
1972. Günter Herburger. *The Eroberung der Zitadelle.*
1976. Nicolas Born. *Die erdabgewandte Seite der Geschichte.*
1977. Alexander Kluge. *Neue Geschichten: Hefte 1–18.*
1980. Christoph Meckel. *Suchbild.*
1982. Peter Weiss. *Die Ästhaetik des Widerstands.*
1983. Paul Wühr. *Das falsche Buch.*
1988. Ingomar von Kieseritzky. *Das Buch der Desaster.*
1989. William Genazino. *Der Fleck, Die Jacke, Die Zimmer, Der Schmerz.*
1991. Ror Wolf. *Nachrichten aus der bewohnten Welt.*
1995. George-Arthur Goldschmidt. *Der Unterbrochene Wald.*
1996. Reinhard Lettau. *Flucht von Gästen.*

German Democratic Republic (Heinrich Mann Literaturpreis der DDR)

(Award is given to writers and not for specific books; books listed were published around the time of the award.)
1955. Franz Fühmann. *Kameraden.*
1955. Gotthold Gloger. *Philomena Kleespiess trug die Fahne.*
1959. Heiner Müller and Inge Müller. *Geschichte aus der Produktion 1.*
1960. Dieter Noll. *Die Abenteuer des Werner Holt.*
1963. Christa Wolf. *Der geteilte Himmel.*
1964. Johannes Brobowski. *Levin's Mühle.*
1968. Wolfgang Joho. *Das Klasse Treffen.*
1969. Jürek Becker. *Jakob der Lügner.*
1972. Ulrich Plenzdorf. *Die neuen Leiden des jungen W.*
1974. Irmtraud Morgner. *Leben und Abenteuer der Trobadora Beatriz nach Zeugnissen ihrer Spielfrau Laura.*
1976. Joachim Nowotny. *Ein gewisser Robel.*
1979. Rudolf Fritz Fries. *Mein spanisches Brevier.*
1981. Peter Hacks. *Pandora.*
1983. Friedrich Dieckmann. *Orpheus, eingeweiht.*
1984. Helga Schubert. *Blickwinkel.*
1987. Luise Rinser. *Silberschuld.*

Spain (Premio Nacional de Literatura: Narrativa)

1951. Ramón Ledesma Miranda. *La casa de la fama.*
1953. José María Gironella. *Los cipreses creen en Dios.*
1955. Miguel Delibes. *Diario del cazador.*
1957. Alejandro Nuñez Alonso. *El lazo de púrpura.*
1959. Ana María Matute. *Los hijos muertos.*
1961. Bartolomé Soler. *Los muertos no se cuentan.*
1963. Salvador García de Pruneda. *Encrucijada de Carabanchel.*
1967. Luis de Castresana. *El otro árbol de Guernica.*
1969. Luis Berenguer. *Marea escorada.*
1971. Angel Palomino. *Torremolinos, Gran Hotel.*
1973. José Luis Martín Abril. *El viento se acuesta al atardecer.*
1977. José Luis Acquaroni. *Copa de sombra.*
1979. Jesús Fernández Santos. *Extramuros.*
1981. Gonzalo Torrente Ballester. *La isla de los jacintos cortados.*
1983. Franciso Ayala. *Recuerdos y Olvidos. 2. El exilio.*
1984. Camilo José Cela. *Mazurca para dos muertos.*

1987. Luis Mateo Díaz. *La fuente de la edad.*
1989. Bernardo Atxaga. *Obabakoak.*
1991. Manuel Vázquez Montalbán. *Galíndez.*
1993. Luis Goytisolo. *Estatua con palomas.*

List of Textbooks
United Kingdom

1952. [First published in 1932]. Catherine Firth (Ed.) *History.* Edinburgh: R&R Clark, Ltd.
1966. David Arnold. *Britain, Europe, and the World: 1870–1955.* Edinburgh: Edward Arnold Publishers.
1977. Paul Richardson. *Britain, Europe, and the Modern World, 1918–1977.* London: Heinemann.
1988. [1977]. John Stokes and Gwenneth Stokes. *Europe and the Modern World, 1870–1983.* Harlow: Longman.
1988. Howard Martin. *Britain since 1800: Towards the Welfare State.* London: Macmillan.
In addition to these books:
1984. [1974]. F. M. Batty. *Revision Notes for Ordinary Level Economic and Social History (from 1760).* London: Bell & Hyman.
1978. Peter J. Broster and David R. Jones. *Revision Notes for Ordinary Level and CSE: Twentieth Century World History.* London: Bell & Hyman.
1990. Department of Education, History Working Group. *National Curriculum: Final Report.*

Federal Republic of Germany

1955. Hans Ebeling. *Deutsche Geschichte.* Braunschweig: Georg Westermann Verlag.
1969. Hans Ebeling. *Die Reise in die Vergangenheit.* Band IV: *Unser Zeitalter der Revolutionen und Weltkriege.* Braunschweig: Georg Westermann Verlag.
1985. Hans Ebeling and Wolfgang Birkenfeld. *Die Reise in die Vergangenheit.* Band IV. Braunschweig: Georg Westermann Verlag.
1995. [1993]. Hans Ebeling and Wolfgang Birkenfeld. *Die Reise in die Vergangenheit.* Band 4. Braunschweig: Georg Westermann Verlag.

German Democratic Republic

1952. Wissenschaftlichen Mitarbeitern des Instituts für Gesellschaftswissenschaften beim ZK der SED. *Lehrbuch für den Geschichtsunterricht. 8. Schuljahr.* Berlin: Volk und Wissen, Volkseigener Verlag.

1962. Ministerium für Volksbildung der Deutschen Demokratischen Republik. *Lehrbuch für Geschichte der 10. Klasse der Oberschule und der erweiterten Oberschule.* Berlin: Volk und Wissen, Volkseigener Verlag.

1964. Ministerium für Volksbildung der Deutschen Demokratischen Republik. *Lehrbuch für Geschichte der 9. Klasse der Oberschule und der erweiterten Oberschule.* Berlin: Volk und Wissen Volkseigener Verlag.

1984. Zentralinstitut für Geschichte and der Akademie der Wissenschaften der DDR. *Geschichte: Lehrbuch für Klasse 10.* Berlin: Volk und Wissen, Volkseigener Verlag.

1986. Zentralinstitut für Geschichte an der Akademie der Wissenschaften der DDR. *Geschichte: Lehrbuch für Klasse 9.* Berlin: Volk und Wissen, Volkseigener Verlag.

Spain

1954. José L. Asián Peña. *Manual de Historia de España.* Barcelona: Bosch.

1957. José Ramón Castro. *Historia Moderna y Contemporánea. Cuarto Curso.* Zaragoza: Editorial Librería General.

1965. José L. Asián Peña. *Historia Universal y de España. Cuarto de Bachillerato.* Barcelona: Bosch.

1977. José J. Gutiérrez, Guillermo Fatas, and Antonio B. Borderías. *Geografía e Historia de España. 3° de BUP.* Zaragoza: Edelvives.

1978. Jesús María Palomares, Celso Almuiña, Juan Helguera, Mateo Martínez, and Germán Rueda. *Historia del Mundo Contemporáneo.* Madrid: Anaya.

1986. [1984]. Julio Valdeón, Isidoro González, Mariano Mañero, and Domingo J. Sánchez Zurro. *Geografía e Historia de España y de los Países Hispánicos. 3° de BUP.* Madrid: Anaya.

1988. Vicente Palacio Atar, Luis Alvarez Gutiérrez, and Ascensión Burgoa. *Historia del Mundo Contemporáneo.* Zaragoza: Edelvives.

1998. Julio Díez Montero (ed.). *Historia de España Contemporánea. 2° curso de Bachillerato.* Zaragoza: Edelvives.

In addition to these books:

1957. Ministerio de Educación Nacional. *Plan de Bachillerato. Programas de Cuarto Curso: Historia.*

Notes

Chapter 1
Introduction

1. For examples of the international relations approach to European integration, see Hoffmann (1966); Moravcsik (1991); Keohane and Hoffmann, (1991); Snidal (1985); Morrow (1994); Stein (1990); Krasner (1991); Fligstein and Mara-Drita (1996); and Garrett and Weingast (1993).

2. About the significant role of country of residence in explaining support for European integration, see Deflem and Pampel (1996). Relevant contributions in the survey research literature to the study of attitudes toward European integration are Gabel (1998b); Wessels (1995); Eichenberg and Dalton (1993); Lindberg and Scheingold (1970); Shepard (1975); Gabel and Whitten (1997); Inglehart (1977a); Janssen (1991); Hewstone (1986); Díez Medrano (1995b); Wessels (1995b); Wessels (1995a).

3. Scholars who study public opinion have certainly been aware of the effect that different conceptualizations of the process of European integration can have on people's attitudes, and of how the effects of particular variables on attitudes toward European integration can vary depending on how people conceive it. They have not, however, integrated this insight in empirical models developed to explain support for European integration. For examples, see Inglehart (1977a) and Hewstone (1986).

4. For a conceptualization of the term, see Bateson (1955) and Goffman (1974). Regarding the concept of schema, see also Fiske and Taylor (1984) and Graber (1988). For examples of how frames affect behavior, see Tversky and Kahneman (1981), Boudon (1996), and Fillieule (1996). Lindenberg and Frey (1993). There is also a vast literature in experimental survey research, dealing with the way questions are framed—the order of questions, the order of answer choices, the type of answer choices, whether the question is closed or open-ended—and how this determines responses. See Foddy (1993).

5. See Lamont and Thévenot (2000).

6. On frames, see Goffman (1974); on social representations, see Farr and Moscovici (1984); on the role of knowledge, see Giddens (1984); on the concept of habitus, see Bourdieu (1991 [1972]); on the role of stories or narratives, see Sewell (1980); on the role of memory, see Halbwachs (1975 [1925]), Connerton (1989), and Fentress and Wickham (1992); on worldviews, see Weber (1958 [1904–5]), on the contrast between unconsciously internalized values and a consciously manipulated cultural repertoire, see Swidler (1986).

7. Mayer Zald (1996).

8. Tarrow (1992).

9. Ibid., p. 177.

10. Gamson (1992).

11. E.g., Gamson (1992) and Snow, Rochford, Worden, and Benford (1986).

12. Snow and Benford (1992).
13. Gamson (1992), p. 135.
14. Ibid.
15. Peter Gourevitch (1979), Laitin (1991), 177; Díez Medrano (1995a), Bollen and Díez Medrano (1998).
16. Colley (1992b), Alvarez Junco (2001), and Schulze (1991).
17. In 1999, Germany's GDP/capita was $19,660 and the United Kingdom's was $19,040. Also, both countries conducted 54% of their trade with the European Union.
18. Laffan (1996), Deflem and Pampel (1996), and Álvarez-Miranda (1996).
19. Gabel and Palmer (1995).
20. Álvarez-Miranda (1996).
21. Laffan (1996).
22. Laffan and Álvarez-Miranda (1996).
23. Mommsen (1994a), Loth (1994), Laffan (1996), Bulmer and Paterson (1987), Katzenstein (1997), and Hassner (1983).
24. Mommsen (1994a), Loth (1994), Richter (1993), and Bulmer and Paterson (1987).
25. Bulmer and Paterson (1987).
26. Colley (1992b), p. 375.
27. Mommsen (1994a), William Wallace (1994), and Helen Wallace (1997).
28. William Wallace (1994), p. 108, Katzenstein (1997), William Wallace (1986), and Nuggent (1992).
29. Colley (1992b).
30. Katzenstein (1997) and Bulmer (1992).
31. Laffan (1996), p. 87, William Wallace (1992), and Bulmer, (1992).
32. Blank (1978).
33. Deflem and Pampel (1996), William Wallace (1992), and Sanders (1990).
34. William Wallace (1986), p. 82; Nuggent (1992); and Bulmer (1992).
35. Although it may have well contributed, as she argues, to more support of membership among Spanish Communists than among Portuguese and Greek Communists.
36. Hewstone (1986).
37. See the appendices for further details on the different sources described below.
38. Corse (1997), pp. 1, 11.
39. Corse (1997), p. 101.
40. Eugen Weber (1981).

Chapter 2
Ways of Seeing European Integration

1. Mosse (1975).
2. When asked how often they think about the European Union, about 1 in 3 ordinary respondents said "Never" or "Sometimes." Moreover, 3 out of 4 said that the opinions about the European Union that they know the best are those from journalists, politicians, and political parties, as transmitted by the media.

Germans were more prone to get their news from local newspapers, Britons obtained them most often from tabloids and quality newspapers, and Spaniards obtained them mostly from TV reports and quality newspapers.

3. See Wetherall and Potter (1988) and Gamson (1992a). For detailed presentations of this methodology, see Hewstone (1986), Carroll and Ratner (1996), and Babb (1996).

4. The analysis that follows builds people's comments into an aggregate collective cognitive frame that very likely reflects the images and evaluations about the European Union and European unification to which they have been exposed over time. The approach does not, however, assume that all individuals rely on their city's or country's frame or that they are consistent in their answers. See Carroll and Ratner (1996).

5. In order to come up with a manageable list of frame categories, I proceeded as follows: I wrote down all descriptive and evaluative comments respondents made when justifying their answers to my questions about European integration. Then, since the list was extremely long, I calculated a frequency distribution to see what comments were mentioned more frequently. Based on this frequency distribution and on content similarity, I created a set of broader categories. The categories mentioned in the text are only those whose frequencies were non-negligible. More information available from the author upon request.

6. Local elites are identified by a number, the city where the interview took place, and their title or occupation; ordinary respondents are identified by a number, the city where the interview took place, their age group, and their level of education.

7. See Horst (1996).

8. The differences were statistically significant at the 0.05 level, two-tailed test.

9. See appendix III for full results.

Chapter 3
Good Reasons for and Attitudes toward European Integration

1. See Boudon (1996) on the topic of rationality and "good reasons."

2. For a thorough theoretical review, see Sinnott (1995).

3. See Haas (1958), Haas and Schmitter (1964), Haas (1971), and Schmitter (1971).

4. See Key (1961), and Lindberg and Scheingold (1970).

5. Much of this empirical research draws from Easton's (1975) distinction between the concepts of "diffuse" and "specific" support. The standard three items used to measure support for European integration are:

1. Generally speaking, do you think that (your country's) membership in the Common Market is a good thing, a bad thing, or neither good nor bad?

2. In general, are you for or against efforts being made to unify Western Europe? If so, are you very much for this, or only to some extent? If against, are you only to some extent against or very much against?

3. If you were told tomorrow that the European Community (the Common Market) had been scrapped, would you be very sorry about it, indifferent, or relieved?

6. These percentages of support, especially with respect to the question on membership and Great Britain, are slightly higher than those normally found in national representative surveys.

7. The European Community Study of 1973 collected similar but not identical information. Respondents were asked to justify why they thought it was good or bad that their country was a member of the European Economic Community. Most favorable answers referred to aspects related to the Common Market. German respondents emphasized more than British respondents, however, the fact that the European Economic Community facilitated closer political links with European countries (21% and 11% respectively, of those who said that membership was a good thing). Most negative answers also referred to economic consequences of the Common Market: in particular, the fact that the cost of living would go up. The loss of political identity and sovereignty was mentioned by 3% and 0% of those British and German respondents respectively who thought that membership was a bad thing.

8. To be sure, the Eurobarometers have periodically included questions that more or less directly address the issue of the transfer of sovereignty, whether by asking people if they want a political union or by asking them about the desirability of strengthening the role of the European Parliament. But these questions have changed over time, thus preventing the development of time-series that would allow for sophisticated quantitative analyses of the factors underlying variation in responses.

9. The principle of subsidiarity means that the European Union should let states keep those functions that they can adequately perform on their own.

10. EMU required states to meet some criteria:

- two-year membership in the European exchange-rate mechanism
- inflation within 1.5% of the three countries with the lowest rate
- long-term interest rates within 2% of the three lowest rates in the EU
- budget deficit below 3% of gross domestic product
- public debt below 60% of gross domestic product

11. The percentages per city especially ought to be seen as merely orientative, since in some cases only one respondent has been classified as "integrationist" or as "free-trader." I have tried other, less strict, classifications of respondents, to increase the number of cases in the Centralized Integration and Decentralized Cooperation categories, and in no case did the results differ in a way that would change the interpretation developed below.

12. Gabel (1998b).

13. Inglehart (1977a), Janssen (1991), and Gabel (1998b).

Chapter 4
Journalists and European Integration

1. It is not this book's purpose to develop or test a theory of Elite-Mass Diffusion processes. The literature on European integration, however, takes it for granted that elites—e.g., the media, political parties—have a greater impact on

public opinion's views of European integration than vice versa. See Dalton and Duval (1981) and Wessels (1995b). Wessels demonstrates quite convincingly that party elites and party supporters influence each other and that the influence of the former is greater than that of the latter. See also Deutsch (1968) and Rosenau (1961). Empirical tests of Rosenau's general model can be found in Peterson (1972). More generally, the literature on frames, while emphasizing the two-way influence between the media and public opinion, has noted the significant role that the media can play in transmitting frames when topics are rarely discussed at the interpersonal level or when there is ample elite consensus on a particular way of framing a problem: Gamson and Modigliani (1989), Klandermans (1992), Gitlin (1980), Hallin (1994), Gahnem (1997), and Zaller (1998).

I determined that the frames that distinguish British, German, and Spanish respondents are more prevalent among more educated and more informed respondents than among less educated and less informed ones through logit statistical models performed with information provided by the respondents with which I conducted in-depth interviews. Results available from the author.

2. I examined the content of articles on European integration and the European Union in the main local newspapers of the cities in which I conducted my fieldwork, published in the first fifteen days of every month in the years 1951, 1957, 1972, 1985, 1991, and 1992. I focused on these years because they are key years in the process of European integration and it was therefore more likely that these local newspapers would have reported more frequently on European integration. I also focused on all articles rather than only on editorials and opinion articles to obtain bigger samples. Contrary to what I find in the op-ed articles in the quality press, articles in local newspapers hardly ever expressed enough regarding the EU to discern the kinds of frames that help distinguish British, German, and Spanish popular frames on European integration. News reporting in these newspapers tended to be factual. Thus, if these local newspapers shaped the opinions of their readers, it must have been more through the selection of the news items that were published than through the framing of those news items. Meanwhile, quality newspapers are a better source of information to examine frames.

3. This was typical especially during the entry negotiation process in the late 1970s and early 1980s, when most editorials simply summarized the state of the negotiations or evaluated the behavior of the different country delegations.

4. In an additional analysis of editorials and opinion articles in the SPD-oriented *Frankfurter Rundschau*, I found that 19% of them (17 out of 90 articles) expressed support for transfers of sovereignty. None of the articles was opposed to a transfer of sovereignty.

5. Significant at the .05 level, N = 16.

6. Both are significant at the .05 level, N = 16. One observes the same contrasts by comparing the correlation between the content of newspaper articles and the content for informed respondents with that between the content of newspaper articles and the content for uninformed respondents (the correlations are 0.71 and 0.66 respectively).

7. One must be careful with the comparisons because of the different conditions under which this information was obtained. The interviews were directed, to the extent that the same questions, covering a wide variety of topics, were asked of

every respondent, whereas the articles' content was decided by their authors. Therefore, one should not expect very high percentages for these categories.

8. The percentages of op-ed articles that mention this theme in *Die Zeit* and the *Frankfurter Allgemeine* are 19.5% and 5.2% respectively. In the extra sample of ninety op-ed articles from the *Frankfurter Rundschau* that I also analyzed, the percentage was 5.6%. The surprisingly high number of *Die Zeit* editorials concerned with other countries' misgivings about Germany was mostly due to former German Chancellor Helmut Schmidt's high number of contributions on the subject of monetary unification in the period immediately following German reunification.

9. Voltmer (1998).

10. Ibid.

11. The percentages presented in tables 9 and 10 concerning sovereignty and national identity are different from those reported at the beginning of the section. Those reported in tables 9 and 10 refer to explicit statements about the positive or negative effects that European integration or membership in European institutions are expected to have on national sovereignty and identity. They do not include statements supporting or opposing developments that would de facto involve a transfer of sovereignty (e.g., the strengthening of the European Parliament). The latter measure is therefore a more restrictive way of measuring opposition to transfers of sovereignty. The percentage obtained through my analysis of a sample of op-ed articles from *The Times* was 7.9%, higher than the 2.8% obtained for *The Economist* and the 14.6% obtained for *The New Statesman*.

12. Data available upon request.

13. Data available upon request.

14. Markus Kiefer has analyzed the content of discussions about German national identity and European integration in West German quality newspapers during the 1949–55 period. See Kiefer (1992), pp. 9–13, 73–95, 120–59, 202–304, 364–409, 581–86, and 660–95.

15. Hans Baumgarten, "Der aktuelle Schuman Plan," *FAZ*, Aug. 7, 1950; Heinrich Kost, "Im europäischen Rahmen," *Die Zeit*, Sept. 13, 1951; "Der aktuelle Schuman Plan," *FAZ*, Aug. 7, 1950; "Europa ohne Angina Pectoris," *Die Zeit*, July 4, 1957.

16. Marion Grafin Dönhoff, "Frischer Wind in Strassbourg," *Die Zeit*, Jan. 15, 1953.

17. See Kiefer (1992) for a discussion of internal debates within both newspapers (e.g., between Paul Sethe on the one side, and Hans Baumgarten and Eric Dombrowski on the other, in the *FAZ*); these debates do not, however, negate the summary view presented in the text.

18. "Nowadays, Europe feels that its nation-states are no longer suited to the reality of technical developments,... the claims to power, the general longing for peace. Thus, agreements toward supranational communities are pursued." Hans Baumgarten, "Aus der Geschichte lernen, ist schwer," *FAZ*, Oct. 8, 1952.

"Even people of international stature find it ludicrous, when they [opponents of integration] come with all this nonsense against market integration and the unification of the whole European economic and political life ... do the critics really believe that one can achieve a unified Europe without topping it with sovereignty powers?" W. O. Reichelt, "Laika starb für Europa," *Die Zeit*, Dec. 26, 1957.

19. Katharina Focke, "De Gaulles' politische Union," *Die Zeit*, July 19, 1963.

20. See also "Frankreichs Europa," *FAZ*, Feb. 14, 1972.
21. *Die Zeit*. "Das Erbe De Gaulles," *Die Zeit*, July 4, 1969.
22. See Fritz Ulrich Fack, "Europa als Rest Posten," *FAZ*, Feb. 13, 1974.
23. See Rolf Zundel, "Europas Stunde?," *Die Zeit*, June 29, 1973; and Theo Sommer, "Europa—bloss ein Spektakel?," *Die Zeit*, Dec. 14, 1973.
24. See "Das EWS muss flexibel bleiben," *FAZ*, July 26, 1993; and Peter Hort, "Ein anderes Europa," *FAZ*, Oct. 15, 1993.
25. See "Europa muss die Weichen stellen," *Die Zeit*, Dec. 6, 1991.
26. "This straight acceptance of the European community should be the centerpiece of British policy." "Keep Right On," *The Economist*, Jan. 21, 1967.
27. One example: "Of all nations, Germany and Italy are not the first to which Britain should cede political most-favoured nation treatments." (Douglas Jay, MP, May 26, 1962.)
28. Paul Johnson was editor of *The New Statesman* between 1964 and 1970. In another article, published on Feb. 21, 1975, "The Ad-Man's Europe," Johnson expressed his utter dislike for the EEC: "I have always believed that the real question at issue is not so much 'Should the EEC exist at all?' In my view, it is a phoney organization, and in some respects a dangerous one.... The abandonment of nationalism does not mean greater confidence in a wider entity called 'Europe', 'European civilizations', and so forth. On the contrary, it is evidence of a collapse of confidence in a racial and cultural system of which the European nations formed essential parts.... There is no case for a bogus super-state called 'Europe,' lacking inner convictions but acting as though it were the custodian of the best human values. This is a fraud and Britain should have nothing to do with it."
29. See "The Paper and Europe," *The New Statesman*, May 12, 1972.
30. See "Saving the EEC," *The Economist*, Nov. 28, 1981.
31. The findings for the period before 1962 mirror those obtained by Antonio Moreno Juste in his extensive analysis of the literature about Europe published in Spain between 1945 and 1962: Juste, (1990). See also García Pérez, (1990). The author traces the transition among Spanish nationalist intellectuals from an anti-European to a pro-European ideology in the years following the Spanish Civil War (1936–39) and stresses the role that the Nazi ideological conception of a "New Europe" played in this transition.
32. See Antonio Garrigues, "El Plan Schuman," *Abc*, Jan. 28, 1956.
33. See also Alfredo Kindelán, "España y Europa," *Abc*, Aug. 11, 1954.
34. See Alfredo Kindelán, "El español y el europeo," *Abc*, Feb. 24, 1955.
35. Also, Alfredo Kindelán, "Europa, en trance letal,¿puede salvarse?," *Abc*, Oct. 26, 1960.
36. The letter read: "I am honored to request, in the name of my government, the opening of negotiations in order to assess the potential association of my country to the European Economic Community, in the form that best suits our reciprocal interests." In Nemesio Fernández Cuesta, "España y Europa," *Abc*, Dec. 2, 1975.
37. See J. M. de Areilza, "Acercarse a Europa," *Abc*, Jan. 14, 1970, and J. M. Alfaro, "Los desdenes de Europa," *Abc*, March 9, 1978.
38. See "La bofetada europea," *El País*, Sept. 18, 1979.
39. See "Una idea de Europa," *El País*, Oct. 26, 1987.
40. Paper in the private collection of the author.

Chapter 5
Spain: Europe as a Mirror with Two Reflections

1. "España y la Comunidad Europea," Oct. 17, 1972.
2. Unamuno (1986 [1895]).
3. Maeztu (1998 [1931]).
4. Franco Bahamonde (1985 [1939]).
5. In 1948, France allowed the reopening of commercial relations with Spain; in 1950, the United Nations lifted Resolution 39 (I) that prohibited Spain from belonging to international organizations and that limited diplomatic relations with Spain; in 1953 the Spanish government signed an economic-military agreement with the United States and a Concordat with the Vatican; finally, in 1956, Spain became a UN member.
6. On the role of social and political conditions in the 1940s in the process of modernization in the 1950s and 1960s, see Richards (1995).
7. Basic references are: Fusi (1999), Graham and Labanyi (1995), Mainer (1980), Abellán and Gómez (1977), Elías Díaz (1974), and Abellán (1971).
8. Castro (1957), p. 289.
9. Ibid., p. 337.
10. See Franco's 1955 New Year's address.
11. See for instance Franco's New Year's addresses of 1950, 1955, 1960, 1965, 1970, and 1974; for more articulated vision of this ideology, see Calvo Serer (1949).
12. See for instance Franco's New Year's addresses of 1955, 1960, 1965, and 1974.
13. See for instance Franco's New Year's addresses of 1960, 1966, and 1970.
14. See Franco's 1974 New Year's address.
15. The "Black Legend" was the tradition of negative stories spread about Spain in other countries starting in the seventeenth century.
16. Castresana (1967), p. 169.
17. Franco borrowed here extensively from Ramiro de Maeztu's blend of Catholicism and praise of Spain's American colonization as developed in *Defensa de la Hispanidad*.
18. See Franco's 1950 and 1970 New Year's addresses.
19. Castro (1957), p. 358.
20. See Franco's 1960 and 1965 New Year's addresses.
21. García Pérez (1990), Castro Real (1942), Escobar (1943), and Aunós (1943).
22. Escobar (1943), p. 176.
23. Castro (1957), p. 358.
24. See Franco's 1970 New Year's address.
25. "Centenario de la Carrera de Ingeniero Industrial: 2-25-1952," vol. 2, p. 608 in Franco Bahamonde (1975).
26. Florentino Pérez-Embid, "Ante la nueva actualidad del 'problema de España,'" *Arbor* 45–46(1949): 149, 159; cited in Díaz (1974). Another representative study of this way of thinking is Fernández de la Mora (1965).
27. Franco actually showed himself quite open about the legitimation payoffs he expected from economic development when he said in an *Abc* interview pub-

lished on April 1, 1964: that "economic development increases the value of, gives prestige, and solidifies the [regime's] political movement and motivates its evolution and improvement."

28. "Avilés, Asturias: 9-25-1957," in Franco Bahamonde (1975), vol. 2, p. 613.
29. This last plan was never implemented.
30. "Hermandad de Alféreces Provisionales—Cerro Garabitas—Madrid, 5-27-1962," and "Valencia—6-17-1962," in Franco Bahamonde (1975), vol. 2, p. 636 and 639.
31. Palomino (1971).
32. Some representative works are: Brenan (1943); Braudel (1949); Herr (1958); Elliott (1963); Jackson (1966); Raymond Carr (1966); Vicens Vives (1957–59); Artola (1959); Tuñón de Lara (1966).
33. Maravall (1978) and Díez Medrano (1995a).
34. Arguably the most thorough analysis of the topic of Europeanization in twentieth-century Spanish culture is Beneyto (1999).
35. The most significant contributions to this debate were: Unamuno (1986 [1895]), Angel Ganivet (1996 [1897]), and Maeztu (1967 [1899]).
36. Ganivet (1996 [1897]), pp. 53–54, 73.
37. Unamuno (1986 [1895]), pp. 137–43.
38. Ortega y Gasset (1998 [1914]) and Ortega y Gasset (2000 [1922]).
39. While retaining this concern with the need to Europeanize Spain, Ortega moved on in *España Invertebrada* and *La rebelión de las masas* to emphasize that Spain's crisis was due to the absence of a project for the future that would capture the Spanish population's imagination (Ortega y Gasset [1935 (1930)]). This was also his diagnosis of the spiritual crisis of Europe, the main cause according to him of the rebellion of the masses. To overcome this crisis, he proposed the unification of Europe, a project he would later elaborate on and justify in *Europa y la idea de nación*, a compilation of articles and lectures from the late 1940s and early 1950s Ortega y Gasset (1986).
40. Laín Entralgo (1948).
41. See Pablo Fusi (1999), p. 135.
42. Details about the broader intellectual debates of the 1950s and 1960s in Fusi (2000), pp. 116–47; Díaz (1974), pp. 87–239; and Abellán (1971), pp. 9–50. On the literary scene, Luis Martín Santos had already expressed this generational change in novels of the critical realist school such as *Tiempo de Silencio* (1961).
43. Fusi (1999), pp. 150–52 also, Amando de Miguel (1980), pp. 82–89.
44. In fact, the initiative to found this newspaper came from Ortega y Gasset's family (José Ortega Spottorno, his son, and several relatives). See Miguel (1980), p. 104.
45. The Director of *El País*, Joaquín Estefanía, stressed this view when I interviewed him on February 17, 1993.
46. On the 1970 General Education Law, see Alted (1995); on recent trends in Spanish historiography, see Fusi (1999), pp. 182–85. In 1977, the year of the first democratic election after Franco's death, Spanish history was taught separately from world history in 3° de BUP (junior high school) and together with geography. Whereas Asián Peña's well-known 1954 textbook on the history of Spain only devoted 18 out of 375 pages (4.8%) to the period between 1874—End of First Republic and Monarchic Restoration—and the present, the content of Edelvives's

1977 history textbook already devoted 59 pages or 12.4% of its content to this period (39.2% if one includes the book's sections on economic and human geography). In the 1990s, the history curriculum for 2° de Bachillerato (second year of high school) was only devoted to contemporary Spanish history, so that 207 or 52.9% of a typical textbook dealt with post-1874 history. See Asián Peña (1954), Gutiérrez, Fatas, and Borderías (1977), and Montero Díaz (1998).

47. Gutiérrez, Fatas, and Borderías (1977), p. 246.

48. Ibid., p. 257; Valdeón, González, Mañero, and Sánchez Zurro (1986), p. 346; Montero Díaz (1998), p. 251.

49. Gutiérrez, Fatas, and Borderías (1977). When discussing the Regeneracionistas and the Krausista philosophy that inspired their teachings and policy proposals, the textbook refers to "great" people such as Giner de los Ríos and Costa (p. 259); when discussing Cánovas, the most representative political leader of the Restoration period, the textbook dismisses Cánovas's claim that he favored a foreign policy of "retreat" and says that it was, properly speaking, an "isolationist" policy (p. 262); see also discussions of the late-nineteenth-century crisis and the reactions to it (pp. 264, 268, 306, 307). See also p. 326 in Valdeón, González, Mañero, and Sánchez Zurro (1986), where the authors praise the vitalist, Europeanizing, and modernizing spirit of the young members of the Generación del 98; the same applies to Montero Díaz (1998), p. 233.

50. Valdeón, González, Mañero, and Sánchez Zurro (1986), p. 376, italics added.

51. Gutiérrez, Fatas, and Borderías (1977), p. 443.

52. Julio Valdeón et al. (1986), p. 385.

53. Antonio Cuadra (1943), Lissarrague (1943), and Ignacio Escobar (1943).

54. Some examples are the following speeches by Franco, compiled in Franco Bahamonde (1975, Vol. 2): October 1969, "Los españoles de América, vínculos de unión entre los pueblos hispánicos" (p. 1350); December 1969, "Colaboración con los pueblos hispánicos" (p. 1353); October 1970, "Homenaje a Simón Bolivar. La genuina interpretación de la emancipación americana y la herencia cultural de España" (p. 1361); October 1970, "Homenaje a Isabel la Católica. Madre de América. La tradición histórica y la comunidad de destino hispano-americana" (p. 1362); February 1973, "La comunidad de pueblos hispánicos" (p. 1369).

CHAPTER 6
West Germany: Between Self-Doubt and Pragmatism

1. Reuter, (1990).

2. Naumann (1915). According to Droz, the book enjoyed the largest sales since the publication of Bismarck's *Memoires*. Barely six months after publication, it had already sold 100,000 copies; in July 1916 a paperback edition was published; soon, the book was translated into several languages (Jacques Droz [1960], p. 208).

3. See Meyer (1955). Droz (1960), and Rider (1996).

4. The British example is clearly present in the following quote from Neumann, in which he refers to Cecil Rhodes: "One thinks, like a certain Cecil Rhodes

expressed it, in 'Earth portions'. He who wants to be small and isolated will be dependent, however, on the changes that take place in the great powers" [from the German original]. Cited in Krebs (1931).

5. Krebs (1931), p. 3.
6. Schmitt (1941).
7. Rider (1996), pp. 7-9.
8. For a detailed account of the philosophical conceptions underlying German historiographic trends, see Iggers (1983). For recent American contributions to the study of German national identity that emphasize cultural continuities in Germany, see Greenfeld (1995) and Brubaker (1992).
9. E.g., Röpke (1946), Meinecke (1947), and Ritter (1962). Eich (1963).
10. Iggers (1983).
11. Kohn (1962) and Dahrendorf (1965).
12. Lorenz (1995).
13. Blackbourn and Eley (1980).
14. Nolte (1986) and Hillgruber (1986). On the historical context, see Evans (1987).
15. Habermas (1986). On this debate, see Evans (1987), and Mommsen (1990), and Augstein et al. (1987).
16. Goldhagen (1996). Michael Schneider (1997), Heil and Erb (1998), and Shandley (1998).
17. Röpke (1946) Adorno et al. (1950). For an analysis of the how publicists dealt with this topic, see Steinle (1995).
18. Almond and Verba (1963).
19. Almond and Verba (1980), Rausch, (1983), and Reuter (1990).
20. E.g. Manabe and Onodera (1999).
21. Schmidt (1991).
22. Christopher Classen reaches basically the same conclusions reported below after a thorough analysis of TV reporting about the Nazi period. Classen (1999).
23. This discussion is based on a detailed examination of the following contemporary history textbooks used in the *Realschule:* Ebeling (1955), Ebeling (1969), and Ebeling and Birkenfeld (1985). Ebeling and Birkenfeld (1995 [1993]). The post-World War II textbooks I examined (years 1955, 1969, 1985, and 1995 [1993]) devoted around 18% of their pages to the 1933-45 period and around 34% of their pages to the 1918-45 period. The only exception to this was the 1955 textbook, which devoted as much as 28% and 71% of the pages respectively to the periods 1933-45 and 1918-45.
24. This discussion has also been prevented by the use of World War I as a starting point rather than 1871, with the only exception of the 1969 textbook examined here.
25. This discontinuity is further buttressed through an extremely positive description of the history of the FRG, which focus on the "economic miracle" and in which no links to the Nazi period are made.
26. Dahrendorf (1965), p. 30.
27. "The threat of war was now made clear to Germany. There were still one, two telegraphs sent from Berlin to Petersburg, expressing the willingness to demobilize.... Germany fulfilled its promised alliance obligations toward Austria.... On

August 1st, the German envoy to Paris asked whether France would want to remain neutral." Ebeling (1955), p. 7.

28. Comments made in previous versions of the textbook (Ebeling [1955], pp. 5–7, 8, 12–13, 20, 21–23, and 37), insisting on Germany's peaceful intentions, on its feeling of betrayal when Britain entered the war, and on the vulnerability of a surrounded Germany, are now gone. Comments about the burden and injustice of the reparations are far shorter and less emotional than in the 1955 textbook (e.g., comments made in pp. 38–40 have been removed). On the contrary, the achievements of the Streseman period, which substantially alleviated the burden of the reparations, are emphasized in the 1969, 1985, and 1995 textbooks (e.g., Ebeling, [1969], pp. 174–78. The fact that the 1985 and 1995 textbooks no longer begin before World War I but, rather, in 1918 (Ebeling and Birkenfeld 1985; 1995) contributes to the dedramatization of the Versailles Treaty. The question of Germany's "objective" responsibility for World War I is thus removed from the narrative.

29. "It became easy now for those who from the beginning had opposed the Republic. The economic crisis was worldwide—there were also millions of unemployed in the USA—but he who declared that unemployment in Germany was due to democracy, found a receptive and gullible audience!" (Ebeling and Birkenfeld [1985], p. 89).

30. All textbooks contain an occasional reference to the lack of democratic culture in Germany, but the topic is not developed—e.g., "The German people had not yet attained a sufficient level of political maturity in the short period of democratic self-administration." Ebeling (1955), p. 74.

31. Arendt (1993 [1966]), p. 27.

32. Jaspers (1947).

33. Reuter (1990), p. 174.

34. Steinle (1995), p. 111.

35. Ibid., and Markovits (1990).

36. Frei (1996); Reichel, (2001).

37. Reichel, (2001), p. 83.

38. Ebeling (1955).

39. "What did the German people say? The majority of the German citizens had heard here and there something about the existence of these camps. Only a minority knew, however, what went on inside—since every person who was released was sworn to strict secrecy—only a minority suspected the extent of this mass annihilation." In Ebeling (1955), p. 109. "[The people] believed unconditionally, passionately, it followed 'its Führer' with all the enthusiasm it was capable of, since it saw only the shiny exterior, the staged good and beautiful and noble in all this activity." Ibid., p. 114.

40. Ibid., p. 114.

41. "For Hitler the war was a struggle for the rise and victory of the Aryan race against the world's Jewry that hid behind the 'lazy' democracies and, especially, behind the Soviet Union, it was a struggle between the good and the evil. This crazy idea was not believed and shared by the people and the military; but the fight in Russia was especially ferocious because of years of demonization of the enemy number 1." Ibid., p. 138.

42. Clasen (1999) and Liebhart (1971).
43. In fact, Günter Grass was in the end denied the award for his book *Die Blechtrommel* (*The Tin Drum*) because, against the jury's recommendation, Bremen's Senate, which had the final say, decided to withhold it on grounds that the novel was too obscene. See Emmerich (1999).
44. Schroers (1957), pp. 146, 153.
45. Grass (1989), pp. 124.
46. Lenz (1961).
47. Ibid., p. 27.
48. Michelsen (1965).
49. Classen (1999).
50. Reichel (2001), p. 154.
51. Ibid., pp. 158–81.
52. Ebeling (1955) and (1969).
53. Herburger (1972) and Born (1976).
54. Jens Schneider (2001), pp. 196–97.
55. Meckel (1980).
56. Weiss (1981).
57. Goldschmidt (1995).
58. In addition to this, the 1978 Bremer Literaturpreis went to the East German writer Christa Wolf, for her book (1978 [1976]) about growing up in Nazi Germany, *Kindheitsmuster*, which broke a taboo in the literature of the German Democratic Republic by departing from the usual focus on the antifascist Resistance and directly and, in this case, autobiographically confronting the past.
59. Ebeling (1969), p. 254. Some reluctance to accept responsibility for the Nazi past was indeed still evident in the critical way the 1969 textbook evaluated the denazification measures: "It's just that it triggered too much personal hate and dislike; people were made to some extent to feel ashamed. Very soon it was clear that this type of purification was inadequate." Ibid., p. 256.
60. Ebeling and Birkenfeld (1985), p. 113.
61. p. 107 in ibid.
62. Genazino (1989) (1990 Bremer Literaturpreis).
63. In Noelle-Neumann and Köcher (1993).
64. Ebeling (1955), p. 152.
65. Schöllgen (1999), p. 20.
66. Majonica (1965), pp. 22–28.
67. Pp. 41, 49–50, 56–57, 68 in ibid. In the late 1950s and early 1960s, German reunification was not a priority for the U.S.; this and the U.S.'s new strategic concept developed by Secretary of Defense McNamara led to a crisis in the relations between the U.S. and the FRG; Richard Davy (1990).
68. The German-Russian Treaty signed in 1922 that meant the end of Russia's diplomatic isolation and Germany's loosening of its ties to the West.
69. Pp. 66–67 in Majonica, (1965).
70. Noack (1981) and Joffe (1979).
71. According to Genscher, the SPD government fell on account of the decision to deploy Pershing II and Cruise missiles. Schöllgen (1999), p. 160.
72. Joffe (1979), p. 722.

73. E.g., Schöllgen (1999), Bredow (1985), Joffe (1979), Heimann (1990), Staden (1990), and Wolffsohn (1991).
74. Schöllgen (1999), p. 81.
75. Bredow (1985), pp. 73, 118.
76. Wilhelmine Lübke, New Year's address of Dec. 31, 1961.
77. Brandt (1971), p. 442.
78. Helmut Schmidt (1991), pp. 613–14; also, Helmut Kohl in Daniel Vernet. (1997), p. 17.
79. E.g., Walter Schütze. (1990), Kolboom (1991), and Lützeler (1997), Vernet (1997), and Brock (1997).
80. Davy (1990).
81. Noelle-Neumann (1977), p. 56, Noelle-Neumann (1983), p. 188.
82. Noelle-Neumann and Köcher (1997), p. 500.
83. Ibid., p. 1100.
84. Ibid., p. 376.

CHAPTER 7
East Germany: A Different Past, a Different Memory

1. Noelle-Neumann and Köcher (1997), p. 504.
2. Trommler (1990).
3. Brinks (1992).
4. Trommler (1990).
5. The history textbooks discussed here are listed in appendix 4. Secondary school contemporary history textbooks in the GDR were considerably longer than those in the FRG. The teaching of contemporary history was also structured somewhat differently. In the years 1962–64, it was divided between the 9th and 10th grades, so that 9th grade covered history from the Russian Revolution to 1939 and 10th grade covered history from 1939 to the present. In 1984, the division was redefined so that 9th history covered from the Russian Revolution to the end of World War II. A combined consideration of the material contained in the textbooks for 9th and 10th grade together, reveals that, proportionally speaking, the space devoted to the 1933–45 and the 1918–45 periods in contemporary history textbooks was similar in the FRG and the GDR.
6. "The fascist terror against the Jewish people began with racist campaigns and ended with the murder of millions of Jews in the extermination camps. ... Even more cruel effects resulted from the racist campaign against the Slavic peoples, against Poland, and especially against the Russian people." Wissenschaftlichen Mitarbeitern, *Lehrbuch für Geschichte* (1952), p. 233. The 1984 edition simply lumps the Jews together with other groups: "More than eleven million people from different nations and classes, foremost workers, communists, Soviet citizens, Poles, progressive members of the intelligentsia and Jews, were cruelly assassinated in the concentration camps." Zentralinstitut für Geschichte (1984), p. 162. See appendix 4 for full list of textbooks discussed.
7. Zentralinstitut für Geschichte (1986), p. 146.
8. Zentralinstitut für Geschichte (1984), p. 50.
9. Gotthold (1955), p. 350.

10. Noll (1960).
11. Ibid., p. 530.
12. Wolf (1978) and Fühmann (1973).
13. Schubert (1984), p. 18. Christa Wolf, in *Der geteilte Himmel*, also introduces, if only briefly, themes such as the inner suffering of many East Germans and their subsequent inability to communicate with their children, that would later be portrayed in West German novels such as *Die Eroberung der Zitadelle*, *Die Erdabgewandte Seite der Geschichte*, and *Suchbild*, discussed above. At some point in the story, the main character's companion, Manfred, says of his father: "Who was my father then? A burdened person with deadly wounded feelings about himself." P. 50 in Wolf (1963).
14. Hermann Weber (1999), pp. 62–63.
15. Müller and Müller (1996 [1959]), p. 76.
16. Walter Ulbricht's 1966–67 New Year's address, published in the newspaper *Neues Deutschland*.
17. Klessmann (1988), pp. 431–68.
18. Bender (1999).
19. Klessmann (1988).
20. Noelle-Neumann and Köcher (1997), p. 500.

CHAPTER 8
The United Kingdom: Reluctant Europeans

1. Newman (1997 [1987]), p. xxiii. The quote from Alan MacFarlane is taken from his book *The Origins of English Individualism: The Family, Property, and Social Transition* (New York: Cambridge University Press, 1979), p. 165.
2. Colley (1992b). Brockliss and Eastwood (1997, p. 6), focusing on the 1814–54 period, conclude, however, that "there is no question of Britishness being constructed from hatred of or contempt for the Continental 'other'."
3. See Alvarez Junco (2001), Schulze (1991) and Greenfeld (1995).
4. See Grainger (1986).
5. Stuart Anderson (1981).
6. Mackenzie (1986b), and Constantine (1986).
7. Thus, David Saunders, for instance, says that "Britain had not yet suffered the sort of external trauma (such as defeat in war) usually associated with a fundamental role reappraisal." Saunders (1990), p. 72.
8. Wallace (1992). On the relations between Empire and English and British identity, see Kumar (2000); also, Cannadine (2001).
9. Grainger (1986), p. 140. The quote by Grainger comes from Montgomery and Cambray (1906), p. 198.
10. Grainger (1981).
11. P. 151 in ibid.
12. P. xxiii in Samuel, (1989a).
13. Orwell (1947).
14. Robbins (1998).
15. Samuel (1989a). On the "Little Englandism" of British social science before the 1970s, see Perry Anderson (1992b [1968]).

16. P. lii in Samuel (1989a).
17. P. xxiii in ibid. Similar descriptions of British attitudes toward foreigners and everything foreign have been made over the years by American observers well acquainted with British life and culture and otherwise strongly sympathetic to it: e.g., Middleton (1957) and Gelb (1982).
18. Baucom (1999).
19. Gikandi (1996), p. xvii.
20. Scott (1968), p. 245. Cited in Gorra (1997).
21. Colley, (1992a), p. 325, cited in Gikandi (1996), p. 29.
22. Colley (1992b), p. 6.
23. Ibid., p. 160.
24. Ibid., p. 165.
25. Taylor (1993), pp. 48, 50.
26. Gindin (1969).
27. Barker (1948).
28. Orwell (1947), p. 40.
29. Amis (1955). p. 181.
30. Calhoun (1994), Brewer (1993), and Brewer (1999).
31. Hogg and Abrams, (1988).
32. Newby (1968).
33. Ibid., p. 10.
34. Ibid., p. 240.
35. Ibid., p. 12.
36. Ibid., p. 16.
37. Ibid., p. 52.
38. Ibid., p. 76.
39. Ibid., p. 203.
40. Lively (1987).
41. See also Gelb (1982), and Middleton (1957) for additional references to this negative attitude.
42. Department of Education, History Working Group (1990).
43. In 1952, Elizabeth delivered the address even though she had not yet been crowned.
44. The differences are statistically significant at $p = 0.05$.
45. Deutsch (1957).
46. Gellner (1983) and Hechter (1975).
47. Gindin (1969), p. 48; Raphael Samuel says also that "the idea of the British as a chosen or specially-favored race has not survived the loss of imperial power" (Samuel 1989a, p. XIX).
48. See Newman (1997), Middleton (1957), Gelb (1982), and Stuart Anderson, *Race and Rapprochement*.
49. See Orwell (1947), Samuel (1989a), Gouldbourne (1991), and Middleton (1957).
50. Amis (1955), p. 209.
51. Samuel (1989a), pp: xxxii–l.
52. Nairn (1994 [1988]).
53. P. 24 in ibid.

54. P. 371 in ibid.

55. E.g. 1948 (25th wedding anniversary and birth of grandson), 1952 (upcoming coronation of Queen Elizabeth), 1954 (account of the previous Christmas celebration in New Zealand), 1956 (Queen Elizabeth's joy over talking on the phone with her husband while he traveled in the South Pacific), 1970 (recollection of previous travels around the world), 1972 (words of gratitude for those congratulating Queen Elizabeth on the occasion of her silver wedding anniversary), 1976 (report on trip to the United States), 1992 (Discussion of how much Queen Elizabeth likes spending time at Sandringham; reflections on difficult times experienced by the Royal Family and gratitude to those who showed sympathy), 1994 (discussion of Queen Elizabeth's personal memories of war).

56. With three exceptions: The queen's visits to the United States, Spain, and Russia.

57. E.g., 1952, 1962, 1970 Christmas addresses.

58. E.g., 1956, 1968, 1979 Christmas addresses.

59. One finds the following characterizations of the United Kingdom and its people: Old People (1948), Old Country (1952), determined people (1952), great power for good (1952), courageous spirit of adventure (1952), love of freedom (1952), great past achievements (1968), inventors of parliamentary democracy (1974), gifted with genius (1974), defenders of liberty (1976), inventors of modern trade (1982), imbued of philosophy of individual freedom, democratic government, and rule of law (1982), proud military tradition (1996). One also finds the following historical references: American Declaration of Independence (1976), traditional U.S.-UK partnership (1976), William the Conqueror (1982), Queen Elizabeth I (1982), Armada defeat (1982, 1988), defeat of Napoleon at Trafalgar (1982), Normandy (1984, 1994), Glorious Revolution (1988), Australia's independence (1988), Dunkirk, Battle of Britain (1990).

60. 1960 Christmas address.

61. Firth (1952 [1932]), p. 308.

61. P. Arnold (1966), p. 271.

63. Richardson (1977), p. 248.

64. For the construction of this myth, see Calder (1991).

65. The differences are statistically significant at $p = 0.05$.

66. On this point, see Anderson (1992a [1964]).

67. Samuel (1989a), p. xxvii.

68. E.g., Hobsbawm (1968). Floud and McCloskey 1994.

69. E.g., Weiner (1981); for a critique of this thesis, see Raven (1989).

70. E.g., Barratt Brown (1988).

71. E.g., O'Brien, (1999) and Warwick (1985).

72. A revised synthetic version of this thesis appears in Perry Anderson (1987); a follow-up to this thesis applied to the most recent years is presented in Nairn (2000). For alternative metatheories, see Warwick (1985); for a critique of the Anderson-Nairn thesis, see Thompson. (1978) and Barratt Brown (1988).

73. Richardson (1977), p. 23.

74. David Arnold (1966), pp. 1–6, Stokes and Stokes, (1988 [1977]), p. 197; Broster and Jones (1978); and Martin (1988).

75. Saunders (1990).

76. Taylor, (1993), p. 51.
77. Ronald Camberton, *Scamp* 1950, Emyr Humphreys, *Hear and Forgive* (1971 [1952]); Kingsley Amis, *Lucky Jim* (1955); Allen Sillitoe, *The Loneliness of a Long Distance Runner* (1967 [1959]); Storey, *Saville* (1976); James Kelman, *How Late It Was, How Late* (1994); A. L. Barker, *Innocents* (1948); Bernice Rubens, *The Elected Member* (1983 [1969]); Graham Swift, *Last Orders* (1996); Knopf. Robert Shaw, *The Sun Doctor* (1961); P. H. Newby, *Something to Answer For* (1968); William Golding, *Rites of Passage* (1980). Roy and Gwen Shaw (1992 [1988], p. 19) have also commented on the sense of dislocation of lower- and middle-class individuals conveyed by novels from the 1950s and 1960s, and on the role of the alienated individual in these novels. Gilbert Phelps (1992 [1988] p. 198) says also: "In charting the general course of the literary struggle and outlining the main tendencies and themes of the period, one broad generalisation will serve as a starting point: that all post-war English literature has been overshadowed by a sense of social and cultural disintegration and of the ever present threat of violence and chaos."
78. Phelps (1992 [1988]).
79. See also Nairn (1973).
80. For discussions of Powell's ideas, see Baucom (1999) and Cohen (1994).
81. See Nairn 1994.
82. Barnett (1982).

CHAPTER 9
Frames and Attitudes toward European Integration: A Statistical Validation

1. The degree of attachment to Europe is not an indicator of the affective dimension of support for European integration, as claimed by Gabel and other authors who build on Easton's distinction between affective and utilitarian dimensions of political support; see Easton (1975), Ronald Inglehart (1977b), and Gabel (1998b). Europe and the European Union are conceptually two different things. Consequently, only a measure of attachment *to the European Union* could be said to capture the affective dimension of support for the European Union. The discussion of political culture in the United Kingdom in the previous chapter should have made it clear that the issue of a country's European identity has historically predated and run parallel to the debate about European integration. Also, to posit a causal effect of the degree of attachment to Europe on support for membership in the European Union is consistent with the empirical literature on peripheral nationalism. This literature has also analyzed the causal relationship between feeling of membership in a culturally distinct community and support for peripheral nationalist parties organized in the name of this community.

2. Easton (1975); Gabel (1998b); see also Gabel (1998a) and Eichenberg and Dalton. (1993). The question read: "Generally speaking, do you think that (our country's) membership of the European Union is ... ?" The answer categories were "A good thing," "A bad thing," and "Neither good nor bad." For simplicity of discussion and in order to exclude respondents whose views are not clearly defined, I have excluded respondents who chose the option "Neither good nor bad" from the analysis. Ordered-probit analysis performed with the same data did not contradict the results discussed below.

3. Variables are from Gabel (1998c). The index of Postmaterialist/Materialist values included in Gabel's models is missing because the battery of items needed to develop this index was not included as part of the Eurobarometer 51.0 questionnaire. What follows is a list of the independent variables included in the analysis:

- *Cognitive mobilization*: Two dichotomous variables based on the question "When you get together with friends, would you say you discuss political matters frequently, occasionally, or never?" The omitted category in the table is "Occasionally."
- *Income*: Based on classification into 10 deciles (relative to their country's income distribution). I have divided respondents into 4 income quartiles. The omitted category in the table corresponds to the second lowest quartile.
- *Occupation*: I used Eurobarometer study 51.0 categories.
- *Education*: Based on age in which respondents stopped studying. Cutoff points are 15, 19, and 20 or more. I assigned those still studying to the highest category if they were 20 or more. The omitted category was "Stopped studying between the ages of 16 and 19."
- *Age*: Age reported by the respondent.
- *Vote for bourgeois party*: Based on answers to the question about vote intentions. Coding information comes from Gabel (1998c), completed with information from the *Comparative Manifesto Project*, conducted at the Wissenschaftszentrum Berlin für Sozialforschung.
- *Vote for leftist party*: The same as above, but applied to leftist parties.
- *Vote for party in power*: Party in power in each country at the time of the survey, March–April 1999.
- *Objective 1 regions*: from: Comisión Europea, *Sexto informe periódico sobre la situación y la evolución socioeconómica de las regiones de la Unión Europea* (Luxembourg: Oficina de publicaciones oficiales de las Comunidades Europeas, 1999).
- *Region's distance from Brussels*: I used a map of Europe that included region demarcations; I then drew concentric circles, each 100 km wider than the previous one, until the circles encompassed all regions in the European Union. I assigned to each region the mean distance corresponding to the circle in which it fell. When a region encompassed several circles, I used the distance corresponding to the average of the mean distance for each circle. For the Canary Islands, the Azores Islands, and Madeira, the value corresponds to the distance from Brussels to the main island in each group of islands, as obtained through the Internet.
- *Deaths in World War II*: From: J. Keegan, *The Times Atlas of the Second World War* (New York: Harper & Row, 1989). I used estimates of the countries' prewar populations to estimate the number of military and civilian deaths per capita.
- *Percentage of a country's total trade with the European Union*: From OECD, *Foreign trade by commodities and main economic indicators* (Paris: OECD, 2000).

- *Economic growth and inflation*: From Eurostat, *Annuaire 2000* (Luxembourg: Office des publications officielles des Communautés européennes, 2000).
- *Catholic country*: I have coded as Catholic those countries in which the large majority of the population is Catholic.
- *New democracy*: I have coded as new democracies Spain, Portugal, and Greece.

4. The coefficient -1.20 in Column 2 means that the odds of supporting membership in the European Union among those who do not hold such fears are about 3.3 times greater ($1/\exp[-1.20]$) than they are among those who hold such fears. The coefficient -0.40 in column 4 means that the average support for transfers of sovereignty and competences to the European Union is 0.40 units greater among respondents who do not hold fears of losing their national identity than among those who do.

5. The coefficient 0.95 in column 2 means that for every unit increase in how close respondents feel to Europe, the odds of supporting membership in the European Union become 2.6 times greater ($\exp[0.95]$). The coefficient 0.35 in column 4 means that for every unit increase in how close respondents feel to Europe, the average level of support for transfers of sovereignty and competences to the European Union increases by 0.35 units.

6. See Bryk and Raudenbush (1992) for a justification of this approach when the independent variables are measured both at the individual and the aggregate levels. I estimated the model using HML 5.04.

I have not conducted a similar analysis using the general measure of support for European integration for statistical reasons. Methods for the estimation of 3-level hierarchical linear models with dichotomous dependent variables are still in their infancy. One major problem is that although programs such as MlWin and HML now include procedures for the calculation of unbiased coefficient estimates (e.g., the Laplace6 solution with HML), these procedures are cumbersome and difficult to apply to models with many independent variables such as the one considered here, which includes 23 individual-level variables, three regional-level variables, and six country-level variables. See Rodríguez and Goldman (2001), Yang and Goldstein, (2000), and Raudenbush and Yang. (1998). My estimation of simpler models than the ones discussed here, with those independent variables that showed the greatest explanatory power, provided results that are comparable to the results presented here. In particular, residence in a Catholic country and distance from Brussels were, as in the analysis below, the variables with the strongest influence on support for European integration.

7. In the past, Gabel used a measure of the different regions' income per capita with the expectation that poorer regions would be more supportive of membership than would wealthier regions.

The rationale behind the inclusion of the "Distance from Brussels" variable is that respondents in the United Kingdom and the press of many countries often criticize European unification by saying that Brussels is "too far away," both metaphorically and geographically. They thus claim that the European Commission is unable to understand the problems affecting the regions where respondents live. One could note, in addition to this, that nationalist movements (e.g., Catalonia, Basque country, Brittany, Corsica, Scotland, Wales) in existing states often take place in the periphery. One would thus expect that the farther away from Brussels people live, the less they support membership in the EU. The rationale behind the inclusion of the predominant religion variable is that the literature often refers to the role of Catholicism in fostering European unification. Both the universalism of the Catholic religion and the goal of re-creating the long disappeared Holy Roman Empire are mentioned as the reasons behind this support. Furthermore, the literature on British national identity often emphasizes the defining role of the fight of the British Crown against Catholicism, foremost represented by France, the major force behind European unification. One could further argue that centuries of religious wars in Europe shaped cultural affinities and enmities, as well as networks of interaction, that are currently reflected in the reception of the European Union, initially a project sponsored by Catholic parties or Catholic political leaders. Finally, the rationale behind the inclusion of a variable measuring whether respondents live in a country that has only recently become a democracy is that the desire to consolidate newly democratic regimes is often invoked as a reason behind support for European integration.

8. The residuals obtained for Great Britain after estimating a model that excludes the variables "Fear of Losing National Identity" and "Closeness to Europe" are on average 34% greater than those obtained in a model including them.

CHAPTER 10
Conclusions

1. Benedict Anderson (1983).
2. E.g., Deflem and Pampel (1996), pp. 123–124, and Laffan (1996), p. 87.
3. E.g., Mommsen (1994a), p. 6, and Bulmer and Paterson (1987), p. 110.
4. E.g., William Wallace (1994), p. 131, and Colley (1992b), p. 375.
5. E.g., Gabel and Palmer, (1995), p. 16; Alvarez-Miranda (1996); and Laffan (1996), p. 87.
6. E.g., Mommsen (1994a), p. 6, Loth (1994), p. 46, Laffan (1996); p. 86; Bulmer and Paterson (1987), p. 110; and Hassner (1983); p. 299.
7. E.g., Colley (1992b), p. 375; William Wallace (1994), p. 131, William Wallace, (1992), p. 424; Blank 1978. Katzenstein (1997), and Laffan (1996), p. 87.
8. I interviewed the following persons: Joaquín Estefanía (Editor of *El País*), Carlos Fernández Lerga (member of the Juridical Division of the Department for the European Communities at the Ministry of Foreign Affairs, 1978–84), Fernando Morán (former Minister of Foreign Affairs as part of the first Socialist government formed after this party's electoral victory in 1982), Apolinar Rodríguez (leading member of the Socialist union, UGT), Inocencio Arias (official at the Foreign Affairs Ministry; currently Spanish ambassador at the United Nations), María Teresa Estevan (Conservative EP member and former official with the centrist [UCD] government in the early years of Spain's democratic transition), José Antonio Gallego Grevilla (major negotiator of Spain's 1970 Preferential Agreement with the EEC), Pedro J. Ramírez (editor of *El Mundo*), Luis Angel Lerena (director of the Research Department of the former Banco de Bilbao—now BBVA), Luis Ullastres (Spanish ambassador to the EEC in the 1960s and major

negotiator of the 1970 Preferential Agreement with the EEC), Marcelino Oreja (former Foreign Affairs minister with the centrist [UCD] government; later on, member of the European Commission, among other posts).

9. Seven out of the eleven respondents that I interviewed mentioned the topic of Spain's modernization, six mentioned the topics of breaking with Spain's isolation, and five mentioned topics related to Spain's prestige. Globally considered, the elite representatives I interviewed conveyed that breaking with isolation is or has been seen as necessary for Spain's modernization (economic, cultural, political) and Spain's standing in the world. This applies as much to top journalists, such as a former editor of the newspaper *El País*, as to two former ministers of Foreign Affairs, one Conservative, the other Socialist. Furthermore, respondents emphasized repeatedly the strong autonomy of the political elites and their motives vis-à-vis the economic elites when dealing with European integration issues, both before and after entry in the European Union.

10. See Brubaker (1996).

11. See definition in chapter 3.

12. An analogy with Kuhnian explanations of scientific revolutions is in this sense appropriate. It takes many and major contradictory findings before a scientific paradigm begins to be seriously questioned. See Klandermans (1992).

13. On the role of crises in progress toward European integration, see Neil Fligstein and Mara-Drita (1996).

APPENDIX 4

Sources for Part II: Novels, History Textbooks, and Head of State Addresses

1. For a year-by-year history of this prize, see Emmerich (1999).
2. See Emmerich (1996).
3. About the Booker Prize, see Todd (1996).

References

Abellán, José Luís. 1971. *La cultura en España (Ensayo para un diagnóstico)*. Madrid: Cuadernos para el Diálogo.
Abellán, José Luis, and Martínez Gómez, Luis. 1977. *El pensamiento español: de Séneca a Zubiri*. Madrid: UNED.
Adorno, Th. W., E. Frenkel-Brunswik, D. J. Levinson, and R. N. Sanford. 1950. *The Authoritarian Personality*. New York: Harper.
Alférez, Antonio. 1986. *Cuarto poder en España. La prensa desde la ley Fraga 1966*. Barcelona: Plaza & Janés.
Almond, Gabriel A, and Sidney Verba. 1963. *The Civic Culture: Political Attitudes and Democracy in Five Nations*. Princeton: Princeton University Press.
Almond, Gabriel A, and Sidney Verba (eds.). 1980. *The Civic Culture Revisited*. Boston: Little, Brown.
Alted, Alicia. 1995. "Educational Policy in Democratic Spain." In Helen Graham and Jo Labanyi (eds.), *Spanish Cultural Studies: An Introduction*. Oxford: Oxford University Press.
Alvarez Junco, José. 2001. *Mater Dolorosa. La idea de España en el siglo XIX*. Madrid: Taurus.
Alvarez-Miranda, Berta. 1996. *El sur de Europa y la adhesión a la Comunidad: Los debates políticos*. Madrid: CIS.
Amis, Kingsley. 1955. *Lucky Jim*. London: Gollanz.
Anderson, Benedict. 1983. *Imagined Communities*. London: Verso.
Anderson, Perry. 1987. "The Figures of Descent." *New Left Review* 161 (January–February): 20–78.
———. 1992b [1968]. "Components of the National Culture." In Perry Anderson, *English Questions*. London: Verso.
———. 1992a [1964]. "Origins of the Present Crisis." In Perry Anderson, *English Questions*. London: Verso.
Anderson, Peter J., and Anthony Weymouth. 1999. *Insulting the Public? The British Press and the European Union*. London: Longman.
Anderson, Stuart. 1981. *Race and Rapprochement*. London: Associated University Presses.
Antonio Cuadra, Pablo. 1943. "Política internacional y política universal de España." *Revista de Estudios Políticos* 9: 161–66.
Arendt, Hannah. 1993 [1966]. *Besuch in Deutschland*. Hamburg: Rotbuch Verlag.
Arnold, David. 1966. *Britain, Europe, and the World. 1870–1955*. Edinburgh: Edward Arnold Publishers.
Arnold, Heinz Ludwig. *Die Westdeutsche Literatur: 1945 bis 1990*. Munich: DTV.
Artola, Miguel. 1959. *Los orígenes de la España contemporánea*. Madrid: Instituto de Estudios Políticos.
Asián Peña, José L. 1954. *Manual de historia de España*. Barcelona: Bosch.

Augstein, Rudolf, et al. 1987. *Historikerstreit: Die Dokumentation der Kontroverse um die Einzigartigkeit der nationalsozialistischen Judenvernichtung.* Munich: Piper Verlag.
Aunós, Eduardo. 1943. "Las tres columnas de la unidad europea." *Revista de Estudios Políticos* 11: 1–53.
Babb, Sarah. 1996. "Frame Resonance in the U.S. Labor Movement, 1866 to 1886." *American Sociological Review* 61,6: 1033–53.
Barker, A. L. 1948. *Innocents: Variations on a Theme.* New York: Charles Scribner's Sons.
Barnett, Anthony. 1982. "War over the Falklands." *New Left Review* 134: 5–70.
Barratt Brown, Michael. 1988. "Away with All the Great Arches: Anderson's History of British Capitalism." *New Left Review* 167 (January–February): 22–53.
Bateson, Gregory. 1955. "A Theory of Play and Phantasy." *Psychiatric Research Reports* 2: 39–51.
Baucom, Ian. 1999. *Out of Place: Englishness, Empire, and the Locations of Identity.* Princeton, NJ: Princeton University Press.
Bender, Peter. 1999. "Rahmenbedingungen deutscher Politik 1949–1989." In Christoph Klessmann (ed.), *Deutscher Vergangenheiten: Eine gemeinsame Herausforderung.* Berlin: Ch. Links Verlag.
Beneyto, José María. 1999. *Tragedia y razón.* Madrid: Taurus.
Blackbourn, David, and Eley, Geoff. 1980. *Mythen deutscher Geschichtsschreibung.* Frankfurt am Main: Ullstein Materialen.
Blank, Stephen. 1978. "Britain: The Politics of Foreign Economic Policy, the Domestic Economy, and the Problem of Pluralistic Stagnation." In Peter Katzenstein (ed.), *Between Power and Plenty: Foreign Economic Policies of Advanced Industrial States.* Madison: University of Wisconsin Press.
Bollen, Ken, and Díez Medrano, Juan. 1998. "Who Are the Spaniards? The Effects of Ethnic Origin, Economic Development, Economic Specialization, and Cognitive Skills on Attachment to the Nation-State in the Spanish Context." *Social Forces* 77,2: 587–623.
Born, Nicholas. 1976. *Die erdabgewandte Seite der Geschichte.* Hamburg: Rowohlt.
Boudon, Raymond. 1996. "The 'Cognitivist Model': A Generalized 'Rational-Choice Model.'" *Rationality and Society* 8,2: 123–50.
Bourdieu, Pierre. 1991 [1972]. *Outline of a Theory of Practice.* Cambridge: Cambridge University Press.
Brandt, Willy. 1971. "Aktuelle Fragen der deutschen Aussenpolitik." *Europa-Archiv* 13: 437–42.
Braudel, Fernand. 1949. *La Méditerranée et le monde méditeranéen à l' époque de Phillippe II.* Paris: Armand Colin.
Bredow, Wilfred von. 1985. *Deutschland: Ein Provisorium?* Berlin: Siedler Verlag.
Brenan, G. 1943. *The Spanish Labyrinth: An Account of the Social and Political Background of the Civil War.* Cambridge: Cambridge University Press.
Brewer, M. B. 1993. "Social Identity, Distinctiveness, and In-Group Homogeneity." *Social Cognition* 11,1: 150–64.
———. 1999. "Multiple Identities and Identity Transition: Implications for Hong-Kong." *International Journal of Intercultural Relations* 23,2: 187–97.

Brinks, Jan Herman. 1992. *Die DDR-Geschichtswissenschaft auf dem Weg zur deutschen Einheit.* Frankfurt am Main: Campus Verlag.
Brock, George. 1997. "Geht von Deutschland eine Bedrohung aus?" *Internationale Politik* 2: 23–28.
Brockliss, Laurence, and David Eastwood. 1997. "Introduction: A Union of Multiple Identities." In Laurence Brockliss and David Eastwood (eds.), *A Union of Multiple Identities: the British Isles, c1750–1850.* Manchester: Manchester University Press.
Bröder, Friedrich J. 1976. *Presse und Politik. Demokratie und Gesellschaft im Spiegel politischer Kommentare der "Frankfurter Allgemeinen Zeitung," der "Welt" und der "Süddeutschen Zeitung."* Erlangen: Palm & Enke.
Broster, Peter J, and David R. Jones. 1978. *Revision Notes for Ordinary Level and CSE. Twentieth Century World History.* London: Bell & Hyman.
Brubaker, Rogers. 1992. *Citizenship and Nationhood in France and Germany.* Cambridge, MA: Harvard University Press.
———. 1996. *Nationalism Reframed: Nationhood and the National Question in the New Europe.* Cambridge: Cambridge University Press.
Bryk, Anthony S., and Stephen W. Raudenbush. 1992. *Hierarchical Linear Models.* Newbury Park: Sage Publications.
Bulmer, Simon. 1992. "Britain and European Integration: Of Sovereignty, Slow Adaptation, and Semi-Detachment." In Stephen George (ed.), *Britain and the European Community.* Oxford: Clarendon Press.
Bulmer, Simon, and William Paterson. 1987. *The Federal Republic of Germany and the European Community.* London: Allen & Unwin.
Calder, Angus. 1991. *The Myth of the Blitz.* London: Jonathan Cape.
Calhoun, Craig. 1994. "Social Theory and the Politics of Identity." In Craig Calhoun (ed.), *Social Theory and the Politics of Identity.* Cambridge, MA.: Blackwell Publishers.
Calvo Serer, Rafael. 1949. *España sin problema.* Madrid: Rialp.
Camberton, Ronald. 1950. *Scamp.* London: John Lehmann.
Cannadine, David. 2001. *Ornamentalism: How the British Saw Their Empire.* London: Penguin Press.
Carr, Raymond. 1966. *Spain 1808–1939.* Oxford: Clarendon Press.
Carroll, William K., and Robert S. Ratner. 1996. "Master Frames and Counter-Hegemony: Political Sensibilities in Contemporary Social Movements." *CRSA/RCSA* 33,4: 407–35.
Castresana, Luis de. 1967. *El otro árbol de Guernica.* Madrid: Prensa Española.
Castro, José Ramón. 1957. *Historia moderna y contemporánea.* Cuarto Curso. Zaragoza: Editorial Librería General.
Castro Real, Juan Manuel. 1942. "El problema de la realidad de Europa." *Revista de Estudios Políticos* 12: 492–503.
Cela, Camilo José. 1983. *Mazurca para dos muertos.* Barcelona: Seix Barral.
Classen, Christopher. 1999. *Bilder der Vergangenheit: Die Zeit des Nationalsozialismus im Fernsehen der Bundesrepublik Deutschland 1955–1965.* Cologne: Böhlau Verlag.
Cohen, Robin. 1994. *Frontiers of Identity: the British and the Others.* Essex: Longman House.

Colley, Linda. 1992a. "Britishness and Otherness: An Argument." *Journal of British Studies* 31: 309–29.
———. 1992b. *Britons: Forging the Nation: 1707–1837.* New Haven: Yale University Press.
Connerton, Paul. 1989. *How Societies Remember.* Cambridge: Cambridge University Press.
Constantine, Stephen. 1986. "Bringing the Empire Alive. The Empire Marketing Board and Imperial Propaganda, 1926–1933." In John M. Mackenzie, *Imperialism and Popular Culture.* Manchester: Manchester University Press.
Corse, Sarah M. 1997. *Nationalism and Literature: The Politics of Culture in Canada and the United States.* Cambridge: Cambridge University Press.
Dahrendorf, Ralph. 1965. *Gesellschaft und Demokratie in Deutschland.* Munich: R. Piper & Co. Verlag.
Dalton, Russell J., and Robert Duval. 1981. "The Political Environment and Foreign Policy Opinions: British Attitudes toward European Integration, 1972–1979." *British Journal of Political Science* 16: 113–34.
Davy, Richard. 1990. "Grossbritanien und die deutsche Frage." *Europa-Archiv* 4: 139–44.
Deflem, Mathieu, and Fred C. Pampel. 1996. "The Myth of Postnational Identity: Popular Support for European Unification." *Social Forces* 75,1: 119–43.
Department of Education. History Working Group. 1990. *National Curriculum: Final Report.*
Deutsch, K. W. 1957. *Nationalism and Social Communication.* New York: John Wiley.
———. 1964. "Social Mobilization and Political Development." *American Political Science Review* 55,2: 493–514.
———. 1968. *Analysis of International Relations.* Englewood Cliffs, NJ: Prentice-Hall.
Díaz, Elías. 1974. *Pensamiento español: 1939–1973.* Madrid: Cuadernos para el Diálogo.
Díez Medrano, Juan. 1995a. *Divided Nations.* Ithaca: Cornell University Press
———. 1995b. *La opinión pública y la integración europea: 1994.* Madrid: CIS.
Droz, Jacques. 1960. *L' Europe centrale. Evolution historique de l' idée de "Mitteleuropa."* Paris: Payot.
Easton, David. 1975, "A Re-Assessment of the Concept of Political Support." *British Journal of Political Science* 5: 435–57.
Ebeling, Hans. 1955. *Deutsche Geschichte.* Braunschweig: Georg Westermann Verlag.
———. 1969. *Die Reise in die Vergangenheit.* Vol. IV: *Unser Zeitalter der Revolutionen und Weltkriege.* Braunschweig: Georg Westermann Verlag.
Ebeling, Hans, and Wolfgang Birkenfeld. 1985. *Die Reise in die Vergangenheit.* Vol. IV. Braunschweig: Westermann.
———. 1995 (1993). *Die Reise in der Vergangenheit.* Vol. IV. Braunschweg: Westermann.
Eich, Hermann. 1963. *Die unheimlichen Deutschen.* Düsseldorf: Econ-Verlag.
Eichenberg, Richard, and Russell J. Dalton. 1993. "Europeans and the European Community: The Dynamics of Public Support for European Integration." *International Organization* 47: 507–34.

Elliott, John. 1963. *Imperial Spain: 1469–1716.* London: Edward Arnold.
Emmerich, Wolfgang. 1996. *Kleine Literaturgeschichte der DDR.* Leipzig: Kiepenheuer.
———. 1999. *Der Bremer Literaturpreis 1954–1998. Reden der Preisträger und andere Texte.* Eine Dokumentation. Bremerhaven: Wirtschaftsverlag NW. Verlag für neue Wissenschaft.
Escobar, José Ignacio. 1943. "La Hispanidad ante el actual momento histórico." *Revista de Estudios Políticos* 11: 163–78.
Evans, Richard J. 1987. "The New Nationalism and the Old History: Perspectives on the West German Historikerstreit." *Journal of Modern History* 59: 761–97.
Farr, Robert M., and Serge Moscovici (eds.). 1984. *Social Representations.* Cambridge: Cambridge University Press.
Feld, Werner, and John K. Wildgen. 1976. *Domestic Political Realities and European Unification.* Boulder, CO: Westview.
Fentress, James, and Chris Wickham. 1992. *Social Memory.* Oxford: Blackwell.
Fernández de la Mora, Gonzalo. 1965. *El crepúsculo de las ideologías.* Madrid: Rialp.
Fernández Santos, Jesús. 1978. *Extramuros.* Barcelona: Argos Vergara.
Fillieule, Renaud. 1996. "Some Light on the Controversies about Rationality." *Rationality and Society* 8,2: 151–56.
Firth, Catherine B. (ed.). 1952 (1932). *History* Edinburg: R&R Clark, Ltd.
Fiske, Susan, and Shelley Taylor. 1984. *Social Cognition.* New York: Random House.
Fligstein, Neil, and Iona Mara-Drita. 1996. "How to Make a Market: Reflections on the Attempt to Create a Single Market in the European Union." *American Journal of Sociology* 102,1: 1–33.
Floud, R., and D. McCloskey (eds.). 1994. *The Economic History of Britain since 1700.* Cambridge: Cambridge University Press.
Foddy, William. 1993. *Constructing Questions for Interviews and Questionnaires: Theory and Practice in Social Research.* Cambridge: Cambridge University Press.
Ford, Boris (ed.). 1992. *The Cambridge Cultural History.* Cambridge: Press Syndicate of the University of Cambridge.
Franco Bahamonde, Francisco. 1975. *Pensamiento politico de Fanco.* 2 vols. Madrid: Ediciones de Movimiento.
———. 1985 [1939]. "Fundamentos y directrices de un plan de saneamiento de nuestra economía, armónico con nuestra reconstrucción nacional." *Historia* 16,115: 44–49.
Frei, Norbert, 1996. *Vergangenheitspolitik.* Munich: Beck.
Fühmann, Franz. 1973. *22 Tagen oder die Hälfte des Lebens.* Frankfurt am Main: Suhrkamp.
Fusi, Juan Pablo. 1999. *Un siglo de España: La cultura.* Madrid: Marcial Pons.
Gabel, Matthew. 1998a. "Economic Integration and Mass Politics: Market Liberalization and Public Attitudes in the European Union." *American Journal of Political Science* 42,3: 936–53.
———. 1998b. *Interests and Integration: Market Liberalization, Public Opinion, and European Union.* Ann Arbor: University of Michigan Press.
———. 1998c. "Public Support for European Integration: An Empirical Test of Five Theories." *Journal of Politics* 60,2: 333–54.

Gabel, Matthew, and Harvey Palmer. 1995. "Understanding Variation in Public Support for European Integration." *European Journal of Political Research* 27,1: 3–19.

Gabel, Matthew, and Guy D. Whitten. 1997. "Economic Conditions, Economic Perceptions, and Public Support for European Integration." *Political Behavior* 19,1: 81–96.

Gahnem, Salma. 1997. "Filling the Tapestry: The Second Level of Agenda-Setting." In M. McCombs, D. Shaw, and D. Weaver (eds.), *Communication and Democracy: Exploring the Intellectual Frontiers in Agenda-Setting Theory.* Mahwah, NJ: Lawrence Erlbaum.

Gamson, William. 1992a. "Social Psychology of Collective Action." In Aldon Morris and Carol McClurg Mueller (eds.), Frontiers of Social Morvement Theory. New Haven: Yale University Press.

———. 1992b. *Talking Politics.* Cambridge: Cambridge University Press.

Gamson, William, and André Modigliani. 1989. "Media Discourse and Public Opinion on Nuclear Power." *American Journal of Sociology* 95: 1–38.

Ganivet, Angel. 1996 [1897]. *Idearium Español.* Madrid: Biblioteca Nueva.

García Pérez, Rafael. 1990. "La idea de la 'Nueva Europa' en el pensamiento nacionalista español de la inmediata postguerra 1939–1944." *Revista del Centro de Estudios Constitucionales* 5: 203–40.

Garrett, Geoffrey, and Barry Weingast. 1993. "Ideas, Interests, and Institutions: Constructing the EC's Internal Market." In Judith Goldstein and Robert Keohane (eds.), *Ideas and Foreign Policy.* Ithaca: Cornell University Press.

Gelb, Norman. 1982. *The British: A Portrait of an Indomitable Island People.* New York: Everest House.

Gellner, Ernest. 1983. *Nations and Nationalism.* Ithaca, NY: Cornell University Press.

Genazino, Wilhelm. 1989. *Der Fleck, Die Jacke, Die Zimmer, Der Schmerz.* Hamburg: Rowohlt Verlag.

George, Stephen (ed.). 1992. *Britain and the European Community.* Oxford: Clarendon Press.

Giddens, Anthony. 1984. *The Constitution of Society: Outline of a Theory of Structuration.* Cambridge: Polity Press.

Gikandi, Simon. 1996. *Maps of Englishness: Writing, Identity in the Culture of Colonialism.* New York: Columbia University Press.

Gindin, James. 1969. *Post-War British Fiction.* London: Cambridge University Press.

Giner, Juan A. 1983. "Journalists, Mass Media, and Public Opinion in Spain, 1938–1982." In Kenneth Maxwell (ed.), *The Press and the Rebirth of Iberian Democracy.* Westport, CT: Greenwood Press.

Gitlin, Todd. 1980. *The Whole World Is Watching: Mass Media in the Making and Unmaking of the New Left.* Berkeley: University of California Press.

Glaser, Hermann. 1999. *Deutsche Kultur, 1945–2000.* Berlin: Ullstein.

Goffman, Erving. 1974. *Frame Analysis: An Essay on the Organization of Experience.* Cambridge, MA: Harvard University Press.

Goldhagen, Daniel J. 1996. *Hitler's Willing Executioners: Ordinary Germans and the Holocaust.* New York: Knopf.

Golding, William. 1980. *Rites of Passage*. London: Faber and Faber.
Goldschmidt, George-Arthur. 1995. *Der unterbrochene Wald*. Frankfurt am Main: Fischer.
Gorra, Michael. 1997. *After Empire*. Chicago: Chicago University Press.
Gotthold, Gloger. 1955. *Philomena Kleespiess trug die Fahne*. Berlin: Aufbau Verlag.
Gouldbourne, Harry. 1991. *Ethnicity and Nationalism in Post-Imperial Britain*. Cambridge: Cambridge University Press.
Gourevitch, Peter. 1979. "The Reemergence of 'Peripheral Nationalisms': Some Comparative Speculations on the Spatial Distribution of Political Leadership and Economic Growth." *Comparative Studies in Society and History* 21,3: 303–32.
Graber, Doris. 1988. *Processing the News: How People Tame the Information Tide*. Lanham, MD: University Press of America.
Graham, Helen and Jo Labanyi (eds.). 1995. *Spanish Cultural Studies: An Introduction*. Oxford: Oxford University Press.
Grainger, J. H. 1986. *Patriotisms. Britain: 1900–1939*. London: Routledge and Kegan Paul.
Grandes, Almudena. 1995. *Las edades de Lulú*. Barcelona: Tusquets.
Grass, Günter. 1959. *Die Blechtrommel*. Darmstadt: Luchterhand Verlag.
———. 1989. *The Tin Drum*. Trans. by Ralph Manheim. New York: Vintage Books.
Greenfeld, Liah. 1995. *Nationalism: Five Roads to Modernity*. Cambridge: Harvard University Press.
Gutiérrez, José J., Guillermo Fatas, and Antonio B. Borderías. 1977. *Geografía e Historia de España. 3° de BUP*. Zaragoza: Edelvives.
Haas, Ernst. 1971. "The Study of Regional Integration: Reflections on the Joy and Anguish of Pre-Theorizing." In L. Lindberg and S. Scheingold (eds.), *Regional Integration: Theory and Research*. Cambridge, MA: Harvard University Press.
Haas, Ernst. 1958. *The Uniting of Europe*. Stanford, CA: Stanford University Press.
Haas, Ernst, and Philip Schmitter. 1964. "Economics and Differential Patterns of Political Integration: Projections about Unity in Latin America." *International Organization* 18: 705–37.
Habermas, Jürgen. 1986. "Eine Art Schadenabwicklung: Die apologetischen Tendenzen in der deutschen Zeitgeschichtsschreibung." *Die Zeit*, July 11, 1986.
Halbwachs, Maurice. 1975 [1925]. *Les cadres sociaux de la mémoire*. Paris: Mouton.
Haller, Max. 1994. "Europe as a New Nation or a Community of Nations." *International Journal of Sociology* 24,2–3: 166–212.
Hallin, Daniel. 1994. *We Keep America on Top of the World: Television Journalism and the Public Sphere*. New York: Routledge.
Harms, Kathy, Lutz R. Reuter, and Volker Dürr (eds.). 1990. *Coping with the Past: Germany and Austria after 1945*. Madison: University of Wisconsin Press.
Hassner, Pierre. 1983. "Zwei deutsche Staaten in Europa. Gibt es gemeinsame Interesse in der internationalen Politik?" In Werner Weidenfeld (ed.), *Die Identität der Deutschen*. Munich: Carl Hanser Verlag.

Hechter, Michael. 1975. *Internal Colonialism: The Celtic Fringe of British National Development, 1536–1966*. Berkeley: University of California Press.
Heil, Johannes, and Rainer Erb (eds.). 1998. *Geschichtswissenschaft und Öffentlichkeit: der Streit um Daniel J. Goldhagen*. Frankfurt am Main: Fischer Verlag.
Heimann, Gerhard. 1990. "Die Auflösung der Blöcke und die Europäisierung Deutschlands." *Europa-Archiv* S: 167–172.
Herburger, Günter. 1972. *Die Eroberung der Zitadelle*. Darmstadt: Luchterhand.
Herr, Richard. 1958. *The Eighteenth-Century Revolution in Spain*. Princeton, NJ: Princeton University Press.
Hewstone, Miles. 1986. *Understanding Attitudes to the European Community*. New York: Cambridge University Press.
Hillgruber, Andreas. 1986. *Zweierlei Untergang: Die Zerschlagung des Deutschen Reiches und das Ende des europäischen Judentums*. Berlin: Corso bei Siedler, Wolf Jobst Siedler Verlag.
Hobsbawm, E. J. 1968. *Industry and Empire: An Economic History of Britain since 1750*. London: Weidenfeld and Nicolson.
Hoffmann, Stanley. 1966. "Obstinate or Obsolete? The Fate of the Nation-State and the Case of Western Europe." *Daedalus*: 862–915.
Hogg, M. A. and D. Abrams. 1988. *Social Identification*. London: Routledge.
Horst, Alfred Heinrich. 1996. "Generationsbedingte zeithistorische Erinnerung in Deutschland. Ergebnisdokumentation einer computergestützten Inhaltsanalyse mit INTEXT." *Arbeitsberichte aus dem DFG-Projekt "Nationale Identität der Deutschen." Messung und Erklärung der Veränderungsprozesse in Ost und West* 10: 1–62.
Humphreys, Emyr. 1971 [1952]. *Hear and Forgive*. London: Macdonald.
Iggers, Georg G. 1983 [revised from 1968]. *The German Conception of History*. Middletown, CT: Wesleyan University Press.
Inglehart, Ronald. 1977a. "Long-term Trends in Mass Support for European Unification." *Government and Opposition* 12: 150–77.
———. 1977b. *The Silent Revolution*. Princeton, NJ: Princeton University Press.
———. 1997. *Modernization and Postmodernization*. Princeton, NJ: Princeton University Press.
Jackson, Gabriel. 1966. *The Spanish Republic and the Civil War: 1931–1939*. Princeton, NJ: Princeton University Press.
Janssen, Joseph I. H. 1991. "Postmaterialism, Cognitive Mobilization and Support for European Integration." *British Journal of Political Science* 21: 443.
Jaspers, Karl. 1947. *The Question of German Guilt*. New York: Capricorn Books.
Joffe, Joseph. 1979. "Die Aussenpolitik der Bundesrepublik Deutschland im Zeitalter der Entspannung." *Europa-Archiv* 23: 719–30.
Katzenstein, Peter (ed.). 1978. *Between Power and Plenty: Foreign Economic Policies of Advanced Industrial States*. Madison: University of Wisconsin Press.
———. 1997. *Tamed Power: Germany in Europe*. Ithaca, NY: Cornell University Press.
Kelman, James. 1994. *How Late It Was, How Late*. New York: Norton.
Keohane, Robert, and Stanley Hoffmann. 1991. *The New European Community*. Boulder, CO: Westview Press.

Keohane, Robert, and Stanley Hoffmann. 1992. "Conclusions: Community Politics and Institutional Change." In William Wallace (ed.), *The Dynamics of European Integration*. London: Pinter.

Key, V. O. 1961. *Public Opinion and American Democracy*. New York: Knopf.

Kiefer, Markus. 1992. *Auf der Suche nach nationaler Identität und Wegen zur deutschen Einheit. Die Deutsche Frage in der Überregionalen Tages- und Wochenpresse der Bundesrepublik 1949–1955*. Frankfurt am Main: Peter Lang: 9–13.

Klandermans, Bert. 1992. "The Social Construction of Protest and Multiorganizational Fields." In Aldon D. Morris and Carol McClurg Mueller (eds.), *Frontiers of Social Movement Theory*. New Haven: Yale University Press.

Klessmann, Christoph. 1988. *Zwei Staaten, eine Nation*. Göttingen: Vandenhoeck & Ruprecht.

Kohn, Hans. 1962. *Wege und Irrwege: Vom Geist des deutschen Bürgertums*. Düsseldorf: Droste Verlag.

Kolboom, Ingo. 1991. "Die Vertreibung der Dämonen: Frankreich und das vereinte Deutschland." *Europa-Archiv* 15–16: 470–75.

Krasner, Stephen D. 1991. "Global Communications and National Power: Life on the Pareto Frontier." *World Politics* 43,2: 336–66.

Krebs, Hans. 1931. *Paneuropa oder Mitteleuropa?* Munich: Fr. Eher Rachf.

Krugman, Paul and Maurice Obstfeldt. 1994. *International Economics*. New York: Harper Collins.

Kumar, Krishan. 2000. "Nation and Empire: English and British National Identity in Comparative Perspective." *Theory and Society* 29: 575–608.

Labanyi, Jo. 1995. "Postmodernism and the Problem of Cultural Identity." In Helen Graham and Jo Labanyi (eds.), *Spanish Cultural Studies*. Oxford: Oxford University Press.

Laffan, Brigid. 1996. "The Politics of Identity and Political Order in Europe." *Journal of Common Market Studies* 34,1: 81–102.

Laín Entralgo, Pedro. 1948. *España como problema*. Madrid: Seminario de Problemas Hispanoamericanos.

Laitin, David. 1991. "The National Uprisings in the Soviet Union." *World Politics* 44,1: 139–77.

Lamont, Michele, and Thévenot, Laurent (eds.). 2000. *Rethinking Comparative Cultural Sociology: Repertoires of Evaluation in France and the United States*. New York: Cambridge University Press.

Lenz, Siegfried. 1961. *Zeit der Schuldlosen*. In Siegrfried Lenz, *Schauspiele*. Hamburg: Hoffmann und Campe, 1998.

Liebhart, Ernst H. 1971. *Nationalismus in der Tagespresse: 1949–1966*. Meisenheim am Glan: Verlag Anton Hain.

Lindberg, L., and S. A. Scheingold. 1970. *Europe's Would-be Polity*. Englewood Cliffs, NJ: Prentice-Hall.

Lindenberg, Siegwart, and Bruno S. Frey. 1993. "Alternatives, Frames, and Relative Prices: A Broader View of Rational Choice Theory." *Acta Sociologica* 36: 191–205.

Lissarrague, Salvador. 1943. "Sentido de la Hispanidad." *Revista de Estudios Políticos* 9: 167–73.

Lively, Penelope. 1987. *Moon Tiger.* New York: Grove Press.
Lorenz, Chris. 1995. "Beyond Good and Evil? The German Empire of 1871 and Modern German Historiography." *Journal of Contemporary History* 30: 729–65.
Loth, Wilfried. 1994. "The Germans and European Unification." In Wolfgang Mommsen (ed.), *The Long Way to Europe.* Chicago: Edition q.
Lützeler, Paul Michael. 1997. "'Grossmacht' Deutschland: Essay über die Perspektive von aussen." *Internationale Politik* 2: 8–12.
Mackenzie, John M. 1986a. *Imperialism and Popular Culture.* Manchester: Manchester University Press.
———. 1986b. "In Touch with the Infinite: The BBC and the Empire, 1923–53." In John M. Mackenzie (ed.), *Imperialism and Popular Culture.* Manchester: Manchester University Press.
Maeztu, Ramiro de. 1967 [1899]. *Hacia otra España.* Madrid: Rialp.
———. 1998 [1931]. *Defensa de la Hispanidad.* Madrid: Rialp.
Mainer, José-Carlos. 1980. "La vida cultural (1939–1980)." In Domingo Ynduráin (ed.), *Época contemporánea: 1939–1980. Historia y crítica de la literatura española,* vol. 8. Barcelona: Crítica.
Majonica, Ernst. 1965. *Deutsche Aussenpolitik.* Stuttgart: W. Kohlhammer Verlag.
Manabe, Kazufumi, and Noriko Onodera. 1999. "A Cross-National Comparison of National Identity: From an ISSP Survey." *Broadcasting Culture and Research* 10: 7–15.
Maravall, José María. 1978. *Dictadura y disentimiento político.* Madrid: Alfaguara.
Markovits, Andrei. 1990. "Coping with the Past: The West German Labor Movement and the Left." In Kathy Harms, Lutz R. Reuter, and Volker Dürr (eds.), *Coping with the Past: Germany and Austria after 1945.* Madison: University of Wisconsin Press.
Martin, Howard. 1988. *Britain since 1800: Towards the Welfare State.* London: MacMillan.
Martín Santos, Luis. 1961. *Tiempo de silencio.* Barcelona: Seix Barral.
Maxwell, Kenneth (ed.). *The Press and the Rebirth of Iberian Democracy.* Westport, CT: Greenwood Press.
Mateo Díaz, Luis. 1986. *La fuente de la edad.* Madrid: Alfaguara.
Meckel, Christoph. 1980. *Suchbild.* Düsseldorf: Claassen.
Meinecke, Friedrich. 1947. *Die Deutsche Katastrophe.* Wiesbaden: Eberhard Brockhaus Verlag.
Meyer, Henry Cord. 1955. *Mitteleuropa in German Thought and Action: 1815–1945.* The Hague: Martinus.
Michelsen, Hans Günter. 1965. *Helm.* Frankfurt am Main: Suhrkamp.
Middleton, Drew. 1957. *These Are the British.* New York: Knopf.
Miguel, Amando de. 1980. *Los intelectuales bonitos.* Barcelona: Planeta.
Ministerium für Volksbildung der Deutschen Demokratischen Republik. 1962. *Lehrbuch für Geschichte der 10. Klasse der Oberschule und der erweiterten Oberschule.* Berlin: Volk und Wissen Volkseigener Verlag.
———. 1964. *Lehrbuch für Geschichte der 9. Klasse der Oberschule und der erweiterten Oberschule.* Berlin: Volk und Wissen Volkseigener Verlag.
Mitscherlich, Alexander, and Mitscherlich, Margarete. 1967. *Die Unfähigkeit zu trauern. Grundlagen kollektiven Verhaltens.* Munich: Piper.

Mommsen, Wolfgang. 1990. "The Germans and their Past: History and Political Consciousness in the Federal Republic of Germany." In Kathy Harms, Lutz R. Reuter, and Volker Dürr (eds.), *Coping with the Past*. Madison: University of Wisconsin Press.

———. 1994a. "Introduction." In Wolfgang Mommsen (ed.), *The Long Way To Europe*. Chicago: Edition q.

Mommsen, Wolfgang (ed.). 1994b. *The Long Way to Europe*. Chicago: Edition q.

Monleón, José (ed.). 1995. *Del Franquismo a la Posmodernidad: Cultura Española 1975–1990*. Madrid: Akal.

Montero Díaz, Julio (ed.). 1998. *Historia de la España contemporánea. 2° Curso de Bachillerato*. Zaragoza: Edelvives.

Montero, Rosa. 1995. "Political Transition and Cultural Democracy: Coping with the Speed of Change." In Helen Graham and Jo Labanyi (eds.), Spanish Cultural Studies. Oxford: Oxford University Press.

Montgomery, H, and P. G. Cambray. 1906. *A Dictionary of Political Phrases and Allusions*. London: S. Sonnenschein.

Moravcsik, A. 1991. "Negotiating the Single Act: National Interests and Conventional Statecraft in the European Community." *International Organization* 45,1: 19–56.

Moreno Juste, Antonio. 1990. "Algunos aspectos sobre la unidad europea en la bibliografía española de 1945 a 1962." *Hispania* 176: 1453–73.

Morris, Aldon D., and Carol McClurg Mueller (eds.). 1992. *Frontiers of Social Movement Theory*. New Haven: Yale University Press.

Morrow, James D. 1994. "Modelling the Forms of International Cooperation: Distribution versus Information." *International Organization* 48,3: 387–423.

Mosse, George. 1975. *The Nationalization of the Masses*. New York: H. Fertig.

Müller, Heiner, and Inge Müller. 1996 [1959]. *Die Korrektur*. In Heiner Müller and Inge Müller. *Geschichte aus der Produktion* 1. Nördlingen: Rotbuch Verlag.

Nairn, Tom. 1973. *The Left against Europe?* Middlesex: Penguin Books.

———. 1994 [1988]. *The Enchanted Glass*. London: Random House.

———. 2000. "Ukania under Blair." *New Left Review* 1 (Jan–Feb): 69–103.

Naumann, Friedrich. 1915. *Mitteleuropa*. Berlin: G. Reimer.

Newby, P. H. 1968. *Something to Answer For*. London: Faber and Faber.

Newman, Gerald. 1979. *The Origins of English Individualism: The Family, Property, and Social Transition*. New York: Cambridge University Press.

———. 1997 [1987]. *The Rise of English Nationalism: A Cultural History 1740–1830*. London: MacMillan Press.

Noack, Paul. 1981. *Die Aussenpolitik der Bundesrepublik Deutschland*. Stuttgart: Kohlhammer.

Noelle-Neumann, Elisabeth (ed). 1977. *Allensbacher Jahrbuch der Demoskopie: 1977*. Munich: Molden.

———. 1983. *Allensbacher Jahrbuch der Demoskopie: 1978–1983*. Munich: K. G. Saur.

Noelle-Neumann, Elisabeth and Köcher, Renate (eds.). 1993. *Allensbacher Jahrbuch der Demoskopie 1984–1992*. Munich: K. G. Saur.

Noelle-Neumann, Elisabeth, and Köcher, Renate (eds.). 1997. *Allensbacher Jahrbuch der Demoskopie: 1993–1997*. Munich: K. G. Saur.

Noll, Dieter. 1960. *Die Abenteuer des Werner Holt*. Berlin: Aufbau-Verlag.
Nolte, Ernst. 1986. "Vergangenheit, die nicht vergehen will: Eine Rede, die geschrieben, aber nicht gehalten werden konnte." *Frankfurter Allgemeine Zeitung*, June 6, 1986.
Nuggent, Neil. 1992. "British Public Opinion and the European Community." In Stephen George (ed.), *Britain and the European Community*. Oxford: Clarendon Press.
O'Brien, Patrick. 1999. "Imperialism and the Rise and Decline of the British Economy, 1688–1989." *New Left Review* 238 (November–December) 48–81.
Ortega y Gasset, José. 1935 [1930]. *La rebelión de las masas*. Madrid: Revista de Occidente.
———. 1986. *Europa y la idea de nación*. Madrid: Revista de Occidente.
———. 1998 [1914]. *Meditaciones del Quijote*. Madrid: Cátedra.
———. José. 2000 [1922]. *España invertebrada*. Madrid: Austral.
Orwell, George. 1947. *The English People*. London: Collins.
Ossorio-Capella, Carles. 1972. *Der Zeitungsmarkt in der Bundesrepublik Deutschland*. Frankfurt am Main: Athenäum Verlag.
Palomino, Angel. 1971. *Torremolinos Gran Hotel*. Madrid: Alfaguara.
Peterson, S. 1972. "Events, Mass Opinion, and Elite Attitudes." In R. L. Merritt (ed.), *Communications in International Politics*. Urbana: University of Illinois Press.
Phelps, Gilbert. 1992 [1988]. "Literature and Drama." In Boris Ford (ed.), *The Cambridge Cultural History*. Cambridge: Press Syndicate of the University of Cambridge.
Raudenbush, Stephen W., and Meng-Li Yang. 1998. "Numerical Integration via High-Order, Multivariate Laplace Approximation for Generalised Linear Multilevel Models." *Multilevel Modelling Newsletter* 10,2: 10–13.
Rausch, Heinz. 1983. "Politisches Bewusstsein und politische Einstellungen in Wandel." In Werner Weidenfeld (ed.), *Die Identität der Deutschen*. Munich: Carl Hanser Verlag.
Raven, James. 1989. "British History and the Enterprise Culture." *Past and Present* 123 (May): 178–204.
Reichel, Peter. 2001. *Vergangenheitsbewältigung in Deutschland: Die Auseinandersetzung mit der NS-Diktatur von 1945 bis heute*. Munich: Beck.
Reuter, Lutz. 1990. "Political and Moral Culture in West Germany: Four Decades of Democratic Reorganization and Vergangenheitsauseinandersetzung." In Kathy Harms, Lutz R. Reuter, and Völker Dürr (eds.), *Coping with the Past*. Madison: University of Wisconsin Press.
Richards, Mike. 1995. "Terror and Progress: Industrialization, Modernity, and the Making of Francoism." In Helen Graham and Jo Labanyi (eds.), *Spanish Cultural Studies*. Oxford: Oxford University Press.
Richardson, Paul. 1977. *Britain, Europe, and the Modern World, 1918–1977*. London: Heinemann.
Richter, Emmanuel. 1993. "German Unification and European Integration: Points of Tension in Community Building." In Heinz D. Kurz (ed.), *United Germany and the New Europe*. Hants: Edward Elgar Publishing.
Rider, Jacques Le. 1996. *La Mitteleuropa*. Paris: Presses Universitaires de France.
Ritter, Gerhard. 1962. *Das deutsche Problem*. Munich: R. Oldenbourg.

Robbins, Keith. 1998. *Great Britain: Identities, Institutions, and the Idea of Britishness.* Essex: Addison Wesley Longman.

Rodríguez, Germán, and Noreen Goldman. 2001. "Improved Estimation Procedures for Multilevel Models with Binary Response: A Case Study." *Journal of the Royal Statistical Association* 164,2: 339–55.

Röpke, Wilhelm. 1946. *The Solution of the German Problem.* New York: Putnam's Sons.

Rosenau, J. N. 1961. *Public Opinion and Foreign Policy: An Operational Formulation.* New York: Random House.

Rubens, Bernice. 1983 [1969]. *The Elected Member.* London: Hamish Hamilton.

Samuel, Raphael. 1989a. "Introduction: Exciting to be English." In Raphael Samuel (ed.), *Patriotism: The Making and Unmaking of British National Identity*, vol. 1. London: Routledge.

Samuel, Raphael (ed.). 1989b. *Patriotism: The Making and Unmaking of British National Identity.* Vols. 1–3. London: Routledge.

Sanders, David. 1990. *Losing an Empire, Finding a Role: British Foreign Policy since 1945.* London: MacMillan.

Schmidt, Helmut. 1991. "Deutschlands Rolle im neuen Europa." *Europa-Archiv* 21: 611–23.

Schmitt, Carl. 1941. *Völkerrechtliche Grossraumordnung mit Interventionsverbot für raumfremde Mächte. Ein Beitrag zum Reichsbegriff im Völkerrecht.* Berlin: Deutsche Rechtsverlag.

Schmitter, Philip. 1971. "A Revised Theory of Regional Integration." In L. N. Lindberg and S. A. Scheingold (eds.), *Regional Integration: Theory and Research.* Cambridge, MA: Harvard University Press.

Schneider, Jens. 2001. *Deutsch sein: Das Eigene, das Fremde, und die Vergangenheit im Selbstbild des vereinten Deutschland.* Frankfurt: Campus.

Schneider, Michael. 1997. *Die "Goldhagen-Debatte": Ein Historikerstreit in der Mediengesellschaft.* Bonn: Forschungsinstitut der Friedrich-Ebert-Stiftung, Historisches Forschungszentrum.

Schöllgen, Gregor. 1997. "Geschichte als Argument: Was kann und was muss die deutsche Grossmacht auf dem Weg ins 21. Jahrhundert tun?" *Internationale Politik* 2: 1–13.

———. 1999. *Die Aussenpolitik der Bundesrepublik Deutschland.* Munich: C. H. Beck Verlag.

Schroers, Rolf. 1957. *In fremder Sache.* Cologne: Kiepenhauer & Witsch.

Schubert, Helga. 1984. *Blickwinkel. Geschichten.* Berlin: Aufbau Verlag.

Schulze, Hagen. 1991. *The Course of German Nationalism: From Frederick the Great to Bismarck, 1763–1867.* Cambridge: Cambridge University Press.

Schütze, Walter. 1990. "Frankreich angesichts der deutschen Einheit." *Europa-Archiv* 4: 133–37.

Scott, Paul. 1968. *The Day of the Scorpion.* New York: William Morrow and Company.

Secretaría General del Movimiento and Ministerio de Información y Turismo. *Pensamiento político de Franco.* 2 vols. Madrid: Ediciones del Movimiento.

Sewell, William. 1980. *Work and Revolution in France: The Language of Labor from the Old Regime to 1848.* Cambridge: Cambridge University Press.

Seymour-Ure, Colin. 1968. *The Press, Politics and the Public*. London: Methuen & Co.
———. 1991. *The British Press and Broadcasting since 1945*. Oxford: Blackwell.
Shandley, Robert R. (ed.). 1998. *Unwilling Germans? The Goldhagen Debate*. Minneapolis: University of Minnesota Press.
Shaw, Robert. 1961. *The Sun Doctor*. Portway: Cedric Chivers Ltd.
Shaw, Roy, and Gwen Shaw. 1992 [1988]. "The Cultural Setting." In Boris Ford (ed.), *The Cambridge Cultural History*. Cambridge: Press Syndicate of the University of Cambridge.
Shepard, Robert. 1975. *Public Opinion and European Integration*. Lexington, MA: Lexington Books.
Sillitoe, Allen. 1967 [1959]. *The Loneliness of a Long Distance Runner*. New York: Alfred A. Knopf.
Sinnott, Richard. 1995. "Bringing Public Opinion Back In." In Oskar Niedermayer and Richard Sinnott (eds.), *Public Opinion and Internationalized Governance*. Oxford: Oxford University Press.
Snidal, Duncan. 1985. "Coordination versus Prisoner's Dilemma: Implications for International Cooperation and Regimes." *American Political Science Review* 79,2: 923–42.
Snow, David, and Robert D. Benford. 1992. "Master Frames and Cycles of Protest." In Aldon D. Morris and Carol McClurg Mueller (eds.), *Frontiers of Social Movement Theory*. New Haven: Yale University Press.
Snow, David A., E. Rochford, Jr., Steven K. Worden, and Robert D. Benford. 1986. "Frame Alignment Processes, Micromobilization, and Movement Participation." *American Sociological Review* 51,4: 464–82.
Staden, Berndt von. 1990. "Das vereinigte Deutschland in Europa." *Europa-Archiv* 23: 685–90.
Stein, Arthur A. 1990. *Why Nations Cooperate: Circumstance and Choice in International Relations*. Ithaca, NY: Cornell University Press.
Steinle, Jürgen. 1995. *Nationales Selbstverständnis nach dem Nationalsozialismus*. Bochum: Universitätsverlag.
Stokes, John and Gwenneth Stokes. 1988 [1977]. *Europe and the Modern World, 1870–1983*. Harlow: Longman.
Storey, David. 1976. *Saville*. London: Jonathan Cape Ltd.
Swidler, Ann. 1986. "Culture in Action: Symbols and Strategies." *American Sociological Review* 51: 273–86.
Swift, Graham. 1996. *Last Orders*. New York: Alfred. A. Knopf.
Tarrow, Sidney. 1992. "Mentalities, Political Cultures, and Collective Action Frames." In Aldon D. Morris and Carol McClurg Mueller (eds.), *Frontiers of Social Movement Theory*. New Haven: Yale University Press.
Taylor, D. J. 1993. *Notes from After the War*. London: Chatto and Wyndus.
Thompson, E. P. 1978. *The Poverty of Theory and Other Essays*. London: Merlin Press.
Tilly, Charles. 1978. *From Mobilization to Revolution*. Reading, MA: Addison-Wesley.
Todd, Richard. 1996. *Consuming Fictions: The Booker Prize and Fiction in Britain Today*. London: Bloomsbury.

Torrente Ballester, Gonzalo. 1980. *La isla de los jacintos cortados*. Barcelona: Destino.
Trommler, Frank. 1990. "The Creation of History and the Refusal of the Past in the German Democratic Republic." In Kathy Harms, Lutz R. Reuter, and Volker Dürr (eds.), *Coping with the Past*. Madison: University of Wisconsin Press.
Tunstall, Jeremy. 1996. *Newspaper Power. The New National Press in Britain*. Oxford: Clarendon Press.
Tuñón de Lara, Manuel. 1966. *La España del siglo XIX: 1808–1914*. París: Librería Española.
Tversky, Amos, and Daniel Kahneman. 1981. "The Framing of Decisions and the Psychology of Choice." *Science* 221: 453–58.
Unamuno, Miguel de. 1986 [1895]. *En torno al casticismo*. Madrid: Alianza.
Valdeón, Julio, Isidoro González, Mariano Mañero, and Domingo J. Sánchez Zurro. 1986. *Geografía e historia de España y de los países hispánicos*. 3° de BUP. Madrid: Anaya.
Vázquez Montalbán, Manuel. 1990. *Galíndez*. Santo Domingo, Dominican Republic: Taller.
Vernet, Daniel. 1997. "Europäisches Deutschland oder deutsches Europa?" *Internationale Politik* 2: 15–28.
Vicens Vives, Jaume. 1957–59. *Historia social y económica de España y América*. Barcelona: Teide.
Voltmer, Katrin. 1998. *Medien Qualität und Demokratie*. Baden Baden: Nomos Verlagsgesellschaft.
Wallace, Helen. 1997. "At Odds with Europe." *Political Studies* 45: 677–88.
Wallace, William. 1986. "What Price Independence? Sovereignty and Interdependence in British Politics." *International Affairs* 62,3: 367–89.
———. 1992. "British Foreign Policy after the Cold War." *International Affairs* 68,3: 423–42.
———. 1994. "The British Approach to Europe." In Wolfgang Mommsen (ed.), *The Long Way to Europe*. Chicago: Edition q.
Wallace, William (ed.). 1990. *The Dynamics of European Integration*. London: Pinter.
Warwick, Paul. 1985. "Did Britain Change? An Inquiry into the Causes of National Decline." *Journal of Contemporary History* 20: 99–133.
Weber, Eugen. 1981. *Peasants into Frenchmen*. Berkeley: University of California Press.
Weber, Hermann. 1999. *Geschichte der DDR*. Munich: DTV.
Weber, Max. 1958 [1904–5]. *The Protestant Ethic and the Spirit of Capitalism*. New York: Scribner's.
Weidenfeld, Werner (ed.). 1983. *Die Identität der Deutschen*. Munich: Carl Hanser Verlag.
Weiner, M. J. 1981. *English Culture and the Decline of the Industrial Spirit: 1850–1980*. Cambridge: Cambridge University Press.
Weiss, Peter. 1981. *Die Ästhetik des Widerstands*. Frankfurt: Suhrkamp.
Wessels, Bernhard. 1995a. "Development of Support: Diffusion or Demographic Replacement?" In Oskar Niedermayer and Richard Sinnott (eds.), *Public Opinion and International Governance*. Oxford: Oxford University Press.

Wessels, Bernhard. 1995b. "Support for Integration: Élite or Mass-Driven." In Oskar Niedermayer and Richard Sinnott (eds.), *Public Opinion and International Governance*. Oxford: Oxford University Press.

Wetherall, M., and J. Potter. 1988. "Discourse Analysis and the Identification of Interpretive Repertoires." In C. Antaki (ed.), *Analysing Everyday Explanation*. London: Sage.

Wolf, Christa. 1963. *Der geteilte Himmel*. Halle: Saale.

———. 1978 [1976]. *Kindheitsmuster*. Berlin: Aufbau Verlag.

Wolffsohn, Michael. 1991. "Deutschland: Eine verwirrte und verwirrende Nation." *Europa-Archiv* 7: 211–14.

Yang, Min, and Harvey Goldstein. 2000. "Multilevel Models for Repeated Binary Outcomes: Attitudes and Voting over the Electoral Cycle." *Journal of the Royal Statistical Association* 163,1: 49–62.

Zald, Mayer. 1996. "Culture, Ideology, and Strategic Framing." In Doug McAdam, John D. McCarthy, and Mayer N. Zald (ed.), *Comparative Perspectives on Social Movements*. Cambridge: Cambridge University Press.

Zaller, John. 1998. *The Nature and Origins of Mass Opinion*. Cambridge: Cambridge University Press.

Zentralinstitut für Geschichte an der Akademie der Wissenschaften der DDR. 1984. *Geschichte: Lehrbuch für Klasse 10*. Berlin: Volk und Wissen, Volkseigener Verlag.

Zentralinstitut für Geschichte an der Akademie der Wissenschaften der DDR. 1986. *Geschichte: Lehrbuch für Klasse 9*. Berlin: Volk und Wissen, Volkseigener Verlag.

Index

Abc (newspaper): decentralized cooperation supported by, 260; on democratization in Spain, 159–60; editorial and op-ed articles in, 145–54; selection, sampling, and coding procedures for, 268; support for transfer of sovereignty in, 109
Die Abenteuer des Werner Holt, 207–8
accountability, 82
Adenauer, Conrad, 119, 194; press criticism of, 268
agriculture: policies on, 93; in Spain, 150–51. *See also* Common Agricultural Policy (CAP)
alienation, British, 294n.77
Allensbach survey, 201
Allensbacher Jahrbuch, 197
Allies: denazification policies of, 182–83, 187–88, 193–94; reeducation policies of, 182–83
Álvarez-Miranda, Berta, 11–12, 13
Amis, Kingsley, 220, 222
Amsterdam, Intergovernmental Conference of; Maastricht Treaty amendments of, 139
Anaya's history textbook, 176
Anderson, Perry, 232, 293n.72
Anglo-Saxon community, 216, 254
anti-Americanism, 78–79; in Spanish newspapers, 146
antibourgeois student movement, German, 190–91
anti-foreign sentiment. *See* xenophobia
anti-parliamentarism, 254
anti-Semitism: collective responsibility for, 187–88; in German textbooks, 290n.6; in Germany, 183; in Nazi regime, 187–88, 288n.41
Aranguren, José Luis, 175
Arendt, Hannah, 186
argumentation, modes of, 22–26
Arriba, selection, sampling, and coding procedures for, 268
Asián Peña, 285–86n.46
Atlantic Alliance, 119; and European Community, 138; political and military cohesion of, 134
Atlantic Community, 130
Atlantic Treaty, signing of, 163
Auschwitz trial, 190
Austria: identification with Europe in, 240; support for EU membership in, 247–48, 261
autarkic Francoist Spain, 175; economic policy of, 163; policies of, 177
authoritarian modernization project, Franco's, 162–71
authoritarianism: in East Germany, 213; in Germany, 205; of Spain, 148–49

backwardness, glamour of, 229–30
Bahr-Brandt Ostpolitik, 195
balkanization process, 55
Barker, A. L., 219–20
Baumgarten, Hans, 282n.18
Belgium, in European Union, 247–48
belief systems: aligned with frames, 7; shared, 6
Berlanga, Luis García, 170
Berlin, Holocaust monument in, 191
Berlin wall, fall of, 83
Blackbourn, David, 183
Blair, Tony, 139; on adoption of euro, 257
Blairite revolution, 139
Die Blechtrommel, 188–89. See also *The Tin Drum*, 289n.43
Blickwinkel, 191, 208–9
border region residence, 246–47; in support of EU membership, 242
borders, removal of, 1, 30–31, 103–4, 110
Bosnia: crisis of, 152; EU peacekeeping role in, 54
Brandt, Willy, 196; Warsaw ghetto visit by, 191
Braumberger, Gerard, 124
Breton-Woods monetary system, breakdown of, 138
Britain in the Twentieth Century, Core History Study Units, 223–24

British character, 293n.59; attributes of, 225–26; monarchy and, 226–28; racism of, 229; sense of distinctiveness of, 217–19, 232–33, 236
British Empire, 14, 60, 216–17, 230; in British history texts, 228–29; British singularity and, 217–19; nationalism and supranationalist identity in, 254; positive and negative views of, 62–63; Spain's economic competition with, 162; supranational identities of, 233, 236; unraveling of, 258
British history: celebration of, 228–29; idealized view of, 129, 136–37
British national identity: satisfaction with, 232–33; sense of singularity of, 217–19, 232–33, 236, 292n.47
British traditions, 226–27, 228, 234
Brussels: dislike of government of, 38; distance from, 242–43, 246, 295n.3, 296n.7
Brussels Treaty, 119, 130
budgetary reform, 139–40
bureaucracy, European Union's: criticism of, 25, 31–33; dictatorial, 51–52

Cambio16 (newspaper): editorial and op-ed articles in, 145–54; selection, sampling, and coding procedures for, 268; support for transfer of sovereignty in, 109
Cánovas, 286n.49
Carlist Wars, 55
Casticistas, 147, 259
Castresana, Luis de, 166
Catadell, views of European Union in, 34
Catholicism, 247; modernization and, 173, 174–75; of Spain, 173–75, 284n.17; in support for EU membership, 242, 243, 246, 296n.3; in support for European integration, 261, 297n.7
Cela, Camilo José, novels of, 172
Central European federation, 180
Central European Union, proposal for, 128
centralized cooperation model, 71, 73, 251–52
centralized integration model, 70–71, 74–75, 251–52; and defending European social model, 86–87; economic and monetary union in, 72; on eliminating European wars, 79–81; versus free-traders, 73; journalists' expression of, 106; percentage of support for, 73, 74; respondents supporting, 280n.11; on socially and environmentally conscious Europe, 83–86; on strengthening and streamlining Europe, 75–79; on strong, peaceful, socially conscious Europe, 81–83, 87–89
Chamberlain, Joseph, 229
Chernobyl accident: environmental impact of, 85; international conference on, 83
China, EU competition with, 30
Christian Democratic Union, 267
Christian universalism, 177
Christian values, 146–47
The Civic Culture, 184
civil wars, 55
Classen, Christopher, 287n.22
cognitive frames, 100–5, 279n.4(ch.2)
cognitive mobilization, 295n.3
Cold War: German reunification and, 258–59; Spain during, 163; West Germany during, 194–95
collective cognitive frame, 279n.4(ch.2)
collective guilt: denial of, 191–92; over Nazi past, 186–92, 208–9; for World War II, 288n.39
collective identity, 253–54; construction impact of, 257–58; in Spain, 48
collective memory, 15, 25–26; culture and, 34; of East Germans, 201–4; of historical events, 60–61; national, 249–50; of Nazi past, 197–98; in shaping images of European integration, 58–63
Colley, Linda, 218, 222, 227
colonies, emotional ties to, 11
Comisiones Obreras, 28
Common Agricultural Policy (CAP), 5, 22, 102*t*; attitudes toward, 68*t*; editorial opinions on, 110–11, 252; farmer subsidization by, 138; German lack of interest in, 54; journalistic criticism of, 110–11, 117; journalistic versus popular views on, 116; need to focus on, 139–40; percentage of articles and in-depth interviews on, 112*t*; Spanish views of, 44–45, 116; United Kingdom's view of, 52–53
Common Defense/Security policy, 238
Common Fisheries policy, 22
common interest, cooperation around, 97

Common Market, 102*t*. *See* European Economic Community (EEC); attitudes toward membership in, 279n.5(ch.3); benefits of, 26–29, 103–4; British distinctiveness and, 234; editorials on impact of, 110–11; Franco's Spain in, 169; in free-trade model, 69–70; percentage of articles and in-depth interviews on, 112*t*; Spain's membership in, 148, 170, 255; support for, 68*t*; survey on support for, 280n.7

Commonwealth, 60; advantages of ties with, 135–36; British ties to, 107, 129, 140, 216, 224, 228, 258; economic problems related to, 155; European Community relations with, 134–35; farm product tariffs of, 131; free trade in, 132; as model for Atlantic Community, 130

communism/communists: antifascist legitimating message of, 209–10; defense against, 146; in East Germany, 60, 205; EU membership support by, 278n.35; fall of, 125–26, 260; moral crusade against, 147; in Spain, 165

competences, transfer of, 15, 70–71; degree of support for, 238; economic, social, and other variables in support for, 243–45; region of residence and support for, 246–47

competition, 102*t*; among European countries, 127; attitudes toward, 68*t*; labor costs and, 94; percentage of articles and in-depth interviews on, 113*t*

competitive strength, 30

concentration camps, population's awareness of, 288n.39

Conservative Party (British): decentralists in, 74; press support for, 267; on United Kingdom in EEC, 131–32; victory of, 139

consumers, European Union viewed by, 22

content analysis, 16–17

Continentalists, 136–37

cooperation model, 140; British support of, 138; deciding on form of, 4

corruption, 32

Corse, Sarah, 18

Council of Ministers: control of, 140–41; in decision making, 70, 71; Spain presiding over, 152–53; transparency in, 142–43

Coundenhove-Kalergi, Count, 180

crime, international, 85, 94–95; control of, 85

criminal law, homogenization of, 94–95

cross-cultural understanding, 104; percentage of articles and in-depth interviews on, 112*t*; support of, 67, 68*t*

Cuba: military defeat of Spain in, 259; War of, 55

cultural counterthemes, 7

cultural differences: across Europe, 82; glorification of, 50–51; irreconcilable, 139–40; and opposition to political integration, 93–94; preventing consensus, 90; preventing political integration, 97; in UK versus other European countries, 50–52, 63, 214–25, 257–58

cultural exchange, 94; European unification and, 42–43;

cultural modernization, 161; in Spain, 170–71

cultural preoccupation, concept of, 6–7

cultural resonance, 15–16

cultural values, 87

cultures: in centralizers versus decentralizers, 251–52; changes in, 6; collective memory and, 34; concept of, 6–7; in Decentralized Cooperation model, 90; difficulty defining, 49; of East versus West Germany, 211–13; European integration as threat to, 56–57; in European integration view, 100–1, 106, 259–60, 261; factors shaping, 14; fear of loss of, 15; of Franco Regime, 173–74; of Germany, 287n.8; national and subnational, 249; roles of in UK, Spain, and Germany, 233–34; of United Kingdom versus Europe, 49–51

currency, common, 2; countries opting out of, 2; degree of support for, 238; implementation of, 24

Czechoslovakia, East Germany's relationship with, 211

Dahrendorf, Ralph, 122, 183, 185–86, 206
Dalton, Russell J., 246
Danish referendum, 2
Davy, Richard, 196
de Areilza, J. M., 149
de Cossio, J. M., 147–48

De Gaulle, Charles, 97; European policies of, 120–22; German attitude toward, 120–21; nuclear development by, 133; opposing enlarging European Communities, 120–21; Spanish opposition to, 149; vetoing UK entry, 133–34, 137
decentralized administration, 71
decentralized cooperation model, 71, 155, 251–52, 259; Anglos versus Latins on, 92–94; British support of, 141; characteristics of elites supporting, 89–90; conservative press supporting, 260; efficiency against integration in, 94–95; free trade in, 72–73; journalists' expression of, 106; percentage of support for, 73–74; protecting national identity in, 90–92; protecting national interest in, 95–97; respondents supporting, 280n.11; Scottish Nationalist Party supporting, 74–75; sovereignty issue in, 97–100; support for, 74, 260
decentralized cooperation projects, Spanish newspapers, 145–46
decentralized integration model, 71, 73, 126, 251–52, 259; British support for, 144; percentage of support for, 73–74
decentralized integration project, Spanish newspapers, 153
decentralizers, 251–52
decision making: centralized, 38; in European Union, 70; main locus of, 71; national parliaments in, 95
decolonization, of British Empire, 228–29
Delors project, 141
Democracy: antidemocratic forces and, 107; decision making in, 99–100; in EU institutional reforms, 140–41; in Germany, 288n.30; in Spain, 149–51; in West Germany, 184
democratic deficit criticism, 37–38; percentage of articles and in-depth interviews on, 112*t*
democratization: recency of, 242; in Spain, 159–60, 253
denazification, 193–94; policies of, 187–88
Denmark: European identification of, 240; Maastricht Treaty rejected by, 2, 141; weak support for EU in, 261
Deutsch, K. W., 281n.1
Deutschmark, 48–49
Día de la Raza, 162–63

differentiation, 220–21
diffuse support, 279n.5(ch.3)
directives, 71
Dönhoff, Marion Gräfin, 121, 126
Dunkirk retreat, 229

East Germany: antifascist legitimating message of, 209–10; Catholicism and support for European integration in, 243; cultural differences of with West Germany, 56, 57; dealing with Nazi past in, 203–10; economic liberalization in, 201–2; European integration views in, 41–42; European Union support in, 8–9, 41–42; foreign policy of, 210–11; historiography of, 204–10; history textbooks of, 276; journalistic versus popular views on integration in, 114–15; mistrust of European Communities in, 127–28; novels of, 274, 291n.13; Occupation Statute of, 210; political culture of, 155–56; reunification experience of, 84–85; shifting collective memory in, 201–4; Socialist nations and, 256; Structural Funds targeting, 54; unemployment in, 202–3; variables in EU membership support in, 244–45; view of World War II role in, 200–13; xenophobia in, 85
East-West détente, 194–95
East-West relations, 123
Eastern Europe: during Cold War, 194–95; cultural differences of, 139–40; East German conflicts with, 210–11; East Germany's role in, 212–13; political instability in, 111; transformations in, 126–27
Easton, David, 294n.1
Ebeling, Hans, textbook of, 185–86
economic benefits, common market, 26–29; for Germany, 12; for Spain, 11
economic crisis: global, 288n.29; with oil price crisis, 122–23
economic development: European Communities membership in, 155; of Spain, 284–85n.27; supporting EU membership, 242
economic integration, 98; against world competition, 81–82
economic liberalism, 27–29; of East Germany, 201–2

economic modernization: Franco's preoccupation with, 168–71; of Spain, 160–61
economic monetary union (EMU), 22; British support of, 141–42; criteria of, 280n.10; editorial opinions on, 269; German debate over, 123–25; lack of commitment to, 144–45; opposition to, 97, 152–53; in peace-oriented identification, 80–81; political steering of, 84–85; satisfaction with, 72; Spain's opposition to, 152–53; Spain's support of, 93; support for, 128; United Kingdom and, 48–49
economic-political-cultural bloc, 75
economic strength, 29–31
economics: disrupting German reunification, 41–42; Franco's policy of, 162–71; of poorer EU countries, 54–55; reform of in Spain, 163–64; in support for European integration, 243–45; transnational problems of, 75
The Economist: Atlantic Community defined in, 130; selection, sampling, and coding procedures for, 267; on UK decline, 128–45, 231
Edelvives' history textbook, 176–77, 285–86n.46
editorials: qualitative analysis of, 252–53; selection, sampling, and coding procedures for, 267–69; on sovereignty and national identity, 282n.11; in Spain, 255; on support for European integration, 108–10
education, state control of, 82
efficiency, against integration, 94–95
Eichenberg, Richard, 246
Eichmann trial, 190
Eley, 183
Elite-Mass Diffusion processes, 280–81n.1
elites: conservative, 90; identification of, 279n.6(ch.2); impact of on public opinion, 280–81n.1; on modernization of Spain, 298n.9; versus public opinion, 256–57; supporting European integration, 74
Elizabeth, Queen, Christmas addresses of, 224, 228, 292n.43, 293n.55
En Defensa de la Hispanidad, 162–63

The Enchanted Glass, 227
Enlightenment ideas, eighteenth-century Spain, 173
Entralgo, Laín, 174–75
environmental consciousness, 83–86
environmental problems, transnational, 75
The Era of the Second World War: 1933–1948, Core History Study Units, 223–24
Erasmus fellowship, 22
Die Erdabgewandte Seite der Geschichte, 291n.13
Erhard, monetary reform, 194
Die Eroberung der Zitadelle, 190–91, 291n.13
España como problema, 174
España Invertebrada, 174
Españolistas, 150
ethnic tolerance, European unification and, 42–43
euro coins: elite attitudes toward adoption of, 257; first circulation of, 1; Germany's opposition to, 48–49; UK debate over, 48–49
Eurobarometer 51.0 survey, 16, 18, 265–66; results of, 236–48; variables in, 295–96n.3
Eurobarometer studies, 8–10, 16; first design of, 65–66; questions included in, 280n.8
Europe. *See also* Central Europe; Eastern Europe; Western Europe: barrier-free, 30–31; British dislike of, 220–23, 291n.2; cultural differences in, 50–52, 63; De Gaulle's concept of, 97; degree of attachment to and EU membership support, 238t; degree of British attachment to, 294n.1; economically and politically strong, 122–23; history of, 155; identification with in UK and other European countries, 239–41; irreconcilable cultural differences in, 139–40; need for strengthening and streamlining of, 75–79; need to rebuild postwar economies of, 129–30; Spain's contributions to civilization of, 151–52; spiritual crisis of, 285n.39; spiritual foundation of, 146
Europe of the Fatherlands concept, 120–21

European Atomic Energy Community (EURATOM), 2; creation of, 117, 119; editorial opinions on, 269; German attitude toward creation of, 119; success of, 131
European Coal and Steel Community (ECSC), 2; British attitudes toward, 129, 130, 132; creation of, 163; editorial opinions on, 268–69; opposition to, 132; plans for EURATOM and EEC of, 131; Schuman Plan for, 118–19
European Commission, factors in support of, 296–97n.7
European Communities, 2; British acceptance of membership in, 132–33; change to European Union of, 2–3; conflict over UK membership in, 129, 133–34; creation of, 119; French opposition to UK entry into, 133–34; German attitudes toward, 119–20; opposition to enlargement of, 120–21
European Community. *See* European Union
European Community Study of 1973, 280n.7
European Defense Community (EDC): British attitudes toward, 129, 130, 132; British support for, 130; editorial opinions on, 268–69; French proposal of, 119; opposition to, 132
European Economic Community (EEC), 2; British opposition to, 132, 283n.28; conflict over UK membership in, 127, 129; creation of, 117, 177; defense of, 86–87; economic success of, 133; editorial opinions on, 269; as employers' federation, 77; farmer subsidization by, 138; fear of Nazi control of, 136–37; German attitude toward creation of, 119; Southern Europe, inclusion in, 139–40; Spain's entry in, 283n.36; Spain's Preferential Trade Agreement with, 149, 151–52; success of, 131; survey on support for, 280n.7; before UK accession to, 118, 120–22; UK relationship with, 131–32
European Economic Cooperation, Organization for, 163
European Free Trade Area (EFTA), failure of, 133
European identity, 237–39

European institutions, 110
European integration: aspects of emphasized by supporters versus nonsupporters, 65–69; attitudes toward, 3, 24, 69; British rejection of, 12–13; classification of models of, 15; complexity of attitudes toward, 69; crises in progress toward, 298n.13; cultural benefits of, 94; development of common view of, 26–33; differences in support of, 2–3; different models of, 250, 277nn.3–4; East versus West German views of, 41–42, 211–13, 255–56; economic benefits of, 94; editorial opinions on, 268–69; elite's views on, 280–81n.1; factors in attitudes toward, 65–105, 249–61; factors in support of, 296–97n.7; four models of, 71–105; frames and support for, 5–7; framing country's contribution to, 56–57; future of, 259–61; general patterns of support for, 108–10; German attitudes toward: after Single European Act, 118, 123–25; before Single European Act, 118, 122–23; before Treaty of Rome, 118–20; before UK accession to EEC, 118, 120–22; German reunification and, 125–27; intergovernmental character of, 122; journalists and, 106–56; measures of support for, 279n.5(ch.3); media's role in shaping discussion of, 42; microeconomic theory of, 245–46; modes of arguments about, 22–26; national and city differences in view of, 55–57, 106; national frames of, 8–11; national images and attitudes toward, 33–53; national self-perceptions and collective memory in, 58–63; newspaper images of, 110–18; op-ed positive and negative comments on, 114t; popular perceptions of, 249–50; problems analyzing public support for, 3–5; slow pace of, 25; Spain's contribution to, 145–54; statistical studies of frames and attitudes toward, 236–48; strength in, 29–30; support for in United Kingdom, Germany, and Spain, 11–14; supporters versus nonsupporters of, 101–5, 250–51; suspicion toward, 1; themes justifying attitudes toward, 27, 68t, 102t; United Kingdom and, 214–35; ways of seeing, 21–64; West German views of, 198–99

European Parliament: in decision making, 70, 71; empowerment of, 85–86; in institutional reforms, 140–41; lack of representation in, 98; limiting powers of, 125; strengthening of, 124–25, 153; strengthening of UK role in, 142–43; support for strong role of, 124–25, 153, 280n.8
European single market, 1
European Union (EU): amount of power transferred to, 69–70; attitudes toward membership in, 21, 294n.2; bureaucracy of, 51–52; Central and Eastern Europe in, 142; conceptualizations of, 5–7; Council of Ministers of, 8; decision making in, 70; degree of support for, 294n.1; democratic deficit criticism of, 37–38; different names of, 2; East German attitude toward, 200; editorial opinion on Spain's membership in, 145–54; effects of, 24; enlargement of, 123–24, 142, 152–53; entry negotiation process of, 281n.3; from European Communities, 2–3; evaluating functions of, 24; event triggering movement toward, 2; evolution of, 25; excessive regulation by, 49–50; frames and European identity supporting, 237–39; governance issues of, 24–25, 31–33, 251; institutional crisis of, 122–23; institutional reforms of, 123–24, 139; national support for membership in, 241–45; odds of supporting membership in, 296nn.4–5; in peace, 81–83; popular social representations of, 249; public knowledge and images of, 22–26; self-identities and attitudes toward, 24; Spain's voice in, 48; symbolic dimension of membership in, 11–12; themes justifying attitudes toward, 27, 68*t*; timing of entry in, 55; trends in support for, 9, 10; United Kingdom's support of, 137–45; variable polity of, 1; visibility of, 22; wage and social benefits inequalities in, 34–37
European wars, 55; elimination of, 79–81
Europeanizers, 259; versus Casticistas, 147; in Germany, 225; in Spain, 39, 176, 225, 233–34, 238, 253, 283n.31, 285n.34
Europeizantes, 220
Europhiles, 220

Eurosceptics: opposition to, 76; in United Kingdom, 12–13, 63, 245, 247

Falange, 173, 174
La familia de Pascual Duarte, 172
farm products: from British Commonwealth, 131; quotas for in Spain, 45
farmers: common market support by, 28; EEC subsidies for, 138; European Union viewed by, 22
federalism, 69–70; versus cooperative approach, 138; German and Spanish newspapers supporting, 109–10; German support for, 121–22
federation of states, 81
Final Solution, 183
Finland, 240
fishing rights, restriction of, 52
Der Fleck, Die Jacke, Die Zimmer, Der Schmerz, 193
foreign labor competition: fear of, 64; in Germany, 155
foreign laborers: cheap, 94; concern over in Germany, 36–37, 111; view of in East versus West Germany, 61–62
foreigners, British mistrust of, 217–20, 221–23
frames: alignment of with belief systems, 7, 15–16; analysis of, 1, 250; collective cognitive, 279n.4(ch.2); discriminant analysis of by city, 270; for European integration, 5–7; genealogy of, 106–7; local newspaper opinions and, 281n.2; national differences in, 252; resonance of, 7; role of, 236; selecting categories of, 279n.59(ch.2); in support of EU membership, 237–39
framing scripts, 7
France: British dislike of, 13, 63, 218, 222–23; hegemony in European Community of, 120–21; mistrust of Germany in, 118; negative attitudes toward, 76; as political and cultural model, 10; referendum in, 2; Spanish relations of, 284n.5; support for European Union in, 8–9
Franco, General: attempt of to enter European Communities, 148; authoritarian modernization project of, 162–71; death of, 150; on economic development, 284–85n.27; press under, 268; in Spanish modernization, 178; speeches of, 286n.54

Franco dictatorship, 13, 44, 46–47, 145, 227–28; cultural foundations of, 173–74; opposition to, 173; political and social foundations of, 172–73; represented in Spanish textbooks, 226
Franco-German cultural exchange, 94
Frankfurter Allegemeine Zeitung (FAZ): decentralized cooperation supported by, 260; op-ed articles in, 282n.8; on quest for sovereignty, 118–26, 128; selection, sampling, and coding procedures for, 267
Frankfurter Rundschau: content analysis of, 281n.4; selection, sampling, and coding procedures for, 267–68
free marketers, 89–100
free movement, 102*t*; attitudes toward, 68*t*; percentage of articles and in-depth interviews on, 113*t*
free trade, 69–70; British support for, 130; in Commonwealth nations, 132; in Decentralized Cooperation model, 72–73; support of, 27–28
free trade area: between EEC and United Kingdom, 131–32; European Union as, 67–69; support of, 72–73
free-traders, 101–3, 105; percentages of, 280n.11
French Revolution, 215; principles of, 146
Fühmann, Franz, 208
functions, transfer of, 70–71

Gabel, Matthew, 245–46, 294n.1; criteria of, 296–97n.7; postmaterialist/ materialist values, 295–96n.3
Gamson, William, 7
García Pérez, 283n.31
Genazino, Willhelm, 193
Generación del 98, 173–74, 176
geographic isolation, 11
George III, King: ordinariness of, 227
George VI, King: Christmas address, 224
German character, 182–84; as evil, 187
German Communist resistance, 209
German history: continuities in, 188–89, 199; discontinuities in, 183–86; Nazi period in, 183–86, 212; philosophical concepts of, 287n.8; progressive versus regressive traditions in, 204–5, 213
German history textbooks: confronting Nazi past in, 188, 191–92; persecution of Jews covered in, 290n.6; view of German population in, 205–6
German principalities, 99
German reunification, 12, 41–42, 83–84, 193–94, 260; consequences of in East Germany, 202–3; costs of, 96; debate over, 125; East German attitude toward, 200–4; with end of Cold War, 195; European integration and, 114–15, 125–27; misgivings about, 196, 282n.8; process of, 60; strategy for, 120; trauma associated with, 212–13; U.S. policy on, 289n.67; West German support for, 255–56, 258–59
German-Russian Treaty, 289n.68
German Social Market economy model, 84
German Unity, Day of, 125–26
Germany. *See also* East Germany; German reunification; West Germany: aggression of, 129–30, 182; anti-foreign worker sentiment in, 36–37; anti-foreigner tendencies in, 38–40; anti-parliamentarism in, 254; belief in model of, 61–62; Central European identity in, 254; characterization of country and people of, by city, 59*t*; common market support in, 27–28; criticism of corruption by, 32; cultural continuities in, 287n.8; cultural differences between East and West in, 56, 57; dangerous cultural traits of, 212, 213; De Gaulle's France and, 120–22; dealing with Nazi past of, 179–99, 181–92, 186–92, 226, 233–34; democratic culture in, 288n.30; denazification of, 289n.59; denial of Nazi past in, 289n.59; Deutschmark in national identity of, 48–49; economic and political concerns of, 54–55; economic crisis in, 186; editorial views in, 108, 111, 155, 252–53; elite journalists' views in, 108, 155; EU membership of, 241–45; EU peace role viewed in, 54–55; EU support in, 8–14, 12, 21, 108, 200–13, 260–61; European fear of, 155, 193–99; European identification in versus UK, 239–41; fall of SPD government in, 289n.71; fear of remilitarization of, 118–19; federal tradition in, 85–86; foreign image of, 196–99; globalization support in, 30; hegemonic tendencies of, 38–40, 200; historic

discontinuities in, 287n.25; historical events of, 60*t*; history textbooks in, 287nn.23–25, 288nn.28–30, 290n.5; international image of in foreign policy, 210–11; journalists versus ordinary citizens' attitudes in, 111–15; labor costs in, 94; leadership position of, 54; militarism in, 128, 205; moral responsibility theme in, 38–39, 189–91; national identity of, 34–43, 287n.8; negative attitudes toward, 76; newspapers in. *See* newspapers, German; novels of, 58, 289nn.43; op-ed themes in, 114*t*, 116–17; peace issue in, 79–81, 111; peaceful intentions of, 40–41; political cultures of in West versus East, 155–56; political integration support in, 103; population of as victims of Nazi regime, 206–8; positive self-perceptions of, 58; postwar economic and military constraints on, 143; press in, 260; problematic relations of neighbors with, 107; protecting national interest of, 95–97; respondent classification from, 73–74; responsibility of for World War I, 288n.28; security concerns of, 125; selection, sampling, and coding procedures for newspapers and editorials in, 267–68; self-perceptions, collective memories, and preoccupations of, 249–50; sovereignty issue in, 117, 118–28, 258–59; Soviet Union demonized in, 288n.41; supporters versus nonsupporters of EU in, 67; supranationalist failure in, 216; themes justifying European integration attitudes in, 102*t*; unemployment in, 79–80, 95–96, 288n.29; Volk of, 227; wages and social benefits in, 35; in World War II, 60–61, 62, 64, 96, 181, 212, 287–88n.27; World War II impact on in East versus West, 247–48

Gesellschaft und Demokratie in Deutschland, 185

Der geteilte Himmel, 291n.13

Gikandi, Simon, 218

Giménez, Ruiz, 175

Gindin, James, 219, 225

global economy, adaptation to, 77–78

globalization, 6, 21; economic, 88–89; Spanish support for, 47–48; support of, 29–30, 47–48

Gloger, Gotthold, 206–7

Goldhagen, Daniel, 183–84; history text of, 191

Goldschmidt, George-Arthur, 191

governance issues, 24–25, 31–33; percentage of articles and in-depth interviews on, 112*t*

Grainger, J. H., 219

Grass, Günter, 188–89, 289n.43

Great Britain. *See* United Kingdom

Green Party, 30, 79–80; on lack of citizen input, 37–38

Habermas, Jürgen, 183

Haider, Jörg, 248

harmonization, criticism of, 32–33

heads of state addresses, 18

Helm, 190

Herburger, Günter, 190–91

Los hijos muertos, 172

Hillgruber, Andreas, 183

Hispanidad, 162–63, 177, 254, 259, 284n.17; failure of, 216

Historia de una escalera, 172

historical events: attitudes toward European integration and, 59–60; in national collective memories, 60–61

history textbooks: British, 223–24, 226, 228–29, 275; on British economic and political decline, 231–32; on denazification of Germany, 289n.59; of East Germany, 276; of East versus West Germany, 290n.5; German, 287nn.23–25, 288nn.28–30; on German imperialism, 205–6; Spanish, 226, 276, 285–86n.46, 286n.49; of West Germany, 275

Hitler, Adolf, 182–83, 288n.41; collective guilt and, 191–92; in German textbooks, 185–86; popularity of, 206; reasons for rise of, 205

Hitler's Willing Executioners, 183–84

Holocaust, 183, 196–97; focus on, 191; in German history textbooks, 192; German public discussion of, 190; nazism and, 187

ideational materials, 6

identity. *See* national identity

immigration: quotas for, 35; unemployment problems and, 35–37

imperial supranational project, British, 216–17, 218–19, 228. *See also* British Empire
In fremder Sache, 188
in-group homogeneity, 220–21
inclusion, 220–21
income classification, 295n.3
India, colonization of, 229
industrialization, in Spain, 159
inferiority, of ethnic groups, 92
inflation rates, 246
infrastructural projects, Spanish, 45
Inglehart, Ronald, 65, 294n.1
Innocents: Variations on a Theme, 219–20
institutional reforms, 139; cooperative approach to, 140; democratic approach to, 140–41
Integrationists, 74–75, 101–3, 105; on defending European social model, 86–87; on eliminating European wars, 79–81; percentages of, 280n.11; on socially and environmentally conscious Europe, 83–86; on strengthening and streamlining Europe, 75–79; on strong, peaceful, socially conscious Europe, 81–83, 87–89
intergovernmental cooperation, 4; versus supranational integration, 3
international organizations, 47–48
international prestige, postwar Spanish, 43, 47–48, 164–65, 167–71
international relations: Darwinian conception of, 216; limitations of literature on, 4–5
International Social Survey Program (1995), 224
interviewees, 297–98n.8
interviewing process, 263–66
Ireland, Northern: identification with Europe in versus UK, 239–40; variables in support for EU membership in, 244–45
Iron Curtain countries, 210–11
isolationism, 102*t*; attitudes toward, 68*t*; breaking with tradition of, 107; of British Labour Party, 137–38; of Franco dictatorship, 168–70; international prestige and, 47–48; modernity and, 47, 148; percentage of articles and in-depth interviews on, 112*t*; in Spain, 43–44, 46–47, 115–16, 148–49, 152, 155, 159, 160, 174, 254, 286n.49, 298n.9; Spanish opposition to, 176–77; theme of, 265; in United Kingdom, 58–59, 137–38
Italy, 8–9

Japan: economic competition with, 124–25; EU competition with, 30; versus German productivity, 96
Jasper 1946 Heidelberg Lecture, 187
Johnson, Paul, 136–37, 234, 283n.28
journalists (elite): access of to information, 154–55; centralizing and integrating model of in Germany, 106; content analysis of views of, 268–69; decentralized cooperation model of in UK, 106; European integration views of, 106–56; on European Union, 110–18, 278–79n.2; frames used by, 15; qualitative analysis of opinions of, 252–53
Juan Carlos I, King, 153–54
Jünger, Ernst, 191
Juste, Antonio Moreno, 283n.31

Khruschchev, Nikita, Bonn visit of, 194
Kindelán, Alfredo, 147
Kinderheitsmuster, 208, 289n.58
Kipling tradition, 225
Kohl, Helmut, 196, 202; on European Union, 200; visit to Bitburg cemetery by, 191
Kohn, Hans, 183
Korean War, 130
Die Korrektur, 209
Krausista philosophy, 286n.49
Krebs, Hans, 180

labor competition: controls on, 35; in Germany, 34–37
labor costs, homogenization of, 35
labor unions: high costs of, 94; supporting European integration, 74
Labour movement, British, compromise of, 135–36
Labour Party (British): curtailed autonomy of, 138–39; integrationist position of, 75–79; isolationism and chauvinism of, 137–38; leadership changes in, 142–43; press support for, 267; on socialism and free trade, 132; socialist vision of, 107
Latin America, Spain's ties with, 148

Lebensraum, 180
leftist parties: opposition of the ECSC and EEC, 132; viewpoint of, 5
legislative function, 72–73
Lenz, Siegfried, 189–90
liberal Europeanizing project, Spanish, 171–77
Little Englandism, 217–18, 220, 226, 254
Lively, Penelope, 222
Lübke, President, New Year's address of, 195–96
Lucky Jim, 220, 222, 226
Luxembourg Compromise, 123

Maastricht Treaty, 2, 128, 139; amendments to, 139; approval of, 141; Danish rejection of, 123–24, 141; editorial opinions on, 269
macro-level forces, 3, 6
macroeconomic processes, 3, 241; in support for EU membership, 246
Maeztu, Ramiro de, 162–63, 174, 284n.17
majority decision making: extension of, 85–86; opposition to, 72–73; support for, 73, 80–81; in transfer of functions, 70–71
majority voting procedure, 71
Manual Workers' Chamber, on unemployment and European Union, 35–37
Marías, Julián, 175
market-oriented approach, 143
market principle, 27–29
Marshall Plan, 163, 177
Marxism-Leninism: in East Germany, 204; in United Kingdom, 234
Matute, Ana María, novels of, 172
Matzerath, Oskar, 189
McFarlane, Alan, 214
McNamara, Robert, 289n.67
Meckel, Christoph, 191
media discussions: of European integration, 42, 198–99; of Germany in European Union, 200
Meditaciones del Quijote, 174
Merger Treaty, 2
methodology, 16–18, 296n.6
Michelsen, Hans Gunter, 188, 189, 190
micro-level processes, 3
micro sociological factors, 6
microeconomic theory, 245–46

militarism: British opposition to, 132; of European Union, 128; in Germany, 128, 205; in West Germany, 213
Mitteleuropa, 179–80, 211; failure of, 216
modernization, 102t, 105, 107; attitudes toward, 68t; economic, 160; instrumental-utilitarian view of, 178; isolationism and, 148; percentage of articles and in-depth interviews on, 112t; respondents mentioning, 298n.9; social and cultural, 161; in Spain, 43–47, 88, 151–52, 155, 160–71, 173–75, 233–34, 238, 253, 258; status issues and, 47–48; in support for EU membership, 241, 242; theme of, 265
monarchy: British, 226–28, 226–29, 234, 293n.55; Spanish, 227–28
Monroe doctrine, 180
Moon Tiger, 222
moral issues, German drama, 189–90
Morocco, Spain's war with, 55
Mosse, George, 21
Müller, Heiner and Inge, 209
multinational corporation, economic policy of, 84–85
Murdoch, Rupert, tabloid press of, 137
Mythen Deutscher Geschichtsschreibung, 183

NAFTA, 67
Nairn, Tom, 227, 229–30, 232, 293n.72
nation-states: defense of, 104; versus supranational communities, 282n.18
national barriers, removal of, 113t
national consciousness, differences in, 253
national culture: individual identities and, 254; repertoires of, 14–15; of West Germany, 198–99
national differences, statistical analysis of, 55–57
national dilemmas, 107
national histories, 100–1, 106
national identity, 102t, 105, 249–50, 265; attitudes toward, 68t; British, 234–35; in centralizers versus decentralizers, 251–52; definition of, 91–92; difficulty defining, 49; editorial and op-ed articles on, 282n.11; European integration as threat to, 56–57, 67, 241; in European op-ed articles, 116–17; fear of losing, 6, 12, 15, 50–51, 52, 63, 90, 238t, 239–41, 245, 251–52, 255, 265–66;

national identity (*cont.*)
functions of, 220–21; of Germany, 12, 287n.8; national versus political, 21; nonessentialist conception of, 76–77; percentage of articles and in-depth interviews on, 113*t*; protection of, 90–92; in shaping images of European integration, 58–63; supporting EU membership, 237–39; in United Kingdom, 48–53, 214–25, 229–35, 245; in United Kingdom versus other European countries, 239–41
national images, 33–34; in Germany, 34–43; in Spain, 43–48; in United Kingdom, 48–53
national interest, protection of, 95–97
national parliaments, 95
National Socialism, 186; German historic interpretation of, 205–6; historical context of, 37; manipulation of population by, 207–8; origins of, 212; racist policies of, 42–43
national wealth, 10
nationalism, 296–297n.7; British, 58–59, 144–45, 225–29; collective identity in, 257; desire to fight, 75; in developed regions, 258–59; in developed versus less developed regions, 8–9; in Eastern and Western Europe, 126–27; in popular views of European integration, 249; rejection of, 76–77, 80; in United Kingdom, 135–36, 218–19, 225–29; before World War II, 254–55
Nationalist Party, Scotsburg, 74
nationalization, masses, 21
Naumann, Friedrich, 179, 180
Nazi "New Europe" concept, 283n.31
Nazi period: causes of, 182–86; collective memory of, 80, 212–13; collective responsibility for, 186–92; dealing with and understanding of, 181–92, 196–98, 233–34; denial of responsibility for, 205–6, 289n.59; East Germans' responsibility for, 203–10; German debate over, 186–92; German guilt and responsibility for, 186–92; in German history, 212, 226; German population's behavior during, 205–9; in Germany's image, 179–99; growing up in, 289n.58; guilt over, 186–92, 208–9; historic discontinuity of, 287n.25; moral questions about, 189–90; racist component of, 192
Nazi sympathizers, rehabilitation of, 209
neo-functionalism, 65
Netherlands, 247–48, 261
Neues Deutschland: editorial support for European integration in, 108; on European Communities, 127–28; on Mitteleuropa concept, 180; selection, sampling, and coding procedures for, 268; views on integration in, 115
New Left Review, 234
The New Statesman: on EEC, 283n.28; selection, sampling, and coding procedures for, 267; on UK decline, 128–45, 231
Newby, P. H., 220–22, 226
Newman, Gerald, 214, 227
news media opinions, 278–79n.2
newspapers. *See also* editorials; journalists (elite); op-ed articles: British, 108–9; on British decline, 128–45; conservative, 90; content analyses of, 16–17, 268–69, 281n.2, 281n.5; editorial and op-ed opinions in, 255; German, 108–10; German reunification theme in, 282n.8; images of European integration in, 110–18; local, 281n.2; on modernization in Spain, 161; in opinions on European Union, 278–79n.2; qualitative analysis of opinion in, 252–53; selection, sampling, and coding procedures for, 267–69; supporting European integration, 74, 108–10; thematic content of, 110
Los nietos del 98, 174–75
Noll, Dieter, 207–8
Nolte, Ernst, 183
North Atlantic Treaty Organization (NATO): British opposition to, 132; British parliamentary sovereignty and, 135; British support for, 130; dependence on, 82; distancing from, 139; Franco's regime and, 163; Spanish support of, 47–48
novels: British, 226, 272–73, 294n.77; East German, 274; German, 58, 289nn.43, 291n.13; postwar British, 220–23, 232; selection of, 271–72; Spanish, 274–75; West German, 273
nuclear deterrent, French development of, 133
Nuremberg trials, 194

O'Brien, Connor Cruise, 196
oil crises, 138; of 1973-85, 122
op-ed articles: content analysis of, 281n.2; positive and negative comments on European integration in, 114*t*; qualitative analysis of evolution of, 252–53; selection, sampling, and coding procedures for, 267–69; on sovereignty and national identity, 282n.11; supporting European integration, 108–10; thematic content of, 110
ordinary, cult of, 227
Organization for Economic Cooperation and Development (OECD), 148
Ortega y Gasset, José, 174, 175, 176, 285n.39
Orwell, George, 217, 220, 225
Ostpolitik, 125, 126
Oststadt Zeitung, 201
El otro árbol de Guernica, 166
out-group differentiation, 220–21
Overdevelopment Theory, 8–9, 258–59

El País (newspaper), 260; editorial and op-ed articles in, 145–54; leadership of, 177; modernity message of, 175; selection, sampling, and coding procedures for, 268; support for transfer of sovereignty in, 109
Palomino, Angel, 170–71
Paneuropa oder Mitteleuropa?, 180
Paris Treaties, implementation of, 194
Parliamentarism, British, 218
parochialism, British, 58–59
passport border controls, abolition of, 1
Past and Present, 234
peace, 102*t*; with conflict over distribution of wealth, 84; EU effect on, 68*t*, 79–81; European integration and, 54–55, 67, 104; NAFTA's effects on, 67; as op-ed topic, 111; percentage of articles and in-depth interviews on, 113*t*; in strong Europe, 81–83
permissive consensus model, 65
Philippines: military defeat of Spain in, 259; war in, 55
Phillip II, King, 150
Philomena Kleespiess trug die Fahne, 206–7
Pléven, Prime Minister, 119
Poland-East German border, 211
police cooperation, 85; efficiency of, 94–95

political cultures, 6; post–World War II, 7; of West versus East Germany, 155–56
political guilt, 187
political instability: East European, 111; Spanish, 171–72
political integration: Anglo versus Latin views on, 92–94; British opposition to, 102–3; cognitive frames and, 100–5; efficiency against, 94–95; opposition to, 90, 98–100; skepticism toward, 96–97; support for, 87, 88–89
political parties, 74. *See also specific parties*
political science literature, 4–5
popular opinions, empirically based conceptualizations of, 65–69
Portugal, 152
postmaterialism, 104
postmaterialist/materialist values, 295–96n.3
Powell, Enoch, 234
power, 72
Preferential Trade Agreement, Spanish, 149, 151–52
production, competition for, 22
prosperity, 81–82
protectionism, Spanish, 159
Protestantism, British, 218
public opinion: analyzing international contrasts in, 3–5; versus elite attitudes, 256–57; elite impact on, 280–81n.1; European integration conceptualization and, 277n.3; on European Union, 278–79n.2; in European Union polity, 2–3
public planning, leftist idea of, 77–78

questionnaires, European unification, 65–69

Rabier, Jacques-René, 65
racial tolerance, 42–43
racism, British, 226, 229
Rapallo, 194
recommendations, 71
Regeneracionistas, 173, 174–75, 176, 286n.49
Regional Funds, 142
regional integration theory, 3
resonance, 7

respondents, 297–98n.8; age, education, and city of residence of, 264*t*; conditions of interviews of, 281–82n.7; selection and distribution of, 263–66; themes mentions by, 298n.9
Rhodes, Cecil, 286–87n.4
Ridruejo, 174
The Rise of English Nationalism: A Cultural History, 1740–1830, 214
Rivera, José Antonio Primo de, 174
Rome, Treaty of, 2, 148–49, 177; period before, 118–20
Royal Family, British, 226–28, 293n.55; Christmas Day addresses of, 234

Saar, recovery of, 119
Samuel, Raphael, 217, 218, 227, 231, 292n.47
Saunders, David, 232, 291n.7
Schengen Treaty, 1, 128; United Kingdom opting out of, 2
Schmidt, Helmut, 126, 184, 196, 282n.8; on European Union, 200
Schmitt, Carl, 180
Schroers, Rolf, 188, 190
Schubert, Helga, 208–9
Schuman Plans, 118–19, 131–32
Schutz, Alfred, 65
scientific revolutions, 298n.12
Scotland, national identity of, 91–92
Scott, Paul, 218
Scottish Nationalist Party: decentralist position of, 74–75; supporting national identity, 90–92
secondary sources, 17–18
security concerns, 125
Self-Determinists (British), 136–37
self-images, 15
service-based economy, 164
Silva, Federico, 159–60
Single European Act (SEA), 139; British signing of, 117; period after, 118, 123–25; period before, 118, 122–23
single market. *See also* Common Market: British support for, 141–42; editorial support for, 110; need to focus on, 139–40; with political union, 123; virtues of, 67
social change, resistance to, 21
Social Charter: adoption of, 1; British attitudes toward, 53; United Kingdom signing of, 2

social consciousness, 83–86
social dumping, avoidance of, 84
Social Europe, goal of, 153
Social Funds, 142
social justice, 88–89
social market economy, 75
social model, 86–87
social modernization, 161
social movements, frames used by, 7
social representations, 15, 243–45, 249
social rights/benefits: of European integration, 63; inequalities of, 34–37; percentage of articles and in-depth interviews on, 113*t*; removal of barriers to, 102*t*
social standards, 53
social values, erosion of, 95–96
socialism: British Labour Party's vision of, 107; British support for, 135–36; defense against, 146; progressive tradition and, 204
Sociality Party (Spanish), 151
socially conscious Europe, 87–89
socioeconomic benefits, 44–45
sociological factors, micro and macro, 6
sociopolitical frames, 17–18
sociopsychological theses, 13–14
Something to Answer For, 220–22
Sommer, Theo, 126
Southern Europe, inclusion of, 123–124, 139–40
sovereignty, 15, 102*t*, 105; attitudes toward, 68*t*; breach of, 32–33; concerns about, 107; in Decentralized Cooperation model, 90; decision impinging on, 4; of East Germany, 210; editorial and op-ed articles on, 116–17, 282n.11; fear of losing, 12–13, 63, 104, 230; formal, 139; formal versus actual, 138; percentage of articles and in-depth interviews on, 113*t*; quest for in German newspapers, 118–28; rejection of concept of, 76, 77; support for, 97–100; of supranational institutions, 69–70; supranational organizations in preserving, 139; threat of European integration to, 67; of United Kingdom, 48–53, 49–50, 52, 214–15; of West Germany, 193–96
sovereignty transfer, 70; British opposition to, 134–37, 155, 229–35; degree of support for, 238; economic, social, and

other variables in support for, 243–45; to European institutions, 108–9; German support for, 258–59; partial, 82; region of residence and support for, 246–47; support for, 73, 75
Soviet bloc, European dialogue with, 125
Soviet Union: attitude of toward European Defense Community, 119; evolution of Western relations with, 194; German demonization of, 288n.41; German protection against, 118; need for defense against, 129–30; security against, 125; strong defense against, 146
Sozialdemokratische Partei Deutschlands (SPD), 267–68; fall of, 289n.71
Spain: 1966 Press Law of, 172; agriculture of, 150–51; "Black Legend" about, 166–67, 284n.15; centralizing and integrating model in journalists of, 106; characterization of country and people of, by city, 59*t*; Christian values of, 162–63; collective memories and preoccupations of, 249–50; colonization of America by, 284n.17; Common Agricultural Policy criticism by, 52; common market support in, 27–28; conservative newspapers in, 260; contributions of to European civilization, 151; as cradle of rationality, liberty, and creativity, 147–48; crisis in, 285n.39; criticism of bureaucracy by, 31, 33; cultural contributions of, 146–47, 151; cultural foundations of, 173–74; cultural modernization in, 170–71; democratic deficit criticism in, 38; democratic profile of, 13–14, 149–51, 159–60; Development Plans of, 164, 169–70; economic development of under Franco, 284–85n.27; editorial and op-ed opinions in, 108, 255; EEC membership of, 283n.36; EU membership support in, 8–9, 241–45; European integration support in, 8–14, 11–12, 21, 108; Europeanist hegemony in, 220; Europeanization of, 160, 161, 162, 171–77, 173–74, 174–75, 238, 253, 258; Europeanizers in, 39, 283n.31, 285nn.34; Franco regime in, 43–48, 227–28; Franco's authoritarian modernization project in, 162–71; Franco's foreign policy of, 168–70; French relations with, 284n.5; General Education Law of 1970 in, 285–86n.46; Germanization of culture of, 174; historical events of, 60*t*; history textbooks of, 226, 276, 285–86n.46, 286n.49; identification with Europe in versus UK, 239–41; industrialization failure in, 159; inferiority complex of, 161; integrationists versus free-traders in, 105; international prestige of, 167–71; international role of, 145–54; isolationism in, 148–49, 159, 160–62, 254, 265, 286n.49, 298n.9; journalistic views on European integration in, 115–16, 155; lack of interest of in EU's peace role, 54–55; loss of colonies of, 162; military defeats of, 259; mistrust of foreign ideas in, 165–67; modernization in, 43–48, 88, 160–61, 238, 253, 258, 265, 298n.9; national culture of, 159–78; national identity of, 43–48; national interests of, 153–54; negative image of in Europe, 166–67; negative self-perception of, 58; new democracy in, 253; newspapers in, 108–10, 252–53; novels of, 274–75; obstacles to European Communities membership of, 148–49; op-ed themes in, 111, 114*t*, 116–17; oppositional culture in, 172–73, 175–76; peace editorials in, 111; political and social foundations of, 149, 172–73; political integration support in, 103; political unrest in, 171–72; post–WW II culture of, 164–65; reasons for European integration support in, 11–12; Regeneracionistas in, 286n.49; respondent classification from, 73–74; selection, sampling, and coding procedures for newspapers and editorials in, 268; self-perception of, 62, 249–50; sovereignty issue in, 117; Stabilization Plan of, 163–64; supporters versus nonsupporters of EU in, 67; supranationalism failure in, 216; themes justifying European integration attitudes in, 102*t*; tourism in, 170–72; transition from agrarian to service-based economy in, 164; unemployment and economy of, 62, 86; versus United Kingdom on political integration, 92–94; variables in EU membership support in, 244–45; voting power of, 152–53
Spanish-American War, 55

Spanish Civil War, 14, 145, 168, 254, 259; aftermath of, 177–78; catastrophic consequences of, 163; critique of, 172; cultural configurations and, 260; lack of modernization and, 176; in Spanish textbooks, 226
Spanish Communists, 278n.35
Spanish Conservative Party, 145–46
Spanish Cortes, 170
Spanish history, 226; critique of, 172; rewriting of, 173–74, 175–77; trends in, 285–86n.46
Spanish Socialist Party, 29–30
specific support, 279n.5(ch.3)
standardization, criticism of, 32–33
state power, transfer of, 72, 77–78
statehood, old, 11
states: permeability of boundaries between, 6; size of, 29–30; as socialization agencies, 6
states too small issue, 112*t*
status issues, 6; in Spain, 43, 47–48
Structural/Regional Funds, 102*t*; attitudes toward, 68*t*; British support for, 142; democratic principles of, 242; editorial opinions of, 252; journalistic versus popular views on in Spain, 116; lack of German interest in, 54; percentage of articles and in-depth interviews on, 113*t*; satisfaction with in Spain, 45; Spain's dependence on, 88–89, 153; United Kingdom's view of, 52–53
student demonstrations: in Spain, 171–72; in West Germany, 190–91
students, European Union views of, 22
subnational cultures, 34
subsidiarity principle, 77–78, 82, 280n.9
Suchbild, 291n.13
Suez crisis, 133, 221
supranational cooperation, 4
supranational institutions, 24, 282n.18; creation of, 69–70; polity of, 2; in preserving sovereignty, 139
supranationalism, 3, 104; in British Empire, 233, 236; in Germany, 211; impetus toward after World War II, 143; in postwar Germany, 179–80; in Spain, 177–78; in United Kingdom, 215–16; before World War II, 254–55
surveys: concentrations of research on, 69–105; focused on European unification support, 65–66
Sweden: EU membership support in, 247–48; European identification in, 240

taxation, 35
Taylor, D. J., 219
Tern, Jürgen, 120–21
Thatcher, Margaret, 139, 234; on German reunification, 196
theater, German, 189–90
Third Reich, 19798
The Times, 267
Torremolinos Gran Hotel, 170–71
trade: dependence on, 10–11; European Union membership and, 242; removing barriers to, 2
transnational problems, 84
transparency, Council of Ministers, 141, 142–43
travel, free, 83, 93; eliminating borders for, 1, 30–31, 103–4, 110; between EU countries, 22; obstacles to, 83
"Tremendista" novels, 172
22 Tage oder die Hälfte des Lebens, 208

Ukania, 227–28
Unamuno, Miguel de, 160, 173–74
unanimous decision making, 71; versus majority procedures, 80
understanding, contributions to, 102*t*
unemployment: in East Germany, 202–3; in East versus West Germany, 61–62; in Germany, 35–37, 64, 79–80, 95–96, 288n.29; high levels of, 86; with immigrants to UK, 135–36; in Spain, 62
uniformity, opposition to, 92
union, strength in, 29–30
United Kingdom. *See also* British character; British Empire; British history; British national identity; Commonwealth: Anglo-Saxon community in, 254; anti-European attitudes in, 58–59, 291n.2; anti-European Union rhetoric in, 136–38; antiforeign attitudes in, 292n.17; attitudes toward euro in, 257; broad interests of, 140; characterization of, 293n.59; characterization of country and people of, by city, 59*t*; collective memories and preoccupations of, 249–50; collective psychology of, 253–54; Common Agricultural Policy and Structural Funds criticism by, 52–53;

common market support in, 27–28; criticism of corruption by, 32; criticism of standardization tendencies by, 32–33; cultural differences of, 49–51, 63, 214–25; decline of, 89, 128–45, 138, 229–32, 253–54; democratic deficit criticism in, 38; dismantlement of welfare state in, 139; distrust of EEC in, 136–37; economic decline of, 138, 231–32; editorial support for European integration in, 108; editorials on peace in, 111; elite and public support for supranational solutions in, 3–4; EU membership opposition in, 253–54, 257–58; EU membership support in, 9, 121, 241–45; Euro-enthusiastic editorials in, 141–42; European Community membership of, 137–45; European identification in, 239–41; European integration support in, 8–14, 21; European integration views in, 214–35; European Monetary Union debate in, 48–49; European political integration opposition in, 63; Euroscepticism in, 12–13, 247; exclusion of from European Communities, 120, 133–34; extra-European engagements of, 236; French conflict with, 13, 133–34; as great power, 231–32; historical events of, 60*t*; history textbooks of, 223–24, 226, 228–29, 231–32, 275; immigrants to, 135–36; interest of in EU peace role, 54; journalist views on European integration in, 115–16, 155; Maastricht Treaty debate in, 2; national identity and culture in, 90–92, 229–32, 234–35, 255; nationalism in, 135–36, 144–45, 225–29; New Labour movement in, 143, 144; newspaper editorials in, 252–53; novels of, 272–73, 294n.77; op-ed themes in, 116–17; options of versus Spain, 148–49; Parliamentary model of, 98–99; political culture of, 294n.1; political decline of, 231–32; political integration opposition in, 93–94; positive and negative comments on integration in op-ed articles of, 114*t*; post-WW II role of, 129–30, 143; postwar economic rebuilding of, 129–30; press in, 260; reassessment of identity of, 142; respondent classification in, 73–74; role of culture in, 233–34; selection, sampling, and coding procedures for newspapers and editorials in, 267; self-perception of, 58, 62–63, 249–50; singularity of, 100, 232–33, 236, 255, 257–58, 291n.7, 292n.47; social identity of, 224–25; sovereignty, identity, and welfare state in, 48–53; sovereignty issue in, 98–100, 117, 229–32; versus Spain on political integration, 92–94; structural economic crisis of, 133; supporters versus nonsupporters of EU in, 67; themes justifying European integration attitudes in, 102*t*; U.S. ties of, 107; variables in EU membership support in, 245; Western European views of, 131; world hegemony of, 216; as world power, 106, 130, 133–34, 230; xenophobia in, 76, 217–18, 221–23

United Nations Resolution 39 (I), 284n.5
United States: British opposition to, 132; British relationship with, 107, 133, 216; cultural diversity in, 97; De Gaulle's opposition toward, 120; defense of European culture and values against, 87; economic competition with, 81–82, 124–25; EU competition with, 30; in Europe's defense, 130; federal structure of, 99–100; versus German productivity, 96; German reunification policy of, 289n.67; political integration model of, 98; protecting European social market from, 75; rise of, 232; Spanish opposition to, 146; world hegemony of, 78–79

Der unterbrochene Wald, 191

Vallejo, Antonio Buero, 172
Versailles Treaty, 180, 182, 288n.28; German historic interpretation of, 205; German textbook treatment of, 185–86
voice, in European Union, 102*t*, 105; percentage of articles and in-depth interviews on, 112*t*

wages: German concern over, 111; inequalities of in Germany, 34–37
Walser-Bubis debate, 191
wars: elimination of, 79–81; Spanish involvement in, 55
Warsaw Pact, 210
wealth, allocation of, 88–89

Weber, Eugen, 18
Weber, Max, 65
Weizsäcker, Richard von, 191
welfare state, 105; in United Kingdom, 48–53
Wessels, Bernard, 281n.1
West Germany: Allied troop withdrawal from, 119; antibourgeois student movement in, 190–91; Catholicism and support for European integration in, 243; CDU-SPD coalition government of, 194–95; conditional sovereignty of, 193–96; cultural differences of with East Germany, 56, 57, 211–13; democracy in, 184; denazification in, 209–10; economic mircle of, 190; European integration attitudes in, 41–42; European Union support in, 8–9; foreign relations of, 193–95, 255–56; historiography of, 182–83, 184–85; history textbooks of, 182–85, 275; journalistic versus popular views on integration in, 114–15; monetary reform in, 194; national consciousness of, 183, 253; Nazi past of, 179–99; non-hegemonic designs of, 253; novels of, 273, 291n.13; Occupation Statute of, 194; political culture of, 155–56; post–World War II political culture of, 7, 197–98; regaining international trust in, 250; renazification in, 187–88; supranational identity of, 179–80; variables in EU membership support in, 245; in World War II, 256; World War II casualties in, 247–48
West-Soviet Union relations, evolution of, 194
Western Europe: attitudes toward unification of, 279n.5(ch.3); hegemonic ambitions in, 254–55; view of UK in, 131
Weststadt: Housewives Association of, 94; images of EU in, 34
Wolf, Christa, 208, 289n.58, 291n.13

workers, migration and unrest of, 171–72
World Trade Negotiations, 133
World War I: Continental blockade during, 180; Germany's responsibility for, 186, 205, 288n.28
World War II: British victory in, 12–13, 129, 216–17; collective guilt over, 208–9; cultural configurations and, 260; cultural effects of, 14; East German view of role in, 200–13; EU support and, 241–42, 246; German memory of, 197–98; German sense of responsibility for, 203–10, 212, 256, 287–88n.27, 288n.39; in German textbooks, 185–86; Germany's role in, 38–43, 56, 60–61, 62, 64, 96, 179–99, 250; impetus toward supranationalism after, 143; lessons of, 68t, 102t, 265; nationalist and supranational identity projects before, 254–55; number of casualties in, 247–48, 295n.3; percentage of articles and in-depth interviews on, 113t; political consequences of in West Germany, 179–80; problems faced by FRG after, 118–19; Spain in, 163; West German sense of responsibility for, 245, 247–48
worldviews, 24

xenophobia, 76; in East Germany, 85; in Germany, 36–40; in United Kingdom, 58–59, 217–20, 221–23, 225–26, 292n.17

Yugoslavia, EU peacekeeping role in, 54

Zeit der Schuldlosen, 189–90
Die Zeit (newspaper), 260; editorials on European integration in, 109; European integration views in, 114; op-ed articles in, 282n.8; on quest for sovereignty, 118–28; selection, sampling, and coding procedures for, 267

Princeton Studies in Cultural Sociology

Origins of Democratic Culture: Printing, Petitions, and the Public Sphere in Early-Modern England by David Zaret

Bearing Witness: Readers, Writers, and the Novel in Nigeria by Wendy Griswold

Gifted Tongues: High School Debate and Adolescent Culture by Gary Alan Fine

Offside: Soccer and American Exceptionalism by Andrei S. Markovits and Steven L. Hellerman

Reinventing Justice: The American Drug Court Movement by James L. Nolan, Jr.

Kingdom of Children: Culture and Controversy in the Homeschooling Movement by Mitchell L. Stevens

Blessed Events: Religion and Home Birth in America by Pamela E. Klassen

Negotiating Identities: States and Immigrants in France and Germany by Riva Kastoryano, translated by Barbara Harshav

Contentious Curricula: Afrocentrism and Creationism in American Public Schools by Amy J. Binder

Community: Pursuing the Dream, Living the Reality by Suzanne Keller

The Minds of Marginalized Black Men: Making Sense of Mobility, Opportunity, and Future Life Chances by Alford A. Young, Jr.

Framing Europe: Attitudes to European Integration in Germany, Spain, and the United Kingdom by Juan Díez Medrano